Roger North's
The Musicall Grammarian 1728

Roger North's *The Musicall Grammarian 1728* is a treatise on musical eloquence in all its branches. Of its five parts, I and II, on the orthoepy, orthography and syntax of music, constitute a grammar; III and IV, on the arts of invention and communication form a rhetoric; and V, on history, consists of an etymology. The text is edited here for the first time in its entirety with two substantial introductory chapters by Mary Chan and Jamie C. Kassler.

North's main thesis is that music is a sign of humanity's changing history and habits; hence, his treatise can be seen as a contribution to musical semiotics. But North also assigned an important role to reflection as a means of critically examining not only his own propositions and theories but those of others. Accordingly, his treatise is also a venture of exploration, a process of thinking about musical thinking.

In the two introductory chapters, the editors have attempted to capture a broader understanding of these aspects of North's work. In the first chapter Jamie Kassler places *The Musicall Grammarian 1728* within the context of its companion treatise, *Theory of Sounds 1728*, as well as North's non-musical writings and their relation to the intellectual ferment of the seventeenth and eighteenth centuries. In the second chapter Mary Chan examines physical and textual aspects of the manuscript as evidence of North's processes of composing the treatise.

CAMBRIDGE STUDIES IN MUSIC

GENERAL EDITORS: JOHN STEVENS AND PETER LE HURAY

Frontispiece. Portrait of Roger North by Sir Peter Lely (by permission of the owner, T. F. North).

ROGER NORTH'S

THE
MUSICALL GRAMMARIAN
1728

edited with Introductions and Notes
by
MARY CHAN and JAMIE C. KASSLER

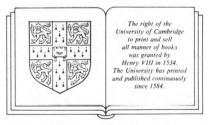

The right of the
University of Cambridge
to print and sell
all manner of books
was granted by
Henry VIII in 1534.
The University has printed
and published continuously
since 1584.

CAMBRIDGE UNIVERSITY PRESS

CAMBRIDGE
NEW YORK   PORT CHESTER
MELBOURNE   SYDNEY

Published by the Press Syndicate of the University of Cambridge
The Pitt Building, Trumpington Street, Cambridge CB2 1RP
40 West 20th Street, New York, NY 10011, USA
10 Stamford Road, Oakleigh, Melbourne 3166, Australia

First published 1990

Printed in Great Britain at the University Press, Cambridge

British Library cataloguing in publication data
North, Roger, *1651?–1734*
Roger North's The musicall grammarian
1728. – (Cambridge studies in music)
1. Music.   Early work
I. Title   II. Chan, Mary   III. Kassler,
Jamie Croy   IIII. The musical grammarian
1728
780

Library of Congress cataloguing in publication data
North, Roger, *1651?–1734*.
[Musicall grammarian]
Roger North's The musicall grammarian 1728 / edited with
introductions and notes by Mary Chan and Jamie C. Kassler.
p.   cm. – (Cambridge studies in music)
Bibliography.
Includes index.
ISBN 0–521–33131–5
1. Music – England – History and criticism – Early works to 1800.
I. Chan. Mary.   II. Kassler, Jamie Croy.   III. Title.   IV. Title:
Musicall grammarian.   V. Series.
ML286.1.N67   1990
780 – dc20
89–1024
CIP
MN

CONTENTS

ILLUSTRATIONS

FOREWORD

The Honourable Roger North (b. 1651?, d. 1734) has been a companionable guide to the intellectual and social ferment of the latter half of the seventeenth and first half of the eighteenth centuries. Through his writings we discovered that responses to the mechanical philosophy of Descartes varied widely; that autobiographical writing may consist of a philosophy as well as deeds or events in a life; and that ethical and critical questions were as central as religious and scientific ones. In return for these benefits, we have made every effort to respect the integrity of North's texts. As in our other volumes devoted to his writings, there has been a division of labour in which Mary Chan has taken responsibility for the physical and textual aspects of the manuscripts and Jamie C. Kassler, the structural and theoretical aspects.

The editors would like to thank the Dean and Chapter of Hereford Cathedral for permission to publish an edition of the manuscript in their possession; the Honorary Librarian of Hereford Cathedral, Miss Penelope M. Morgan, for providing access to the manuscript; Mrs Pamela North for sharing her interest in North and his manuscripts at Rougham Hall; and the Australian Research Grants Scheme and St John's College, Cambridge, for generous fellowships.

Professor Bernard Martin willingly shared his knowledge of languages and classical texts by helping to identify obscure words or phrases. Professor Pierre Lazslo opened up a world of chemical analogies hitherto invisible to our eyes, thereby adding a dimension to our understanding of North. And Dr Graham Pont encouraged and assisted inauguration of the series, North Papers, published at the University of New South Wales. We are indebted also to our respective families, who with grace, good humour and considerable patience have adopted North as a member of the family during the years devoted to studying his writings.

BIOGRAPHICAL NOTE

Roger North was the youngest of ten children of Dudley, fourth Baron North.[1] He was born at Tostock in Suffolk about 1651 and was educated privately and then at the Free Schools of Bury St Edmunds and Thetford. On 30 October 1667 he entered Jesus College, Cambridge, where he was tutored by one of his brothers, John North.[2] On 21 April 1669 Roger North was admitted to the Middle Temple, London; and on 29 May 1674 he was called to the Bar. Another brother, Francis North, was almost fifteen years older and already well-established in London as a lawyer. He sent business to Roger North, who attributed his own success in the law to that brother's influence. Between 1682 and 1685 North's legal practice centred in the Court of Chancery. He held positions of Steward to the See of Canterbury (1679), King's Counsel (1682) and Solicitor General to the Duke of York (1684). After the Duke came to the throne in 1685 as James the Second, North became Solicitor General to the Queen, Mary of Modena, and in 1686 he was appointed her Attorney General. After the Revolution of 1688 and because he refused to take the oath of allegiance, North was forced to resign most of his public appointments.[3]

On 26 January 1679 a fire broke out in the Middle Temple, after which North resided with his brother, Francis, whose wife had died in the previous year.[4] On 30 November 1680 the benchers of the

[1] This Biographical note has been compiled from a number of sources, including unpublished manuscripts and letters of the North family; the unpublished account book at Rougham of North's father; Korsten (1981); North (ed. M. North 1819, ed. Jessopp 1887, ed. Jessopp 1890, ed. Millard 1984); and Wilson (1959). Other sources are noted below, and supplementary data appear in various footnotes to the edited text.

[2] John North acted only nominally as a tutor, as Roger North makes clear: '... a freind lent his name, as tutor, to enable my admission but I read to my self; so a little phisicks, mathematicks, the peacable side of logick[,] some musick, and no conversation were my cursus at the university' (*Preface*: f.3).

[3] Only the most prominent of North's public appointments are listed in this paragraph.

[4] For further details about this period, see North (ed. M. North 1819). There is evidence that North resided with his brother much earlier, even though he used his rooms at the Middle Temple from time to time.

Middle Temple invited Christopher Wren to provide a design for
the new cloisters and, during rebuilding, to pass the workmen's
accounts. On the same day Peter Lely died, and North became one
of the executors of his will and a guardian of Lely's two illegitimate
children. Between 1683 and 1684, when North was Treasurer of the
Middle Temple, the Great Gateway was built which still gives
access to the Temple from Fleet Street. The design for the Gateway,
originally attributed to Wren, was by North himself. After the
death of Francis North on 5 September 1685, Roger North moved
from his brother's house into Lely's house in Covent Garden,
which he leased from the estate until 1690. During this period
North catalogued Lely's collection of art works for auction. He also
began to sort through Francis North's papers, to write notes and
animadversions on some of them, and to commence writing on
philosophical subjects.[5] About 1690, he and his brother, Dudley,
conducted experiments in a 'laboratory' they had set up at Wrox-
ton, the estate of the late Francis North.

On 26 December 1690 North purchased the Yelverton estate in
Rougham, Norfolk, and in 1692 began the rebuilding of Rougham
Hall.[6] On 26 May 1696 he married Mary, daughter of Sir Robert
Gayer of Stoke Poges in Buckinghamshire. Of the seven surviving
children from this marriage, only the dates of birth of his two sons
are recorded. In addition to his immediate family, North's respon-
sibilities extended to the Lely children and to educating and over-
seeing the affairs of various nieces and nephews, whose guardian he
had become on the death of his brothers Francis, Charles and
Dudley. About 1700, North bought another estate at Ashwicken,
Norfolk, and commenced improvements and agricultural experiments. In 1701, he let his Middle Temple chambers to relatives and
acquaintances. Although he still made occasional visits to London,
his time was spent mostly in Norfolk, where, from c. 1704, he acted
as a lawyer for various neighbours, including Sir Thomas Coke of
Holkham, Sir Nicholas L'Estrange of Hunstanton Hall and Sir
Robert Walpole of Houghton. He also established a parochial
library in Rougham Church which was completed in 1709.

The events of North's public life are well documented, but
details of his private life until the time of his death in March 1734 are
less accessible. Insofar as music is concerned, the sources of North's

[5] For a list of North's early writings up to 1703, see *Cursory Notes of Musicke* (ed. Chan and
Kassler 1986: 293–308).
[6] The extensive renovation and rebuilding is celebrated by North in a manuscript, *Cursory
Notes of Building* (ed. Colvin and Newman 1981).

Figure 1. The Great Gateway which gives access to the Temple from Fleet Street, London, built after North's design.

activities derive chiefly from his father's account book for the early
years and from North's own writings begun c. 1688.[7] But North's
reporting of personal events and circumstances is different in kind
from that of Samuel Pepys or John Evelyn. In the first place, North
was not a diarist. Then, because of political events, he was circum-
spect about naming names. And finally, the bulk of his writings are
a record of his thoughts, not an account of his social activities.
Nevertheless, from these writings it is possible to glean some
information about North's activities in music, which may be
regarded as of three kinds: practical, scientific and philosophical.

North's practical experience in music probably began c. 1660,
when he had lessons on the viol with John Jenkins. These lessons
lasted to 1666, during which period Jenkins introduced North to
the principles of music. Contact between the two men continued
into the 1670s, when North's practical musical activities included
lessons on the theorbo with John Lilly; acquaintance, and possibly
lessons on the violin, with Nicola Matteis; and membership in The
Gentleman's Society, a music meeting that gathered at least once a
week in private chambers or taverns to play music in the style of
Lully. North also made a few essays in composition but, with
characteristic irony, judged them worthless.[8] Family correspondence and the bequests in his will indicate that music-making
continued to be important after North's marriage and retirement
from London. In 1709, for example, the family had a visitor, on 27
February, a 'rare harpsi[c]ordiere'.[9] This must have been
'Captain' F. Prencourt, whose treatise on the first principles of
music North transcribed and later recopied with his own
animadversions.[10]

Scattered throughout his writings are many remarks on music
education. These remarks are guided by ideas that are central to

---

[7] North family papers are housed in Cambridge (University Library, St John's College
Library), London (British Library), Oxford (Bodleian Library), Hereford (Hereford
Cathedral Library), and Rougham Hall, Norfolk. Microfilms of some of North's private
papers are available from the Norfolk Record Office in Norwich.

[8] 'I became, as I thought, a master of composition, which was great pleasure, and I essayed
some compositions of three parts, which I cannot commend. Some of two I made airy
enough, which my brother, the Chief Justice [Francis], would be content to play. I was
not out at song neither, for my father translated the Italian old song which his daughters
had learned: "Una volta finira," &c., "Time at last will set me free," &c., and gave it to me
to set, which I did in three parts, imitating somewhat I had heard of Italian: it was in f, fa,
ut, three flats, a solemn key, and I thought succeeded well; my brother gave me the
encouragement to ask where I stole several passages' (Notes of Me ed. Jessopp 1887: 83–4).

[9] Letter to North Foley, 27 February 1708/9, BL Add MS 32501: f.66.

[10] See References and bibliography 1.2: Prencourt Tracts and Musicall Recollections I [Prencourt
Tracts Annotated].

North's conception of human nature and that stem from the neo-Stoic philosopher, Thomas Hobbes.[11] Although North was critical of Hobbes's theory of government,[12] he returned again and again to Hobbes's theory of human nature and, particularly, his theory of pleasure.[13] For example, in advocating that children learn how to sing or play a musical instrument, North wrote:

We know that there is a pleasure in mere action as such, witness the usual running and play of boys, who will not walk on the ground if a rail be near, but they must walk on the top of that. So sliding on skates, riding full speed upon a horse, shuttlecock, tennis (without wager), and many such things are pleasant, merely as action, and a doing of somewhat, though to no end but doing. So if a nail be to be driven, and two or three stand by, each has a mind and would be pleased to do it. Therefore it must be allowed that action itself is a pleasure, and such will be allowed to [musical] performers, which the audience cannot pretend to. Mr. Hobbes to this has affixed another, rejoicing in their own skill, which is witty, and in measure true, and also very lawful, harmless, and satisfactory.[14]

For North, however, practical music was not restricted to performance or composition, for as early as 1663 he spent time constructing an organ.[15] His interest in the technology of musical instruments was revived in February 1683, when he and other benchers of the Inner and Middle Temple invited the organ builders, Bernard Smith and Renatus Harris, to submit designs for a new organ for the Temple Church. Subsequently, the successful competitor, Smith, built North's own organ, which was set up in the long gallery at Rougham Hall. During the time of its construction in the 1690s, North began work on the physics of pipes, a subject which, previously, had been dealt with by only two authors: Marin Mersenne and Hobbes. Neither writer had understood the nature of a wave in the air and the way in which it 'fits' into a pipe. Because North drew on developments in kinematic optics and, in particular, on the work of Christiaan Huygens and Robert

---

[11] For a new interpretation of Hobbes, see Kassler (forthcoming), who argues that Hobbes had recourse to Stoic philosophy as a means of criticising and modifying scholastic Aristotelianism.

[12] See, for example, *Of Etimology*, essay 8, 'Notes relating to the origination of Governement, laws, and their peculiar language', section 4 of which is a critique of Hobbes (ff. 56–61v). The critique is transcribed by Korsten (1981: 217–22), who does not indicate that it is an extract from a larger work.

[13] For some aspects of this theory see the Introduction to, and notes accompanying the text of, *Cursory Notes of Musicke* (ed. Chan and Kassler 1986).

[14] *Notes of Me* (ed. Jessopp 1887: 73).

[15] *Preface*: f.2.

Hooke, his work on the physics of musical pipes constitutes the most important advance on the subject before the work of Jacques Vaucanson in 1737.[16]

In addition to problems that we now term 'scientific', North also grappled with a question of philosophical import: how is knowledge possible? In his attempts to answer this question, North revealed the philosophical and adversarial side of his character. The former, philosophical side had been nurtured by his father, whose influence deserves careful study;[17] the latter, adversarial side was developed by his legal training and was fostered in discussions and disputes with two of his brothers, Francis and John. By nature, however, North was reticent, even shy.[18] Hence, writing became a means of critically examining the philosophical ideas of others and developing his own ideas. The chief catalyst that gave direction to his writing was Francis North's *Philosophical Essay of Musick directed to a Friend*. Although this little tract was published in 1677, it was not until some fifteen to twenty years later that Roger North wrote down his searching criticism of it.[19] From this period music became the focus of North's efforts to solve the problem of knowledge.

Older interpretations of North's work have focused on his writings as sources for performance practice and for the social history of music.[20] In our reappraisals of North's writings, we have taken a different line of interpretation, one which attempts to capture a broader understanding by including those aspects which traditionally have been omitted by musicologists. Such an interpretation is

[16] According to D. Lasocki, 'Vaucanson was the first person to write about the flute's acoustics, and indeed the only person in the 18th century' (Vaucanson 1737/1979). But the flute-type of pipe (flue pipes) was treated by North prior to *c.* 1703 in *Cursory Notes of Musicke* (ed. Chan and Kassler 1986), which includes North's first attempt at a physics of musical pipes.

[17] The character of North's father is admirably sketched by Randall (1983).

[18] At least, this is the way North portrayed himself in *Notes of Me*: 'my character, very recluse'; 'I wanted those abilities that prevail in great men's esteem, that is confidence and put-forwardness' (142); 'I could not have put myself forward, which made me sensible of my incurable unfitness for a Court interest' (180); 'being . . . bashful in nature, as well as not gifted to public oratory' (182); 'Whatever the subject or the occasion be, I had rather write than speak' (197). Behind his reticence and shyness, however, was an awareness of various 'defects', so that North wrote: 'If I should go about to observe all my indiscretions which were incidental in . . . transient businesses, I should have work enough. It was my comfort and affliction that I was sensible of them either immediately or soon after, and not only so but of my incapacity of being much wiser. This was the affliction; the comfort was, that being thus sensible argued me not a senseless sot, but one that was not wise in my own eyes, therefore within the pale of hope' (*ibid.*: 138).

[19] See Hine, Chan, Kassler (1987).

[20] The traditional approach to North's writings is exemplified by past editorial practices, which have been surveyed by Chan (1986).

provided in Introduction I. But there is another aspect of North's work that has yet to be more widely recognized, and this aspect· derives from the important role North assigned to reflection. As we have argued elsewhere, North regarded reflection as a means of critically examining not only his own but others' propositions and theories before giving assent to them. During the course of such an examination, North hoped to root out error, confusion and prejudice. Because of this reflective aim, North's writings may be regarded as a venture of exploration, a process of thinking about musical thinking. Physical evidence for this process is treated in Introduction II.[21]

J. C. K.

---

[21] The basis for our interpretation of North is set out in the Introduction to *Cursory Notes of Musicke* (ed. Chan and Kassler 1986); the methods for reconstructing his processes of thinking are demonstrated in the detailed studies of various manuscripts in Hine, Chan, Kassler (1987) and Chan, Kassler, Hine (1988).

INTRODUCTIONS AND
EDITORIAL GUIDELINES

INTRODUCTION I

Jamie C. Kassler

PREFACE

In a draft for the work edited and presented here, North writes as a courtier, speaking of music as his mistress:

A musicall family, conversation with the best masters of the time, and a pittance of formall teaching, made me a professor; and from a medler with most sorts of instruments (not excluding the voice,) a buisy body in transcribing, transposing, and composing, and a meeting-hunter of musick in London for divers years. I found my self drawne in to such a familiarity with the prattique, that performing at sight, was to me like speaking, walking, or running; and there lyes the secret of a true lover, who is never so undone, as when his mistress is easy, and smiles.[1]

Of the various types of lovers of music, North associated himself with 'the most gallant', namely, 'those who aim at the whole art scientifick, and practick'.[2]

The results of North's aspirations are three pioneering theories of musical cognition. The first theory was written between *c.* 1698 and *c.* 1703 as a single treatise, *Cursory Notes of Musicke*. The second theory, expanded into three separate treatises, was written some-time after 1708 and before *c.* 1720 with the overall title, *Musicall Recollections*. The final theory consisted of two separate treatises, *Theory of Sounds 1728* and *The Musicall Grammarian 1728*.[3] These three theories are not merely rewritings of similar material, as has been previously supposed,[4] for they differ in structure, emphasis and detail. Moreover, there are developments from one theory to the next.

As a theorist of musical cognition, North is concerned with the twofold problem of how we acquire knowledge and act on it. To solve this problem, North had to develop a philosophy of physical

---

[1] *MG c. 1726* (f.2).
[2] *Ibid.* (f.28v).
[3] See References and bibliography 1.
[4] For example, Wilson (1959: vii), Clifford (1963: 276) and Korsten (1981: 29).

3

and human nature. This philosophy cannot be extracted from any single text, because it was worked out over a period of some forty years. For example, North's first treatise on music also happens to be the first synthesis of his philosophy of nature; hence, it has an important status within his writings generally. But in this treatise North left undeveloped a number of aspects of his philosophy and theory of musical cognition. Some of these aspects may be traced through his writings on music, which provide the best overview of his philosophy; but other non-musical texts must be consulted for details which are unclear, omitted or vaguely stated in the writings on music.[5]

Vagueness is not the only difficulty, for North is not rigorous in developing a consistent scientific nomenclature. For example, in some texts he may use the terms 'mind' and 'soul' interchangeably, while in other texts he may employ the terms 'spirit' and 'soul' interchangeably. Yet, in his philosophy mind (soul) and spirit are not the same thing. Although North does present a consistent philosophy of nature, the inconsistency of his terminology presents a considerable challenge to the interpreter of North's texts.[6] It may well be that North sacrificed scientific nomenclature to the requirements of style, for he speaks directly to the reader and signals much about his own opinions through the use of irony and other literary devices. On a 'surface' reading, therefore, his writings have considerable charm. But on a 'deeper' reading, there are numerous failures which a more rigorous and less literary style would have prevented. Nevertheless, North's writings are of the greatest importance in presenting a philosophy that, until recently, had been ignored by scholars of seventeenth- and eighteenth-century science.

When North first began writing, it was in response to the work of René Descartes (b. 1596, d. 1650). By the time he began composing his first theory of musical cognition, he had studied the works of a number of writers who had modified Descartes' philosophy. North regarded some of these writers as controversial, so that he sometimes assented to only parts of their work. The process of giving or withholding assent may be traced through the many texts, musical and non-musical, preparatory to North's second and third theories of musical cognition. In those texts North examines

---

[5] For a list of non-musical topics treated by North, see 'Appendix A' in *Cursory Notes of Musicke* (ed. Chan and Kassler 1986) and Korsten (1981a).
[6] My interpretation differs from that of Korsten (1981) and other writers who have labelled North a 'Cartesian'.

the ideas of others, modifies or extends aspects of his own philosophy, struggles to find the right nomenclature and structure for expressing his ideas and labours to refine his style of writing. To trace the development of North's philosophy and theory of musical cognition, therefore, requires thorough grounding in all North's writings, as well as a detailed knowledge of the works of others to whom he alludes, often covertly.

Such a study is beyond the scope of this Introduction, in which I have sought to provide a background and context for understanding North's work, to outline the main features of his science of music and to indicate the philosophical tradition into which his work falls. To date, only one of North's musical texts has been edited in its entirety so as to include aspects of natural science that are an integral part of his theories of musical cognition.[7] The still widespread acceptance that 'art' and 'science' are two separate 'cultures' has militated against presenting the 1728 theory in its entirety. For this reason I have attempted to place *The Musicall Grammarian 1728* within the context not only of the *The Theory of Sounds 1728* but also within the context of North's non-musical writings and their relation to the intellectual ferment of the seventeenth and early eighteenth centuries. The main problem then becomes: how can one accurately capture past arguments without immersing oneself in the historical context in which the discussions in North's texts arise? I believe that without that context one cannot know whether one has or has not identified the issues.[8]

1. INTRODUCTION

1.1. The seventeenth-century background

In the seventeenth century, various issues were brought into prominence concerning the role of music and, in particular, its utility: how can music provide the greatest pleasure to the greatest numbers?[9] These issues were addressed in the context of two

---

[7] See *Cursory Notes of Musicke* (ed. Chan and Kassler 1986).

[8] See the 'Introduction' (*ibid.*) for contents.

[9] Hollander (1970) provides the only detailed study of the English background relating to the role of music. He argues that between the time of the Reformation and the Revolution of 1688 in England, there was a change in the status of music. He interprets this change in status as a decline, supporting his thesis from the evidence of literary sources. A number of recent, shorter studies suggest that Hollander's thesis may need alteration when other, non-literary evidence is considered. See, for example, Carlin (1973), Gouk (1980) and Kassler and Oldroyd (1983).

debates. One debate attempted to decide whether music was an intellectual or a sensual pleasure. The other debate focused on whether ancient or modern music was the more affective.[10]

The intellectualist/sensualist debate stemmed from problems bequeathed by Descartes, who constructed a mechanistic philosophy of nature in which he regarded particles as impenetrable, matter as extension, space as completely filled, motion as relative and mind as non-physical. But if the mind is non-corporeal, how can it affect and be affected by the body to which it is united? Descartes' answer to this question seems to have proceeded along the following lines. In human sensation there is, first, the mechanical conveyance of physical stimuli from external organs of sense to a common sensorium and, second, there is internal perception of these mechanically-conveyed stimuli by a higher 'spiritual' principle.[11]

Even though Descartes asserted that mind uses body as an instrument, his dualist approach seemed to deny any interaction between mind and body. Some philosophers attempted to meet this inadequacy by reinterpreting substance. For example, Thomas Hobbes (b. 1588, d. 1679) reduced mind to matter; George Berkeley (b. 1685, d. 1753) assimilated matter by mind; and Benedict Spinoza (b. 1632, d. 1677) regarded mind and matter as metaphysically parallel.[12] The intellectualist/sensualist debate in music was a direct result of the substance question, as is clear from 'A Letter concerning Love and Music', written by the Cambridge Platonist, John Norris (b. 1657, d. 1711).

Norris argued that before a decision could be made in the debate, the 'Idea of a Sensual and Intellectual Pleasure must be stated',

...[for] the better conceiving of which it is here to be consider'd that since Matter is not capable of Thought, it must be the Soul only that is the proper Subject both of Pleasure and Pain. And accordingly it will be necessary to say that the true difference between Intellectual and Sensual Pleasure does consist, not in this that Intellectual Pleasure is that which is perceiv'd by the Soul, and Sensual that which is perceiv'd by the Body; for the Body perceives not at all. Nor yet . . . in this, that Sensual Pleasure is when the Body is primarily affected, and the Soul secondarily, or by

---

[10] Both debates are of considerable importance for understanding developments in musical science during the early modern period, although neither debate has been the subject of a special study.

[11] This two-step process implies that everything except consciousness and will can be explained in terms of matter and motion. See Kassler (1984) and the sources cited there.

[12] For various solutions to the problems bequeathed by Descartes, see Fearing (1930/1964), Gardiner, Metcalf, Beebe-Center (1937) and Morris (1966).

participation; and that Intellectual Pleasure is when the Soul is primarily affected, and the Body secondarily, or by participation, (the Soul being the only true percipient in both) but rather in this, that Sensual Pleasure is that which the Soul perceives by the mediation of the Body, upon the occasion of some Motion or Impression made upon it; whereas Intellectual Pleasure is that which the Soul perceives immediately by it self, and from her own Thoughts, without any such occasion from the Body.[13]

The two sides in the debate, then, seem to have been organised along the following lines: the 'intellectualists' argued that music had to work on the passions by informing the mind; the 'sensualists' claimed that music had to affect the passions mechanically by movements of sound coinciding with the motions of the passions.[14]

The other debate, which was related to the first, attempted to decide whether ancient or modern music was the more affective. This debate stemmed from a controversy between those who supported the ancient philosophies and those who championed the new philosophies of nature. Because the 'ancients' were concerned to preserve the *status quo*, their most prominent spokesmen tended to be 'high-church clerics, relentless foes of Latitudinarianism and dissent, enemies of toleration and comprehension, staunch Royalists and Tories'.[15] The 'moderns' allied themselves with the ideological programme of Francis Bacon (b. 1561, d. 1626), whose call for the 'advancement of learning' had included a number of features, one of which – the conception that moderns were better than ancients – embodied an embryonic notion of progress. Although the moderns shared certain beliefs and values, they were divided into what one historian has called 'left-Baconians' and 'right-Baconians':

The first group . . . were primarily concerned with changing the social and natural environment by means of utopian planning, agricultural improvement, radical reform of the educational system, and the humanitarian goal of the control of nature for the benefit of the people. The right-Baconians . . . accepted traditional social values and rejected any notion of a basic

---

[13] Norris (1678/1710: 312). As a Platonist, Norris held that music is an intellectual pleasure (see Kassler 1979: ii/798).

[14] See Mace (1964). Some of the broader issues of the intellectualist/sensualist debate are treated by Williamson (1935), who provides a survey of the spirit/matter controversy in the 1650s; Leyden (1968), who deals with metaphysical issues; and Yolton (1984), who gives a brief summary of the controversy insofar as it affected theories of cognition. See also the 'Introduction' to North's *Cursory Notes of Musicke* (ed. Chan and Kassler 1986: (36)–(42)).

[15] Wood (1983: 89). Gaukroger (1986) surveys the English responses to the new philosophies.

reordering of society. They envisaged science in terms of personal fulfil-
ment and a revelation of the order and regularity of the universe as an
expression of God's great design.[16]

In those aspects of the ancient/modern debate relating to music,
two authors were of particular importance: the Rev. John Wallis (b.
1616, d. 1703), a 'right-Baconian', and the Rev. Isaac Vossius (b.
1618, d. 1689), an 'ancient'. In an appendix to his edition of *Claudii
Ptolemaei Harmonicorum Libri Tres* (1682), Wallis provided a comparison of the theories of ancient Greek music with that of his own
day.[17] Some of the opinions expressed there in Latin were
expanded in 1698, when he observed that the reports of ancient
writers were 'highly *Hyperbolical*, and next door to *Fabulous*'.
According to him, music in ancient times was 'a *Rare* Thing, which
the Rusticks, on whom it is reported to have had such Effects, had
never heard before'. Moreover, since harmony alone belonged to
modern music, it equalled, if not exceeded, the powers of ancient
music in pleasing the ear. But, he continued,

... if we would have our Musick so adjusted as to excite particular
Passion, Affections, or Temper of Mind (as that of the Ancients is
supposed to have done) we must then imitate the Physician rather than the
Cook; and apply more simple Ingredients, fitted to the Temper we would
produce. For in the sweet Mixture of compounded Musick, one thing
doth so correct another, that it doth not operate strongly any one way.
And this, I doubt not, but a judicious Composer may so effect, (that with
the Help of such Hyperbole's, as with which the Ancient Musick is wont
to be set off) our Musick may be said to do as great Feats as any of theirs.[18]

---

[16] Wood (1983: 85). The so-called 'left' Baconians included Samuel Hartlib and John
Webster. The so-called 'right' Baconians included Robert Boyle, Ralph Cudworth, John
Locke, William Petty and John Wilkins. Wood (1983) points out that the two groups did
not live and work in isolation, for there were shared values and beliefs as well as frequent
association among a number of the individuals.

[17] Wallis' edition was an important work of musical scholarship, for it made available in
Latin Ptolemy's treatise on harmonics. In the appendix Wallis covered briefly the ancient
harmonics according to the different sects, Aristoxenian and Pythagorean, comparing
these doctrines to the modern theory of coincidence of pulses. A favourable notice
appeared in the *Philosophical Transactions of the Royal Society* (1683) 13: 20–1; and the work
was reprinted in Volume 3 of Wallis' *Opera Mathematica* (1693–99), along with two new
commentaries on the music theories of Porphyrius and Manuel Bryennius.

[18] Wallis (1698: 302–3). If the question posed had been 'whence it comes to pass that *Musick*
hath so great an Influence or Efficacy on our Affections, Passions, Motions, &c.', Wallis
would have had to discourse on 'the Nature of Sounds, produced by some Subtile
Motions in the Air, propagated and continued to the Ear and Organs of Hearing, and
thence communicated to the Animal Spirits; which excite suitable Imaginations, Affections, Passions &c. and these attended with conformable Motions and Actions, and
according to the various Proportions, Measures, and Mixtures of such Sounds, there do
arise various Effects in the Mind or Imagination, suitable thereunto' (*ibid.*: 297).

Vossius took a position diametrically opposed to that of Wallis. In a large tome entitled *De Poematum Cantu et Viribus Rithmi* (1673), he argued that motion communicated to the mind by means of the body pleases us if that motion is regular; that the ancient philosophers perceiving this took care to cultivate their language and make it harmonious by the number and combination of long and short syllables; that to this end they invented metrical feet as the foundation of ancient versification; and that the whole effect of ancient music is ascribable to the power of that particular arrangement and interchange of quantities which he called 'rythmus'. Since the knowledge and application of this rhythmus had been lost for over a thousand years, so too, claimed Vossius, had the power of exciting the affections by music.

Decisions in each debate hinged on the nature of evidence. In the case of the intellectualist/sensualist debate, the evidence for the effects of music rested on conceptions of the passions and affections. These words were of common coin in the seventeenth century, but in systematic writings their meaning derives from one or another philosophy of nature. For example, in Descartes' philosophy the passions were defined as experiences of the soul derived from alien causes, whereas in Hobbes's philosophy the passions were treated as tendencies, not feelings, and were closely connected with the bodily motions of pleasure and pain.[19] In the case of the ancient/modern debate, the evidence of the effects of ancient music resided chiefly in the testimony of authors, since only a few fragments of the music itself had been preserved.[20]

The problem of evidence was addressed first by Roger North, a lawyer experienced in evaluating testimonial as well as circumstantial evidence.[21] North attempted to demonstrate that music is an intellectual as well as a sensual pleasure, since it exercises all our powers – mental and physical. Hence, in his first treatise on music, *Cursory Notes of Musicke*, written between *c.*1698 and *c.*1703, he argued that music:

---

[19] For various conceptions of the passions and affections in the seventeenth century, see Gardiner, Metcalf, Beebe-Center (1937), who stated that no writer of the seventeenth century attributes to the passions such significance for the whole life of man as Hobbes. In his theory they sustain thought, constitute will, determine the intellect and moral character and are the sole springs of action. Without the passions the train of our thought would be unregulated, since direction is given by the endeavour to reach a desired end.

[20] Other problems included understanding the Greek system of music and deciphering the notation.

[21] For North's legal procedures, see the 'Introduction' to *Cursory Notes of Musicke* (ed. Chan and Kassler 1986: (14)–(22)); see also *MG 1728* (f.103 below). For changing conceptions of evidence during North's lifetime, see Shapiro (1983).

... exceeds all arts, and means upon earth, that ever were knowne, and practist, for the immediate and copious enterteinement of all our facultys together abstract[ed] from all relation to nutriment or exoneration, which an heterodox philosopher [Hobbes] will have to comprehend all pleasure whatever.[22]

North was already steeped in the contemporary philosophical literature when he wrote *Cursory Notes of Musicke*. Moreover, he also had read the works of Wallis and Vossius. In an unpublished critique of Vossius' treatise, North sided with Wallis who allowed 'what I contend for', since, as to the effects of ancient music, Vossius had 'taken the hyperbolicall, or retoricall expressions, that orators, such as most historians then were, used to prays what they thought comendable and usefull, and therefore to be recomended to practice'.[23] Vossius supposed that music had attained perfection in antiquity and had since been corrupted. North supposed the contrary: 'the world improved their [the Ancient's] musick, and it went on advancing in variety and compas of notes, and comodiousness of instruments'. After assessing this and other 'errors' of Vossius, North concluded that it was presumptuous for that author to value his own 'science':

... yet sure wee may claime the priveledg that is allowed to the veryest fools in the proverb, which says their [*sic*] know more within their owne houses, then wise men doe, who come not there. And according to this priviledg I venture to say the author of this charg, writes of the moderne musick, with as much ignorance as ever yet abased a subject in print, and with a doctorall supersiliousness equall to, if not exceeding his ignorance.[24]

After North's death, the evidence was evaluated by another lawyer, Sir John Hawkins (b. 1719, d. 1789), whose critical account of both the intellectualist/sensualist and ancient/modern debates forms the preliminary discourse to *A General History of the Science and Practice of Musick* (1776 rev. 1853/1963), the first modern history of music to provide what Hawkins himself described as:

... an explanation of fundamental doctrines, and a narration of important events and historical facts, in a chronological series, with such occasional

[22] *Cursory Notes of Musicke* (ed. Chan and Kassler 1986: 151).
[23] *Vossius de viribus Rithmi* (ff. 56 and 53v).
[24] *Ibid.* (f. 58).

remarks and evidences, as might serve to illustrate the one and authenticate the other. With these are intermixed a variety of musical compositions, tending as well to exemplify that diversity of styles which is common both to music and speech or written language, as to manifest the gradual improvements in the art of combining musical sounds.[25]

1.2. The context of the Enlightenment

The work of North and Hawkins demarcates the period called the 'Enlightenment'.[26] Despite the many differences of outlook during this period, there was widespread acceptance of the reality of natural law – that civilized or cultured humankind is essentially the same, despite local, regional or national variations. The reassertion of natural law led to the notion that European music is a universal 'language' with local, regional or national 'dialects' (i.e., idioms, styles). Hence, efforts were made to understand the 'grammar' of this European language, the dialects of which were regarded as deviations from, or variations of, the universal central core. Accordingly, it was thought that a logically connected structure of laws and generalisations susceptible of demonstration and verification could be constructed and would replace ignorance, prejudice and dogma.

The efforts to formulate such laws and generalisations led to grammars of what now is called 'tonality', the musical language that has governed most Western music from the seventeenth to the end of the nineteenth centuries.[27] This new science of music needs to be understood in the context of developments in the seventeenth century, when the increasing subordination of mathematics to

---

[25] Hawkins (1776 rev. 1853/1963: i/xix). Hawkins, who aligned himself with the intellectualists and the moderns, provided details about each debate in his preliminary discourse, as well as in the body of his work (see Kassler 1979: i/475–80). Musicologists have ignored the importance of the preliminary discourse as a key to the issues which contributed to the emergence of early modern musical science.

[26] Although there is some dispute about the dates of the Enlightenment, I have adopted the dates c. 1700–c. 1780, with some allowance for an earlier manifestation of the ideology in England. The generalisations made here about trends in writings on music stem in part from my book (1979) which contains data for a study of the conceptual impact of different texts, an important but ignored area in the history of musical science and musical pedagogy. The bulk of the data stems from textbooks, which provide the best evidence for the spread of ideas at a particular time.

[27] The word 'grammar' was used in a number of different ways by writers on music of the seventeenth and eighteenth centuries. For musico-grammatical developments in England, see Atcherson (1973), Chenette (1967) and Kassler (1979).

experience, and the discovery of unexpected laws through close observation, led to the modern natural science of acoustics.[28] In acoustics we find a genuine school of science, the soundness of whose hypotheses, and accuracy of whose computations, were increasingly established. Since the task of acoustics was restricted to establishing the physical and mathematical antecedents of sounds in general, without regard to their beauty or deformity, *musical* science was still to be sought.

The new science of music was to emerge through efforts of writers to determine accurately the scope of music. The first writer to undertake this task was Roger North,[29] whose writings reflect a tendency of the Enlightenment period to take language as the model for thought. This practice was influenced by the 'Messieurs du Port-Royal', who held that grammar illustrates logic and that both disciplines describe how the mind works.[30] In particular, the Port-Royal *Grammaire Générale et Raisonée*, by the clarity and time-liness of its method, assisted North to give English voice to a new idea of musical grammar and musical understanding in his own country. This new idea was based on the Port-Royal's connection between language and thought.

North regarded musical grammar as the study of musical signs and their proper disposal through human thought and experience so as to answer the several purposes of instruction and utility, the two ends of science. In his educational theory, North adopted the two cardinal principles of Bacon: regardless of the differences of students to be educated, materials should be placed before their senses and further enlightenment should derive from the proper methods of instruction.[31] The methods of instruction North uti-lised were based on a model, derived from botany, of growth,

[28] See, for example, Hawkins (1776 rev. 1853/1963: ii/719–24). The history of musical acoustics had little attention from scholars until the work of Hunt (1978). This study, incomplete at the author's death, has been followed by a number of special studies that focus on the seventeenth and eighteenth centuries; see, for example, Cohen (1981), Cohen (1984), Dostrovsky (1974–75), Gouk (1982), Kassler (1979) and the 'Introduction' to *Cursory Notes of Musick* (ed. Chan and Kassler 1986: (22)–(27), (36)–(53)).

[29] In the 1728 theory, for example, North attempts to distinguish sound from other motions, music from other sounds, singing from other vocal noises, and so on.

[30] For studies of the Port-Royal grammar and logic and their influence in England, see Arnauld and Lancelot (tr. Rieux and Rollin 1676/1975), Arnauld and Nicole (tr. Dickoff and James 1685/1964), Cohen (1977) and Howell (1956).

[31] See *MG 1728* (ff. 13v, 15, 16, 56v, 57, 69, 75v, 79, 87 *et passim.*); see also Kassler (1976). In *Notes of Me* (ed. Jessop 1887: 75), North writes: 'beginners should be trained as in manufacture and trades, first taught to provide the material and then to put it together, and lastly to finish it'.

increase and decay.[32] According to this model, students were not to be burdened with matters unsuitable to their age, comprehension or physical development. Instead, they were to be cultivated by means of a proper method of instruction which would lead them from darkness into light.

To establish a proper method of instruction, North sought for natural principles in physico-mechanics and physiological psychology and from these deduced rules for musical criticism and for the structure of musical composition. A similar (but by no means identical) approach was adopted by the French composer and writer, Jean-Philippe Rameau (b. 1683, d. 1764).[33] Later, attempts were made to form abstract systems of music by stating and exemplifying a series of rules thought to be the general expressions of the practice of great composers. This type of approach is exemplified in the work of the German writer, Johann Philipp Kirnberger (b. 1721, d. 1783).[34]

Musical 'grammarians' were concerned chiefly with the 'syntax' of music, for their main task was to provide rules for the connection of musical elements treated as simple (notes, rests) or as compound (intervals, chords, periods). Hence, rules were needed for note-to-note relations as well as for relations of larger structures. Comparisons were made to language, for the grammarians treated the different levels of musical structure like syllables (notes), words (chords) and phrases (periods) of language. Although structures analogous to the sentence and the paragraph were identified by a few grammarians, rules for these structures were not established until after the period of the Enlightenment.[35]

In establishing rules for unity and variety, the grammarians adopted a combinatorial approach, in which the elements, regarded as '*materia musica*', merely change their position and arrangement in time. The combinatorial doctrine of changes was applied first to chords, whereby the notes constituting a triad change their position and arrangement to form the first and second inversions of that

[32] See *ibid.* (ff.8v, 13v, 14v, 28, 30, 30v, 54v, 60v, 64v, 73, 84v, 94v, 98v, *et passim*.). The botanical model also underpins North's theory of history (see below I.2.2.).

[33] For the transmission of Rameau's ideas in England, see Kassler (1979).

[34] Kirnberger's theory was introduced into England at the end of the eighteenth century by Augustus Frederick Christopher Kollmann and Thomas Young (see Kassler 1979: i/646–71, ii/1088–96).

[35] North refers to one of his musical examples as 'an uncouth sentence' (*MG c. 1726*: ff.112–112v), but from the context it is clear that he means paragraph ('strain', 'verse'). Hence, he identified larger structures, although he did not systematically treat them. In England the larger structures were also identified by John Casper Heck and were afterwards systematically treated by Kollmann (see Kassler 1979: i/492–8, 646–71).

PATTERNS OF REPETITION

UNIFORMITY Imitation of Period★	VARIETY Variation of Period	
	Music	*Mathematics*
1 Repetition on the same (or on a different) note of the scale	1 Change of key and mode	1 Change by transposition
2 Repetition in notes of the same (or of different) lengths	2 Change of measure	2 Change in magnitude by augmentation or diminution
3 Repetition in the same (or in a different) motion	3 Change of movement	3 Change in shape by inversion or 'reversion'
4 Repetition in the same (or in a different) form	4 Change in the divisions of the harmony and air	4 Change in form by division

★ Imitation includes the ideas of same and similar; that is, strict imitation and free imitation.

Figure 2. Patterns of Repetition.

triad. Roger North was the first musical grammarian to attempt an explication of what is now known as the principle of chord inversion and to present a system of harmonic progression based on that principle.[36] Towards the end of the Enlightenment, the doctrine of changes was applied also to periods, the rules for which are schematically represented in Figure 2.[37]

Despite their focus on musical syntax, the musical grammarians did not exclude the semantics of music. But the problem of musical

[36] In North's vocabulary the terms for inversion are 'change' and 'counterchange', but he has difficulty finding appropriate terms to distinguish between a chord in root position and a chord in first or second inversion. In *Some Memorandums, concerning Musick* (f.21v), he adopts the terms 'natural or true base' and 'forct or assumed base'. In *Cursory Notes of Musicke* (ed. Chan and Kassler 1986: 200 *et passim*), he changes his nomenclature to 'proper' and 'improper' base. In his 1728 theory he settles upon 'proper' and 'consort' (also called 'intermediate') base notes.

[37] The combinatorial approach of musical grammarians contributed to the modern conception of musical analysis which proceeds from the assumption that a piece of music may be decomposed into its material elements and recomposed or generated again from those elements. For some of the historical background relating to combinatoriality and analysis, see Kassler (1987); see also below I.2.1.

meaning – how was music to signify? – was addressed in relation to music's function. The consensus was that music's function, like that of other imaginative arts, was moral: to please and to instruct (*utile dulce*).[38] Hence, the proper subject for music was imitation of human nature. Traditional theories of imitation had given primacy to vocal music, so that signification could be conveyed by means of the text. In the neo-classical aesthetic that dominated the period of the Enlightenment, music with words continued to be regarded as the principal vehicle for conveying musical meaning. Hence, the rules laid down for such vocal genres as oratorios, operas and cantatas were merely reaffirmations of a much older tradition deriving from Hellenistic times.

The rapid growth of purely instrumental music and the development of instrumental genres such as sonatas, symphonies and concertos, demanded that some modification be made to the traditional aesthetic. Such a modification is found in the work of Roger North, who indicated how human nature could be imitated in purely musical terms without relying on texts, since in his theory 'harmony' and 'measure' may be used to depict, respectively, human thoughts and human actions.[39] Later, the moral philosopher, Adam Smith (b. 1723, d. 1790), provided a justification for the value of instrumental music in an essay 'Of the Nature of that Imitation which takes Place in what are called the Imitative Arts', written before 1780 but published posthumously in 1795.[40]

The procedures employed in the new musical grammars provided a rule of reason, which gradually came to be associated with deductions of logic concerning beauty and deformity from supposed principles and feelings of human nature.[41] Grammars using this rule were intended to replace older, more authoritarian grammars which had been prescriptive, not descriptive. In the older grammars, freedom still meant special exemption from a general rule of compulsion; liberty still implied a special privilege to do something forbidden to others. In the new grammars, freedom

---

[38] *Utile dulce* (Lat.): The useful with the pleasant. According to contemporary opinion, to say that someone has combined the *utile dulce* is to give the very first praise to a writer or composer (see Borgerhoff 1950/1968, Clark 1925/1965 and Pocock 1980).

[39] This notion was mooted in North's first treatise and developed in subsequent writings. See *Cursory Notes of Musicke* (ed. Chan and Kassler 1986: 151 *et passim*); *Musicall Recollections III* (ff. 52v–56 *et passim*.); *MG 1728* (ff. 64–66 *et passim*.).

[40] See Smith (ed. Black and Hutton 1795: 179–244); for his contributions to music, see Kassler (1979: ii/942–6).

[41] For some of these procedures, see Kassler (1979).

was understood in the modern sense of the term as the power to do as one thinks fit unless restrained by law.[42]

Law was established by precedent – the compositions of the best masters – and not by authority of grammarians. Hence, in their explications of the technical 'secrets' of composers, the grammarians' precedents were usually passages from, and sometimes entire pieces of, music. The passages, in particular, were regarded as patterns illustrative of good and bad usage, or as material to take up and use as occasion required. But the grammarians acknowledged that some passages in music were inexplicable (*'je ne sais quoi'*): being divinely inspired, the transcendent or sublime passages could only be shown and not described.[43]

Despite the rule of reason, then, there remained certain aspects of music that were regarded as beyond rational explication. Nevertheless, contemporary opinion recognised the importance of the new science of music, for there was public awareness that a person who had completed such a study would be equipped to compose correctly or to judge accurately the works of others. But by the end of the Enlightenment, musical composition and criticism were considered of too great magnitude and intricacy for the grasp of immature, amateur or female intellects: the exercise of a vigorous and discerning male mind was requisite to the acquirement of profound theoretical knowledge and the attainment of excellence in

[42] The new conception of freedom is already apparent in a number of treatises written in England during the early part of the seventeenth century. For an analysis of the new conception, see Hobbes (ed. Macpherson 1651/1986: Part II, Chapter 21). By the middle of the eighteenth century, Hawkins observed: 'That we are at this time in a state of emancipation from the bondage of laws imposed without authority, is owing to a new investigation of the principles of harmony, and the studies of a class of musicians, of whom Geminiani seems to have been the chief' (1776 rev. 1853/1963: ii/902). According to Hawkins' account, Francis (Francesco) Geminiani, in his *Guida Armonica* (*c*.1742), first laid bare the secrets of composers, thereby causing the old, choir-trained musicians to stand 'aghast at the licences which it [the treatise] allowed' and to predict 'little less from the work than the utter ruin of musical science' (*ibid.*: ii/907). See also Kassler (1979: i/ 381–5) and (forthcoming).

[43] In his first theory North points out that 'however hard it is to anatomise beauty in any thing so as to shew in what the grace of an action, or turne of an hand, eye, or foot lys; yet nothing should be done with a designe of becoming without knowing why; but if no reason of doing appear, doe nothing, and it's likely the best grace will be in that. So tho it is hard to say why a certein air some musick hath above other, is so considerable, yet there is some reason for it, which one with comparing and reflecting may a little more or less guess at. And a world of such je ne scay quois there are in matters of pleasure' (*Cursory Notes of Musicke* ed. Chan and Kassler 1986: 206). North's writings to *c*.1703 contain a number of remarks about *'je ne sais quoi'* or what North also refers to as 'inexpressible'. These remarks may be traced in Hine, Chan, Kassler (1987). See also below *MG 1728* (ff.78v, 82v, 87, 92). For historical background to the concept, see Borgerhoff (1950/ 1968: 186–200).

these fields.[44] Precocious talent, such as Mozart's, was recognised, of course; but evidence of such a talent was considered to be as rare as the discovery of a new planet.[45]

2. ROGER NORTH'S SCIENCE OF MUSIC

2.1. Musical cognition

Roger North's contributions to the science of music fall within the early part of the Enlightenment and constitute a direct response to issues raised and debated in the seventeenth century. Two such issues have already been mentioned,[46] each of which presents a decision problem. Is music a particular kind of pleasure? Are some kinds of music more affective than other kinds? Since the evidence in each case is inconclusive, answers to these questions can only be probable, not certain. What, then, constitutes a convincing argument? In North's form of argument, which reflects his training in the law, general propositions are assumed, from which all sorts of consequences are deduced by the aid of logic and other material assumptions. Some of, if not all, the consequences are verified empirically; and it is concluded with probability that the propositions are applicable to the case at hand.[47]

In all three theories of musical cognition, North assumes two general propositions: elasticity and goodness.[48] According to the first proposition, his thesis is that sound depends on, and proceeds from, the elasticity ('spring') of the air: unless the air is made to spring, there can be no production or perception of sound.[49]

---

[44] Women were excluded from training in composition for reasons detailed in Kassler (1972).

[45] North himself refers to such talents as 'rarities' (*MG 1728*: f.10). For English writings describing such prodigies, see Kassler (1979: i/52–4, 132–3 *et passim*).

[46] See above I.1.1.

[47] For a discussion of North's method, see the 'Introduction' to *Cursory Notes of Musicke* (ed. Chan and Kassler 1986: (14)–(17)). For historical background relating to questions of probability and certainty, see Leeuwen (1963), Shapiro (1983) and Kassler (1986).

[48] The discussion here focuses chiefly, but not solely, on North's 1728 theory, although non-musical texts have been consulted for reasons indicated above (I. Preface).

[49] By the term 'spring' North denotes the reversible expansion and contraction of physical bodies. In *Cursory Notes of Musicke*, he never uses the term 'elasticity', even though he employs it in a text preparatory to that treatise (see Hine, Chan, Kassler 1987: 6). In the seventeenth century this term and its variants ('elatery') were taken over by various English writers from French authors; but the term 'spring' was preferred by Boyle and Hooke (see Webster 1962–66: 453–4 and 'Introduction' to *Cursory Notes of Musicke* ed. Chan and Kassler 1986: (36)–(53)).

According to the second proposition, his thesis is that the basis of a judgement that *x* is good is the link between goodness (i.e., decorum, congruity) and pleasure. The propositions of elasticity and goodness enable North to provide an equilibrium analysis of the process of musical cognition and to reach critical conclusions that are deducible strictly from the premises.

For musical knowledge to take place, however, there must be a knowing subject, as well as a knowing process. North conceives of the former as body and the latter as mind ('soul'). But it would be a mistake to construe North's meaning in Cartesian terms, as other scholars have done, for North adopts a modified form of Hobbism.[50] Instead of two substances, corporeal and incorporeal, North posits only one substance: matter. Accordingly, he holds that 'all the varietys of sence, may be produced by simple matter onely moved'.[51] If motion is the natural state of matter, human individuals may be reduced to the effects of a mechanical apparatus consisting of sense organs, nerves, muscles, memory, imagination and reason, which apparatus moves in response to the impact (or imagined impact) of external bodies on it.

In Hobbes's philosophy, the human apparatus is not, strictly speaking, self-moving; but it is always in motion, because other things are always impinging on it. In a less strict sense, it is self-moving, because it has built into it an endeavour to maintain its motion. People's most complex and refined actions can be explained as effects of the operation of this mechanical system, not by treating them all as mere reflex actions, but by treating voluntary or willed actions ('intentions') as a process of computation which calls into play the external as well as internal senses and puts them all to work in service of the in-built endeavour.[52]

North's in-built endeavour is tension, for he holds that all bodies, artificial and human, are like

---

[50] See, for example, Korsten (1981), who did not study North's writings on music. For a brief comparison of the theories of Hobbes and North, see *Cursory Notes of Musicke* (ed. Chan and Kassler 1986: 273–4 (151:3) *et passim.*).

[51] *Prejudices* (f.4v). Elsewhere, North writes: 'Cartesius saying cogito, was mistaken, it being more proper to say, percipio ergo sum. For what the vulgar means by thinking as ruminating, meditating, etc., is onely a secondary act of sense, called remembrance owing to the economy of parts in the sensorium. Therefore wee resort to primary sensation, as the passion of the mind, which we have to consider' (*Change of Philosoficall Methods*: f.99). Accordingly, North holds that all human capacity lies '1. in the use of our senses, 2. in the movement of our members, and from these two are to be deduced the understanding of all humane things' (*Of Humane Capacity*: f.34v).

[52] This summary is from Hobbes (ed. Macpherson 1651/1986), but see Kassler (forthcoming).

... a box of springs of infinite sorts, sizes, and vigor but all allyd by connexions so that, scarce any can be moved, but the whole more or less is affected[.] Or suppose [body to be like] a tree of wire growing by a strong stem and branching out[,] and at the end of each wire grew a lead bullet, which weighing downe all hang as upon springs, not touching. If you take this up in your hand, you shall see all the bulletts play in a sort of counterpois to each other, or if you move one, all will move more or less; and if this were an animall, and the sensorium [were] at the root, nothing would happen att the extremitys, which would not make a sensible influence there.[53]

In his explanation of body in motion, North has recourse to the pendulum condition, that is, the isochrony of 'springs' such as taut strings and other systems having equilibrium configurations along axes, for he is fully aware that, physically, no pendulum is truly isochronous.[54] Accordingly, he regards every body as a tensional field made up of outward and inward action, expansion and contraction; through this double movement, the utility and existence of body is preserved.

People are like musical instruments, for both kinds of body have the potential to sound. But in order to sound, such bodies, or parts of them, must first become agitated so as to shake all the contiguous air.[55] When the agitation is equal-timed, the pulses occasion the simple harmonic motion of air particles, the particles then acting on each other according to the laws of impact. By means of the air, an invisible and impalpable body, sound spreads around the spot where it has been produced by a vibratory movement which is passed on successively from one part of the air to another. The spreading of this movement, taking place equally rapidly on all

---

[53] *Of Humane Capacity* (f.41v).

[54] See the 'Introduction' to *Cursory Notes of Musicke* (ed. Chan and Kassler 1986: (24)–(27) *et passim.*) and Ariotti (1971–72). According to Cannon and Dostrovsky, systems having equilibrium configurations along axes 'were observed to undergo simpler motions when the motions took them through their equilibrium configurations, that is, when all parts of a system reached its axis simultaneously. Thus, the motions that were studied were those having the properties of isochronism and simultaneous crossing of the axis. The connection between isochronism and the simple pendulum was familiar in the work of Beeckman, Galileo, and Huygens. It was clearly assumed that isochronism meant the restriction to the case of small vibrations. But furthermore, it was assumed that isochronism and simultaneous crossing of the axis meant that each element of the system would move as a simple pendulum, that is, each element would undergo simple harmonic motions having the same period' (1981: 5–6). Before the middle of the eighteenth century, it was believed that isochronism and simultaneous crossing of the axis always implied the 'pendulum condition', and it was Jean Le Rond D'Alembert who showed that the vibrating string itself provides a counter example.

[55] In the case of the voice and wind instruments, it is not the instrument but an enclosed quantity of air which vibrates.

sides, forms spherical surfaces or waves. These waves, ever enlarging, strike our ears. Sound, therefore, is transmitted by pulses.

For immediate knowing to take place, sensible presence, by itself, is insufficient, for there also must be attention. Hence, pulses must be notable, that is, they must engage the attention and lead to sustained reflection and thought. In North's theory, notable pulses consist of indistinguishable ('insensible') moments of time, because they are so swift. When pulses meet this condition, they excite the tympanum of the ear,[56] the chain of events taking place internally in human bodies being the same as that which happened externally. The vibrating tympanum transmits the pulses to the nervous system. The nervous system, in turn, vibrates and transmits the pulses to the brain, which co-ordinates the various pulses and elevates them into consciousness as images. The mind, by its presence to the brain, then 'reads' the images in the act of perception.

The images represented to, and seen by, the mind are the rules of vibrations, which North exemplifies in a series of 'punctations', one of which is illustrated in Figure 3 (see p. 22). In this punctation the parallel vertical lines represent the flow of time, and the points represent the pulses. The lowest row represents the pulses that correspond to the fundamental tone ('key'); the pulses above correspond to the intervals of the octave, 12th, 15th, 17th, 19th and 22d. These intervals form what North calls the 'full accord' (he never uses the terms 'harmonic' or 'overtone series'), which, with some octave transposition, is represented in current common musical notation below the punctation.

From this punctation alone, it is clear that sounds co-exist and do not obliterate each other, because they are dynamic processes in the air, of which each of them is a certain modification. Such modifications can undergo what now is called 'superposition' without losing their identity, whereas a superposition of static states does away with them. We may conclude, therefore, that in North's theory the brain is not a wax tablet on which images are impressed or a piece of paper on which creases are made.[57] North himself suggests that the

[56] In his writings generally North has little to say about the external senses, leaving details to the 'anatomists'. In *TS 1728* he simply remarks that 'The fabrick of the ear is very considerable, with regard, not onely to the perceiving, but judging of sounds. The place of the sensible touch, is reputed to be the drum membrane, for by the modes of attaque upon that, wee judg the modes of the percussion, as quik, dull, continued, or otherwise as the case is' (f.95).

[57] Both images were used by Descartes, who regarded the brain as a soft substance in which animal spirits leave traces. These traces are preserved, the animal spirits passing through

brain or 'residence of thought' is like a reflecting telescope.[58] According to this comparison, the concave mirror or speculum is the cerebellum ('sensorium'); the eyepiece or combination of lenses for magnifying an image is the cerebrum ('brain'); and the eye is the mind. But North insists: 'I doe not argue extention, or locality of the mind otherwise then it hath power over this particular matter, to which in every humane body it is affix't'.[59] Mind, therefore, differs from the instruments of body only in its function as 'a president to determine among the capacitys of the body, which shall be imployed, and which not'.[60]

To fulfill its function as president, the mind scans the images transmitted to the brain. Despite the rapidity with which it performs this action, the mind can attend to only one image at a time, because in the act of perception the mind must perform various computations on the data represented to it.[61] In performing these computations, the mind employs three powers: the ear, the memory and the imagination. These powers are not separate faculties; rather, they are different functions of mind. The first power, the ear, processes data communicated as notable or indistinguishable pulses, the computation of which occurs subconsciously ('without science', 'incogitanter') and involves counting. The method may be illustrated in the Key to Figure 3 (see p. 23), showing North's punctation in numbers, followed by the mechanical derivation on the monochord. In the punctation and its computational model, the bass or fundamental tone (1 in the computational model) is the normative sound in determining the character of harmonic sonorities, all the upper parts being more or less perfect as they have more or fewer pulses that coincide with pulses of the bass.

In the computational model and in the mechanical derivation shown in the Key, the ratios of simple consonances stop at 6:5, because in North's theory we know only the numbers 1 to 6 by forming ideas of so many bodies. Beyond this, we know only

them again and again, thereby endowing the living creature not only with sensory perception but also with memory. The conception of cerebral traces of impressions of ideas became known as *engrams*, which until the nineteenth century were conceived as static imprints. The implication of such models is that function is localisable in some portion of the brain (see Kassler 1984). North does not hold this view.

[58] *Some Essays* (ff. 13–15). The reflecting telescope was invented by Isaac Newton.
[59] *Ibid.* (f. 15).
[60] *Ibid.*
[61] North explicitly states that 'the mind is not capable of observing more then one thing at a time'; it 'seems to observe more onely by a swift passage of the attention from one thing to another, and so passing and repassing seems to dilate the observation' (*Power of Humane Understanding*: f. 89).

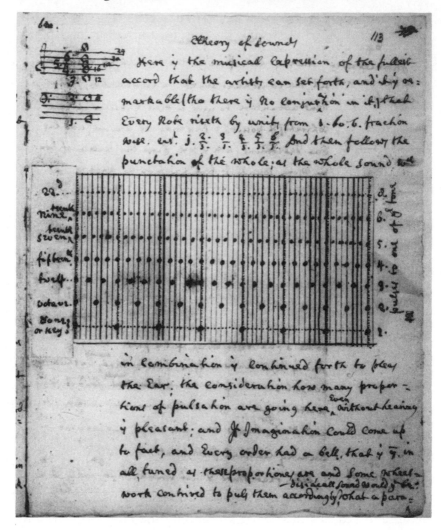

Figure .3. North's 'Punctation' or language of thought (*Theory of Sounds 1728*: f. 113).

hypothetically and 'by names where of the signification is granted'.[62] Hence, the mind's power of distinguishing natural things is limited,

... and the measure is given from our faculty of moving some part of our bodies which is done, actually or mentally, when ever wee mark or

---

[62] *Cursory Notes of Musicke* (ed. Chan and Kassler 1986: 152).

```
                    1
                  1 2
                1 2 3
              1 2 3 4
            1 2 3 4 5
          1 2 3 4 5 6
```

Monochord dividend	Intervals produced	Ratios of frequencies	Order of perfection
1	Unison	1:1	(Most perfect)
2	Octave	2:1	
3	Fifth	3:2	
4	Fourth	4:3	
5	Third ♯	5:4	
6	Third ♭	6:5	(Least perfect)

Key to Figure 3. Computational model and mechanical derivation.

number things passing by us. And if the transits are so quick wee cannot attend them with our reall action, then the idea of a continuation emergeth. And in like manner the waves of pulses that follow so swift, that we have no corporeall means to distinguish them, become a continued sound, and we call it noise.[63]

When pulses strike us faster than we can count, the mind is unable to separate them in conscious thought into preceding and succeeding moments of time. In processing such pulses, memory,

---

[63] *TS 1728* (ff.99–99v). Before North, numerous writers attempted to explain why the ratios of simple consonances stop after 6:5. Starting with the scenario of Gioseffo Zarlino, the various explanations are detailed and critically examined by Cohen (1984). None of the writers surveyed by Cohen seem to offer North's explanation, which is based on the 'dullness of our materiall engin' (*Untitled Essay*: f.254v), a point he reiterates in a number of other texts. In one text, for example, North writes: 'It is very well knowne how and where indistinction begins, for our members are of a stated demension, and moved by stated powers, and it being a law of nature that things shall move equably . . . whereby pendulums, as so quallifyed, swing isocronically. In like manner wee can swing our armes, and hardly if at all otherwise; and wee can nodd, and point with such a swiftness, and no faster, and when objects pass faster than wee can accompany with the motion of any of our members (and mentall is the same as actually) a continuation indistinguishable begins' (*Change of Philosoficall Methods*: f.100v). And in another text, he states: 'If motions have returnes swifter then any motion of our bodys can keep pace with, all distinction ceaseth, and the idea is confused, and the sensation is as of a thing continued. So wee distinguish the movement of the musitian's hands, but not the vibrations of his strings; and the like' (*Untitled Essay*: f.254).

the second power of mind, gathers them into larger units, which North regards as appearances or mental fictions.[64] Appearances consist of distinguishable pulses, the computation of which occurs consciously and involves comparison. Pitches, for example, do not merely exist at the moment they are heard, they also endure in the memory and relate to what came before and what follows after. The mind accepts a pitch as harmonically functional by a process of comparison, as North insists when he writes:

Experience tells us ... that some tones are proper, and others very improper, to succeed each other. And this is discovered by certein mutuall relations or habitudes. As if two tones are made to sound together the compound effect, to our sence may be gratefull, or harsh and offensive: and thereupon it must be concluded that tones which accompany well, are best qualifyed to succeed one and other, for so near as immediate succession, memory doth as it were joyne them.[65]

The names by which we designate appearances are conventional, for North acknowledges that 'wee have little else, but names, to be concerned with in this theory . . .[and] it must be no surprise if some termes occurr, without a sufficient vocabulary, but I shall take care, whatever names are assumed, the things shall be clear enough'.[66] Accordingly, names such as 'noise' and 'tone', 'accord', and 'discord', 'high' and 'low', 'harsh' and 'smooth' are common terms for various combinations of vibrations that are impressed on our organ of hearing and transmitted to the mind to read. That is, high and low, etc., are not intrinsic to bodies. Nevertheless, there is a correspondence between reality and appearances, for, as North himself states:

It is very remarkable that altho the mind hath no distinction of the elements of continued sounds, yet there is a resentment of the reall propertys that attend them, but yet in different ideas, whereby every alteration or variety amongst them is vertually perceived and one composition is distinguish't from another . . .[67]

---

[64] This conception is similar to a notion of Helmholtz (tr. Ellis 1887/1954), who argued that when we listen to a series of four or more consecutive harmonic vibrations we do not hear a series of partial tones. Our hearing faculty blends the partial tones into a compound whole (whence their name) and perceives a single musical tone of definite pitch. Phenomena such as musical tones, therefore, are the products of sensory perception.

[65] *MG 1728* (f.15v). Memory enables the mind to compare pitches, and it is by comparison that the scale is formed. Hence, North writes: 'to the ear all sounds are indifferent, till some consecution determines the indifference, and institutes the scale, which is to rule the following tones' (*MG c. 1726*: f.25).

[66] *TS 1728* (f.105v).

[67] *Ibid.* (ff.99v–100).

Once the mind is stocked with data from immediate sensation and memory, it forms new ideas by means of its third computational power, imagination, which combines the data in order to yield new ideas. North explains this computational process by recourse to a logical calculus of ideas conceived as a combination of simple into complex concepts. In his version ideas are like pitches: we all employ the same musical lexicon, and musical thinking is merely the concatenation of pitches according to a rudimentary probabilistic mechanics – the art of combinations and permutations. Simple ideas consist of single pitches, as well as pitches in relation, for, as North insists, it is the scale 'out of which all variety of harmony and melody is derived'.[68] Complex ideas consist of larger levels of structure, starting with the formation of chords, whereby the notes may counterchange their positions by means of the combinatorial procedure we now call 'chord inversion'.

In the knowing process just described, the imagination plays a major role, for it serves to represent the images received from the external sense of hearing; to bring the images back into consciousness from the memory in the absence of the sensed object; and to combine the images in order to yield new ideas.[69] In each of these roles the imagination provides images for the mind to read. Nature, therefore, is a visible language, for it can be seen by the mind. But to exist as a sign, nature must be interpreted. In North's account, reading involves interpreting, for although he holds that sense presentations are necessary for knowledge in that they form the raw material in which the knowing power exercises itself, his emphasis is on the way the sense material is handled and articulated, for he details how the mind follows certain patterns in action. Forms are automatically imposed on sense input by the person receiving, thus enabling the knowing subject to order reality.

The forms imposed are judgements, for they concern relations between things. Indeed, counting, comparing and combining all involve different kinds of relation. The tendency to perform judgements is active from the first moment of contact between people and their environment. But what are the criteria of such judgements? According to North, the criteria derive from our ability to

---

[68] *MG 1728* (f.15v).
[69] North's solution to the problem of whether matter can think, feel or judge seems to be found in the important role assigned to imagination. In a text from his middle period of writings, he indicates the lines along which this problem might be solved. According to him, only the mind can create new ideas which are not found in body. That is, North ascribes all 'sensible formes' to the 'workings' of the imagination rather than to the nature of objects. See *Change of Philosoficall Methods* (ff.94–102v, especially f.95v).

feel pleasure and pain, for he holds that nature constituted all creatures with an instinctive attraction towards those things which promote their own well-being and a complementary aversion towards their opposites.[70] Hence, pleasure is motivational, for it is analysed in terms of realisation of the good – the object of striving. On this view, the affections and passions of the mind can be defined in terms of endeavour. Although the foetus has the capacity to feel pleasure and pain, experience alone brings on endeavour, for, as North writes:

... wee bring onely the instruments of motion, a little determined by instinct. But wee have not power to move any member or part to the porposes of life or arts, but by slow degrees and tryalls ... so that all that wee doe in life, is acquired, as musick is.[71]

Since knowledge is entirely empirical, the truth of what people apprehend depends on external impressions of a sufficiently clear and distinct kind. But people are prone to err, and there are two principal sources of error. One source is from the mind itself as subjective delusions occasioned by disorders in the body.[72] The other source is from hasty or excited inference.[73] Hence, judge-

---

[70] In *Notes of Me* North asserts: 'certeinly Nature calls for that which is good for itself. And setting aside wantonness, which is easy to be perceived and may be as easily checked in children, their appetites are the best Indications of what is good for them' (ed. Jessopp 1887: 3).

[71] *Of Humane Capacity* (ff.42–42v). The foetus does not come into the world with innate knowledge. Indeed, before people can govern their own economy, they must first know and be acquainted with their members. Accordingly, North writes: 'It is a comon fancy, that wee bring into the world with us, as innate, the knowledg of our hands, fingers, etc. and that a child new borne can tell which finger is pricked, and the like. But I thinck otherwise, and that naturally and originally we have no knowledge of our selves and our parts, and that wee learne it all by experience; all that wee bring is to know wee are well, or ill. I need not appeal to nurses, to declare how long it is before an infant can make both ey[e]s point to a candle, or ceas to wonder at its litle hand, or to point at any thing. And much of this sort of philosofy would be had from children's processes, if men had as much to doe with them, as weomen have. But the state they are in at first is no more or other than this: they have members which from occasions of nature move, without order or government of them; and those being touched makes them sensible' (*ibid.*: f.37). Hence. 'the more children are tost[,] danc't and playd with, the faster they come on, and have more knowledg and spirits. [But] ... if they always ly dull ... they grow up to be more stiff and inept, and almost uncapable of learning the infant skill of it self, and so it becomes dull, and approaching to that, they call changeling' (*ibid.*: f.37v).

[72] In *Notes of Me* North recommends that we avoid pleasures that destroy health, for once our nature is weakened, we cannot form adequate images of reality. Disease occasions false images, which, North remarks, 'are strange things and few that are sick observe them, but think the reality is according to their sense' (ed. Jessopp 1887: 147). Instead of choosing pleasures that lead to sickness, therefore, we should gratify our inclinations by pursuing pleasures such as music that preserve health.

[73] When the image is a true impression, it is firmly held by reason and assented to. But the sense image can be rejected as untrue or as held weakly. In the latter case, assent is merely

ments made in response to our environment provide us with an understanding of what is only apparently good and apparently evil. What, then, are the criteria for judging what is really good and really evil? According to North, the basis of moral choice is a causal understanding of events and the consequences which follow from them.

By a causal understanding, North signifies analysis ('resolution'); and he conceives analysis as an exercise of the imagination, whereby simple motions or forces are imagined which, when logically compounded, provide a causal explanation of complex phenomena. What, for example, makes a person tick? One cannot find the answers as a watch repairer can do, by taking the watch apart. But one can take a person apart in imagination, that is, hypothetically. In so doing, North writes, the power of the human understanding 'is magnifyed, and proved by algebra',[74] which is like the watch repairer's art – a taking apart in order to show the pieces. Accordingly, North describes algebra as

... a method of working a proposition, without ideas of the subject matter, ... wherein the demonstration and the method of working it, is rather, as the word imports, a shewing things in peices, like explaining a watch, then proving. For it deals altogether in present existent certein quantity.[75]

opinion, the source of which is unregulated passions. North sometimes refers to such passions as 'humours', 'whims', 'caprices' or 'conceits'. To live in harmony with nature (that is, in a state of equilibrium), the passions must be 'sublimed' or regulated. There are several means of doing this, one of which is a proper course of education. The wise man is one who knows for certain and not by opinion: avoiding precipitancy and error, the wise man withholds consent from the sense image until it has been tested by scientific methods. See *Prejudices* (ff. 2v–7v), which is a short argument for living in harmony with nature by examining the roots of prejudices which are alien to reason (i.e., nature).

[74] *Power of Humane Understanding* (f. 88v).

[75] *The World Part I* (f. 9); see also *MG 1728* (f. 40v). At least two writers propounded such a notion: Hobbes and Gottfried Wilhelm Leibniz. Hobbes, who held that ideas have their origin in sensation, attempted to differentiate between understanding and imagination. In so doing, he identified understanding with formal logical reasoning, which in turn is reduced to a pure combination of names established by rules of agreement. But the influence of the algebraic calculus is clear in Hobbes' conception of definition based on the definition of a quantity by means of a formula, whereby definition is 'the resolution of a compound into parts' (ed. Molesworth 1656/1962: 83, 85–6). Leibniz attempted to extend the language of algebra to all rational sciences by his 'combinatory art' or 'general characteristic', that is, by universal symbolism. He regarded definitions as being similar to an expression of a quantity by means of an algebraic formula; and he also conceived the decomposition or analysis of a complex concept into simple ones after the fashion of the decomposition of a whole number into its prime factors. North's conception is closer to that of Hobbes than of Leibniz. For some background relating to these issues, see Kassler (1986) and the sources cited there.

Hence, North consistently explains all stages of the knowing process as computations.

2.2. Musical grammar

In his writings on musical grammar North is concerned with music as communication: as the outward expressions of inner processes which parallel rather than account for them. Of the two treatises constituting his 1728 theory, the second represents North's final essay towards a comprehensive musical grammar.[76] In the first treatise, *Theory of Sounds 1728*, North sets forth the two general propositions of elasticity and goodness. In the second treatise, *The Musicall Grammarian 1728*, he assumes that these general propositions are true, and he proves the truth of other propositions by demonstrations presented as suppositions imposed by hypothesis. These are then confirmed by experiment (experiences) which serve to validate the hypothesis. North, therefore, is indebted to Baconian 'dissection' or 'anatomy' which proceeds by reasoning and induction with experiments as aids.[77] But the 1728 theory also evinces a developing argument in which new technical terms are introduced gradually in a significant order and ideas are adjusted and refined as the work proceeds.

In *The Musicall Grammarian 1728* the main argument is that music is the invention of humans and is the representation of their changing history and habits ('fashions'). In constructing his argument, North divides the treatise into two parts consisting of the 'Grammarian' proper and 'Memoires of Musicke', each of which begins with an 'Advertisement'. But, as he specifically states in the first

---

[76] In *TS 1728* North is concerned chiefly with reality. He states his purpose as follows: 'Least musical instructions should be expected here, I must precaution that the following essay is purely phisicall, designing onely a research of the naturall, and, (as near as I can,) mechanicall causes of all agencys that usually affect us by means of hearing; and whither this be a slight undertaking, or not, will appear after it is considered that the whole subject is invisible, and by no means (hearing onely excepted) sensible' (f.74v). In *MG 1728* North does 'not formalize upon phisicall speculations' but takes matters 'just as our sence informes us' (f.7). Hence, in this treatise he focuses on appearances.

[77] North himself uses the word 'anatomy' in the Baconian sense; see, for example, Hine, Chan, Kassler (1987: 4, 42, 93) and Chan, Kassler, Hine (1988: 84). Bacon set forth his conception of natural history in a number of places, including the 'Introduction' to *Sylva sylvarum* (1626/1818), which includes a 'Catalogue' of necessary and useful histories to be prosecuted. A comparison of North's published and unpublished writings with listings in Bacon's 'Catalogue' is instructive. For example, North wrote natural histories on the following topics listed in the fourth division of the 'Catalogue': sleep and dreams, human generation, sounds and hearing, music, pleasure and pain in general, intellectual faculties, architecture in general, fish-ponds and breeding of fish.

'Advertisement', the 'Grammarian' is not a 'sume of rules sufficient to instruct an art'; rather, it presents the interpretations of a grammarian, who reasons upon those rules and shows 'the principles of them derived upon nature and the positive truth of things'.[78]

North's twofold division does not reflect the structure of the treatise, which, with its two advertisements, may be divided into an introduction, five parts and an appendix as follows:

'Advertisement' (f. 1v)
Introduction (ff. 7–9)
Part I. Elements of performance (ff. 9–36v)
Part II. Elements of thorough bass (ff. 37–58v)
Part III. Composition (ff. 59–81v)
Part IV. Genres (ff. 82–98v; 99–101v are blank)
'Advertisement' (f. 102v)
Part V. History (ff. 102–142v; 143–144 are blank)
Appendix of music (ff. 144v–147v)

Parts I and II deal with the elements treated as the groundwork or foundation of the practice of music. Four assumptions guide North's treatment of Parts I and II: (1) the elements of music must be studied as if for the first time; (2) the steps of this study must begin with the basic constituents of which all music is constituted; (3) whatever is distinctive will appear from the classification of these constituents; and (4) 'meaning' will ultimately derive from these basic constituents of music. In Part I it is the orthography and orthoepy of the elements themselves (pitch, scale, beat) and in Part II, the syntactic combination of these elements (intervals, chords, cadences, ornaments) that are described. In both Parts North proposes 'reformations'.

The reformation in Part I relates to North's concern for phonetic specificity, namely, to provide a uniform orthography for 'pronouncing' pitches in the scale.[79] Traditionally, vocal and instrumental scales had been treated separately, for the vocal scale was pronounced by solmisation syllables, whereas the instrumental scale was pronounced (silently or mentally) by letters of the alphabet. North's reformation of this practice results from his aim to

---

[78] *MG 1728* (f. 1v), the principles of which are derived from *TS 1728*.
[79] In a number of his writings North exhibits a distaste for solmisation of the four- as well as the six-syllable variety. There are two principal reasons for this. First, the manner of 'pronouncing' the notes is different for voice and for instruments, the latter being 'named' by the letters of the alphabet. Second, solmisation tends to encourage learning by rote rather than by exercising judgement (see, for example, *Some Memorandums, concerning Musick*: ff. 12–12v; *Cursory Notes of Musicke* ed. Chan and Kassler 1986: 169, and *MG 1728*: f. 21 *et passim*.).

establish one scale (letters and sounds) of 'universal intention', thereby making music accessible and useful to students by removing misery, toil and perplexity. He achieves this aim by assigning letters of the alphabet to both scales. But he acknowledges that the pronunciation of these letters in singing requires some accommodation, since vowels, for example, require an accompanying consonant, else there would be no proper distinction between one intoned pitch and another. Hence, North proposes the following orthography for the vocal scale: Gho, Ar, Be, Ça, Do, El, Fa.[80]

The reformation in Part II relates to North's concern, manifest in all his theories of musical cognition, to seek in the physical nature of sound a natural, or rational, connection between music (appearances) and pulses (reality). In *The Musicall Grammarian 1728* North neither deals with the mechanism of the production of ideas in the mind by the impressions on the nervous system nor even studies that system's operations. Instead, his main effort is to analyse the contents of consciousness into units and to trace those units to an irreducible association with the constant properties of sounding bodies: the order and 'time' of pulses that strike our ear. The consequence of this effort is a new classification of musical sounds.

Traditionally, musical sounds had been divided into concords and discords, and concords had been further divided into perfect/ imperfect or primary/secondary. North rejects the traditional classification, for in his theory no pitch of the scale is discord. Rather, concords are graded by degrees of perfection ('more or less').[81] Nevertheless, North makes two distinctions between concord and discord. When he writes that 'harmony is positively good so that [discord] is positively bad, as being direct contraries to each other', he uses the terms 'harmony' and 'discord' as cognates of good and evil, pleasure and pain.[82] Discord, in this context, means sounds unusable in music.[83] But when he writes of 'harmony' and 'dis-

[80] See *MG 1728* (f.22).
[81] The gradation is the result of North's theory of harmony by the coincidence of pulses (see above I.2.1.). Although Chenette (1967) provides an admirable summary of North's theory of harmony, he is not to be relied on for the intellectual context.
[82] *MG c. 1726* (f.12v).
[83] In *TS 1728* North provides the natural basis for this distinction as follows: 'And when wee come to reflect upon sounds, wherof the elements are indistinguishable, wee find egregious differences with respect to pleasures of sence, or pain. . . . The only account I think possible to be given of such various effects is that the ingredients of harmony, that is the pulses from whence the comprest waves are emitted, (and by being blended instill our sence of continuance) are in some sort regular, orderly co-assistant and symmetrically compounded, from whence flows our idea of harmony. And on the other side when the pulses are unequall, immetrical, opposite and disorderly, as contingents usually are, the compound nois is most disagreeable, and scarce to be borne with' (f.101).

cord' in a musical context, the term 'discord' means (1) out-of-tune playing, (2) a pitch having no orientation to a key or to an accord of a key, or (3) melodic parts not agreeing.[84]

Parts III and IV deal, respectively, with the invention and communication of music. The principal assumptions guiding North's interpretations in both parts relate to his conception that music has a moral purpose, and this purpose is the *utile dulce* of neo-classical criticism. The word '*dulce*' embraces the delight afforded by various compositional techniques, such as the 'invitatory manner'. But it also means the emotions induced by specific compositions named by North. The word '*utile*' covers the representation, in music, of moral behaviour, as well as the socialising function of music in performance. Taken together, the words '*utile dulce*' capture the effect of music on the listener, an effect that is so powerful but so difficult to define. It is to be noted, however, that the effect in question relates not only to *pathos* but also to *ethos*.

In Part III, *utile dulce* pertains to the art of the composer. The elements ('ingredients') having been prepared (in Parts I and II), they are to be combined ('mixed', 'joined') together to form various movements ('manners'), of which there are gradations, slow to fast. None of the combinations are to be random, for North stresses the importance of intention: the 'design' of music is to please and to instruct by representing the whole personality ('humanity'), thoughts as well as actions. This representation takes place in a social and, specifically, rhetorical context, for North's stress is on the communication of intention through signs associated with passions and affections. Accordingly, he holds that music must never be 'inconsistent' with 'humanity',

... which ... consists in thinking, and acting; and so musick consists of harmony, and measure, which is called time. And in effect harmony works upon the thoughts, and the time upon the actions of humane kind. And consequently, from the thoughts it passeth to affections, and passions and so to actions in conformity with the time . . .[85]

North enumerates two universal rules for the treatment of 'harmony' and 'measure'. The first rule is that combinations of accords

---

[84] See *TS 1728* (ff.110v–111 'Whence discords better and wors', ff. 114v–116 'Discords without the scale'). In examining the notions of various writers on music, North sometimes is forced to follow traditional usage of the term 'discord'. But he tends to distance himself from this usage by qualifying the term with 'as it is called' or 'as they say' (see *MG 1728*: ff.48, 50v).

[85] *MG 1728* (f.66v).

must succeed 'wors' and 'better' alternately.[86] The second rule is that time must be 'acted', else it is not legitimate.[87] North provides a number of passages as exemplars. These passages, he points out, may be taken up and used when invention fails a young composer. But in an earlier text he warns that a piece made up of such passages 'would be like a dish drest with rocambo and juice of onion sauce'.[88]

In Part IV, *utile dulce* relates to the efficacy and use of musical entertainments, solitary, social, ecclesiastical and theatrical. In this part, North focuses on the auditory, for whom the efficacy of music derives from a special kind of *dulce*, namely, notable pleasure.[89] In entertainments of all kinds, public or private, notable pleasure may be achieved by following a universal rule, which North summarises in an early text as follows:

... the master must contrive that the beginning be moderate, for the least thing at first serves and then other parts enter with a noise and fire perpetually increasing, and the greatest fury must be at the last, and then all expire at once. This draws the spectators from one degree of amazement to another, without any relapse or flagging, till it arrives at the acme, and then to cease; for the least pause or abatement, nay non-progression, spoils all.[90]

Utile arises chiefly from a social context, for by practice of music in this context, unruly inclinations of human individuals may be brought into harmonious consent so as to achieve the aim of social sympathy.[91] North allows some utility to solitary music, but he

[86] *Ibid.* (ff.47v, 54).
[87] This rule is clearly stated in the penultimate draft, where North writes: 'Now since time in musick, and comon humane actions are found to agree so well, that the one inconsistent or contrary to the other is not well accepted, I may affirme that ... all movements that are quicker then wee can comand our members to move, or cannot be distinguisht into the confines of such our capacity, are direct absurditys. For it is impossible that a chattering movement, which cannot by any means be complyed with, can fasten upon our facultys so as to affect our minds; and without that, the nois is rather a jingle, like bells upon a team of horses, then musick. And from hence it is that straines are denominated according to men's acting. As andante, is the measures of the step in walking. And so currant, and jigg a species of running, and others relating to the art of dancing inumerable' (*MG c. 1726*: ff. 62v–63).
[88] *MG c. 1726* (f.98).
[89] For details of North's theory of notable pleasure, see the 'Introduction' to *Cursory Notes of Musicke* (ed. Chan and Kassler 1986: (30)–(34) *et passim.*).
[90] *Notes of Me* (ed. Jessopp 1887: 71). For other aspects of North's conception of unity and variety, see *Some Memorandums, concerning Musick* (f.24 'As to designe', f.26v 'As to the designe'); *Cursory Notes of Building* (ed. Colvin and Newman 1981: 56–9 'Of unity and variety'); and *Cursory Notes of Musicke* (ed. Chan and Kassler 1986: 227–34 'Of operas').
[91] In *Notes of Me*, North indicates that music is useful chiefly for 'diverting noble families in a generous way of country living' (ed. Jessopp 1887: 71). In *Cursory Notes of Musicke* he begins to emphasise the broader social implications.

limits its utility to the practice necessary 'to make a hand' and to the 'releif of an active mind distressed either with too much, or too little employment'.[92] In the case of an active mind distressed with too much employment, music is a remedy for melancholy.[93] In the case of an active mind distressed with too little employment, music is a remedy for 'sottishness and vice'.[94]

With Part IV North concludes the 'Grammarian' division of the treatise. In this, the most extensive of the two divisions, North posits the ideals of discipline, competence and elegance of expression. He also mentions a number of specific points related to these ideals. For example, he holds that the meaning of music must be clearly conveyed. To begin with, there must be a regular movement of the bass. In the case of music with text, the text must be heard. Hence, the composer should aim for distinct speech rhythm and avoid the manner of instruments. But even in untexted music, note-against-note counterpoint is the desideratum, for, as North writes in his penultimate draft,

... that kind of composition is best which least needs harsh notes to sett it off as in oratory, the plainest and least figurate style is the best; so the plainest notes put together i[f] masterly done, makes the best musick; and as the corrupters of oratory instead of familiar, and explicite arguments, affect art, and out-of-the-way language, so injudicious composers, affect hard notes, thinking all is well, if done with a regular preparation and fetching off, as they cant it. But the soveraigne composers, have more regard to the nature and state of the harmonia, than to such pedanterios.[95]

In each of the four parts, North also holds that there are certain proprieties or decorums that must be observed, for there are

---

[92] *MG 1728* (f. 82v).

[93] When writing about his neurotic brother, John, North claimed that 'The doctor had no favourite diversion or manual exercise to rest his mind a little, which he held bent with continual thinking. His parents, who were much addicted to music, recommended that to him for a diversion, and particularly the noble organ, as the fullest and not only a complete solitary consort, but most proper for an ecclesiastic. And indeed if study had not had the upper hand of all his intendments, he must of course have taken up in that way *quasi ex traduce*, for after the care of prayers and meals, nothing was more constant and solemn than music was in that family. He was sensible the advice was very good, and accordingly got a small organ into his chamber at Jesus College, and suffered himself to be taught a lesson or two, which he practised over when he had a mind to be unbent. But he made no manner of advance, and one accident put him out of all conceit of it' (*Life of John North* ed. Millard 1984: 109). After recounting the 'accident', North concluded: 'The pleasure of music is like that of books, never true and good unless easily and familiarly read or performed, and then nothing is more medicinal to a crazy and fatigued mind than that – *musica mentis medecina moestae*' (*ibid*.).

[94] *Notes of Me* (ed. Jessopp 1887: 74).

[95] *MG c. 1726* (ff. 97v–98).

'virtues' (fitness and congruity, pleasantness and gravity) as well as 'vices' (solecism and barbarity; dullness and ostentation) in music. But it is by virtues alone that music may work such force upon the mind and thereby become an art of eloquence. For example, North points out that music must be congruent stylistically to the subject matter ('intention') as well as to the place of performance. In identifying three styles – high, middle and low – he follows critical convention in assigning to sacred music the best or most sublime style. Because of the transcendent subject matter of the text, sacred music should represent lofty matters, not trivial ones, for, as North himself writes, such music must keep 'within the bounds of decency, suiting the place, and intention'.[96]

In Part V, separately titled 'Memoires of Musicke', North adopts a naturalistic explanation by outlining a vocalic theory of the origin of music. He then argues that historical change comes chiefly through innovation and technology. In treating the changes that take place in music, North divides historical time into four broad periods: (1) antiquity; (2) the fall of the Roman Empire to the twelfth century ('Gothick' times); (3) the twelfth century to the Reformation; and (4) the Reformation to his own day. North refers to the changes from one period to the next as 'revolutions', a term that denotes 'egregious' or very noticeable changes.[97] He subdivides the four periods by 'ages', usually identified with the reigns of different rulers.

In his treatment of change North reveals something about his own historiographic principles, for he writes:

... the grand custome of all is to affect novelty and to goe from one thing to another, and despise the former. And it is a poorness of spirit, and a low method of thinking that inclines men to pronounce for the present, and allow nothing to times past. Cannot wee put ourselves in loco of former states, and judg pro tunc? Therefore as to all bon gusto wee ought to yeild to the authority of the proper time and not determine comparatively where one side is all prejudice. It is a shallow monster that shall hold forth in favour of our fashions and relishes and maintaine that no age shall come wherein they will not be despised and derided. And, if on the other side, I may take upon me to be a fidling profet, I may with as much reason declare, that the time may come when some of the present celebrated musick will be as much in contempt as John come kiss me now now now,

[96] *MG 1728* (f.91).
[97] *Ibid.* (ff. 109v, 118v, 125, 134v).

and perhaps with as much reason, as any is found for the contrary at present.[98]

Here we have the statement of a contextualist and anti-'Whig' historian.[99] But that North has a progressive notion is clear from an earlier text, where he writes: 'It must be granted that better, and better is endless, and things are not to be rejected becaus they improve, and that some improving alwais carrys difficulty with it'.[100] History is not continuous improvement, however, for North imposes a pattern of cyclical change, the motor of which is corruption: like a plant, music may 'decay' as well as 'grow'.[101]

Corruptions of music are redressable, for they arise chiefly from failures identified not only in Part V of *The Musicall Grammarian 1728*, but also in other parts of the treatise. In particular, North singles out failures in innovation ('extravagances', 'difficulties') and in pedagogy (rote methods). To redress the corruptions brought about by these failures, musical composers and music teachers must proceed on a rational basis, namely, an understanding of human needs and human ends. North's aims, therefore, are ethical and critical. But his moral sentiments or judgements are not idiosyncratically individual or particular: they are not a function of mere self-interest, nor are they arbitrary or whimsical. Rather, his ethical and critical judgements are predicated on two presuppositions: that there is such a thing as a common and universal human nature; that part of human nature is some degree of social feeling (sympathy) for the welfare of others.

[98] *Ibid.* (ff. 132v–133).
[99] The Whig interpretation of history devotes attention to seemingly modern ideas and movements regardless of their importance in their own time, refusing historical understanding to all opposing tendencies. North is close to the origins of this kind of interpretation, which originally meant history interpreted from the viewpoint of the English Whig party whose historians wrote in a partisan way favouring certain causes as progressive movements in history. North's eldest brother, Francis, was slandered by the early Whig historians, and some of Roger North's writings are an attempt to put events in their context.
[100] *Musicall Recollections III* (f. 80v).
[101] In *MG c. 1726* (f.61v), North refers to the Roman historian, Polybius (tr. Paton 1960), who contrived a model of a cycle based on a psychology of power: political power tends to erode the probity of rulers so that monarchs in time degenerate into tyrants, who are overthrown by disciplined aristocrats, who become lax oligarchs, who are in turn replaced by law-abiding democrats, who lapse into mob rule, at which point a new monarch takes charge of the disoriented polity. Only a mixed constitution, in which monarchical, aristocratic and democratic elements are combined, can break the cycle with built-in checks on the infirmities that afflict the rulers of the pure forms of government. The motor of cyclical change is corruption, a mixture of self-interest, loss of martial vigour and of loyalty to the régime.

3. ROGER NORTH'S PHILOSOPHY OF MUSIC

3.1 The linguistic model

The Musicall Grammarian 1728 deals with musical eloquence in all its branches. Parts I and II, on the orthoepy, orthography and syntax of music, constitute a grammar; and Parts III and IV, on the arts of invention and communication, form a rhetoric. Although Part V is separately titled, this part is integral to North's plan, for it deals with the 'etymology' of music, thereby continuing the linguistic orientation of the treatise.[102] Indeed, within the treatise itself there are many comparisons between music and language,[103] and North also asserts that the principles of oratory and music are the same.[104]

The most probable immediate sources for North's linguistic model are three works identified with Port-Royal in France. Although these works are usually described as 'Cartesian', North's adaptation of them does not make him a Cartesian, as we shall see. Rather, it exemplifies the way in which he uses various sources and modifies them for his own purposes.[105] The works in question are *Grammaire Générale et Raisonée*; *L'Art de Parler*; and *La Logique, ou l'art de penser*. Taken together, they deal with the external expression of our ideas in speaking and writing, as well as the internal operation of these ideas in thinking. North turns these concerns to musical account not only in *The Musicall Grammarian 1728* but also in *Theory of Sounds 1728*.

Only one of the three Port-Royal sources is actually identified by North: the *Grammaire* composed by Antoine Arnauld (b. 1612, d.

---

[102] The twofold division of 'Grammarian' and history is reminiscent of two of Cicero's works which were sometimes printed together. The first, 'On oratory', treats the art of eloquence; the second, 'Brutus; or, remarks on eminent orators', 'contains a few short, but very masterly sketches of all the speakers who had flourished either in Greece or Rome, with any reputation of eloquence, down to [Cicero's] own time; and as he generally touches the principal incidents of their lives, it will be considered, by an attentive reader, as a concealed epitome of the Roman history' (Cicero tr. Watson 1896: 402). North refers several times to Cicero ('Tully') and, specifically, to Cicero's 'Brutus' (see Hine, Chan, Kassler 1987: 19).

[103] See, for example, *MG 1728* (ff. 1v, 12v, 27, 56, 60v, 63, 65, 72, 81, 88v, 93, 93v, 94, 97v).

[104] *Ibid*. (f.60v).

[105] The work of John Locke, for example, is not labelled 'Cartesian', although he, too, was indebted to Port Royal. Indeed, the commonality between Locke and North stems from their common sources, which include Boyle, as well as Port Royal. See Locke (1690/1985), Alexander (1985) and Cohen (1977).

1694) and Claude Lancelot (b. 1615, d. 1695).[106] According to its title-page, the *Grammaire* was to cover the foundations of the art of speaking explained in a clear and natural manner; the reasons for what is common to all languages, and for the principal differences among them; and several new remarks concerning the French language. But the treatise itself consists of two parts on (1) the letters and characters of writing and (2) the principles and reasons on which the various forms of the signification of words are founded.

In Part I, the shortest of the two parts, Arnauld and Lancelot deal with letters and words as sounds and written signs. Stressing that 'sounds have been adopted by men as signs of thoughts, and that men have also invented certain figures to serve as signs of these sounds',[107] they lay down four rules by which characters may signify sounds:

(1) That every figure mark some sound; that is to say, that no thing is written which is not pronounced.
(2) That every sound is marked by a figure; that is to say, that no thing is pronounced which is not written.
(3) That each figure mark only one sound. . . .
(4) That the same sound is not marked by different figures.[108]

Part I of the *Grammaire*, therefore, is concerned with phonetic specificity, a concern shared by North in Part I of *The Musicall Grammarian 1728*.

In Part II, the longest part of the *Grammaire*, Arnauld and Lancelot treat the use we make of speech and writing for signifying our thoughts by the

. . . marvelous invention of composing from twenty-five or thirty sounds an infinite variety of words, which although not having any resemblance in themselves to that which passes through our minds, nevertheless do not fail to reveal to others all of the secrets of the mind, and to make intelligible to others who cannot penetrate into the mind all that we conceive and all of the diverse movements of our souls.[109]

---

[106] The *Grammaire* was published in a first edition on 28 April 1660; a second edition appeared in March 1664; a third edition, revised was printed in 1676; and a fourth and a fifth edition appeared in 1679 and 1709, respectively (see Arnauld and Lancelot tr. Rieux and Rollin 1676/1975 and below f.8v, note 2).
[107] Arnauld and Lancelot (tr. Rieux and Rollin 1676/1975: 56).
[108] *Ibid.*
[109] *Ibid.* (65–6). See also Locke (1690/1985: 132).

The main focus in Part II, however, is on the parts of speech, the discussion of which begins with words that signify the objects of thought (nouns, etc.) and moves on to words that signify the manner of thought (verbs, etc.). This twofold division finds its most explicit reflection in Part III of *The Musicall Grammarian 1728*, where North treats harmony as signifying objects of thought and rhythm as signifying manners of action, the two together constituting signs of humanity. But he lays the groundwork for his treatment in Part II, where he deals with the 'parts of harmony', namely, accords, intermixtures of accords and cadences.

The whole of the *Grammaire* concludes with a brief chapter devoted to syntax, 'or the construction of words put together'.[110] In this chapter syntax is 'distinguished' into two parts: 'agreement, when words ought to agree with one another, and government, when one of two words causes a variation in the other'.[111] According to the authors, the first is mostly the same in all languages, whereas the second, being totally arbitrary, is different in all languages. In North's development of these ideas, it is the underlying chordal structure which provides 'agreement' (i.e., determines the semantic interpretation) and the ornamenting of that structure that results in 'government' (i.e., determines the phonetic interpretation).

The remainder of the chapter is given over to a discussion of figures, or 'modes of speaking', of which the authors identify four: *syllepsis* (conception), *ellipsis* (omission), *pleonasm* (abundance) and *hyperbaton* (reversal). The first figure 'agrees' more with our thoughts than with words in a discourse, but the three remaining figures are traceable in North's treatment of cadential passages (*pleonasm*, as in his 'consort of cadencys') and his identification of two kinds of semi-cadences, one of which omits the proper bass (*ellipsis*), the other of which moves from V to I back to V again (*hyperbaton*).[112]

The concerns of the *Grammaire* are most apparent in Parts I and II of *The Musicall Grammarian 1728*, the parts constituting North's musical grammar, although they have some impact on Parts III and IV, North's musical rhetoric. But the subject matter of these latter parts is closer to *L'art de parler* of Bernard Lamy (b. 1640, d. 1715),

---

[110] *Ibid.* (170).
[111] *Ibid.*
[112] See Introduction II.

which the English translator referred to as the 'Port-Royal Rhetoric'.[113] Although Lamy repeated and paraphrased some of the
material in the *Grammaire*, he treated (1) the physiological bases of
speech, or how speech is formed, (2) functional grammar, or the
role of art in speech, (3) the science of poetic, or pronunciation and
versification, (4) the differences between styles – high, middle, low,
and (5) the art of persuasion, or invention and communication.[114]
The difference between Lamy's structure and North's is that in *The
Musicall Grammarian 1728* North incorporates the third topic, composition, in his treatment of invention and the fourth topic, style, in
his treatment of communication.

The authors of the *Grammaire* and the 'Rhetoric' dealt with
external expression, whereas the authors of *La Logique*, Arnauld
and Pierre Nicole (b. 1625, d. 1695), focused on the internal operations of the mind; (1) conception, (2) judgement, (3) reasoning and
(4) ordering.[115] According to Arnauld and Nicole, 'words are
distinct and articulate sounds used by men as signs of mental
activity. Since all mental activity can be reduced to conceiving,
judging, reasoning, and ordering ... words may be signs of any
one of these activities'.[116] But the authors gave the highest role to
judgement, for as Dickoff and James have pointed out:

Ideas are joined to form judgments; reasoning is but a kind of judging; and
ordering is a marshaling of thoughts to arrive at some judgment. Conceiving, reasoning, and ordering are in this sense subordinate to judging. To
classify judgments on the basis of the ways in which man comes to know
the certain or probable truth of the judgment, then, amounts to identifying the ways of man's knowing. And to realize that for each mode of
knowledge distinguished the *Logic* suggests a method for arriving at such
knowledge and for avoiding its common defects is to have some apprecia-
tion for the scope of the work.[117]

---

[113] See Lamy ed. Harwood (1676/1986), Ehninger (1946), Howell (1956), Waite (1970) and
Wood (1972).

[114] The contents have been differently classified by Ehninger (1946), Howell (1956) and
Wood (1972).

[115] The Port Royal *Logique*, which complements and augments the *Grammaire*, was published in a first edition at Paris in 1662 and reprinted twice more. A second edition
appeared in 1664 and was reprinted; a third edition was published in 1668; a fourth
edition, in 1674, reprinted 1675; a fifth edition, in 1683, reprinted twice in 1684; and a
sixth edition, in 1685, reprinted six times, the last reprint appearing in 1730 (see Arnauld
and Nicole tr. Dickoff and James 1685/1964).

[116] *Ibid.* (99).

[117] *Ibid.* (xlvi).

Under the first topic, conceiving, the authors discussed the nature of ideas and their relation to things, knowers and expression; identified the main sources of defective ideas; and explored remedies for these defects. That North sought after such remedies is suggested by his awareness of a 'defect' in his own thinking. In *Notes of Me*, for example, he admits to judging this defect

... by comparison of my own performances with those of others; for I have observed in some so steady a faculty of discharging their minds by speaking as if all their matter were prepared and produced like wares to be shewn with greatest advantage, and no emotion or passion, interruption, or any outward disturbance, puts them by, but [they] can immediately resume the thread and proceed; whereas I could never, though dealing in things of perfect familiarity to my mind, relate without omissions and oversights of considerable articles.[118]

North attributes the defect to a childhood illness, the result of which was that

... my discourse was confused, and from thence I inferred my thinking was so too. And that is a great truth; men's words, as to clearness or obscurity, declare the justness or confusion of their thoughts. And, generally speaking, men who think well either speak or write well, and that according to the power and measure of justness in their thinking.[119]

As North 'feared nothing but my own doubts and failings and the consequences of my own actions',[120] he agrees with Arnauld and Nicole that judging should be the goal of all thinking.

But North identifies two kinds of judgements.[121] The first kind are those which we make in response to our environment and which provide us with criteria for what is only apparently good and

[118] *Notes of Me* (ed. Jessopp 1887: 22). The assistance that could have been rendered by a study of *La logique* is apparent in the full title of the English translation: *Logic; or the Art of Thinking: in which, besides the common, are contain'd many excellent new rules, very probable for directing of reason, and acquiring of judgment, in things well relating to the instruction of a mans self, as of others. In four parts. The first consisting of reflections upon ideas, or upon the first operation of the mind, which is called apprehension, &c. The second of considerations of men about proper judgments, &c. The third of the nature and various kinds of reasoning, &c. The fourth treats of the most profitable method for demonstrating or illustrating any truth, &c. To which is added an index to the whole book. For the excellency of the matter, printed many times in French and Latin, and now for public good translated into English by several hands* (Arnauld and Nicole tr. Anon 1685).
[119] *Ibid.*
[120] *Ibid.* (198).
[121] See above I.2.1.

apparently evil. The second kind of judgements are those which we make on the basis of a causal understanding of events and the consequences that follow from them. But there are problems with the first kind of judgements. For example, as the mind cannot observe more than one thing at a time,[122] North argues that 'offense will produce what is offensive and pleasure the contrary, because it is impossible to be offended and pleased at one and the same time'.[123] The implication is that one sensation confirms or discredits another; that is, that pleasure and pain are relative, not absolute, expressions of comparable experiences. What, then, provides the criterion?

North worries over this question in a number of places. For example, in the penultimate draft of *The Musicall Grammarian 1728*, he writes:

> It is an hard task to pronounce upon the different manners, between the musick of these ancient times and of our owne, which of the two is really most valuable or best . . . Must we resort . . . to the general gusto? . . . is that a criterium of better and wors abstractedly? It would be hard to get the savages to determine, for could the caus be brought to tryall upon that foot, it would be found that even those have bin used to sounds which thro prejudice would corrupt their tast[e].[124]

If all 'prejudice' and 'humour' could be taken away, North continues,

> . . . the true intrinsic goodness of musick . . . must be gathered from the copia, and of that the pure naturall meliority, which one sort or other is found to contain. For if any reallity, or true subsistence, renders musicall sounds eligible before such as are wholly immusicall, where that (whatever it is) abounds in right judgment, the best musick is found; altho the being pleased or not pleased[,] that is [,] the caprice or humour of many at a certain conjuncture[,] says nay.[125]

An understanding of what is really good and really evil, therefore, must derive from the second kind of judgements, for, as North himself states: 'in order to find a criterium of good musick we must . . . look into nature itself, and the truth of things'.[126]

[122] See above I.2.1.
[123] *Cursory Notes of Musicke* (ed. Chan and Kassler 1986: 149).
[124] *MG c. 1726* (ff. 161v–162).
[125] *Ibid.* (f. 162).
[126] *Ibid.* (f. 162v).

3.2. The 'chemical' model

North's conception of nature proceeds from the assumption of the immanence of life and function in organised matter, neither of which can exist independently of each other. In his philosophy, life or animating principle is a creative world spirit, immanent in everything and directing events by expansion and contraction (elasticity) to achieve worthy ends (goodness). These are Stoic tenets, which North extends by recourse to a book-of-nature metaphor.[127] In his version, the book of nature is written in acoustical signals, and nature itself is a large-scale model of a musician. Body (including the body politic) is a consort of musical instruments that has the potential to play together harmoniously. Mind is the conductor of the consort, for it has the potential to read the musical score and direct which instrument, or group of instruments, is to play at appropriate times.[128] The potential of body (including mind) is made actual by spirit, which is composer as well as musical score that the unity of body and mind expresses.

In North's interpretation of body in motion, there are two kinds of cause: primary and secondary. When, for example, he writes of 'mechanicall causes of all agencys that usually affect us by means of hearing',[129] North denotes secondary causes ('occasions'), for he holds that:

As to the operations of the mind, I look upon the action of things sensible to be occasions onely, and not causes of those ideas that are framed in the imagination. As pulses indistinguishably quick, in the proportions of time, as 3 to 2, excites in the mind an idea of what musicall men call a fifth, so for [a] 3d sharp and flatt, so peculiarly delicious sounds, as are not to be found in the material acting that is the occasion of such harmony.[130]

---

[127] For the Stoic legacy, see the 'Introduction' to *Cursory Notes of Musicke* (ed. Chan and Kassler 1986: (37)–(42), (66)–(69)). The Stoic tradition has yet to be fully analysed for its contributions to early modern science and scientific method. For some information about the transmission of Stoic ideas to the seventeenth century, see Barker and Goldstein (1984), who state that Stoic ethics led to a revival of interest in Stoic physics as part of the attack on Aristotle's matter theory and particularly his distinction between heaven and earth. A number of Stoic tenets also appear in Bacon's pneumatic cosmology, developed at the end of the sixteenth century (see Gregory 1938, Rees 1975, 1980, and Rees and Upton 1984).

[128] The implication is that music also should have a conductor, and North in fact proposes this. See *Some Memorandums, concerning Musick* (f.24v) and *Cursory Notes of Musicke* (ed. Chan and Kassler 1986: 233). See also *MG 1728* (f.36v).

[129] *TS 1728* (f.74v).

[130] *Change of Philosoficall Methods* (f.95).

An account of nature based on secondary causality leaves us in the realm of what is only apparently good and apparently evil. To understand what is really good and really evil, recourse must be had to primary causality.

North's conception of primary causality is a cosmic one, for he adopts a thoroughgoing monism: the world is a plenum filled with particles of matter. But matter has two principles, a passive and an active principle. The manifold variety in the world is explained by reference to these two features of matter. The passive principle is unqualified body; the active principle is subtle matter, which North also calls 'the spirit of the world'.[131] Spirit is responsible for all activity, change and variety and, therefore, for knowing.

To explain how spirit accomplishes its creative and regulative functions, North has recourse to the newly emerging field of pneumatics or gas chemistry.[132] He describes spirit as a very tenuous, invisible, elastic medium extended throughout the universe:

... if we would consider the perfection of that nature [body], it consists in extension or space in infinitum, as philosofers now hold: and the other nature spirit which consists in power, may be all alike as to essence [i.e., extended in space], yet is spirit or (as the most wee can say) non body. The advances are in power and the perfection is in the Allmighty.[133]

The assumption of its extreme tenuity is in strict accordance with North's hypothesis that spirit is omnipresent not only within body but also within the apparent emptiness of the space between bodies.

---

[131] See *Cursory Notes of Musicke* (ed. Chan and Kassler 1986: 1–25), in which North details his matter theory. After *c.* 1703 North tends to omit explanations of subtle matter, a primary cause, and to focus on secondary causes. Thus, in *MG 1728* he makes only passing reference to subtle matter, which he obliquely terms 'interstitiall' or 'finer' matter (ff.80, 90–91). But it would be a mistake to conclude that at the end of his life North relinquished the subtle-matter hypothesis, for in the final summary of his natural philosophy, written *c.* 1726, he clearly states that 'subtle matter is no figment' (the statement occurs in North's own holograph and not in his son's copy of *Physica*).

[132] Although the word 'gas' (literally, chaos) had been coined in the first part of the seventeenth century by J. B. van Helmont, the chemical nature of the air was not understood (see Kassler 1987 and sources cited there). The work of Boyle is regarded as the starting point for the development of pneumatics or gas chemistry and for the discovery of particular gases. In North's day this incipient science was still part of physico-mechanics.

[133] *Change of Philosoficall Methods* (f.97). North's spirit is not to be confused with the 'animal spirits' of the physiologists and physicians, for he writes that Thomas Willis 'and others that use the terme, animall spirits, seem to intend the same as I doe, but yet I subtileize more' (*Some Essays*: f.14). Willis, an English physician and contributor to anatomy, provided the most extensive treatment of the nervous system to his day.

As the active principle of matter, spirit functions:

. . . like a spark firing the power in a mine: it is not the spark that heaves the bastion, but some other mechanicall power derived from the latent energie of matter at large in the world. And if the globe of earth were of like composition as gunpowder is, it were the same thing.[134]

Hence, spirit works 'just at the incoation of the power of body, and then in the way of explosion is disperst over the whole, by the machination of the organs and parts of it'.[135] But body is not merely a passive recipient: it actively and vitally collaborates with spirit in that it undergoes certain dispositions, for, North writes:

What signifies the matter of nitre sulfur, and charcoal, without a disposition, whereby it may explode, and such are humane bodys which from very insensible touches are made to move an immense weight, whereof the opperations are manifestly mechanick in all respects but the occasion, which is lodged like a spark of steel till it exerts itself, and produceth a spacious effect.[136]

Body's potential, then, is made actual by spirit.

In addition to creating life and motion, spirit regulates the world by pneumatic action, for its component particles endeavour – that is, have a tendency – to move by pressing inward from the surfaces of ordinary bodies or by pressing outward from the interspaces of those bodies. By means of these two opposing tendencies, spirit maintains ordinary bodies in a dynamic state of equilibrium ('balance', 'posture of rest'). Thus North writes: 'By the ballance of impulses, I mean when the force imprest by the subtile matter tends to drive the body one way as much as another . . . so long it must needs rest'.[137] When ordinary bodies are displaced from their positions of equilibrium by some additional or external force, the particles of spirit behave like the restoring forces acting on a bent spring or oscillating pendulum.

By these same pneumatic actions, spirit mediates between the properties of external objects and the consciousness of the perceiving mind. In North's account of the knowing process, every stimulus from the outside is conducted from the specific sense organ

---

[134] *Essay on the Reciprocall Forces of Body and Spirit* (f.80v).
[135] *Change of Philosoficall Methods* (f.97v).
[136] *Ibid.*
[137] *Cursory Notes of Musicke* (ed. Chan and Kassler 1986: 8).

excited by it to a central processing unit which co-ordinates the various impressions, elevates them into consciousness and then releases the impulse reacting to the sensation. The mind ('soul'), North writes, 'gives the inception that occasions the whole [body] to work with its proper forces; and the externall incidents of the body, or sense, administers objects to affect the soul, and so returnes are reciprocally made'.[138] The vital function of the central processing unit, therefore, unifying all the activities of body and maintaining and regulating its contact with the external world, clearly defines a dual direction of communication. But it is only through the incessant movement of spirit that this two-way communication is established.

To prove the universal law of causality, it is necessary to look for observational sources of evidence. North relies on inferences based on signs and events in his physical surroundings. Since modifications of spirit take place in body as modifications of tension or 'tone', nerves and muscles may be either tensed or relaxed, just as the mind may be 'nerved up' or 'enervated'.[139] The effect of tonicity and flaccidity, therefore, is visible not only in objects such as pendulums, springs and musical strings but also in the external movements of the human body, including the countenance of the face. Internal and external movements together result in an 'air' or sign of a particular passion or affection. The word 'air' here means external manner, appearance or mien, but it is the result of an internal character; a tense or relaxed spirit.[140]

North is the first writer on music to bring together the concepts of external manner and internal character to form an original

---

[138] *Essay on the Reciprocall Forces of Body and Spirit* (f.81).

[139] See, for example *MG 1728* (f.12 and n.2; f.82). Even today, the word 'tone' (*tonus*), in physiology, denotes the tension (contraction) of the muscles as the condition by which health and vigor are maintained. More specifically, it refers to the usually moderate physiological activity of a tissue or organ, for example, the striated muscle, which, as a result of continuous nervous stimulation, is normally in a state of moderate contraction by which posture is maintained.

[140] Cartesian mind-body dualism left the visible face of human nature as a tantalising illusion, for if 'the ego is hidden, if mind was but a ghost in a machine, how could inspecting the outside of the machine tell you about the ghost?' (Porter 1985: 386). In attempting to solve the problem of the ghost in the machine, North posits an internal character which may be 'read' by external signs. It has been suggested that the question of signs was one of the focal points of the ancient Stoic–Epicurean debate. According to Markus (1957), the Stoics conceived signs as intellectual and the Epicureans as sensible entities. North occupies a middle ground, perhaps because the distinction between Stoicism and Epicureanism had become blurred during the seventeenth century (see Barker and Goldstein 1984).

conception of musical 'ayre'.[141] In his theory the term 'ayre' has a specific as well as a general sense. In its specific sense it may mean melody, song or tune; or it may mean the 'complexion' or 'ayre' of a key, that is, its tonality'; or it may refer to the 'character' of a key, that is, its mode, major or minor; or it may refer to the various 'manners' of a piece, that is, its tempi, slow to fast. In its general sense ayre signifies 'common measure', that is, harmonic rhythm, which maintains the interaction (sympathy) between the different parts (melody and harmony) of a composition, making ayre analogous to spirit, which mediates between mind and body.[142]

In his first theory, North does not always make a consistent distinction between these various uses, for his conception of musical ayre is not yet fully formulated.[143] In his second theory, North develops his conception within the confines of a separate treatise, in which he explicitly states that 'time' represents actions and melody, thoughts and affections; that is, these two aspects of music represent the whole personality ('humanity') – the actions of the body as well as the passions and affections of the mind.[144] But for music to have 'life', there must also be 'harmony', that is, harmonic rhythm, for 'harmony . . . runs thro the whole work and like the soul [i.e., spirit] animates the mass, which would be dead without it'.[145]

In that treatise North also merges the notions of ayre and sublimity. By sublimity he means the 'wit' or 'anima' of a great composer which is imprinted on a work and which gives that work its 'ayre', that is, its style or excellence of expression.[146] Wit, for North, is not a sudden flash of 'conceipt' or 'humour'.[147] Rather, it

[141] The word 'ayre' seems to have originated in England and France in the sixteenth century and commonly was used loosely as a synonym for song or tune. North's unusual usage cannot be understood from the miscellany of extracts provided by Wilson (1959).

[142] North's meaning is clearer when he refers to harmonic rhythm as 'current measure' (see, for example, *MG 1728*: f.30v). Underpinning his conception of harmonic rhythm are the notions current of air ('spring') and common measure ('pulse').

[143] See *Cursory Notes of Musicke* (ed. Chan and Kassler 1986: 199–208 *et passim.*).

[144] According to North, 'musick is a true pantomime, or resemblance of humanity in all its states, motions, passions and affections. And in every musicall attempt reasonably designed, humane nature is the subject, and so penetrant that thoughts, such as mankind occasionally have, and even speech it self, share in the resemblance so that an hearer shall put himself into the like condition, as if the state represented were his owne. It hath been observed that the termes upon which musicall time depends, are referred to men's active capacitys. So the melody should be referred to their thoughts and affections' (*Musicall Recollections III*: f.48v).

[145] *Ibid.* (f.52v).

[146] *MG 1728* (ff.12v–13, 64v), '*Anima*', of course, is material; hence, North sometimes uses the term 'vein', that is, a quality or strain traceable in music (see, for example, *ibid.*: ff.132, 133v, 134, 135, 135v, 137).

[147] See above I.2.1.

is a settled, constant, habitual sufficiency of the understanding, whereby the aspiring composer is enabled to achieve sharpness in invention, subtlety in expression and dispatch in execution.[148] Wit, then, is 'sublimed' by habitual acquaintance with the rules, just as the rules need wit to produce something more – that *'je ne sais quoi'* which makes great music more than the sum of its parts.[149] Judgement without wit is dull: but judgement with wit 'transcends', as in the case of the great masters. Their 'bold strokes', however, are not to be models for beginners to emulate, 'becaus novices are disposed allwais to think excellences lye in difficultys and exoticks, and esteem not what is plain altho true excellence for the most part lyes in that'.[150]

North's treatment of musical ayre in this sense is reminiscent of Longinus, author of the classic work on the sublime.[151] Longinus defined sublimity as a certain distinction and excellence of expression by which authors have been enabled to win immortal fame. In considering whether there was such a thing as an art of sublimity or profundity, Longinus observed:

Genius, they say, is innate; it is not something that can be learnt, and nature is the only art that begets it. Works of natural genius are spoilt, they believe, are indeed utterly debased, when they are reduced to the bare bones of rules and systems. However, I suggest there is a case for the opposite point of view when it is considered that, although nature is in the main subject only to her own laws where sublime feelings are concerned,

---

[148] North's conception of wit was first stated in relation to the 'composing' of words, for in *Notes of Me* he wrote: 'It is a happiness I have admired and envied that some will speak or write, and at the same time be contriving forwards to compose what is to succeed in form, and beating about for new matter, till there is a full persuasion nothing considerable is omitted, and not be disturbed, but pursue the method proposed, as if a discourse were premeditated. So also to have such quickness of thought, that no sooner is an objection started and understood but a true, or, for want of that, a witty answer is uttered. These are felicities to be admired and essayed, but not to be acquired, being the produce of natural strength improved by the practice of the mind and its performances. And by how much I have understood this in others I have so been conscious of my own wants' (ed. Jessopp 1887: 23).

[149] North states this most clearly when he uses an analogy from medicine (i.e., pharmacy and dietetics): 'It is to be remembered that the values of these mixtures are shortly represented in abstracto and universally, but in formed musick will be as the cook's provisions for a choice dish of meat, or the ingredients of a medicin, which put orderly together in composition, with salvo to the proper effect of each, shall acquire transcendencys not found in the simples' (*MG 1728*: f.40). Literary critics (e.g., Monk (1960), Wood (1972)) tend to ignore the 'chemical' analogies that abound in discussions of the sublime and that become increasingly important with the transformation of alchemy into chemistry.

[150] *MG c. 1726* (ff.80v–81); see also *MG 1728* (f.43).

[151] The work of Longinus was especially popular amongst French neo-classical critics. Clark (1925/1965) treats the transmission of their ideas to England.

she is not given to acting at random and wholly without system. Nature is the first cause and the fundamental creative principle in all activities, but the function of a system is to prescribe the degree and the right moment for each, and to lay down the clearest rules for use and practice. Furthermore, sublime impulses are exposed to greater dangers when they are left to themselves without the ballast and stability of knowledge: they need the curb as often as the spur.[152]

In *The Musicall Grammarian 1728*, which contains echoes of Longinus,[153] North sets out the limits within which composers have freedom. These limits are based on the physiological limitations of human nature, or, more strictly, on what North conceives as the limits necessary for the maintenance of individual and social equilibrium. Although his theory of cognition, as well as his method, force him to use contraries, opposites or extremes, he continually cautions that contraries must be tempered, opposites reconciled, and extremes avoided. Hence, North's universal rule is moderation.[154] The corollary is that there must be a balance between the varieties taken up and used by composers.

CONCLUSION

In *The Musical Grammarian 1728*, North's aim is to provide the means for enabling musical goodness to become natural, that is, akin, to the aspiring composer. Musical goodness, for North, is the beautiful, which resides in the true, simple and natural. The beautiful may be recognised by those whose cultivated taste enables them to do so, but what are the rules for achieving it finally? In a number of places in the treatise, North suggests that the rules are ultimately mysterious, because the beautiful is linked with the sublime. Yet, even if we cannot have certain knowledge of the rules, we can have probable knowledge of them, because nature (God, spirit) creates and regulates the universe so as to move equably, thereby producing and maintaining goodness; harmonious equilibrium.[155]

---

[152] Longinus (tr. Dorsch 1965: 101).
[153] See, for example, *MG 1728* (ff. 80v–81).
[154] According to North, the aspiring composer should avoid 'all manner of extremes, for such exceed the power of [human] nature in those things which are to be represented' *MG c. 1726*: ff. 144–144v.
[155] The probable bases of North's philosophy and theory of cognition are the principles of the Good, for which see the 'Introduction' to *Cursory Notes of Musicke* (ed. Chan and Kassler 1986: (66)–(69)).

Accordingly, 'God wills the good of all creatures, and pain is evil'.[156]

Although the universe as a whole develops in an ordered pattern, determined by immanent providence, this does not remove human responsibility for good and evil. It is the proper function of human nature to grasp the cosmic order so as to live in harmony with nature, that is, to live consistently with the will of nature. Such a life will be productive of happiness and goodness. But how can we set about the task of grasping the order of nature? North's writings provide an answer to this question, for they are attempts to bring the light of nature to those who sit in darkness and to leave a record for the enlightenment of posterity.[157] But those same writings indicate that North himself was one who sat in darkness and struggled to see the light. That he never published either his science of music or his writings on the philosophy of nature must be attributed partly to this struggle. But there may be another reason why these works remained unpublished, for North's philosophy is heterodox.[158]

The heterodoxy is to be found in the materialistic and deterministic features of North's philosophy, features which he extended to account for generation: the human soul, he wrote, is transmitted by the parents to the children.[159] This theory of generation, known as 'traducianism', was (and still is) considered heretical in both Roman Catholic and Anglican doctrine.[160] But North's heterodoxy is to be found also in his conception of the deity as material, immanent and continuously creative in the universe. According to this pan-

---

[156] *Notes of Me* (ed. Jessopp 1887: 155).

[157] For example, in *TS 1728* North provides a 'phisicall' account, because he thinks various other writers had brought forth 'more of cloud, then light, whereby plain truths might be discerned' (f.75). Although some of his own countrymen had 'come neerer the mark', these had relied so much on mathematics 'that nature is confounded and lost amongst them' (*ibid.*: f.75v). Hence, North's purpose is 'to develope the subject, which is wholly of audibles, and to shew it puris naturalibus, with all the plaine and explicit descriptions, using as much of vulgar speech, and intelligible experiments, as I can materially adapt, supposing it were not to describe, but to bring the matter forth, and to shew it above board' (*ibid.*: f.75v). Although North holds that mentation is computational, his supposed distaste for mathematics has been commented on by various writers (e.g., Korsten 1981) who have failed to identify accurately the grounds for it. Because of his holism and pantheism, North believes that nature is lost by using abstractions. A similar view was adumbrated later in the century by Johann Wolfgang von Goethe.

[158] North's first editor was his second son, Montagu North, who took holy orders and so would not have published material that went against orthodox theological views.

[159] See the digression, 'Of generation', in *Some Essays* (ff.24v–28v), which Korsten (1981) did not edit, as being 'too vague and speculative' (1981: 309).

[160] In North's day, those who identified the creating principles of the universe with God were called 'atheists'.

theistic view, human individuals are not atoms or pieces of matter cut off from other pieces of matter, nor are they body without spirit. Such separations, in North's view, are merely appearances, mental fictions, convenient for purposes of classifying and understanding reality.

INTRODUCTION II

Mary Chan

PREFACE

When Roger North sat down to write *The Musicall Grammarian 1728*, he evidently believed he was writing the final version of the texts he had entitled 'The Musicall Grammarian', and set out to make his manuscript look as much like a printed book as possible. On folio 1 he wrote a title-page, formally laid it out, and dated it 1728. The leaves which follow (excluding those at the back of the manuscript which are ruled for music and contain 'Amante che ditte', ff. 145–148) he folded in half lengthwise and then in half again lengthwise before he wrote on them in order to create a wide and uniform left-hand margin for each page of the manuscript.

If one's first acquaintance with the manuscript is through photographs or microfilm, its appearance is close to that of a 'fair copy', for only those additions above the line or in the margin show up. But when one looks at the actual manuscript one is struck by the amount of revision and alteration North made to his original text: by scraping text off the page and writing over the top, by pasting additional material on to a page, by pasting two leaves together, by removing whole leaves and pasting new ones on to the stub of the old leaf. Indeed, it is apparent that if North began writing *The Musicall Grammarian 1728* in 1728, then he revised it extensively in the following years and may have continued revision until 1733.[1]

The purpose of this essay is twofold: (1) to provide a physical description of the manuscript and (2) to illustrate and discuss the ways in which knowledge of the manuscript, and inferences which can be drawn about its compilation, make clear to the reader the significance of not regarding the manuscript as either an isolated treatise or a fixed and final text – as one might regard a printed book, for instance. In seeing North's writing here as part of a process, a continual struggle to clarify his ideas, the reader can understand the problems and issues facing North in writing his last theory of musical cognition, and thus gain a fuller understanding of

---

[1] See below, II.1.2.

the work itself and of North's achievement. Evidence which places the manuscript in the light of an ongoing struggle for clarity also helps the reader to locate those parts of the text where difficulties of interpretation lie.

I discuss first (in Sections 1 and 2) the physical characteristics of the manuscript in its present state. In Section 3, I draw on evidence provided by the physical characteristics of this manuscript and compare it with the other 'Musicall Grammarian' manuscripts (*The Musicall Grammarian c. 1726* and *The Musicall Grammarian Fragments*) which preceded it, in order to illustrate North's method of composition. The structure and physical composition of these two earlier manuscripts are discussed in detail in Chan, Kassler, Hine, (1988). Finally I look at some of the problems of terminology North himself encountered and those likely to be encountered by a reader unaware of musical terminology which is now obsolete or changed in meaning. My discussion throughout relies on the definition of the structure of *The Musicall Grammarian 1728* (its division into five parts) discussed in Introduction I.

1. PHYSICAL ASPECTS OF THE MANUSCRIPT

1.1. Provenance and transmission of the text

Hereford Cathedral Manuscript R.11.xlii. is a quarto volume bound during the nineteenth century and containing two distinct title-pages, *The Musicall Grammarian 1728* and *Memoires of Musick 1728*. The modern binding includes leaves of nineteenth-century paper at the front and back and on the first of these, at the front, is the following inscription:

> Original Manuscript of the Hon*our*able
> Roger North. Bequeathed to the
> Dean & Chapter of Hereford Cathedral
> by George Townshend Smith.
> Organist for 34 years & six months.
> Aug*ust* 3rd 1877.

On the first leaf of the original manuscript, three leaves further in from that describing Hereford Cathedral's acquisition of the manuscript, is written:

MSS of the Hon*ourable* Roger North of
Rougham, Norfolk –
Presented to
G. Townshend Smith
org*a*nist of Hereford Cathedral
upon his leaving, Lynn, Norfolk.
by
Robert Nelson.
Jan*uary* 18. 1843.

A different hand has added, above this note,

Musical Grammarian Musical Memoirs

and after 'Norfolk'

Attorney General to King James 2.

Little is known about Robert Nelson or how the manuscript came into his possession. Peter Millard (1973) has discussed the fate of North's papers after his death and accounted for their dispersal and subsequent appearance in various libraries. The major collectors of North's papers in the nineteenth century were James Crossley and Dawson Turner, but Millard points out that, despite the fierce competition between these two collectors, neither managed to own all the extant North papers. Robert Nelson appears to have been another collector. Millard refers to a letter of Nelson's which 'lists several works in his possession, including the *Memoires of Musick* (now in Hereford Cathedral Library), a work on architecture, and one on the baroscope' (Millard 1973: 286).[2]

The manuscript has suffered at the hands of three early editors. Charles Burney published extracts from Part V, 'Memoirs of Musick', in his *General History of Music* (1776–1789), claiming that access to the manuscript had been granted him by North's 'descendant the late Dr. Montague North Canon of Windsor'.[3] 'Dr. Montague North' was North's second son Montagu (b. 1712, d.

---

[2] Millard claims that the letter is dated 1846, but from the presentation note in the Hereford Cathedral Manuscript, a note presumably in Nelson's hand, this cannot be correct since Nelson gave the manuscript (he thought of it as two manuscripts) to George Townshend Smith in 1843. Rimbault (1846) gives further details of the manuscript's early history. He claims that it passed from Roger North to his son Montagu. At Montagu's death in 1779 it came into the possession of Roger North (the author's grandson) by whom it was given to Henry North of Ringstead, Norfolk. At the sale of Henry North's papers, it was bought by Robert Nelson.

[3] Burney (1789: iii/334. note x).

1779) to whom North left his papers and manuscripts in his will. Montagu North was appointed Canon of Windsor in 1775. North's next editor was Edward F. Rimbault (1846) who edited only that part of *The Musicall Grammarian 1728* which Burney had quoted from, 'Memoires of Musick'. Finally, the same part of the manuscript was edited by John Wilson (1959: 315–59) although not quite complete. He omitted those sections which are numbered 23 and 24 in our edition. Wilson also included some excerpts from earlier parts of the manuscript in his book, but because of the way in which he stitched his excerpts from North's manuscripts together to form a 'portrait' of North, these are not easily identifiable except by close reading of his list of sources. All three earlier editors of parts of *The Musicall Grammarian 1728* present North's work in ways which create serious problems for students of North. These are not dealt with here since they have been already discussed in Chan (1986).

1.2. Paper, binding and handwriting

Before it was given its present binding, and leaving aside consideration of the blank leaves which form part of this binding, the original manuscript was made up of single sheets folded in quarto and measuring approximately 20.5 cm × 15.5 cm.[4] The binding makes it impossible to discern accurately North's original gatherings but it seems that some are incomplete. North himself made alterations to the text as he wrote, or subsequently, by pasting additional leaves on to the inner margin of a leaf, or on to the stub of a leaf removed, or on top of a page already written. Those leaves which have obviously been 'repaired' are: ff.41, 42, 43, 45, 46, 49, 50, 51, 73, 74, 85, 104, 109. Folios 61 and 61v, 62 and 62v, 125 and 125v, 126 and 126v have originally been two leaves, each of which North has pasted one on top of the other. North may have made further additions by inserting completely rewritten leaves or gatherings, insertions which are not evident from the binding of the manuscript. Some evidence for the insertion of new gatherings is seen in inconsistencies in North's pagination (see II.2.1.) and in discrepancies in the numbering sequence of the sections in the text (see II.2.2.).

---

[4] The modern binding also includes a letter, dated 6 October 1952, between ff.56 and 57 from the Department of Manuscripts at the British Museum to F. C. Morgan, the Librarian of Hereford Cathedral at that time. The letter refers to two manuscripts, including the present one, apparently sent to the British Museum for verification of the handwriting.

Those leaves on which the text is written consist of one paper throughout. The watermark and countermark are similar to those in Heawood (1950: no. 3702), that is, a watermark of the *Pro Patria* type with a crowned GR as a countermark. I refer to this paper as *Pro Patria* (1). The paper was used by North in manuscripts which he dated 1726 and 1728.

For the music at the end of the manuscript (ff.145–147v) and the following leaf (f.148 recto and verso which is ruled for music but not otherwise written on) North used a different paper. This paper has a watermark of a fleur de lis, similar to Heawood (1950: no. 178). No countermark is visible in either this or the only other document among North's papers which uses it, BL Add MS 32527: ff.1–107. This latter manuscript contains some entries in the early folios in the hand of Roger North's brother, Francis North (b. 1637, d. 1685), indicating an early date for the paper. In the Hereford Cathedral Manuscript, the paper ruled for music at the end of the volume has been cut to the size of that on which the text of the manuscript is written, but has not been folded in the usual quarto way, for the chain lines run vertically on these folios. The four leaves were originally separate and were joined by North at the middle with a strip of paper. The music on ff.145v–146, 146v–147, was written after the joining of the leaves to be read across the two pages of the opening.

The blank leaves which formed the end-papers to North's original manuscript consist of a third paper, also of the *Pro Patria* type with a crowned GR countermark, but the marks are smaller than those in the paper on which the text was written and are similar to those illustrated in Heawood (1950: no. 3706). I refer to this paper as *Pro Patria* (2). The paper is also slightly smaller in size. I have found only one document in North's hand which uses this paper: BL Add MS 32546: ff.285–286, dated '20 January 1730'. The paper was used by North's son, Montagu, in those folios he rewrote in BL Add MS 32530: ff.5–7 and the following blank leaf, and also ff.84–88 and the blank leaves which follow. The only other occurrence of *Pro Patria* (2) among North's manuscripts which I have examined is as end-papers to some of the volumes of North's *Life of the Lord Keeper North* in St John's College, Cambridge (MS James 613): Volumes 1, 4, 5, 6, 7, 8, 10.

The occurrence of the paper in these volumes and in the Hereford Cathedral Manuscript as end-papers, together with its use by Montagu North in copying some of his father's writings in BL Add MS 32530, suggests that *The Musicall Grammarian 1728* and the *Life of the Lord Keeper North* at least were among those manuscripts to which North referred in a letter to Montagu dated 2 June 1733. There he wrote:

I hope you have a strict care of the MSS which I would not have miscarry in any respect, being a sort of writing slight and slovenly as it is (such a fool I am) pleaseth me to peruse better than any books, of which the best soon tire with me.[5]

If North used this paper as wrapping for the manuscripts he sent Montagu, this would explain its presence as end-papers in those manuscripts and its use in the leaves Montagu copied in BL Add MS 32530. In the latter case, I suggest that Montagu used some of the wrapping sheets in order to recopy those damaged or missing leaves in BL Add MS 32530, a manuscript also included in the parcel of books.

The end-papers of the Hereford Cathedral Manuscript (excluding the nineteenth-century paper) are made up as follows: at the front of the book are seven leaves, the first of which is *Pro Patria* (1) paper. This first leaf contains the presentation note from Robert Nelson and because it was originally loose (that is, not part of a gathering) it may have been taken from any place in the manuscript. The other six are *Pro Patria* (2). At the back of the manuscript, after f. 148 (the last of the leaves ruled for music), there is one blank leaf (f. 149) of *Pro Patria* (1) paper, followed by leaves of the *Pro Patria* (2) paper which North used here only for end-papers, consisting of two separate quarter sheets pasted on to a fold of six leaves made up of a single sheet wrapped in a half sheet.

The manuscript was written entirely by North himself, and the handwriting is of an elderly person. Rimbault (1846: vi) describes it as 'somewhat strange and affected' but this description seems far too subjective an interpretation of what is a plain and clear hand. Figures 4, 5 and 6 illustrate North's hand at various times of his life. We have grouped North's writings into three periods, corresponding to changing circumstances in his life.[6] The handwriting of the 'early' period (*c.* 1680s–*c.* 1703) is illustrated by Figure 4; Figure 5 illustrates North's handwriting in the 'middle' period (*c.* 1704–*c.* 1720); Figure 6, from the present manuscript, illustrates his handwriting in the 'late' period (*c.* 1721–1734).

---

[5] *Notes of Me* (ed. Jessopp 1887: 279).
[6] See *Cursory Notes of Musicke* (ed. Chan and Kassler 1986: (62)–(63)).

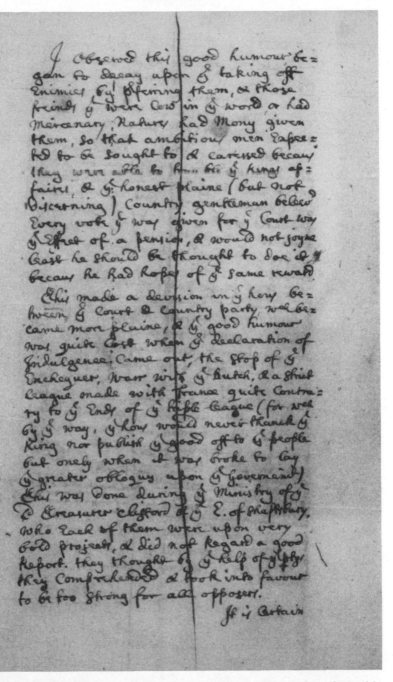

Figure 4. An example from the early period of one of the styles of North's handwriting.

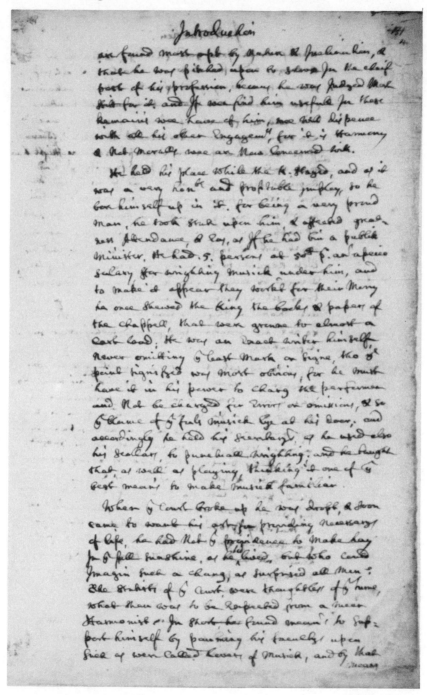

Figure 5. An example from the middle period of North's handwriting.

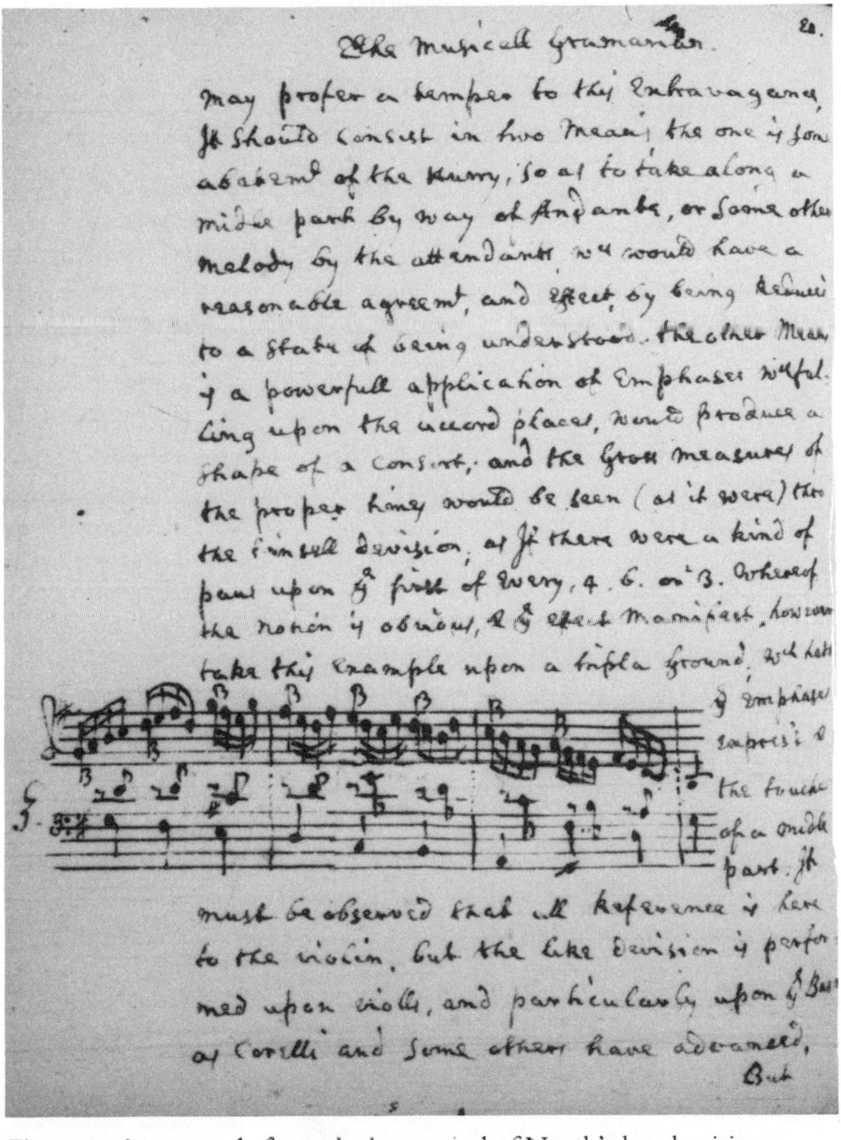
The Musicall Grammarian. 20.

may proper a temper to this Extravagance, It should consist in two Means, the one is some abatemt of the hurry, so as to take along a midle part by way of Andante, or some other melody by the attendants wch would have a reasonable agreemt, and effect, by being reduc'd to a state of being understood. the other Mean is a powerfull application of Emphases wilfulling upon the accord places, would produce a shape of a consort, and the Gross measures of the proper time would be seen (as it were) thro the tinsell devision, as if there were a kind of pause upon ye first of every, 4. 6. or 3. whereof the notion is obvious, & ye effect manifest, howev take this example upon a triple ground, wch hath ye emphases express'd & the touche of a midle part. It must be observed that all reference is here to the violin, but the like Devision is performed upon violls, and particularly upon ye Bass as Corelli and some others have advanced,

But

Figure 6. An example form the late period of North's handwriting.

2. TEXTUAL ASPECTS OF THE MANUSCRIPT

2.1. Foliation, running titles, pagination and catchwords

The manuscript has been foliated since binding in its present form, and this foliation includes numbering of the blank leaves between the end of the text (f.142v) and the music (f.144v) and the nine blank leaves of *Pro Patria* paper which now (with three nineteenth-century leaves) form the back end-papers. The foliation 23 has been given to two consecutive folios; the second is now f.23ª. Our edition uses this, modern, foliation.

North uses running titles throughout, beginning on f.7 for 'The Musicall Grammarian' and on f.103 for 'Memoires of Musick'. 'The Musicall Grammarian' occurs on all pages from ff.7 to 98v, except ff.22v and 36v (whose heading is 'The Musicall Grammer'); 'Memoires of Musick' occurs on all pages from ff.103 to 142v except ff.128 and 135 (whose headings are 'Musicall memoires') and ff.125v and 140 (whose headings are 'Memorialls of musick').

North paginated the manuscript using a form of lettering which can be found in others of his writings. Each page, beginning with f.7, is given a letter name from 'a' to 'z' written in the top inner margin; after 'z' the sequence begins 'aa' to 'az', then 'ba' to 'bz', and so on. North does not use the letters 'j' or 'v' in his sequence. On some pages North has repeated, omitted, or deleted and rewritten, the lettering, thus upsetting the sequence. The following pages contain inconsistencies in lettering:

> ff.26 and 26v: 'ar' on both
> f.29 contains both 'ax' and 'ay'
> f.44v: 'f' [cf]
> f.45: 'ce' [cg] although f.45v has 'ch'
> f.47 has no letters
> f.47v: 'cd'
> f.48: 'ce'

The sequence continues from here to 'co' (f.52v). Then:

> f.53: 'cn'

and the sequence continues to 'cz' (f.58v).

> ff.73v and 74 have no letters although the sequence takes account of their omission on f.74v.

f.85 has no letters: f.85v has two sets of letters which are illegible. ff.86 and 86v have 'fg' and 'fh' respectively, and the lettering continues in sequence from here although all pages from ff.87 to 90v also have two other sets of letters, both deleted. From f.91 the sequence is correct again.

The a–z sequence begins again for the 'Memoires of Musick' and the discrepancies in the sequence here are as follows:

f.104v: 'd' which is correct in the sequence but written on the outside corner of the leaf
f.109: no letter [i]
f.120: 'al' on the outside corner of the leaf
ff.141v–142: 'e'; and 'eg' [cf], [cg]
ff.144v, 145–147v (the text and the music of 'Amante che ditte') are not paginated by North.

Some of the inconsistencies occur on pages which have been 'repaired' in some way before the present text was written on them – that is, either by cutting a leaf back to a stub and pasting a new leaf on to it, or by pasting at the inner margin an additional leaf between original leaves (see II.1.2.). The first group of leaves indicating rewriting of this kind is ff.41 to 51, and North's lettering here is also erratic. Other rewritten leaves (but not those pasted one on top of another) also coincide with problems in the lettering sequence and in the case of the addition of a rewritten folio (f.85 recto and verso) it appears from the lettering that rewriting may have given rise to the insertion (or replacement) of a complete gathering: ff.87–90.

North uses catchwords at the foot of most pages of the main texts (ff.7–98v and 103–142v). In places, however, he omits a catchword or fails to pick it up on the following page and in some cases these pages are also those which other evidence shows were repaired or added, or in some other way emended, at a later date. Some of those pages on which there is no catchword, but which show no other evidence of revision, may indeed be revised pages whose later insertion is not apparent from the modern binding. North's use or omission of catchwords is as follows:

(i) North has continued the text without regard to the catchword, that is, the catchword is not picked up at the top of the next page, so what is written as a catchword, is in fact, part of the text: ff.16v–17, 119v–120.

(ii) On some pages North picks up not only the catchword but the last word of text as well: ff.12v–13, 32–32v, 60v–61,

132v–133. Compare these with ff. 86v–87 where the catch-word itself picks up the last word of text on the page; and compare them also with ff. 57–57v where the catchword consists of two words, the first of which is in fact the last word of the text.

(iii) North has omitted a catchword on the page preceding one beginning with a new section heading: ff. 15v–16, 17v–18, 20v–21, 25v–26, 26–26v, 27–27v, 28v–29, 29v–30, 48–48v, 48v–49, 59v–60, 64–64v, 74–74v, 86–86v, 103–103v, 111v–112, 116–116v, 117–117v, 121–121v, 131v–132, 132–132v, 135–135v, 135v–136, 136v–137, 139–139v, 142–142v; cf. ff. 90–90v.

Despite the fact that North usually writes a catchword before a page beginning with a new section, the large number of places (cited here) where he does not, suggests that he had not decided on a consistent 'policy' in this regard.

(iv) On many pages North has omitted the catchword even when the following page does not begin with a new section. Some of these pairs of pages are among those which other evidence shows contain revisions of the text: ff. 26v–27, 36–36v, 38–38v, 38v–39, 39–39v, 39v–40, 41–41v, 42–42v, 43v–44, 45–45v, 45v–46, 47v–48, 61–61v, 73v–74, 105–105v, 107v–108, 113v–114, 123–123v, 123v–124, 125v–126, 127–127v, 130v–131.

Folio 127 ends with a small flourish of the pen, and although North does not begin a new section on f. 127v, he does begin a new paragraph there.

Neither f. 36 nor f. 73v has a catchword, and, although North has not given the following sections (ff. 36v and 74) new headings, a new section beginning is implied on each by the text and other physical and textual evidence (see II.2.2.).

(v) On two occasions North does not pick up the catchword on the following page: ff. 30–30v, 47–47v.

Despite the appearance in certain sections of the manuscript that North had difficulty reaching a satisfactory final version of his text, parts of the manuscript, and especially those making up Part I (ff. 1–36v) and most of the 'Memoires of Musick', have the appearance of a neat and careful text. Besides the addition of rewritten leaves, North has made alterations to his text by deletion, addition above the line, addition in the margin, and by scraping the ink from the page and writing over the scraped-off words.

2.2. Index and section headings

Besides using a system of pagination, North numbered the section headings of the manuscript in sequence. The sequence begins again for the 'Memoires of Musick'. North also provides an 'Index' for both 'The Musicall Grammarian' and the 'Memoires of Musick' at the front of the manuscript (ff. 2–5v). Both indexes contain inconsistencies in the numbering sequences, some of which appear to be simple errors but all of which indicate revision or rewriting. The discrepancies between North's index entries and his section headings, and the inconsistencies of numbering within each, indicate where the manuscript was revised and passages rewritten and inserted at different times, and also reveal the way in which North composed his work (see also II.3.1.).

In the discussion which follows here and in Section 3 below, I use North's own numbering when referring to section headings in the text or to numbered entries in the 'Index' rather than our editorial section numbers (see Editorial guidelines, section 4). My reason for this is that the discrepancies in North's numbering are some of the clues to his method of composition or revision of the manuscript.[7] In the discussion which follows, the section numbering for this edition is given in brackets following a reference to North's numbering.

Evidence for later revision provided by a comparison of section headings and index entries is found in three places. Each case suggests that the 'Index' was written before revision of the text took place. First, on f. 46 North begins a section, 'Of maintaining the key' which he numbers '61. 62'. (63). The 'Index', however, numbers 'Of maintaining the key' as 61 and gives a separate entry for 62: 'In framing accords the proper base to be considered'. Because in the text as it now stands there is no place for this new section, it seems that the index entry for 62 was made before f. 46 (a 'replaced' leaf) was rewritten.

Second, the numbering of the section headings on ff. 34 and 34v also indicates second thoughts or rewriting of the leaf after the compilation of the 'Index'. The section heading which occurs at the top of f. 34, 'Comon time and tripla distinguisht by emphasis', was originally numbered 48 (which would be correct in the sequence), but it was changed to 47, thus giving two sections with the number

---

[7] A comparison of both 'Index' and section headings is made in Chan, Kassler, Hine (1988: 34–44).

47. On f.34v, the section entitled 'The effect of emphasis' is numbered 48 (49), but the 8 has been heavily scored, suggesting that it covers another figure not now discernible. In the 'Index' North does not list this section at all, going from the text's second 47 (which is numbered 48 in the 'Index', North's original number in the text too) to what in the text is 49 (50): 'Tripla is but a manner of dividing upon equall times'. Again, the lack of correlation between 'Index' and text suggests a change to the text – in this case, the addition of another section – after the 'Index' was compiled.

The third example of revision of the text, after the compilation of the 'Index', is found on f.36v. By the end of Part I, North's section numbering in the text and the 'Index' had been brought to coincide once more after the dislocation of the numbering on ff.34–35: Part II begins in both at Section 51 (53). But it seems that f.36v was left blank when North began Part II on f.37 and was filled later. The evidence for this supposition is that the writing on the page is more crammed than that on f.37, implying limited space; and the material on f.36v really demands a new heading (and in *The Musicall Grammarian c.1726* had been given a section to itself, 59: ff.58v–59v). That North did not give this section a heading in 1728 implies that his discussion of keeping time in consort was not included in his original text, and that having decided to add it, he did not wish to adjust his section numbering for the end of Part I yet again.

It is clear that North had compiled his 'Index' at least before he made those revisions to the text discussed above. But other evidence indicates that North's method of working was to compile the 'Index' as, or before, he wrote even the first version of the text. For instance, in two places North omitted a section number and heading from his text which he listed in his 'Index', although the numbering sequence in the text implies a missing heading and a new paragraph has been begun. That the heading and number are missing from the text but not from the 'Index' suggests that North was working from a list of headings already compiled.

First, on f.60v, North begins a section numbered 79 (81): 'Of keys and their changes'. His next heading in the text occurs on f.62v numbered 81 (83): 'Elegances of an upper part'. The missing section number and heading 80 should come at the top of f.61v. In the 'Index', this Section is numbered 80 and given the title: 'Theory of flat and sharp keys'. Second, in the 'Memoires of Musick', f.125, North begins Section 35 (37): 'Plainsong and figurate musick introduced by the clergy'. His next numbered section begins on f.127: 37 (39), 'The defects of plain-song musick'. Section 36 (38), which is listed in the 'Index' with the title 'Of descanting and In Nomines', begins in the text halfway down f. 126, although North has omitted the number and title there. The fact that North has listed the section in the 'Index' and omitted its heading from the text, while keeping the numbering nevertheless consistent, indicates that he compiled the 'Index' before, or as, he wrote the headings in the text, or that he wrote the numbers and titles for a group of sections in the 'Index' which he then proceeded to write out in his text.

A slightly different, and more puzzling example of 'misnumbering' also provides evidence that North compiled the 'Index' before writing the text. In his 'Index', North omits 99, numbering from 98 (99) to 100 (101), as though intending to fit 99 in later. In the text, however, although he begins a new section where one would expect to find Section 99 (100) (on f.74, a discussion of the sarabanda), it is not given a title nor, in the text, allowed for in the numbering sequence.

3. METHOD OF COMPOSITION AND MATTERS OF STYLE AND USAGE

3.1. Writing by commonplacing

North's method of composing his treatise can be glimpsed in the evidence, already discussed (II.2.2.), that he wrote his index entries before, or at the same time as, he wrote the text of *The Musicall Grammarian 1728*. This evidence has been cited to explain the relationship of index entries to the section headings in the text. North's composition of the 'Index', either completely or in part, before he wrote the text appears to follow the method of composition he refers to in 'The writer's preface' to *The Musicall Grammarian c. 1726*. There he wrote:

At first onely a marginall index, was intended, to be numbred by way of repertory but in the collecting the notes I have cast them into chapters and sections, keeping still the marginall numbers. Whither the text will all along correspond [to] the epigraffs, or not, I cannot say . . .[8]

Here North has set out his method of composition. He began, he says, by writing an index of 'marginall' headings which he then expanded by 'notes' (that is, his text) 'cast . . . into chapters and sections' which he hoped would correspond to the index entries.

[8] *MG c. 1726*: f.2.

The method he describes is that of 'commonplacing', which he had set out in *A Discourse on the Study of the Laws* (ed. Anon 1824: 28). There North encourages the law student to purchase a blank book, write a set of running titles at the top of each page and 'note' or enter in the book. This method of commonplacing was followed by North in *Cursory Notes of Musicke* and possibly in others of his writings.[9] In both versions of *The Musicall Grammarian*, *c.* 1726 and 1728, North simply varied this method, writing not running headings to his pages but an index of section headings before filling out his text.

'The wrighter's preface' to *The Musicall Grammarian c. 1726* was written, or rewritten, after the main text of the manuscript was completed.[10] But it is evident from what North says just before the passage on the composition of the 'Index' that he still did not regard the text as satisfactory or finished: 'It will soon appear that here is rather a bundle of materialls then a just essay, and in order to look somewhat digested, ought to be transcribed more then once,' he wrote.[11] So it seems that North began *The Musicall Grammarian 1728* as a 'digestion' of the earlier work, to make a more 'just essay'.

The text of *The Musicall Grammarian 1728* is based, then, on the other complete text of the same name, *c.* 1726 which, like the present text, is a companion to one entitled *Theory of Sounds*. A comparison of the two 'Musicall Grammarian' texts, taking account also of the fragments or drafts and rewritten leaves which survive (in *The Musicall Grammarian Fragments*), and of the kinds of deletions and additions North made even to his final version, reveals much about the way he worked and also about those parts of his theory which he found more difficult than others to write.

Specifically, a comparison of Part I of *The Musicall Grammarian 1728* with Part I of *The Musicall Grammarian c. 1726* reveals just how North set about his 'digestion'. In writing Part I of *The Musicall Grammarian 1728*, North followed his earlier version closely in the order of his subject matter and certainly in the division into sections up to Section 19 in both texts (*c.* 1726: f.26v; 1728: f.18). Furthermore, writing in 1728, he lifted the opening sentence in eighteen of the first nineteen sections almost verbatim from the *c.*1726 version.[12] It was, therefore, within each section that North made his alterations to the text. This method of revision seems to have

---

[9] See *Cursory Notes of Musicke* (ed. Chan and Kassler 1986: (21)).
[10] See Chan, Kassler, Hine (1988).
[11] *MG c. 1726*: f.2.
[12] Section 17 (*c.*1726: f.24v; 1728: f.17) opens differently in the two versions.

been a common one for North. For example, it is possible to identify discarded leaves from *The Musicall Grammarian c. 1726* in *The Musicall Grammarian Fragments* by the fact that a page in the fragments begins in an identical way to one in *The Musicall Grammarian c. 1726*. In one case, North virtually recopied a whole page of text before branching off into his revision on the following pages.

In sitting down to compose *The Musicall Grammarian 1728*, then, North first wrote his index entries (or at least a group of them); then he began to write each corresponding section of text, using the opening of the similar section in *The Musicall Grammarian c. 1726* as a springboard to launch him into his revised version. Once he was launched into his new treatise, however, North diverged from his earlier text in Sections 20 (20) to 36 (36) of *The Musicall Grammarian 1728*.[13] Nevertheless, that North was still working from the *c.* 1726 text and adapting it, is clear from the way in which, from time to time, he dips into it for a phrase or a sequence of sentences. Although generally this part of the 1728 version gains from the revision, there are now occasional problems of obscurity where it seems that the material was almost too familiar to North, and he consequently elided ideas which previously he had spelt out in detail. An example of this is the passage which begins at the foot of f. 19v in the 1728 text which in the *c.* 1726 version North took three pages to make clear (ff. 29v–31).

Sections 20 to 36 are those sections of Part I North changed most radically. It seems that in 1728 he found his earlier discussion of the gamut and clefs too prolix. Although the material treated is the same in each version, in the later it has been reordered and reduced, resulting in a more logical and less digressive argument. The discussion on organ tuning in *The Musicall Grammarian c. 1726* (ff. 34–34v, Section 29), is one section entirely omitted from the 1728 version and it is clearly a digression in *c.* 1726. Furthermore, North's long discussion in the *c.* 1726 version (ff. 44v–46v) of Salmon's clef system and the debate about it, including the reference to J. F. de la Fond's restatement of it in 1725, has been greatly reduced in the 1728 version, and the treatment in the later manuscript has more relevance to the surrounding material (ff. 23ᵃ–23ᵃv).[14]

One notable example of North's changes to the text in 1728 is his omission of the 'synoptick diagram' which occurs in *The Musicall Grammarian c. 1726*: f. 49, illustrating in 'tabular' form his foregoing

---

[13] *MG c. 1726*: Sections 20 to 49.
[14] See also I.2.2.

discussion of 'the toning and notation of sounds', Figure 7. Had North included such a diagram in *The Musicall Grammarian 1728*, it would have clearly illustrated his discussion to f.25v. Nevertheless, the following folio in the 1728 version, f.26, is the point at which he returned to follow *The Musicall Grammarian c. 1726* more closely, and he may have omitted the 'synoptick diagram' in the later version because he considered his revisions had obviated the necessity of summarising his material visually. Certainly, in the sections of *The Musicall Grammarian c. 1726* which immediately precede his introduction of the 'synoptick diagram', North had digressed from his main line of argument in his long discussion of Salmon's clef system and the 'Ancients'' scales (Sections 40–45). The reason for introducing the diagram at Section 46 (f.48v) may have been to bring his discussion back to the main point. On the other hand, North may simply have baulked at copying such an elaborate table again.[15]

North's use of Part I of *The Musicall Grammarian c. 1726* illustrates, generally and on a large scale, that method of commonplacing which we have observed in his compilation of the 'Index'. It seems that at each level of composition, North used this system. So, the whole of Part I of *The Musicall Grammarian c. 1726* is itself a springboard to launch North into much more thoroughgoing revision of the later parts of his treatise. But first he wrote his 'Index' of section headings to be filled out; and even in the filling out, he used the opening words of each section in the *c.* 1726 version to start him off on the process of recasting.

3.2. Style of writing

From the point of view of the subject matter discussed, North's alterations and revisions of the early sections of *The Musicall Grammarian c. 1726* Part I may appear minor; but from the point of view

[15] In *MG c. 1726*: f.2 North mentions that 'by a misadventrous fall from a starting hors [he] dislocated [his] right shoulder' which prevented him from 'all kinds of brachiall capacity' but not from using his fingers, and so leaving him still with 'free use of the pen'. Stiffness from a healed dislocated shoulder may well have encouraged North to avoid copying and recopying as much as possible in 1728 and this, as much as a change in his text, may be the reason for his omitting the 'synoptick diagram' from *The Musicall Grammarian 1728*. Had he thought it an essential part of his discussion in 1728 however, he could have transferred it from the *c.* 1726 manuscript, a practice of North's for which there is a good deal of evidence in many of his manuscripts. For an instance of a pasted-in diagram, see *MG 1728*: f.73v, Example 1. The 'synoptick diagram' could well have been drawn before the fall from the horse since there is evidence that the *MG c. 1726* was composed over a period of time (see Chan, Kassler, Hine 1988: 21–3).

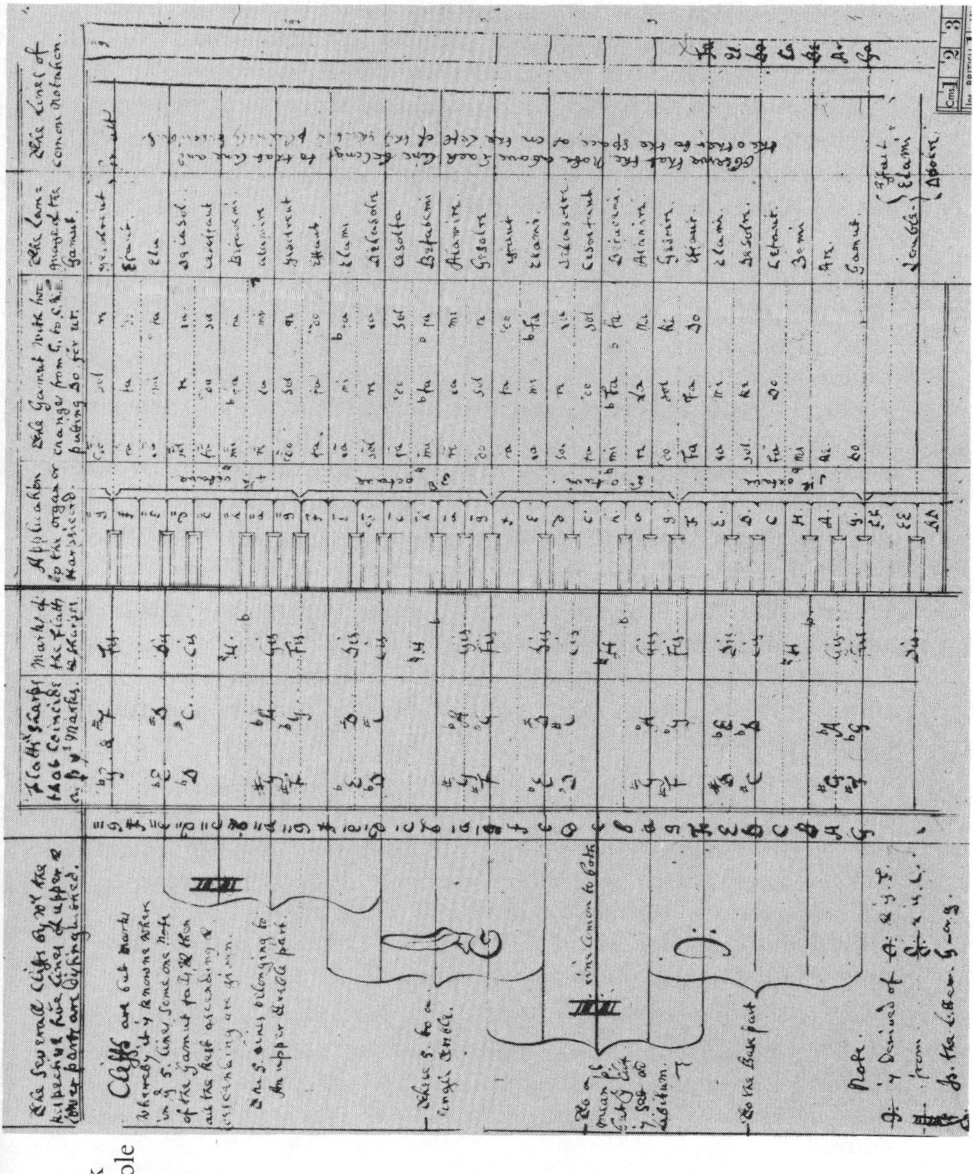

Figure 7.
North's 'Synoptick
diagram of the whole
art of notation'.

of style and treatment, a comparison reveals one of the purposes of rewriting. The major change is in succinctness and in tone, which in 1728 becomes generally more instructional and less conversational. The example which follows illustrates one aspect of this change in tone: the more vigorous style and the greater clarity of the 1728 version (which is given second) in this case does not necessarily mean greater brevity:

... For tho a tone is the first thing to be learnt, it is the last that a voice acquires without exception, and seldome well, till a good and sound judgment, which is the result of a cultivated experience, is added to all other qualifications.[16]

... for altho a tone is the first thing to be learnt, it is the last that a voice acquires without exception, and seldome well, untill the judgment is matured, and that (maturity) grows out of discipline; which discipline hath these two essentials, 1. instruction, 2. example. The former will do litle without the other, and that (other) is the cheif, for example, by force of imitation, may forme [the] voice, when instruction, without example, can do nothing.[17]

Sometimes the rewriting does not create a more assured tone (as in the example above). In the second of the two following passages (from the 1728 version) North succeeds in cutting down the length of the corresponding c. 1726 passage but the result is a confusing ellipsis:

This [i.e., the gamut] consists (principally) of 7 tones continually ascending from the lowest, and then (in effect) returning in the same order again. For after ascending or descending, the same septenarys are found to adjoyne, onely sharper, or flatter, otherwise of the like consonance, as when a boy and a man sing the same tune. These 7 tones that (as it were) turne about and come round againe are the elements, out of which all musick or harmony is flowing or composed.[18]

... and it falls out that after the whole number [of the 7 tones] is past over, the like caus as determined the modallity of the gradation operates upon the further proceeding and so, indefinitely, whereby the musicall scale is but a septenary, out of which all variety of harmony and melody is derived.[19]

The greater formality of the 1728 version means, however, a loss of one of the most notable features of the c. 1726 version: a style which is digressive, full of images and metaphors and, in particular,

[16] *MG c. 1726*: f.20
[17] *MG 1728*: f.13v.
[18] *MG c. 1726*: f.23.
[19] *MG 1728*: f.15v.

which personifies music. North begins this personification even in 'The wrighter's preface' (f.2) where he describes his musical activities as 'acts of courtship' and music as his 'mistress'. On f.106 he writes:

So chast[e] is musick to her native key, that she scarce visits another, unless it be the next neighbour and then not without a penchant to returne soon home again, and that which strays, and keeps too farr off, hath more of a savage then civilised air;

or on f.119:

Here ... wee ... retire from the church to the theater, where in our age musick seems to mount her throne.

The revisions in style in 1728 were, generally, towards a more concise and clear discussion of the subject but also towards a more impersonal (North might have said 'proper') tone.

3.3. Language usage

A study of the physical construction of the manuscript and comparison of this, final, version of the text with both *The Musicall Grammarian c.1726* and *The Musicall Grammarian Fragments* reveals that North had most difficulty in writing those sections in which he attempted to set out his theory of harmonic progression. Because he was working at a new theory and, as he himself points out, a theory 'wholly of audibles',[20] problems of description and expression were paramount for him. 'What difficulty there is,' North cries, 'in transfusing mentall ideas, and imaginary matters by meer words, which are not always and by all persons understood alike.'[21]

That North had most difficulty organising the material in Part II is evident from comparison of the differences in this section between the two texts[22] and from the discarded fragments which survive for the early sections of Part II of *The Musicall Grammarian c.1726*. Even in 1728, as the state of the manuscript suggests, North did not arrive at his 'final' version easily.[23] North's difficulties with this material arose particularly in his discussion of 'key', as can be seen from the evidence of the surviving leaves in *The Musicall Grammarian Fragments*: ff.40–52. In Part II, one of North's major problems – that of nomenclature – is most apparent and this has not

---

[20] *T S 1728*: f.75v.
[21] *ibid.*
[22] *M G 1728*: ff.37–58v; *c.* 1726: ff.67–115v.
[23] Witness the rewritten leaves between ff.40 and 51, and see II.2.1.

been entirely solved in the 1728 version. The lack of a satisfactory solution in 1728 may be partly owing to his commonplacing method of revision which makes him reluctant to move completely away from, and rewrite, an existing text. Nevertheless, he succeeded in reducing the *c.*1726 version of Part II from forty-eight folios to twenty-one in the 1728 version and the gain is, on the whole, in clarity of definition and argument.

The reader thus faces two kinds of problems in reading the text of *The Musicall Grammarian 1728*: first, is that of usage of words which is no longer current. Words in this category are dealt with in our edition by glosses to the text.[24] But even where words are not glossed because their meaning in context is supplied by standard reference books, readers should beware of anachronistic reading, particularly when North is using musical terms common both in his day and ours but whose meanings may have changed. Examples of the possibility of such misreading are to be found in North's use of 'tremolo' (ff. 56v, 67v, 73), or 'cantabile' (f. 33v) for instance, and one whose meaning in *The Musicall Grammarian 1728* is not found in *New Grove*: 'ricercata' (f. 33v). The words we gloss also include those which North appears to have made up, words such as 'cantable', 'vociferacious', 'chachinnatory', or words which he uses in an unusual form, such as 'sigh' as an adjective. Words such as these we term 'Northisms'.

The second problem the reader faces is that North often uses words both with their common, eighteenth-century or modern meaning and with a meaning peculiar to himself. Those words in this second category will be considered separately rather than glossed (see II.3.4. below). They are also Northisms of a kind but they differ from words like 'sigh' in that North's peculiar usage relates specifically to his theory. The purpose of this section of Introduction II is to provide readers with examples of the problems they may encounter when reading the text and to stress the importance of North's context in determining meaning.

Near the beginning of *The Musicall Grammarian 1728*, North writes: 'This subject is incumbred with termes of doubdtfull signification, and need to be distinguished';[25] and in the same place he rehearses some of the issues which will require definition in the pages to follow: what are 'musick', 'melody', 'harmony', 'discord', he asks. Throughout the treatise, and particularly in Parts II and III, on the one hand he constantly uses phrases such as: 'ordinarily

---

[24] See Editorial guidelines, 6.2.
[25] ff. 7v–8.

means', 'it is called', 'in the common language of the professors', 'which is usually called'; and on the other hand (and by contrast) he defines his own terms: 'which wee call', 'which I call'.

All the words in the sections which follow are used by North both with a meaning peculiar to his theory and with their common eighteenth-century (and in some cases also modern) meanings. Their meanings in North's text are discussed here, even when some are still in use today, to point up the ways in which North derived and defined his own usage. The words, discussed in alphabetical order for ease of reference, are: ayre, cadence, consort, intermediate(s), key, proper.

3.4. Appendix of terms

Ayre

Apart from its meaning 'atmosphere', four different meanings of 'air' can be distinguished in *The Musicall Grammarian 1728*, three of which are to be found in the *OED*. These three, common, uses are: (i) 'appearance';[26] (ii) 'vivacity', 'liveliness';[27] (iii) 'melody', 'song'.[28] (iv) North's own usage of 'ayre' is not found in the *OED* and yet is crucial to his theory of music (see I.3.2.).

North uses the word to cover a number of meanings all bearing on musical composition. In *The Musicall Grammarian 1728* he defines the word in several places and from the quotations of these definitions below the reader will see that 'ayre' refers both to the rudiments of music (for example, f.80, the 'air of the key'; f.79v, the 'three points' in which ayre consists) and also to something more: as North says, 'further then wee are ledd by the nature of keys, and their accords . . . the inquiry is after good musick' (f.80v). This is the spirit or 'invention' by which the music will rise above the commonplace.[29] North's definitions are cited here in the order in which they appear in the text.

> f.58: . . . allwais emphasing the accords for that distinguisheth the nature of the notes, and [the] air of the key . . .
> f.59v . . . and by that [air] wee understand a timely movement in the

[26] *OED*, III., f.11v
[27] From the adjective, *OED*, 6.c.: f.48v; cf. 'aiery'/'ayery': f.28.
[28] *OED*, IV.18.: ff.28, 97, 97v; cf. 'ayery': f.97v.
[29] ff.1v, 28v, 43, 43v, 45, 45v, 46v, 52, 52v, 54v, 58, 59v, 60v, 61v, 62, 63, 63v, 64, 64v, 66, 67, 68, 69, 70, 70v, 71, 74, 75, 75v, 76, 79v, 80, 80v, 81, 81v, 86, 87v, 88v, 89, 91, 96v, 97v, 127, 127v, 129, 131v, 133, 133v, 135, 140v; cf. 'aiery'/'ayery': ff.44v, 45, 60v, 62, 71, 72, 76v, 91, 95, 126, 128v, 129v, 131, 131v; 'ayerily': 44; 'unaiery': f.64.

gradations of some key, and that not changing, but according to the rules already given.

f.64v: The matter or, (if I may so call it,) ayre must come cheifly out of pure invention . . .

f.79v: The secret of ayre hath bin allready opened, but may bear a further explication. It consists in two or three points: 1st that the parts shall move in the scale of the key, allways emphasing upon the prime accords; 2[d] that in all changes of the key, (which introduce a new scale), it shall be into some one of the prime accords of the former, and by those I mean the third or fifth, ascending, or descending; and 3[d] that returnes back to the proper key be frequently made, which after a change will be better accepted; unless the spirit moves to ramble, and then allowing time enough, for the memory of the former to wear out, the musick in like order may pass into any key.

f.80: The air of a key is so well knowne or knowable that I am avers to the giving any examples of it. What is more comon then the flourish at the entry of a consort, which is onely a successive striking the key and its prime accords one after another, either distinct, or gradient according to the scale, or intermixt, and (in time) ad libitum, but ever observing to give the advantage, or emphasis upon the prime accords? What is easyer to doe then this? And what els is, or can be the ayre of the key note but this?

ff.80v–81: Now as for ayre, further then wee are ledd by the nature of keys, and their accords, I must suppose, the inquiry is after good musick [(]and I must confess it would be rare if wee could prescribe to that,[)] and just as if one were to be shewed how to make a good speech or a good play, for ayre in musick is like witt in language, which supposing a genius must come by application, and industry, passing into an habit, and not by immediate instruction. There are authors of gramer, shewing how to put words together, and of rhetorick, how to enforce and adorne them; and all very well in ordinè ad, but there is more required to make an orator. So all our gamutts, times, keys, mixtures, fuges, and what els is couched under the musicall termes, are necessary in order to make a good musitian, but the good musick must come from one by nature as well as art compleatly made, who is arrived at a pitch to throw away the lumber of his rules and examples, and act upon the strength of his judgment, and knowledge of the subject matter it self, as if it had bin bred and born in him ab origine.

f.95: . . . if the melody is ayery, or what they call pretty . . .

f.127: I would not have it thought that, by what is here observed, I am recomending this kind of musik [i.e., 'plain-song musick']; for in one principall article, nothing can be more defective, and that is variety or what is called air . . .

f. 131v: His [i.e., Jenkins'] fancys were full of ayery points, graves, triplas, and other varietys . . .

Cadence

The article on 'Cadence' in *New Grove* discusses cadences under two main headings: perfect and imperfect, in each case referring to a progression of two chords. Although the modern meanings of 'cadence' in both American and British usage, discussed in *New Grove*, are in some cases similar to North's, modern usage does not provide a reliable guide to understanding his meaning and can confuse the reader.

In *The Musicall Grammarian 1728* North uses 'cadence' in at least three distinct ways and 'semi-' or 'half-cadence' in two. (i) One of North's common uses of 'cadence' corresponds to what in *New Grove* is called a 'perfect cadence', i.e., a progression V–I in root position.[30] Although North apparently uses 'cadence' to describe V–I progressions in most instances, his own definition of 'cadence' on f. 51v does not state specifically that it is a V–I progression: 'And the full composition of a cadence is a mixture of the key note and its fifth, and the capitall accords of them . . .' Furthermore, in defining a 'semicadence' (f. 53, and see below) by contrast with a 'whole cadence' (f. 53v) North lays emphasis on the fact that the chords of the 'whole cadence' are in root position. (ii) North uses 'cadence' as an adjective, as in the phrase 'cadence note', to indicate a dominant in the bass part.[31] (iii) Sometimes North uses 'cadence' to refer to a cadential passage (of more than two chords). On f. 51v he calls such passages 'prepared' cadences and gives examples of 'preparation' on f. 52.[32]

New Grove defines 'half-cadence' with 'imperfect cadence' as a cadence ending on the dominant, preceded by any chord, but mostly a chord on the tonic or the supertonic in first inversion. The article points out that in American usage, 'imperfect' is sometimes applied to cadences whose chords are not in root position or whose upper parts do not end on the tonic; but it also makes clear that, in modern usage, 'half-' or 'semicadence' is not defined in this way.

---

[30] North uses 'cadence' with apparently this meaning in the following instances: ff. 44, 45v, 50, 51v, 56, 80, 93; cf. 'cadencys': f. 54v.
[31] ff. 51v, 52, 52v, 53, 61, 61v, 63, 80.
[32] See also: ff. 51v, 52, 56 (and Example 2), 58v, 61, 61v, 72, 81v, 126v; cf. 'cadencing': f. 64.

These modern definitions are confusing for a reader of *The Musicall Grammarian 1728* for North uses 'semicadence' in two distinct ways, each of which shares some ground with the modern definitions of 'imperfect' cadences.[33]

In *The Musicall Grammarian 1728*: f.53, North describes two kinds of 'semicadences'. The first is a I–V cadential passage: (i) 'one manner is very solemne and often concludes grave musick; and it is onely by returning from a close [note] to the cadence note back again, and ending with a short flourish thus [Example 2].'

North then goes on to define what he calls 'the ordinary half cadences' which occur (ii) 'when the base falls downe slowly from the key to the cadence note, and the 5th held on breaking onely a 7th upon the last note thus [Example 3].'

In (ii) it is not the progression which distinguishes it particularly as a 'semicadence'; nor is the progression I–V, but rather V–I in inversion, as North goes on to make clear (ff.53–53v) when he says 'the notes are resolvable into an whole cadence, by supplying the proper base in the room of the consort base as is there [f.53, Example 3] obscurely hinted but here [f.53v, Example 1] more distinct.' It is, therefore, the fact that the chords are in inversion which makes the passage an example of a semicadence. North continues: 'But the half cadence is of great use in musick, where the bases are more consort then proper.'[34]

Consort

Three distinct meanings for 'consort' are to be found in *The Musicall Grammarian 1728*. Two are common contemporary meanings, and the third is peculiar to North. The two common meanings and their occurrences are (i) as North himself describes it on f.8: 'harmony is of divers, called consort'. He uses 'consort' with this meaning as both a noun, as in, for example, 'comon tones are often permitted to sound together, but cautiously, and in consort' (f.39) or 'a lively consort' (f.54); and also as an adjective as in, for example, the phrase 'consort notes' (f.27v), referring to notes in harmony.[35] (ii) The

---

[33] What throughout *The Musicall Grammarian 1728* North called a 'semicadence', in an earlier text (BL Add MS 32537: f.225v) he called an 'imperfect cadence'. He does not use this term in *1728*.

[34] See 'Consort', 'Proper' below.

[35] *OED*, II.3., 'the accord or harmony of several instruments or voices playing or singing in tune'; a piece of music in several parts: ff.8, 25v, 27v, 28v, 39, 41, 41v, 45, 47, 48v, 52, 52v, 53, 54, 55, 56, 58v, 62v, 64, 64v, 66, 66v, 68, 69v, 70v, 72v, 74, 75, 75v, 77, 77v, 78,

second common meaning is 'a company or set of musicians, vocal or instrumental, making music together'.[36] (iii) North also uses 'consort' in an unusual way. This usage he defines on f.41 as the lowest note of a chord in inversion. 'Consort' has this meaning in the phrases 'consort base', 'consort note', 'consort base note'.[37]

Intermediate, Intermediates

North uses 'intermediate' in three ways, two of which are common in modern usage. (i) The first sense is (as an adjective) of 'coming or occurring between two things'. He defines this on f.45v: 'it is observable, that these removes of the key skipp over all interme-diate notes, as must happen passing from concord to concord . . .' (ii) The second sense is (as a noun) of 'something intermediate or intervening', for example on f.46v: 'As for the intermediates [Example 2], they are all in accord with the key or its accords, but those descending, as A is a 5th to D the fourth below . . .'[38] (iii) I have drawn attention to these, modern, uses of the word because both examples occur early in Part II where North also uses the word 'intermediates' according to his own definition. When North first states his (idiosyncratic) definition of 'intermediates' (on f.38v) it is clouded by his awkward sentence construction at that point in the text: 'These taken as usuall singly . . . which I call intermediates . . .' Nevertheless, the definition on f.41 makes clear that North equates 'intermediates' with 'consort base notes', that is, the bass notes of chords in inversion:

It is found that in consort, all accords whatsoever (in truth) have for base the key of the scale, but when intermediates happen, the lower note of the accord usurps the place of the key; and is termed the base of that accord . . . For this reason I am forced upon making a distinction between proper, and consort base notes; the former are key notes and the others intermediates.[39]

78v, 81, 83v, 85, 92, 95, 96v, 97v, 113v, 114, 118v, 126v, 127, 127v, 131, 131v, 134, 138, 142; see also 'consort' as an adjective: ff.44, 54v, 63, 91v, 113v, 121, 122v.

[36] *OED*, II.4: ff.28, 33v, 36v, 76, 82, 85v, 91v, 95v, 106, 129v, 134v, 135, 136, 137, 137v, 141; see also 'consort' as an adjective: ff.79v, 124v, 126; cf. 'consortier', a player in consort: ff.44v, 76, 128v.

[37] ff.41, 41v, 44, 45, 46, 53v. See also 'Intermediates' and 'Proper'.

[38] See also f.61. Although North's usage seems clear here, he may have had in mind, *as well*, his own meaning of 'intermediates', see (iii). On f.46 (in a passage quoted below, 'Key') he refers to the 'key' note 'and its full accord as G–B–D–g and the rest intermediate or consort notes, as A, C, E, F.'

[39] See also: ff.39v, 41v, 42. But note f.46, Section 62 where North seems to have confused his own meaning with the common one. The passage is cited under 'Key'.

Key

Besides the use of 'key' to refer to keys of musical instruments,[40] North uses 'key' in two distinct but related ways. Herein lies the possibility of confusion for the reader since it is not always clear precisely which meaning North intends.

(i) North uses 'key' (both as a noun and as an adjective, as in 'key note') in a way not dissimilar to its modern sense (given in *New Grove*) of 'the quality of a musical composition or passage that causes it to be sensed as gravitating towards a particular note called the key note or tonic'.[41] The 'key note' he sometimes also calls the 'leader',[42] the 'leading note',[43] the 'leading tone',[44] and the 'primary tone'.[45] All uses of 'key' in Part I carry this meaning. (ii) North also uses 'key' (again, both as a noun and an adjective) to mean the lowest note of a chord in root position (the 'key' or 'key note'), what he elsewhere calls a 'proper base note'. He defines this on f.41: ' . . . the true base, that is the key note'; and further (f.41): 'For this reason I am forced upon making a distinction between proper, and consort base notes; the former are key notes and the others intermediates.'[46] Earlier, North's definition reveals a confusion of the two meanings of 'key':[47] 'Whereupon the key in musick may be thus defined: the lower or leading tone of that scale which is chosen to determine the accordant notes of the following harmony'; and again, on f.46, we see the problems which arose for North in his attempting to discuss 'key' (i) – what he calls the septenary, i.e., the diatonic scale – in the context of harmonic progression, relative keys and cadences: 'Now to finish this doctrine of accords wee must take in view againe the key and its whole scale, and say it consists of that note and its full accord, as G-B-D-g and the rest intermediate or consort notes, as A, C, E, F.'[48]

Later, in Part III, North himself expresses the problem of definition when he writes (f.62):

[40] f.122v.
[41] ff.20, 20v, 21v, 22, 24, 24v, 25v, 26, 37, 37v, 38, 38v, 39, 41, 41v, 42, 42v, 43, 43v, 44, 44v, 45, 45v, 46, 46v, 47v, 48, 48v, 49, 49v, 50, 50v, 51, 51v, 52, 53, 53v, 56, 57v, 58, 59, 59v, 60, 60v, 61, 61v, 62, 62v, 63, 67, 67v, 68v, 69v, 70, 72, 79v, 80, 81, 81v, 89, 93, 124v.
[42] ff.17, 21v, 37, 42.
[43] ff.25v, 49v.
[44] f.37.
[45] f.37.
[46] See also: ff.39v, 41, 41v, 42, 42v, 45, 46, 46v, 48, 51, 55, 60, 61, 62.
[47] f.37, Section 52: 'The key defined'.
[48] cf. f.38 and Example 1.

Some think it odd if not a fault in the scale, that the 7th is allwais ♭ as [to be] not so harmonious, as if it were ♯, but there is a difference between the order of the scale, which respects one key note, and harmony which respects divers . . . And hereby wee see the importance of the science of keys, that is of base notes such as wee have styled proper.

Proper

North uses 'proper' in at least four senses in *The Musicall Gramma-rian 1728*. Three of these were common usage in the early eigh-teenth century. These are (i) belonging to oneself or itself; (one's or its) own;[49] (ii) 'belonging or relating to the person in question distinctively; special, particular, distinctive';[50] (iii) 'fit, apt, suit-able, appropriate'.[51] (iv) North uses 'proper' in the phrase 'proper base note' to mean the lowest note of a chord in root position.[52] This usage, although peculiar to North, is clearly related to those other senses in which North uses the word, on the one hand with the sense 'peculiar to', 'inherent in', and on the other, with the sense of 'fitness' or 'aptness'.

North uses the phrase 'proper base' early in his writings on music; but in both versions of *The Musicall Grammarian* (*c.* 1726 and 1728) and in *The Musicall Grammarian Fragments* he appears to have experienced problems of definition because of his use of 'key note' as an alternative to 'proper base note'. Furthermore, in all extant versions of 'The Musicall Grammarian': *The Musicall Grammarian c. 1726*, *The Musicall Grammarian Fragments* and *The Musicall Gram-marian 1728*, North also refers to the bass of a chord in root position as a 'proper key',[53] besides using the term 'key note' (as in *The Musicall Grammarian 1728*), 'reall base', 'proper harmony'. North's definition of the bass note of a chord in root position as a 'proper key' indicates the significance North placed in his theory on the inherent qualities of good music, and the fitness of certain kinds of consecution, cadence, and bass movement; but it also appears to have been the cause of the confusion of the two meanings he gives

---

[49] The first two meanings are very close and it is not always possible to be certain of North's exact meaning: cf. note 51, below. (i) *OED*, I.1 · ff 9v, 17, 22v, 23, 37v, 46v, 60, 69, 79v, 104v,

[50] *OED*, I.2.: ff.23ᵃ, 40, 42v, 48, 52, 55, 58, 78v, 117v, 133; cf. 'properly', strictly speaking: ff.41v. 56.

[51] *OED*, III.9.: ff.15, 22, 24v, 26, 27v, 28v, 29, 29v, 35v, 37, 49, 49v, 65v, 69v, 84v, 85v, 86, 92, 95v, 103, 108v, 117v; cf. 'properly': f.80; 'propriety': ff.24v, 66; 'improper': ff.12, 12v, 15, 35v, 90; 'improperly': ff.43, 47v, 55, 96v, 126.

[52] ff.41, 41v, 42, 44, 45, 46v, 51, 52v, 53v, 55v, 62, 75.

[53] *MG c. 1726*: f.71; *MG Frag*: ff.42, 47, 48; *MG 1728*: ff.42, 51.

to 'key' (see above). Other evidence of North's problem of nomenclature here is seen in the many leaves in *The Musicall Grammarian Fragments* which are rewritings of the early part of Part II of *The Musicall Grammarian c. 1726*, where North first defines 'key'; and that this matter was not satisfactorily solved by the time he came to write *The Musicall Grammarian 1728* is seen from the evidence in that manuscript of replacement of pages in Part II of that text too (see II.1.2. and 2.1.).

Conclusion

A study of the physical construction and state of the manuscript reveals that the date on North's title-pages of both 'The Musicall Grammarian' and 'Memoires of Musick', 1728, does not necessarily indicate the date at which North regarded his treatise as complete. Indeed, if my interpretation of evidence is accepted, that is, evidence of North's method of revision provided by his pagination and section headings (see II.2.1. and 2.2.) and of his transmission of the manuscript to his son, Montagu, provided by the end-papers (see II.1.2.), then it is clear that North could have added to, and revised, the manuscript up to the middle of 1733.

We have seen that evidence exists for supposing that some of those parts of the text North found most difficult to put into a final shape were sections in which he was explaining the foundations of his theory. I have attempted here (as we have also attempted in the glosses) to point out the traps North's use of certain words, even in the 1728 text, sets for the unwary reader, although both editors realise that it is impossible to identify all those words which North uses in a special or idiosyncratic way. The problem is, thus, partly North's – a problem of naming – and partly the reader's – a problem inherent in all historical texts. North himself reminds us of the difficulties likely to be encountered by readers of such texts when he asks at the beginning of his own discussion of historical writing: 'who should make the dictionary, or adapt things to the words used by obsolete authors?'[54] The purpose of the last part of my Introduction has been to alert the readers to the ever-present possibilities of misrepresentation in anachronistic reading, even though the 'dictionary' offered there is far from comprehensive.

[54] *MG 1728*: f.104v.

EDITORIAL GUIDELINES

1. INTRODUCTION

The principles followed in editing *The Musicall Grammarian 1728* are based on those worked out for our edition of North's *Cursory Notes of Musicke* and discussed there on pp. ⟨55⟩–⟨62⟩. Unlike that treatise, *The Musicall Grammarian 1728* presents a carefully worked and extensively revised text: the style is more concise and polished, sentence structure more lucid and punctuation more consistent. Consequently, we have found it possible to keep more closely to details of North's punctuation and sentence structure than was possible in our edition of *Cursory Notes of Musicke*.

We do not believe, nevertheless, that a facsimile or close transcription, which presents all North's deletions and indicates additions above the line or in the margin, made at (perhaps) various times after writing the original text, is helpful in presenting *The Musicall Grammarian 1728*. Therefore, in our edition of this treatise we do not draw attention to such textual issues as deletions and insertions unless these give rise to other problems within the text.

Our edition follows North's text page by page, including his catchwords where they occur and using the foliation (not in North's hand) which is on the manuscript, although renumbering North's section headings to form a continuous sequence. We retain the irregular foliation with two folios 23, given as f.23 and f.23ᵃ, respectively. Physical aspects of the manuscript, as well as various textual problems, are dealt with separately in Introduction II.

2. SPELLINGS AND CONTRACTIONS

2.1. We retain North's spelling (which is often consistently irregular), adding where necessary for sound or sense a final or medial letter, e.g., tast[e], her[e]in.

2.2. North uses accents on some Latin words, e.g., è contra, ordinè; he sometimes omits them from French words, e.g., generale, raisonee. We regard accents as part of spelling and follow North's irregular usage.

2.3. All abbreviations and contractions common in the seventeenth and early eighteenth centuries have been expanded: e.g., yt (that), ye (the), & (and), wch (which); the prefix p (pre, pro, per); the suffixes –mt (ment) and q (que). Abbreviations still in common use are retained, as Mr (Master); two other common abbreviations are retained in their modern form: &c. (etc.), vizt. (viz.).

2.4. From ff.7–98v North's running title is 'The Musicall Gramarian' and from ff.103–142v 'Memoires of Musick' (see Introduction II.2.1.). Our running title, 'The Musicall Grammarian', is produced in the spelling as it appears on the title-page, and we retain this running title for the whole manuscript, since the 'Memoires' is not a separate treatise (see Introduction I.2.2.).

2.5. North occasionally uses a singular verb with a plural subject or a plural verb with a singular subject. We retain these verb forms.

2.6. North occasionally uses apostrophe *s* for plural endings and for verb endings in *s*. We follow modern usage in transcribing such words, reserving the apostrophe *s* for possessives and abbreviations and adding it in those cases where North omits it.

2.7. Where North interchanges 'to' and 'too', 'of' and 'off', we transcribe in accordance with modern usage.

3. PUNCTUATION AND CAPITALISATION

3.1. All full stops are dropped from section headings in the text.

3.2. We retain North's punctuation within a sentence, although occasionally, where sense requires it, we break a long sentence at a colon or semicolon.

3.3. Where North added additional passages above the line, he sometimes omitted to alter the original punctuation or covered it with his caret mark. In such cases we punctuate as sense requires.

3.4. North uses capital letters idiosyncratically and not always at the beginnings of sentences. We follow modern practice in beginning all sentences with capital letters and removing them mid-sentence and from words which are not proper nouns. All proper nouns are given initial capital letters whether capitals are given in the text or not.

3.5. North often places a full-stop on either side of an arabic numeral, thus: .1. We omit all full stops with numerals except when they are used to enumerate examples or points of discussion, in which case the full stop is retained after the number only. When North uses full-stops in a sequence of letters or numerals (e.g., 1. 2. 3.), we transcribe these as commas.

3.6. All other editorial punctuation is given in square brackets.

3.7. We retain North's paragraphs; but where a discussion of new material is not indented, we indent if sense requires it.

3.8. North uses an equal sign '=' for words which are broken at the end of a line in the manuscript. We transcribe words so broken as one word. For hyphenated words North uses (in printer's language) an en-dash '–' (e.g., organ–builders f.19). We retain his practice in all cases, even where modern usage might not use a hyphen (e.g., plain-song f.32) or would standardise practice.

4. EDITORIAL EMENDATIONS

Three section headings in the text are editorial: Section 54 (f.36v); Section 82 (f.61v); and Section 103 (f.74). The decision to include these headings was based on a comparison of North's table of contents ('Index') with the section headings in the text, as well as from evidence of his revision of the text (see Introduction II.2.2.). Occasionally, repairs to the pages of the manuscript affect the text in the inner margins. In these cases, editorial additions are given in square brackets.

5. MUSICAL EXAMPLES

Musical examples are transcribed as North wrote them, errors being glossed at the foot of the pages on which the examples occur. In cases where North has deleted a note, this is neither reproduced nor commented on. Some procedures in accordance with modern writing have been followed for clarity.

5.1. Stems of notes are given as in modern practice.

5.2. When North writes notes tied over a bar-line thus ♩, we use modern notation. When two crotchets are tied within a bar, we write them as a mimim.

5.3. North writes the crotchet rest ⌐, but this has been transcribed using the modern sign.

5.4. The order of flats and sharps in key signatures is given according to the order, lines and spaces of current common musical notation. However, when North presents part-writing on one staff rather than in score, we retain his method of indicating key signatures in two places on the staff (see ff.55, 56).

5.5. Time signatures are given according to modern practice; e.g., 3 becomes $\frac{3}{2}$ or $\frac{3}{4}$.

5.6. Figured bass is given below the bass line.

5.7. Letters or names of notes are given below the stave to which they refer.

5.8. North does not break his song texts into syllables. We follow modern practice of text underlay, writing the syllables of a word under the note, or notes, to which they are to be sung.

North usually follows the contemporary practice of naming notes in the first octave of the gamut with capital letters (G, A, etc.) and those in the second octave with lower-case letters (g, a, etc.). We follow this practice and emend where North is not consistent. In the few instances where he employs the sharp sign to cancel the effect of a flat sign, we do not emend to a natural sign. North uses 'shaddowed' notes or what he also refers to as '(obscurely marked)' (f.38) or 'in obscuro' (f.51v) notes. We reproduce these notes, which are drawn in dotted outline and which North uses for various purposes, including to indicate an imaginary bass line produced from the roots of chords in first or second inversion.

6. COMMENTARY

Two types of commentary accompany the text: (1) annotations at the foot of each page, and (2) the Glossary at the end of the text. The first type of commentary is identified by a number; the second type, by an asterisk(*).

6.1. Annotations

Annotations are reserved for North's cross-references within the text, for editorial comment, for interpretations of words and passages in the text which are obscure; for identification of persons, books, music or events mentioned overtly in the text; for clarification of North's allusions to philosophical or music-theoretical issues; and for provision of citations to the companion treatise, *Theory of Sounds 1728*, to which North sometimes refers. Errors of interpretation are left without remark, as, for example, when North provides false etymologies (f.128v).

In *The Musicall Grammarian 1728* North has reworked the musical examples from earlier texts, some of which contain a far richer lode of 'commonplaces' and exemplars to illustrate both good and bad usage. He seems to have devised the majority of the examples, as he hints in a number of places (e.g., f.1v), the longer passages being modelled on those from compositions which North considered touchstones of excellence. But North did take a small number of examples from the works of others. Unfortunately, those which are identified here make no advance on Wilson (1959).

North's texts contain many covert references. The 'signals' for these are sometimes clear, as when he writes about 'an author'. But often the covert references are not at all clearly signalled, and this kind of sub-text emerges only after long familiarity with the manuscripts. Some of the covert references are of an autobiographical nature. Others derive from North's method of commonplacing, which has been detailed in the 'Introduction' to our edition of *Cursory Notes of Musicke*. In that edition an effort was made to trace as many of North's covert references as possible. No similar attempt has been made here, even though a number of his covert references have been identified.

6.2. Glossary

The Glossary is reserved for translations of foreign words or phrases not found in the *Concise Oxford Dictionary*, or whose meaning in North's text is different from the meanings given there. A few words whose meanings are given in the *Concise Oxford Dictionary* are glossed when their common, modern meaning is so different from North's meaning as to be confusing. One example is 'egregious', whose modern meaning of 'shocking' is very different from North's meaning 'remarkable', which is also given in the *Concise Oxford Dictionary*. The Glossary gives the meaning of a word or phrase and then cites other occurrences of the word or phrase with the same meaning.

The *Oxford English Dictionary* (*OED*) has been used for all historical meanings of words. Where more than one usage is given, the *OED* reference is cited in the gloss. In the case of musical terms *The New Grove Dictionary of Music and Musicians* (*New Grove*) has also been consulted. When North's meaning is not found in either source, the musical term has been glossed. Foreign musical terms in common usage, e.g., correnti, galliardo, musica di camera, repien, are not glossed even if their spelling is idiosyncratic. Occasionally, where North's terminology might be confused with modern meanings, we gloss the term as it applies to the context of his theory: e.g., modallity (f.15v).

Latin, French and Italian words and phrases have been glossed from the following sources: C. T. Lewis and C. Short, *A Latin Dictionary*, revised and enlarged edition, Oxford 1969; J. E. Mansion (ed.), *Harrap's Standard French and English Dictionary*, 2 vols., London 1961; and *Sansoni-Harrap Standard Italian and English Dictionary*, 2 vols., Florence and London 1970. For information about contemporary proverbs, we consulted M. P. Tilley, *A Dictionary of the Proverbs in England in the Sixteenth and Seventeenth Centuries*, Ann Arbor 1950 and *The Oxford Dictionary of English Proverbs*, 3d edition revised by F. P. Wilson with an introduction by Joanna Wilson, Oxford 1970.

Some words and phrases not given in standard dictionaries may have been invented by North. Such words are glossed as 'Northisms', although some may not be true neologisms but errors in writing: e.g., manireonico (f.33v). At least two words in the text are cited in the *OED* as used only by North: 'fastidium' and 'tonations'. Selected words which were not invented by North but which he uses in an idiosyncratic way or with a meaning peculiar to himself are not glossed but discussed in Introductions I and II.

The Glossary at the back of this volume lists all the words and phrases identified in the text by asterisk and cites other occurrences in the text of each word. This list is confined to Northisms and to those words and phrases whose dictionary meaning has been given. Words and phrases which are given a more explanatory annotation in the Introductions are excluded from the Glossary.

7. METHODS OF CITATION

Most of the unpublished texts cited in the Introductions and annotations are those written by North. Some of these texts are untitled, some have short titles and some have long titles. In the list of references to North's writings, we assign a short title or abbreviation to each of the texts and use these to cite the text (see References and bibliography: section 1). In the case of published writings the social-science citation style has been adopted (see References and bibliography: section 2). Occasionally, cross reference is made to the Introductions, which are cited by roman numeral and section numbers, e.g., I.2.1.; II.2.2. All quotations from North's unpublished texts are edited according to the principles set out in these Editorial guidelines.

THE MUSICALL GRAMMARIAN

/ The Musical Grammarian
being
a scientifick essay
upon the practise of musick
1728

/ Advertisement

The title here is not Grammar but Gramarian; from the former is
expected a sume of rules sufficient to instruct an art, but the other is
of a superior order, pretending to reason upon those rules, and to
shew the principles of them derived upon nature and the positive
truth of things. This is like etimology to language, or as naturall
reason and history to humane laws, and if any rules happen to
result, they are such as flow, not from comon practise or authority,
but as the very consequences of fact. According to this caracter here
will be found wanting a phisicall account of sounds, which is the
foundation of the whole, and for that I must referre to a former tract
intituled the Theory of Sounds[1] intended [as] a part of this work,
and but for bulkyness, to have bin ioyned, which together make
this designe (quantum in nos★) perfect; the air and compositions
here will shew the writer is no professor;★ to be a well willer
answers his ambition, especially if instead of teaching, he may shew
learners in some measure how to teach themselves.

---

[1] *TS 1728*; for details of this manuscript, see Chan, Kassler, Hine (1988).

Table of Contents

'The Musicall Grammarian'

f.7 /1. The scope of this essay

The action of sound in the air is sensible to us by the effects, which excite in our minds ideas infinitely various, but none more egregious★ then those of acceptance, and aversion;[2] whither it be one or other, and whatever the modifications are, the active caus is no other then pure percussion of the air upon the auricular membrane;[3] whence then proceeds the passions of the mind? I have endeavoured to answer this question, in a former tract designed to give a phisicall account or resolution of the phenomena of sounds, wherein among other varietys, the subject is drawne to lean most upon the distinction of harmony, and discord.[4] Therefore in this designed to be a continuation of the former Theory, wee shall not formalize upon phisicall speculations but take matters just as our sence informes us; and from thence wee hope to derive the principles of a splendid science called musick; wherein the learned, and unlearned have their parts, either to hear or practise; and all humane kind now are, and ever since

the

7v / the creation of the world haue bin, and will be rejoycers in the noble fruits of it. And the practise ever was a symptome of good, and never of evill to human kind; and her[e]in I may include the whole animall race; for no creature in pain ever made an aggreable noise. Therefore I have thought it no derogation of my time, to examine and reduce to wrighting, what I can draw from my observation, and experience concerning the rules, and methods

[2] See I.2.1. The principal contraries in North's philosophy are expansion/contraction (elasticity). Acceptance (pleasure) and aversion (pain), which are derived from these, are affections and passions of the mind; that is, they are secondary properties (appearances) occasioned by primary properties (reality).
[3] *TS 1728* (ff.95–95v).
[4] *TS 1728* (f.101).

whereby the art is or (as I think) may be, to such good porposes, conducted. And here you have my full intent and scope in this essay, which may stand as an appendix to the former Theory [of Sounds].

2. Of melody[,] harmony and discord

This subject is incumbred with termes of doubdtfull signification, and need to be distinguished; and first that all aggreable sounds are not, in our sence, musick: as the speech of an orator, whistling of birds, and the like; but it is confined to that genus [such] as humane kind, by apt means may produce, and qualifie either to

pleas

f.8   / pleas, or as the art may distinguish, to displeas; the former is either melody, or harmony. Melody is the modulation of one production, of such as is commonly called, tune; harmony is of divers, called consort, and is allwais taken in a good sence opposed to discord. And that terme may be ambiguous; for it may intend those sounds which fall on the wrong side of indifference, and are really painfull to hear, as scraping china, cutting cork[,] sharping saws and the like; and to the sence of hearing, are like corruption, odious to the tast[e], and not to be made use of so much as in sauce.[5] And in a milder sence, discord means the same as when wee say out of tune. And of that sort there are degrees of better, and wors; as when made with designe and skill, and when contingent. The latter belong not to musick, and are enimys to it, but others tho of the same quallity, are not utterly rejected, but made us[e] of as an inferior harmony, and artificially★ mixed with better, become comparatively good, and often superlative.[6] The exemplification of all these matters stands refferred

to

f.8v / to the following accounts of them.[7] It is comonly observed that satiety takes place in harmony, as well as in other gratifications of sence, and the best (continuing) will grow more and more fastidious;★ therefore the inferior quallitys must be admitted to give a temper, and sensible refreshment, by some change; for varia, as

---

[5] '. . . and to the sence of hearing . . . as in sauce': 'which are to hearing, like sublimated arsenick in cookery, not to be made use of so much as in sauce' (*MG c. 1726*: f.12v).

[6] *TS 1728* (ff.110v–111, 114v–116).

[7] See ff.9v–36 ('melody') and 37–58v ('harmony').

well as contraria, juxta se,★ set one and other off, and thereby
harmony is exalted to such exquisite pitch; as no simple sounds can
obtain. And it is the office of a good musitian, to marshall his
sounds in such elegant commixture as for the presumed time, and
porposes shall be and continue most gratefull to the hearers.

3. Explanation rather then grammer
  In treating this subject, I designe not to move all together in the
paths of comon grammer, for that is not wanted, nor ever will be,
so long as Mr. Butler's excellent tract is extant.[8] But I aime cheifly
to enter rather as an interpreter, and after the example of a French
author, who wrote a grammer tituled–Generale et Raisonee,[9] to
explicate and distinguish upon the

ordinary

f.9 / ordinary rules, and to render the musicall language, and notation
less misterious, and more usefull, and (perhaps) [more] pleasing,
then comon teaching instructs. For no art is more enveloped in dark
diallect, and jargon, then musick is, all which impedimenta I would
have removed, that the access to the art and practise may be more
recomendable and inviting; and herein if I shall happen to vary from
the comon track, or fancy to have discovered anything new, in
order to encourage persons to enter into or the tyrones★ to continue
in the discipline, I hope it will be accounted no sin or arrogance,
(however failing) to have attempted it.

4. Humane voice to all intents preferred
  Musicall sounds are produced by the voices of animalls, or
otherwise by inflation of tubes, or pulsation of solids.[10] And of
voices, none affects our spirits so sensibly as the humane; nor have
wee power over any other means of sound, to diversifie or forme,
with so much nicety as wee have of that; for which reason I shall

---

[8] I.e., *The Principles of Musik* (see Butler 1636, 1636/1970), lent to North by John Jenkins
  'with a commendation of it that it was the best of the kind' (*Notes of Me* ed. Jessopp 1887:
  83). Charles Butler (b. *c.*1560, d. 1647), divine and schoolmaster, was a proponent of a
  simplified system of phonetic spelling which he used in treatises on grammar, rhetoric,
  oratory and music.
[9] Probably Antoine Arnauld, co-author with Claude Lancelot of the *Grammaire Générale et
  Raisonée* (see I.3.1. and Arnauld and Lancelot tr. Rieux and Rollin 1676/1975).
[10] In *TS 1728* (f.141) North supposes that the voice generates sound in the same way as the
  'reedall' or reed pipe in organs. The bulk of the treatise, however, focuses on the
  production of sounds in tubes (ff.130–146v) and in elastic solids (ff.147–149). The section
  on elastic solids is short, because North employs a 'musical string' (i.e., a monochord)
  earlier in the treatise as an example of elasticity ('springs') (ff.101v–104v *et passim.*).

take it for a foundation to build upon, and from thence as from a naturall principle, instruct most if not all

that

f.9v / that I shall have to say scientifically of musick. As for the other means of sound, by puls or inflation, they have their proper advantages, but never so great as when joyned with voices, which artfully★ combined give the greatest perfection to musick. I must allwais assert the voice to have bin prior, and in a separate estate[11] preferable; for the powers of it have no dependance, and probably did governe before any other instruments (the imperfect imitators of it) were knowne. And at this day, the mechanicks being at a non plus★ of improvement, it is not pretended★ that the voice is to submitt unto, or wait on any instruments, but those are allwais called in to wait upon the voice. That hath no gimcracks★ to tune it, but carrys all tune within it self, and after all means used to imitate the human voice, the devices have failed, and the deteriority★ of the sound allwais discovers the true from the counterfett.

5. The voice the instructor of tune
    Here are reasons enow for musick to enter with the voice, but I have to add, that it is the best if not the onely means to introduce the use

of

f.10 / of the finest, and most courted instruments, I mean violins, flutes, and some others whereof the tones are regulated to an exactness, by a nicety of the breath or touch. I have knowne severall persons attempt musick and have fallen off, becaus they had no knowledg or comand of tune, and not enough to adjust an instrument which had not happened if primarily they had bin taught and exercised in singing; for the initiall cours of that, as will appear,[12] not onely teacheth but inculcates the knowledg of tune, and to conforme the voice accordingly. How should any one finger out of an instrument the genuine musicall sounds, that knows them not when he hears them, nor when he is right, and when wrong. Some industrious persons very attentive and capable, may by meer imitation obtain a tuneableness, and also to touch an instrument not amiss, as the comon learners of tunes doe; but these raritys apart; how many blunder on and never attain any tollerable measure of it? And indeed

---

[11] I.e., before the invention of instruments.
[12] See ff. 10v–17.

many pretenders to instruct others have great failings in this kind, so important

is

f. 10v / is it to learn early what is called an ear; and it seems most securely if not onely acquireable by entring with the voice. Therefore let every one who would acquire the art of musick, to be exercised in any manner, begin with the plaine rules of universall intention, and exercise them vocally, as if singing well were the cheif designe; for after that he may divert to any other kind of practis by instruments with advantage.

6. Errors in singing

But since wee are to begin with the voice, wee will at present suppose that to be the cheif designe of a learner; and as for those who are ambitious to sing, or performe finely in any manner I have a word of advice; and as to singing in particular, that they labour not to sing like them that doe sing finely. There are many not wonderfully advanced, that after hearing a curious* cantata, at the theater (perhaps) send for the master, and fall to work in a designe (under such circumstance) impossible to be accomplish[t]. They doe not distinguish between learning a

song

f. 11 / song, and learning to sing; the former is beginning at the wrong end, as a person that learnes to dance not having strength to walk. There is a peculiar art in pronouncing musically, which must be acquired in order to pronounce cantando.

7. Other failings to be regulated

There are divers other mistakes observable which most people comitt who court a voice, which in the first place are to be obviated; one is that in learning they have cheif regard to ornaments, such as are called graces, and pretty devisions, which makes them neglect the art of sounding full and true, and that onely renders a voice musicall. Such devices should not be thought of 'till a good fund of pronounciation is layd in to be so adorned; els it is but straw drest up with fringe and bone-lace.[13] Another mistake is not sounding with the mouth enough open, and perhaps the teeth litle otherwise then shutt. I knew a servant-maid who sung loud and tuneably holding

[13] I.e., lace, usually of linen thread, made by knitting upon a pattern marked by pins, with bobbins originally made of bone [*OED*, *1*.]. The general sense of the clause is of something worthless decked out with expensive ornaments.

her teeth shutt, and her lipps open, but her song was accordingly, that is – clank clery clank clank clery clee. The Neapolitans say to the Genoese (Zeneze, as that people love to speak,) that they held

allwais

f.11v / allwais in their teeth a lous by the legg; such posture of the mouth is certeinly a vice even in speaking, and much more in singing, for it corrupts the clear tone of the voice. And divers persons will not be perswaded to hold up their heads, but affect to joyne their chin to their necks, which mutes the voice, that ought to have no restraint put upon the organs that forme it. And very few will be prevailed on to enforce their voices in order to pronounce vigorous and loud. What gives some ballad singing weomen such invidious voices, but a constant streining to make the utmost use of their breath? Perhaps such streining may a litle harden the sound, and discompose the air of the countenance, which modest and polite★ persons are much afraid of;[14] but time and use will soften the one, and recompose the other, but never recover a voice, which by a timorous practise is become languid. These precautions are very necessary for learners to observe, for the good or ill success of their undertaking may follow upon their having regard to these, and some other inde-corums which may be hinted to them, but I forbear.

In pro-

f.12 /8. The distinction of flat and sharp

In pronounciation the cours of the voice is either direct or deflected.[15] The latter is perceived by a manifest alteration, which the ear is well acquainted with, and never failes to observe; and it is that which is (musically) termed flatter or sharper, or els (from an arbitrary but improper reference to place or position) lower or higher,[16] and that with respect to the notation, (of which after-wards[17]), appositely enough: the higher is when the passages of the voice, (as in youth) are constricted, and [the] lower when the same, (as in adult and elderly persons) are relaxed, and it may be extended.

---

[14] That women of a certain social rank should not distort their faces is a 'decorum' reaching back into mythology and, in particular, the myths concerned with Athena's inventing and blowing the flute. In *Some Memorandums, concerning Musick* (ff.26–26v), North points out that this decorum impedes vocal production and that the singer and actress, Charlotte Butler, solved the problem by singing with her back to the audience so that she could produce a 'full and true' sound.

[15] I.e., continuous or discrete.

[16] See I.2.1. The issue here is a distinction between the rules of vibration (reality) and what we call 'high' and 'low' (appearances).

[17] See ff.22–25v.

And every person, whither old or young, hath power, by imploy-
ing the muscles of his mouth and throat, to prove this difference, as
comon singer[s] with great facillity, and by habit, without any
direct intention, apparently performe, and meer immitation will
lead other persons less habituated, to exercise the like powers, being
led from essays to full performances, as rusticks learne of one and
other divers vociferations, which they call singing.[18] And these
differences of flatt and sharp being gradatory,⋆ by like

(tho

2v / (tho improper) resemblance to reall quantity, are conceived
according to degrees of more and less in divers proportions,[19]
whereof the termes will be afterwards considered.[20] The smaller
flexures⋆ belong to comon speech, and have bin termed acute, and
grave; but these not belonging to moderne musick, are dropt here,
and wee proceed to what is peculiar, and in the art may be depended
on.

9. A steddy tone principall, in musick

When the ear perceives a sound continuing without any manner
of deflection, it is certein that voice is direct, and in a musicall sence
is called a tone, or (alluding to wrighting) a note, which termes,
meaning the same thing, are often used promiscuously; but sometimes one degree of flexure is called a tone, but of that afterwards.[21]
In the mean time the greatest regard is to be had to a clear continuance of tone without warping⋆ towards flatter or sharper for that is
the unum necessarium⋆ of art, and the holding forth such a tone
with a steddy voice, as long as the breath will conveniently hold
out, is the materia or

rather

13 / or rather anima⋆ of vocall musick, and that from a well tempered
voice is musick of it self. And upon this foundation the whole

[18] Like a musical instrument (wind or stringed) which produces gradations by intension and
remission of sounds, human individuals produce sounds in the same way, as this
paragraph hints. For North, therefore, elasticity (intension and remission) is the
physiological basis of the scale. Once habituated, our corporeal powers automatically
produce the gradations we call 'sharp' and 'flat'.
[19] See *TS 1728* (ff.123–128v). North argues that the natural intonation of the voice is just
intonation (see below ff.14v, 18v, 107, 110v, 112, 112v, 117v); but as instruments are
artificial, not natural, they must be tempered. In *TS 1726* (ff.54v–56v) North presents a
procedure for meantone temperament.
[20] See ff.15–18v.
[21] See ff.14v–15.

science of musick (which[22] consisting of such tones) is erected.
And for that reason the first lesson and practise of a voice is to
performe pure tones true and intensly, and thereby an habituall
sonorousness or rather ringing of the voice, will be acquired.

10. The same exercised may make or perfect a voice
And what is more, such a prolate pronunciation often exercised,
will not onely improve a mean voice, but gradually rais up one that
hath seemed altogether inept for tone, and so made to pass muster.
It is certein that aptitude is not found alike in all persons, for the
respective organs may be differently capacitated; and education,
together with a peculiar attention as well as favour★ to musick, in
divers persons will exceedingly vary; but except the naturally
incapables (if there are any such) no person duely assisted hath
reason to despair, as many are apt

to

f.13v   / to doe; but every one that will apply and persevere may gather his
quota, and become compos★ of a part in vocall consorts, which
altho not much used in our cryed up enterteinements, are in my
judgement the very culmen★ of musicall perfection.

11. Nature without instruction and example not sufficient
I have yet mentioned onely the exercise of pronouncing a single
tone,[23] which one would think a lesson so plain, that any one might
solitarily pra[c]tise it; but really it is not so, for altho a tone is the
first thing to be learnt, it is the last that a voice acquires without
exception, and seldome well, untill the judgment is matured, and
that (maturity) grows out of discipline; which discipline hath these
two essentialls, 1. instruction, 2. example.[24] The former will doe
litle without the other, and that (other) is the chief, for example, by
force of imitation, may forme [the] voice, when instruction, without example, can do nothing; yet that fullfills the example by
admonition;★ for a learner seldome perceives his errors, and without a monitor★ will not know

that

---

[22] MS gives the round brackets before 'consisting'.
[23] See ff.9v–13v.
[24] I.e., the two cardinal principles of Bacon and his followers (see Kassler 1976). In *MG*
c. 1726 North writes: 'there is a natural tendency to imitate, which makes good vocal
example, the best instructor of a voice, and when the patterne it self is not as it should be,
the copy will be wors, for imitation is without judgment' (f.20v). According to North
(*ibid.*: f.19v), judgement 'is the result of a cultivated experience'; therefore, it comes with
maturity.

f.14 / that his voice riseth or flattens, or when instead of filling the tone, it languefies,★ and if once he hath touched the sound, as a string twanged,[25] he thinks he hath done enough. This shews how essentially needfull it is to use a good master, the rather, becaus the naturall excellences of the example will be in great measure carryed over by imitation, so that a master's voice shall be heard in the scollar's; and on the contrary, imperfections will pass in like manner, and perhaps more readly. The use of an instrument will help as to pitch, or tuning, but adds nothing by way of imitation; from thence it is that a learner must acquire a good voice as well as the manner of using it. And as for such as have a genius, or naturall aptitude to voicing, they will so much more improve by imitation; and considering that they seldome tone steddily, and true; but are loos and wavering, the example and monition of a good teacher adds the perfection of art, and skill to that of nature; whence come these excellences, wee admire.

12. The simplicity of a plaine tone most conducing
    Here I am but in the beginning or very entrance of a musicall discipline, and before I take

another

f.14v / another stepp, I shall, by way of apology, owne that what hath bin recomended, with much of what is to follow, will seem to affect overmuch plaineness and simplicity; for learners never think they advance fast enough, and for want of patience, rush on to the midle, or choos to begin (as I sayd[26]) at the wrong end. But I must desire it may be observed, that all erudition whatsoever must enter with intire simplicity, and thereout as from a radix,★ all arts must derive their growth and increas; and nothing flourisheth in conclusion, that begins not in all singleness and distinction. And for that reason plain methods ought not to be despised, or presumed as matter of discouragement. And if it be thought I have made too much adoe about a single tone let it be remembred that Philomel her self is cheifly admired for that,[27] and that the meer tone of a good voice, musically pronounced, is allwais harmonious, and delightfull to those that hear it.

---

[25] '. . . as a string twanged': 'like a string that hath once twanged' (*MG c. 1726*: f.20v).
[26] See ff.10v–11.
[27] Philomel (Philomela), in legend, one of two daughters of Pandion, king of Athens, was transformed into a nightingale.

13. Shifting the tone to be after example

But to proceed, least it become fastidious to dwell over long upon the practise of a single tone loud, just, and steddy, wee will suppose that done

with

f.15   / with, and advance to the next in order, and that is to shift the voice well from one tone to another; and whenever that is done, it should be with some distinction, and not sliding as it were with one breath, or without stop, which so done would be like howling rather then singing. Then supposing that such transitions must be used, it will be infferred that they are not to be in a manner contingent, or without rule. If an ideot were demanded to sing, he would shift his voice, and vary his tone often enough, but being out of all rule, the sound would be more like that of a beast then of a man; what this order or rule must be, cannot be delivered by words onely, but must be referred to example, to be held forth by some competent instructor.

14. The plain gamut the best rule of shifting tones

Experience tells us (for wee enter into no reasons and causes here, but for them referr to the Theory of Sound[s]) that some tones are proper, and others very improper, to succeed each other. And this is discovered by certein mutuall relations or habitudes.[28] As if two tones are made to sound together

the

f.15v   / the compound effect, to our sence may be gratefull, or harsh and offensive: and thereupon it must be concluded that tones which accompany well, are best qualifyed to succeed one and other, for so near as immediate succession, memory doth as it were joyne them, and makes them want very litle of consonance. But of those that may joyne well, there is a choice or preference, which may determine the option rather to one, then to another; for some require less muscular action then others; as to pass 2 or 3 degrees (in musicall account) requires more or stronger action, then those that lye neerer. Now to fix a rule, or graduall order of these transitions, after a scrutiny of nature it self, and the experience of all ages, wee must appeal to the comon scale of tones called the gamut, and this consists of 7 [tones] in succession; and it falls out that after the whole

[28] See *TS 1728* (ff. 108–108v).

number is past over, the like caus[29] as determined the modallity★ of the gradation operates upon the further proceeding and so, indefinitely, whereby the musicall scale is but a septenary,★ out of which all variety of harmony and melody is derived.

f.16   / 15. Learnt onely by imitation

The manner of sounds expressed by counterchanging these 7 tones is matter of example, and not of description;[30] but instruments of musick readily explain them, and as such I may appeal to the observation of comon steeple-bells, which yeild a most sensible impression, and are signally, not onely regarded, but actually imitated by the comon people, who sound the tones as if a master had taught them; and being so comon, their melody is almost ingrafted in our natures, and made the musicall scale as if it were borne with us. For it is at least the first musick wee hear, and the nurse's tunefull voice, whose air is comonly the 5 bells, makes an early impression, whereby musicall learning is exceedingly facillitated; which would soon be found true if a meer barbare★ should be brought to the proof of being taught.[31]

16. The gamut notes most apt for shifting

It is no slight demonstration of the naturall vertues of the musicall scale, that the tones of it haue, as I sayd,[32] a co-sounding relation each to [the] other, and all to the first or leader; for if in the septenary, the 2d 3d 4th 5th 6th and 7th are

made

f.6v   / made successively to sound upon the first; the ear rejects none, but is highly pleased with severall of them; and the like (comparatively) of any two sounding together; which would be manifest, if the experiment were made of any other order of sounds to succeed or joyne, which would be found all to be imusicall if not detestable; and the worst junctures of the gamut tones collated would be thought harmonious. Some notes of the gamut joyne better then others, but all follow well; the first with the 3d and 5th so the 1st with the 4th and sixt, are harmony, and every two, one interposing, which they call a 3d are elegant; but imediates not so well, yet not

---

[29] I.e., comparison.

[30] North provides an example of 'counterchanging' the seven notes in *Cursory Notes of Musicke* (ed. Chan and Kassler 1986: 160–1 and Example 3 facing 160).

[31] The import is that teaching the 'barbare' would be difficult, because early implanting of the pitches of the scale had not taken place (see *MG c. 1726*: f.23v).

[32] See f.15.

rejected, and if the whole septenary were made to sound all together, the blended sound would be disagreeable, becaus it is a confusion, which is good in nothing; yet it would not offend so much as a jargon of contingent sounds such as harvest men's largess.★ These agreements and disagreements are but touched here, and are to be[33] cleared up in another place,[34] but at present they serve to shew that the gamut scale is marked out by nature, and the voice will slip

from

f.17   / one degree to another more aptly, whither per saltum★ or immediately, then in any other, therefore the exercise of this ought to be begun with.

17. The gamut is derived of the first tone

All sounds are to our hearing indifferent, untill some one tone is heard, and then the indifference is determined, and immediately the gamut or septenary, of which that tone is the leader, takes place, and will regulate the succeeding tones; for the ear doth not accept such as are dissonant, but expects consonancys, and that comes by memory. And all these septenary scales have their caracter, and denomination from the proper leader; and as the tones of the same scale by consonances relate to that which leads; so the leaders of divers scales may have relation to each other, and if those are accordant, the tones of their respective scales will not be so dissonant to each other as otherwise [they] would be. And this takes place in the severall degrees of meliority,★ as to instance the scale led[35] from the fifth note, shall agree better then the scale ledd from the sixt note above the leader of the gamut; this also is but touched here but will be found very consequentiall in what follows.[36]

Hitherto

f.17v   / 18. The use of the gamut syllables

Hitherto of pronouncing and shifting of tones,[37] buisness necessary to be dispatched[,] but nothing yet of the practicall meane[s], which follows next.[38] It is impossible for any one to pronounce musicall tones successively without investing the sound with some formall syllables; and it is convenient that consonants as

---

[33] I.e., have been.
[34] See *T S 1728* (ff. 106–121v *et passim.*).
[35] MS has 'lead'.
[36] See ff. 37–41.
[37] See ff. 9–14v ('pronouncing') and 14v–17 ('shifting').
[38] See ff. 17–22.

well as vowells should be made use of in them, for vowells are apt to
run one into another, as the whole 5 may be prolated in one breath,
which consonants intermixt would put a stop to. As to our porpose, it is almost indifferent what syllables are used, provided they
be sonorous, and folks are agreed upon them. And this consideration favours those already found in the gamut, which being in
possession ought not without reason to be changed; but as to that I
have somewhat to say afterwards.[39] At present the scale stands
thus: vt, re, mi, fa, sol, la, pha. This latter sound (the same as fa) was
by Mr. Butler prudently varyed in the orthography, becaus it hath a
different place in the scale.[40] Each of these belong to a severall tone,
and have regard to vt, the leader, as they would have if advanced
from any other sound or tone whatsoever.

18   / 19. Of tones and semitones

The state of these tones as to sharper and flatter, whenever there
is occasion to shift or change them, is determined by concordances,
and not by numbers or mechanick measures, for in the musick scool
there is neither broad, long, nor deep, but the sounds either agree,
or disagree according to their places in some scale or other. Therefore the tonometers have no imployment there.[41] But a gradation,
although there is no comon measure to guide a voice, is necessary in
order to pass from one concord to another, whereby it is perceived
that more sharpening the voice is required to pass from re to mi then
from mi to fa or from la to pha; for which reason use hath introduced the denomination of tones and semitones, and accordingly
re, mi, sol and la are accounted whole tones, and the fa and pha
semitones. Which concludes not that there is any measure of equallity between tone and tone, or of mediety* between the semitones
and tones, but each according to their order are related to each other
by concordances, which the ear must find out and that can be done
no otherwise then by

exercise

8v   / exercise of toning over the scale which will in time create an habit
of tuning the notes justly according to their places. And so they
learne to sound fa as if it were sol[,] that is half a note higher, and sol
as if it were fa which is half a note flatt and by that means the whole

---

[39] See ff.21–22.

[40] Butler, whose system is a movable syllable system, added the syllable 'pha' for the
seventh degree, a semitone above la (1636: 12–22; see also Chenette 1967: 119–23).

[41] A monochord called a 'tonometer' was invented by Ambrose Warren (fl. 1670–1725).
The explanatory booklet accompanying the invention presented a system of
temperament in which the octave is divided logarithmically into thirty-two equal
intervals (see Warren 1725 and Kassler 1979: ii/1045–8).

scale is broke into semitones, and serves to accomodate instruments but litle concernes a voice but when it is tyed to them as I shall shew afterwards.[42]

20. Of the letters in the gamut

It is reported that Pope Gregory first distinguished the musicall scale by 7 letters, beginning with the first letter of his name, as G, A, B, C, D, E, F, and so went on to other septenarys, round again by G and in the reverst order descending.[43] And becaus these letters harping so much upon the vowell E were not so apt for a common musicall pronounciation one Guido stole from a church poem the seven syllables, which have ever since bin nominally joyned with the letter, but pronounced without it.[44] Thus farr very well; for here is the letter scale, which is of universall regard, and is called the naturall, and when any tone used as a member of any other scale is reduced to the naturall it

hath

f. 19   / hath this mark ♮. Then wee have the vocall scale of syllables annexed to this pari passu, which at present I shall not presume to alter, but only by using Go[45] instead of ut, which (vt) making a full stop of the voice, is fitt to be exchanged for another more sonorous. And then the letter and vocall gamut will stand thus;

etc.

a

g

F	Pha
E	La
D	Sol
C	Fa
B	Mi
A	Re
G	Gho

FF

EE

[42] See ff. 19v–20.

[43] Gregory the Great (b. *c.* 540, d. 604), pope and theologian, who, according to North, used 'discretion in keeping musick unperplext' by adopting letters of the alphabet to denominate the scale (*MG c. 1726*: f.43).

[44] According to tradition, Guido of Arezzo (b. *c.* 991–2, d. after 1033) chose the solmisation syllables from a hymn to St John: U T queant laxis R Esonare fibris/M Ira gestorum F Amuli tuorum/S O Lve polluti LAbii reatum.

[45] I.e., one of North's new syllables for 'toning' the scale (see f. 22).

here is no defect, but every note (according to the old Greek manner) hath its letter mark, and vocall appellation, unless it be thought that the superior and inferior octaves are not well distinguished. The letter scale hath found a formed★ distinction, as GG, G, $\bar{g}$, $\bar{\bar{g}}$ for so many octaves but the vocall here wants it, for sol in the upper and lower octaves is the same as in the midle. But I am inclined to think, that in elder times church musick was used in great simplicity, and seldome strayed beyond the plain septenary, and was not perplext with flatts and sharps as more latterly by means of musicall instruments have bin introduced, and so required no further distinction.

21. The letters serve instruments and the syllables voices

Here I may observe that if musick had bin confined to instruments, and voices had not bin joyned with them, the letter scale had bin sufficient, for what had needed more, then the organ-builders use, viz. marks to agree with their sounds?[46]

But

19v / But the necessity of voices following the wanton changes that instruments have affected, hath made it also necessary to add to the letter, more vocall scales then one, which hath bredd such a confusion over the science and practice of musick, as few learners can comport with; and these misterys I propose to unfold with all the clearness that may be; and that is reasonable to be done, because I am in quest of some clear directions how a voice may find the notes that upon shifting the learner may venture to sound.

22. The syllables added follow the change of the key, or leader

The letters and sillables thereto annexed are fixed upon the broad keys of the organ, note for note. But by means of the exotick★ semitones which by the narrower keys are intercaled★ the instrument may pitch a musicall scale upon any other tone, or letter, besides G in the whole septenary; which is but taking two of the semitones, for a whole tone, when the assumed scale requires it; and by using the marks of sharp and flatt for the out-of-the-way semitones, keep the lettered scale fixt in its place. But the vocall scale must remove so, that the Gho shall allwais fall upon the note, or

---

[46] In *MG Frag* (ff. 14v–15v, 18v–20), North devotes attention to the manner in which organ builders mark their pipes. In *MG c. 1726* (ff. 34–35v), he indicates that his account of the accidental marks refers to the practice of German organ builders. His knowledge of this practice probably came from two Germans resident in England: Bernard Smith (see f. 139, n. 483) and 'Capt.' F. Prencourt (see *Cursory Notes of Musicke* ed. Chan and Kassler 1986; *Prencourt Tracts*; and *Musicall Recollections I*).

letter that leads the scale which in using the instrument[47] is
intended to be ruled by, (and that note I shall presume to

call

f.20   / call the key;) as when the instrument makes A and not G to be the
key, the voice must sing it as Gho and so for B, C, etc. whereby if
fancy leads to change the key often, how should a voice tune after it?
Therefore Guido (I suppose) finding that the musick upon one key
was dull, and that provision for some change must be made, he
added to the letters two vocall scales more; one upon C and the
other upon F presuming that the 3 keys G, C and F might afford
change enough for church musick; and to avoid inextricable confusion went no further, and having affixed markes for these
changes, he thought learners with their voices might shift well
enough, and then the gamut stands thus.

				Pha	
				La	
				Sol	
			Pha	Fa	
			La	Mi	
			Sol	Re	
F	Pha	Fa	Gho		
E	La	Mi			
D	Sol	Re			
C	Fa	Gho			
B	Mi				
A	Re				
G	Gho				
	Naturall	Change to C	Change to F		

[47] The whole sentence is obscure, partly because North was working from, and trying to
abbreviate, the corresponding passage in *MG* *c. 1726* (ff. 29v–30v). The meaning is:
. . . Gho shall always fall upon the note or letter that leads the vocal scale, although the
'leader' of the scale, on an accompanying instrument, might not be G but A or B, etc.

23. How the gamut disturbed, and of the mi-cliffs[48]

These alterations were made with as much discretion as was possible, for it was considered what notes lay neerest in harmony to the key, and into which a change would least disturbe the gamut scale, or dislocate any notes in it. And it was found that falling a 5th or (which is the same) rising a 4th would disturb onely one note, and the rest would keep their places, therefore upon the change into C onely B (its 7th) must be flatted. And the next

                                                                   remove

20v   / remove a 4th higher into F flatted further onely the E and it appears by changing round still a 4th higher onely one note more at each change would be disturbed. But to F was farr enough, for altho they had marks by sharps and flatts, in the notation to serve the turne as I shall shew;[49] yet the rending the syllables from their proper letters, and an unreadyness in finding where the key note lay, and other incident doubtings, as the key might change and rechange, made the learners' part so difficult, that nothing but necessity could hold them to it. And at length a neerer and as was thought less perplext way is found out, which is by slighting the key note, and never using the vt and re, but at the entrance, depend wholly upon the mi and that being found[,] the notes ascending and descending are readily named.[50] For from mi the sillables fa, sol, la twice upwards, and the like reverst downwards come again to mi either way and then the gamut stands thus.

---

[48] I.e., the movable system of four syllables used in England from 1600. The four syllables were mi, fa, sol and la. Mi is located by means of the key signature, and the syllables fa, sol, la appear in order both above and below mi. According to Chenette: 'Apparently, the key note was fa directly above mi in the sharp keys – the major mode – and la below mi in the case of flat keys – the minor mode. In this system, the key note was truly a "center," surrounded by the pitches above and below' (1967: 386). Butler (1636) misunderstood the four-syllable system, and this may account for some of North's difficulties here and also at f.20v.

[49] See below and ff.23ᵃv–24.

[50] In *MG Frag* (f.21v) North treats the four-syllable system in more detail; but in *MG c. 1726* he observes: 'And thus by certein rules for finding the mi-cliffs, and inculcating them into the nodles of the poor quire-children, after much contusion, and rigorous ill usage, they are brought to sol-fa (as they call the singing by the syllables) tollerably well, and some I have knowne performe it swift to a wonder. But no ingenuous person that is not by hand and hammer driven thro these briars will ever set foot in them; therefore I do not set downe their rules, nor shew how farr they will carry, not intending that any should (nor doe I intend to) make use of them. But they are to be found in most writers and particularly in Mr. Playford's Introduction' (ff.33v–34; see Playford 1655, various editions).

	Naturall	Change to C	Change to F
f			
e		Mi	
d		La	
c		Sol	
b		Fa	
a		La	Mi
g		Sol	La
F	Pha	Fa	Sol
E	La	Mi	Fa
D	Sol	La	La
C	Fa	Sol	Sol
B	Mi	Fa	Fa
A	Re	La	Mi
G	Gho	Sol	
FF		Fa	
EE		Mi	

And the hunting is for the mi cliffs, as they are called, for the mi found[,] the rest of the syllables lye in fair order ascending and descending. But after all the mi rules, there seems litle redemption for a learner thereby. Wha[t] a stir is there in teaching about B mi, and B molle[51] which in the comon gamuts is wrote B fa ♯mi, for ♭ mi is contradictory. The mistery is onely that whe[n] [the] scale is upon C the B is of cours flatt and so when upon F. But when upon G it is of cours sharp, as the order of the severall scales at G, C and F that compose the common gamut shew [which] so happens to all the notes in the scale if changes were so continued.

f.21   / 24. The hideous task of learning the gamut memoriter,★ layd aside

These puzlements of the voice will appear much more formidable when I come to the manner of notation and dealing with the

---

[51] In the MS the text on f.20v ends here with 'B molle'. North wrote the remaining text on this page at the top of f.21, above Section 24. The continuation is indicated in the MS by the sign + which also follows the words 'B molle'. We transcribe it on f.20v, since North clearly intended it to fill out Section 23.

semitones;[52] but at present I cannot pass by the inconsolable task imposed upon youth (that are forced to learne dans les formes,★) which no ingenuous and free person will submitt to. They add to the letter the sillables that in the gamut stand against it, to make one word which is to be the name of that note; and to give it its due, it helps to distinguish the octaves higher and lower, but it is better done by numbers. For is not G 1st, G 2d, and G 3d better then Gamut, Gesolreut and Glasol? But the poor youths without any explication must be held to repeat their whole gamut, with 3 sillables joyned with most of the letters backwards and forwards, and from any note to any note, upon pain of being most inhumanely used. The drudgery of conning such pedantique gibberish, can scarce be compensated by any good to be had by it; therefore all things considered, I have determined to disband all the furniture of the gamut except the naturall, which conteining nothing enigmatique (for the sake of

the

f.21v / the teachers as well as learners of plain song) may have.[53] For perhaps they may be prejudiced in favour of the fa sol and that being affixt to the letters serves for all teaching intents; and so it was originally designed, before the gamut was corrupted by changes. And perhaps I may produce a vocall scale, composed of the letters and sillables commixt with subsidiary marks, as may be obviously intelligible, practicall, and universall;[54] and if any benefit may be worthily bestowed upon the faculty of musick, it is to render the avenues to the science, as well as practise, easy and not unpleasant.

25. A compound gamut unperplext, proposed

And in order to that it may not be amiss to consolidate the naturall gamut into one plain scale, which shall be both nominall and vocall, and to order it so, that the same letters and syllables shall serve both to name every note whither sharp or flat, and also in singing to use the same syllables thro out. If any one be fond of the vt, re, mi, fa, they may be used as before and be sufficient (as I sayd[55]) for teaching a voice to tune the notes, but then it can goe no

[52] See ff.23–23ᵃv ('notation') and 23ᵃv–25v ('semitones').
[53] '... may have' occurs at the end of the line and is inserted above '⟨shew⟩'; the binding is tight and may conceal another word. We suggest the following emendation: '... which contains nothing enigmatic (for the sake of the teachers as well as learners of plain song)'.
[54] See f.22.
[55] See ff.17v–18.

further then the single key or scale of the leader; and that is

insufficient

f.22   / insufficient to conduct a voice as the use now requires; I mean in
singing at sight from a manner of notation proper for instrumentall
musick, which often changeth the scale, and with great variety
exceeding the 2 scales that are comonly added to the gamut, as hath
bin shewed.[56] Therefore before I come to describe the comon
notation,[57] I shall venture to propose these syllables to stand in the
musicall scale; viz. Gho, Ar, Be, Ça (saving the primer and as in
Spanish, pronouncing it as Sa), Do, El, Fa.

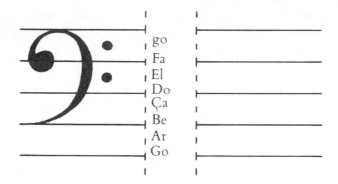

These preserve the scalar letter, and add[58] a vowell, or liquid or
two for clearer distinction; and how these are to be accommodated
to all keys shall be declared;[59] and then wee shall proceed further in
the prattique★ of the voice.[60]

26. The comon notation described

It was observed that in sounding sharp and flat there was a
resemblance of high and low;[61] and for that reason it was naturall to
make the notation of them by some climax of ascent and descent,
and then the notes are distinguisht by place according to order, as
well as by name, according as here [in the example above] they are
applyed in the gamut. Whereby it appears that 5 lines are sufficient

to

---

[56] See ff. 19v–20.
[57] See ff. 22–25v.
[58] MS has 'adds'.
[59] See ff. 23ᵃv–25v.
[60] See ff. 26–29v.
[61] See f. 12 and n. 16.

f.22v   / to comprehend the whole octave scale, for from space to line, and from line to space all the notes are affixt to proper places, by which they may be knowne and pronounced;[62] and by musitians they are usually pricked* down in this manner.

           Go   Ar   Be   Ça   Do   El   Fa

This serves very well for the compass of one octave which a voice seldome exceeds (much) and nothing can be more explicite, and apt for memory then it is; for the lines are few, and create no confusion in the idea, as all multitude must doe. It is seldome that more lines are used, but if there is occasion, some scraps added above or beneath, readily account for it.

27. The notation lines extended to answer all uses

   But in regard the whole musicall compass containes divers octaves, or septenarys of notes continued one above another, it is needfull that the notation should be continued also, and in intire series without interruption. It depends on positive appointment, what septenary, and which are the lines to be made use of, for some voices take it high and some low; which proves the cause of some obscurity, for the whole scale, designed for 3 or more octaves

                                                                will

f.23   / will fall out, as most authors shew them, in this manner,

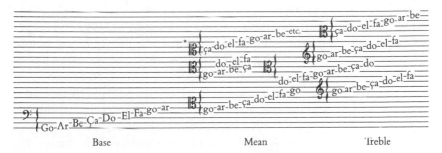

           Base   Mean   Treble

* MS has the clef one space too high. The note names omit 'do' and begin on the line below the clef.

whence any 5 lines may be extracted.

[62] According to North, 'while the musick assigned to one part, doth not exceed the 5 lines, the performer, who is (like a gamester and his pipps) habitually instructed of his places, is easy' (*MG c. 1726*: f.40). About two decades after North's death, Elizabeth Gambarini devised a method of teaching musical notation by the pipps on cards (see Kassler 1979: i/ 369–70).

28. The manner of extracting the comon scales for use

Here the conspic[u]ous marks, 𝄢, 𝄡 and 𝄞, are called cliffs, being to signifye some one note, as it stands in the five lines (to be extracted for use) and if the place of any one note is knowne[,] all the rest follow one way or other. The mark 𝄢 stands upon the upper of the 5 lines but one which is the place of Fa. [The mark] 𝄡 usually stands in the midle line, which is in the place of Ça. And [the mark] 𝄞 stands usually upon the lower line but one, and is the place of Go. The cliffs, 𝄢 and 𝄞, are seldome put upon any other place, but 𝄡 is variously placed according to the pitch of the voices, or kind of instrument. I have extracted the three usu[a]ll pitches, with their proper cliffs which in

comon

f.23v / comon notation stands thus,

Treble 2 places or a 3d higher

Mean 1 place higher*

Base

* MS has '2 places higher'

and are the parts knowne by the names of base, mean, and treble, which make a continuall rising of the notes thro 3 octaves and might be carryed further, as the use is. Whereby if any part in rising comes to exceed its lines, changing the cliff to the next above, gives a new compass. And that change of the cliff is a great cross to the unready performer who often is at a non plus by the surprize; for the action is not so ready, as the notion; and it requires great exercise, and habit to bring them together; such changes will fall out in this manner and in favour of beginners. Masters are content rather then change the cliff to add supplementary scrapps of lines as in this latter example.

Cliffs changing

Not changing

This

23ᵃ   / 29. Salmon's project to disband the cliffs, rejected

This inconvenience is so considerable, that some coniseurs have bent their witts to remove it; and particularly one Salmon, who about 50 years since published a project in print,[63] which hath bin revived by a late author.[64] And it is no more but this. The 5 lines proper to all octaves, superior and inferior, should have the notes, according to the letter, in the same places, so that G should be upon the lower line, D upon the midle line, and A upon the first [line], and so of spaces, etc. And to distinguish the severall octaves, or parts; a mark should be put at the head of the lines, as B for the base part[,] M for the mean, T for the treble, and A for the alt[65] thus.

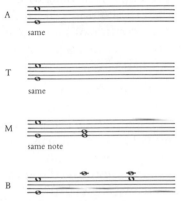

And by this means all cliffs being taken away, the changes were not to be any more troublesome, and any voice could indifferently,* as to tune, performe any parts. But this device however plausible hath bin found unreasonable, and unprofitable. Unreasonable, becaus the septenary is an odd number so that the same note shall stand both upon lines and spaces as G in the base, and G in the octave, and then again in the treble, and the alt, so that if

additionall

3ᵃv   / additionall lines are intercaled the notes will clash fouly as a line added between B and M is E to the first and C to the latter. But let

---

[63] Thomas Salmon (b. 1648, d. 1706), divine and fellow of the Royal Society, proposed to reform musical notation in four ways: (1) the first seven letters of the alphabet would replace the Guidonian syllables; (2) the five-line staff would be reduced to four lines, (3) the clefs would be discarded in favour of the symbols B (bass), M (mean) or T (treble); and (4) lute and other tablatures would be replaced by the new staff notation (see Salmon 1672).

[64] John Francis de la Fond (fl. 1716–1725), teacher of languages and music, was author of two tracts, both of which proposed reforms (c.1724, 1725; see also *MG* c. 1726: ff.45v–46 and Kassler 1979: i/271–3, ii/1242–3).

[65] I.e., high tone; usually the octave above the treble stave beginning with G.

that pass, it will be needfull when the parts sweep a great compass
for t[he] mark equally confounding to be brought in to serve the
turn, thus.

    F   a   d   f   a   f*   a   a   F   D   A

* MS has d
† MS omits barline

And without more words, I may appeal to any artist, whither this
way would not disturb and check the carriere* of a performer as
much, if not more, then the comon scale and cliffs; and if so, wee
depart from order, and a continuall series to no porpose. I had not
layd out so many words upon this whimm if I had not found that
some ingenious persons had a better opinion of it then it deserves.[66]

30. The application to the semitonian scale

    Hitherto wee have bin enterteined with our gamut,[67] and
reduced it to a scale of letters, and 7 notes[68] cantable* accordingly,
without much notice of flatts and sharps; that is the semitonian
scale, as it is expressed upon organs and clavicall instruments; and
now the buissness will be to shew how the vocall part of our lettered
scale may be accomodated to answer so

much

f.24   / much variety, as by keys changing among the semitones of an
octave may be introduced. And first of the marks ♭ and ♯ whereof
the first is to signifye a semitone flatter, and the other a semitone
more sharp. And the signall of the naturall scale which is G is (as
was touched[69]) thus ♮ . The occasion of all which is from the organ
builders, for they tune all from C which they account naturall, and
the order of that key requires B to be flat, and the B♮ in the gamut,
they call H or K which in the G key is the naturall. And becaus the

---

[66] Wilson (1959: 240) speculated that one of the 'ingenious persons' was Malcolm, author of
a treatise on music (1721; see Kassler 1979: ii/732–8). There is no evidence that North was
acquainted with Malcolm's treatise before 1730, when he does mention it (see *Notes of Me*
ed. Jessopp 1887: suppl.). It is probable, therefore, that North's allusion is to John Wallis
(see I.1.1 and Kassler 1979: ii/1039–42). Because Wallis and Salmon were advocates of
syntonic tuning, North may have inferred that Wallis supported Salmon. Hawkins,
however, suggested that Wallis' response to Salmon's notational reforms was ironic (see
Hawkins 1776 rev. 1853/1963: ii/716–7 note).

[67] See ff.15–18v.

[68] See ff.18v–23ᵃv.

[69] See ff.18v–19.

organs make B to be flat, that letter, viz. B is taken for the flat mark thro out, and is so used on all occasions; and then the mark H restoring B♮ to the gamut or G key, that letter corrupted, viz. ♮ is made the mark of naturall thro out, that is a restorer of every note de[s]turbed back to the scale of the gamut, as was touched before.[70] And by a further corruption the same mark turns to ♯ which signifies the raising any note a semitone higher.

31. The syllables applyed as the letters to flatts and sharps

It was considered that of equally sonorous syllables, it was indifferent which were to be used

with

f.24v / with the voice, provided folks were agreed upon them.[71] Therefore the syllables I use with the letters of the gamut, shall be cantable to both the sharp, and the flatt of any note, as there is occasion to use one or other. And by that wee gaine a vocall syllable adapted to every semitone. And let the musick be set [in] any key ordinary or extraordinary, the voice shall never be at a loss to find the proper syllable to every note, and so have the same propriety as the letters which never change place but by flatts and sharps distinguish all the semitones. This shall be fully exemplifyed by the following specimens.

Here may be observed an importune multitude of the flat and sharp marks, which as the scale deviates from the naturall will more or

[70] See above and ff. 18v–19.
[71] See f. 17v.

less obtrude. Therefore it is used as a laudable expedient instead of marking every

note

f.25   / note, to mark the place at the beginning of the lines, in which the extraordinary flatts and sharps will fall; and that keeps the lines clean, the notes more distinct, and for the most part discovers, upon which tone or semitone of the gamut, the scale of the musick is pitcht, or at least with a slight perusall it may be found out; and of such cases these may be examples.

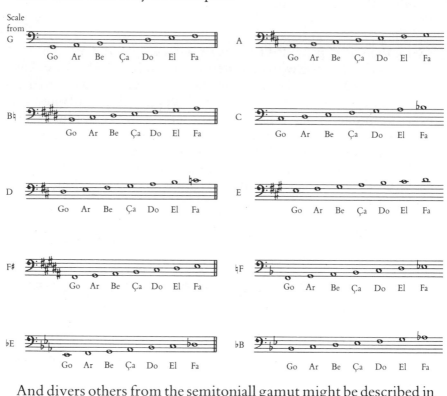

Scale
from
G   Go Ar Be Ça Do El Fa
A   Go Ar Be Ça Do El Fa
B♮   Go Ar Be Ça Do El Fa
C   Go Ar Be Ça Do El Fa
D   Go Ar Be Ça Do El Fa
E   Go Ar Be Ça Do El Fa
F♯   Go Ar Be Ça Do El Fa
♮F   Go Ar Be Ça Do El Fa
♭E   Go Ar Be Ça Do El Fa
♭B   Go Ar Be Ça Do El Fa

And divers others from the semitoniall gamut might be described in like

manner

f.25v   / manner. Here note that in the scale C a flatt is set to B[,] and in the scale D a ♮ is set to F,[72] and in the scale ♮ F a ♭ is also set in B,[73] and

[72] I.e., C.
[73] I.e., E.

in the scale ♭ E the like is set in D, and [in] ♭ B it is also set in A, all which notes in the cours of the severall scales are required to be so, but in the cours of the musick the occasion to use them comes so seldome, that masters often choos to mark them at the note, rather then at the line which might occasion other marking of as much trouble.

32. Objection for the [four syllable] sol-fa answered

It may [he] sayd by way of objection, that to find the m[i] cliffs is as easy, as to find the leading note[74] of the scale. I grant that the mi is allwais the 2d note above the key note; and that (key note) found[,] the mi and every other note follows in order; but of itself the mi is a rote–lesson, [and] leads to no understanding, as may be had by a knowledg of an universall musicall scale. For that helps to know concords (of which hereafter[75]) wherewith the mi hath nothing to doe. A flourish of the musick at the beginning of a consort, declares the key note and then the flatts, without other puzle, arc soe knowne. And to conclude, the knowing any one syllable of the scale, gives all the rest, but the la and sol are twice in every octave, and the knowing either, concludes nothing certein as to the others, which is a defect in the method by mi cliffs.[76]

f.26 / 33. Lesson rising and falling from the key

But as to method of teaching, let every one be pleased, and provided the learners are not discouraged, but gaine the point of a voice sounding clear, full, and true, all is safe and well; and then it will be proper to proceed in practise of lessons of more variety then the plaine scale; and this I choos to advance before I bring under examination the modes of time in musick,[77] becaus wee propose no variety to be used in plain song, but onely notes of equall duration, as a longer minum or shorter sembreif, spending about 4 seconds of time, but in exact equallity if possible, and that may be procured by the motion of a hand up and downe as the notes pass, for a corporall movement falls into equabillity naturally, as will be further declared.[78] Then it is recomended for the first lesson to rise from thc key to the severall notes in the gamut ascending and descending in this manner.

[74] I.e., the note which leads.
[75] See ff.37v–41.
[76] In the four-syllable system ut and re are changed into sol and la; therefore, they are repeated twice in every octave (see f.20 and n.48).
[77] See ff.30–36v.
[78] See ff.30–31v.

Ascending

Descending

2d   3d   4th   5th   6th   7th   8th

f.26v   / 34. Manner of securing leaps

This task in the neerer degrees as to the 2d, 3d and 4th is easier
then [in] the more remote, as the 5th, 6th and 7th, but the continuall
rising easyest of all. Therefore it is recomended to pass the mean
degrees with a low voice, or rather mentally,[79] till it comes at the
intended stage,★ and then to sound out, and custome will bring the
saltations of the voice to be sudden and exact. The manner may be
thus expressed, ascending and descending.

Ascending

Go   Do   Go   El   Go   Fa   Go   go

Descending

go   Ça   go   Be   go   Ar   go   Go

The small points shew how the fancy is to touch the notes passant★
in their places, which will not be at first jumped into without such
help.

35. Divers initiall lessons

There are divers other lessons commonly recommended to practise, and allwais profitable, as the rising and falling by accords, and
first by thirds which is next to the plaine gradation thus.

Ascending

Go   Be   Ar   Ça   Be   Do   Ça   El   Do   Fa   El   go

Descending

go   El   Fa   Do   El   Ça   Do   Be   Ça   Ar   Be   Go

The like by fourths, fifths, sixts, and sevenths as in the following
examples.[80]

---

[79] The phrase, 'low voice', hints at an extreme empiricist position more characteristic of the
counter-Enlightenment, when it was supposed that language and thought were
inseparable: to think is to speak low; to speak is to think aloud.
[80] See f.27, Example 1.

f.27 / These

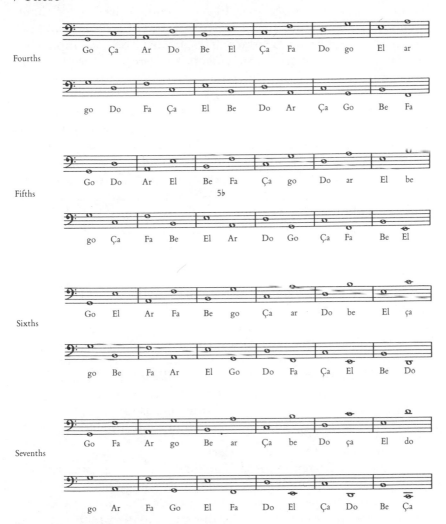

Fourths

Go Ça Ar Do Be El Ça Fa Do go El ar

go Do Fa Ça El Be Do Ar Ça Go Be Fa

Fifths

Go Do Ar El Be Fa Ça go Do ar El be

5♭

go Ça Fa Be El Ar Do Go Ça Fa Be El

Sixths

Go El Ar Fa Be go Ça ar Do be El ça

go Be Fa Ar El Go Do Fa Ça El Be Do

Sevenths

Go Fa Ar go Be ar Ça be Do ça El do

go Ar Fa Go El Fa Do El Ça Do Be Ça

with many more of like sort are to be found in all musicall instructions and serve to tune the voice[,] strengthen the tone, and in time
make a learner capable to gather any thing at first sight, a talent so
desirable, that no paines are too much to acquire it; and as a
readiness in reading languages, common as it is, can never be
acquired without much, and almost continuall exercise, so musick.
And neither can be pleasant without it.

27v / 36. The benefit of sounding consort notes
      There is therefore no need here to multiply initiall lessons, so

well by others prescribed, and by masters further prescribable ad infinitum; but one thing I would recomend to the best of them; which is that when they find a scollar compos of his tones, and can sound his gamut firme, he (the master) fall off from accompanying in unison, and take into some plain and proper accords; as in descending the scale from Go[,] the master fall in with a 3d[,] that is begin with Go following upon El, and accompany some notes downe, and so ascending. This will surprise and amaze the learner, who will not soon be brought to bear the novelty, and to keep his tone, but after some exercise, he will become exceedingly pleased and desire more of it; and in conformity it will engage him to swell his voice, and endeavour to fullfill the harmony. The benefits of this practise are incomparable, for besides the creating a love for musick, and desire for practise, it will firme and steddy his tone, and make it more musicall[,] for sounds in consort will draw each other,[81] and the

effects

f.28   / effects of harmony are so strong, that it will be perceived in a single voice that is used to it. For such will not onely ring, but as it were act a consort, when the most plausible★ singers, not so exercised, shall warble well, and as the wild notes of birds be pretty and diverting, but void of harmony. This discours directed to all masters of song perhaps may not be well accepted by some that esteem themselves tout accomplié;★ but if there are any not quali-fyed for teaching in that manner, I must needs say it is great pitty, for the meer teaching a song by rote, is but a pittyfull imployment.

37. Somewhat to follow more aiery

But it must be remembred that this plaine-song practise will grow tedious, and it will be fitt to intercale somewhat that shall be accounted more ayery, to recreate a learner; but allwais avoiding quick graces and devisions, or any thing that may instill bad habits, which at first are propens★ to grow of themselves. There are certein grave aires to be found, or composed for the porpose, and some used in the cathedrall services

very

f.28v   / very proper, as the versicle between the commandement which may be bounded in this manner.

---

[81] Francis North had argued that the unison, a single tone, is made more loud and full by the addition of other tones (1677; see f.82v, nn.270, 271). In *TS 1726* (ff.47–48v) and *TS 1728* (ff.120–121v), Roger North adumbrates the same argument. For the challenge posed by Isaac Newton, see Chan, Kassler, Hine (1988: 58).

Lord have mer - cy up - on us, and in - cline our

hearts to keep this law.

* MS illegible at this point. Upper line could read

I might instance further in the Gloria patri, and other of the ecclesiasticall hymnes, which are short and plain, and are readily to be acquired, as also such manner of cantatas may be composed for the porpose, rising in air from one degree to an other, as the genius of the learner invites, ever intermixing consort as occasion prompts; and as a pattern I have shadowed a consort part to the hymne above, which I guess would gratifye a learner. This is set for a lower part, but the same methods serve for the superiors, the notes being disposed accordingly. And to say truth the master ought to be qualifyed with a voice adequate to that of the person to be taught, for the imitation of a deep base mu[st] needs vitiate the delicate tone of one superior.

f.29 / 38. Of the attendance of an instrument

This may introduce the reflexion, how farr the attendance of an instrument may be usefull in teaching regularly to sing; and I think at the first entrance when the whole work is imitation, it is best to have none; but after some advance, and the learner begins to be sensible of tune, and hath tasted of harmony, it becomes needfull to joyne some instrument; and it ought to sound by a touch mildly, as a guittare, or rather a base viol[,] lute fashion and this as much for the sake of the teacher, as of the learner, that the former might not sink, or vary his tone but both one and other hold up to the proper pitch. But such as are vociferacious,* I mean organs, harpsichords, loud viols, hautbois, should never accompany learners, for they by imitation will carry off a tincture of the instrument. Once it was a mode in London to learne to sing of a famous violin master, who had no manner of voice, but had the corrupting of many good ones.[82] And it hath bin a misfortune, that most of our great masters of musick have wanted good voices, whereby it is become prover-biall to say any one sings like an

organist.

[82] Probably the elder Matteis (see f. 57, n. 189), who issued *A Collection of New Songs . . . made purposely for the use of his scholers . . .* , London 1696 and 1699.

f.29v / organist. A flute is most unfit to be used with the voice of a learner, becaus it hath a shuffling and incertein tone, and very rarely holds out a blast well,[83] and for that reason cannot be proper for an early imitation; and in fine, [there is] no [other][84] means to make a singer, as a teacher in whom a competen[t] voice, skill, and discretion meet.

39. Against solitary teaching

And as to the learning of musick in generall I must out of my experience say, that of those persons who are so happy to acquire it, more teach themselves, then are taught; and all that advantage is from society. For all arts are more effectually learnt under a sociall then under a solitary discipli[ne] and none more eminently so then musick. For of that the learning is imitation, and the exercise society; and ambition no less then emulation are the procurers. It is an unhappyness in England that there are not musick scools for yong people to be taugh[t] as well as reading and wrighting scools;[85] but chambe[r] teaching, for reasons moving from the teachers, as well as from the learners, rarely and that not without an immens charge ever makes an accomplisht scollar.

f.30 / 40. Time keeping depends on equallity

It is not to be expected that persons of spirit and vivacity of humour, ambitious of the pleasures that the exercise of musick is expected to afford, should be long held back among dull formalitys, but on the contrary, whither by the voice, or some musicall instruments, to fall upon practise, esteeming also difficultyes a choice enterteinement. And of those difficultys none are found greater then to attain a true knowledg and setled habit of keeping musicall time.[86] I have yet but just touched upon the subject,[87] becaus the initiall practise needed onely a plain equallity, to be expressed by moving the hand at every note, per arsin et thesin* as authors love to express it. And so far there was no mistery nor difficulty. For equallity takes place in our most thoughtless actions,

---

[83] See *TS 1728* (ff.141v–144).

[84] MS is illegible at this point.

[85] Elsewhere, North writes: 'in England, where there are scarce any open musick scools, at least not such as are regularly conducted, as they are in most forrein cittys, ... masters and scollars meet on horary termes' (*MG c. 1726*: f.53). He probably refers here to houses of music masters which were called 'schools' and which offered private, hourly tuition to individual students. The first 'public' music school in England was founded in 1822 (see Kassler 1972).

[86] In *Notes of Me* North describes his own difficulties in mastering 'the practical counting, which wee call keeping time' (ed. Jessopp 1887: 82).

[87] See f.26.

as when wee walk, run, strike, act with our fingers, or swing an arm, all run in equallity. And as for the arme in swinging, I shall appeal to it as governed by pendulum law.[88] Nothing unequall timed is pleasing, as if equallity had planted its capitall residence in our vitall facultys.

And[89]

30v / 41. The practis without helps difficult

This simple equallity is the root, out of which all the varietys of musicall time spring; and altho wee are so naturally addicted to it, yet in the artfull practise, no part is so hard to acquire with sufficient exactness, as that which belongs to time; and many, even of the professors, are not so punctuall at it as they should be. And nothing of failure is less excused then missing time; for the audience being once possest of a current measure, esteem it an injury to be interrupted by any fracture, and are apt to continue it in their minds in its due cours as it should have bin till turned adrift by the miscarriage, and they can get a new hold to conduct them.[90] This generall ineptitude proceeds from a misapplication of thought. For most expect that time may be judged by opinion, which hath nothing to doe in the matter, for who can opine the length of a day[,] hour[,] minuit or second, withou[t] attendance upon some reall cronometers, such as in musick must also be appealed to?[91] And the use of that means[92] is what is here proposed to be explained, as the best assistance to practise.

Al[l]

f.31 / 42. All varietys reducible to equallity

All expression of melody or tune is the result of distinguishable sonorus pulsations in a series continued, and all leaning upon some gross equallity of time. As when at distance wee hear a company

---

[88] I.e., having the properties of isochronism (see I.2.1. and n.9). In *MG c. 1726* North clearly states that 'all iterated agency of matter' is subject to the pendulum law, adding that 'as for the why, let the phisico-mathematicall gentlemen look out' (ff. 54v–55). For his own physico-mechanical account, see *TS 1728* (ff. 85–87v).

[89] MS does not pick up the catchword on f. 30v.

[90] In *MG c. 1726* North points out that 'the disorder by breaking time (as it is called) is least of any musicall miscarriage endured' (f. 55v). By this statement he means a 'fracture' in the beat or tactus. When time is broken, it must be healed again, a metaphor North uses when treating tempo rubato (see, for example, *Cursory Notes of Musicke* ed. Chan and Kassler 1986: 192, 219, 221).

[91] Most of the early musical chronometers consisted of a bullet tied to a string. For a discussion and illustration of these and other types, see Harding (1938) and Kassler (1979).

[92] I.e., unit note value.

dancing litle is perceived but equall timed stepps, and being present wee can scarce forbear pulsing the like, and the effect of art is onely diversifying these measures by affected subdevisions, which they call tunes, and those must not without great fault impeach the comon measure instituted for the whole. And these comon measures artists have subdevided onely in two manners, of which one is termed dupla or common time, the other tripla where three comes in the place of two upon one. The former is plain to be understood, the other is more intricate, and will occasion some nicer reflections.[93] I shall dispatch the duple first, becaus that is most generall, and the tripla will be found built up upon it.

43. The description and manner of time keeping
     It is necessary to all accounts and measures whatsoever that some defined quantity shall stand as a unit to be a comunis mensura★
                                                                          where

f.31v   / whereby all other homogene quantitys may be compared. So of time, when there is a certein duration prefixt, that by dupling and subdupling gives all other measures of that denomination, as in the way of increas [as] 1, 2, 4, 8, 16, 32 and of decreas as 1, 1/2, 1/4, 1/8, 1/16, 1/32. And it is found by experience that our active powers may execute these proportions readyer then any other whatsoever. As first[,] the unite most familiarly [known] by a pendulous motion of the arm may be iterated as often as wee pleas; and then if it be demanded to swing as fast again, which is dupling, it is easily done and continued as before, and so quadrupling and octupling one, after another. And in like manner it being demanded to swing less quick by one half, it is readily done, and so on as before subdupling and dupling gradatim;★ but as to 4 or 8 times as fast or slow it is not to be done saltuatim★ without the help of art. But to remove from one to 5, 7 or the like it is absolutely impossible, for in such attempts our active powers faile us, and the measures being thereby impracticable, would be offensive to all.
                                                                          Now

f.32   / 44. The estimates and values of time
     Now seeing that all distinction of time in musick is made by pulses successively, which may be taken separately or in some totum★ collected; it is contrived that the totums shall be distinguished by some manifest signall, whither by touch or (as in

---

[93] See ff.34–36.

plain-song) movement. And there is a gage whereby the performers may know whither accounts of their devisions fall right or
not, and these signalls allwais conclude an equall duration as prescribed;[94] which is called an whole time, and in the notation is
marked out by a line struck cross the scale, and that is called a barr,
and in comon time is noted by a ⌂ . There are markes for multiplying this called long, large, and breif, but being antiquated I forbear
to express them, and begin with the sembreif (or barr). I have
adioyned this sinoptick diagram,

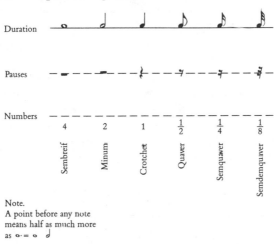

Duration

Pauses

Numbers

4   2   1 $\frac{1}{2}$ $\frac{1}{4}$ $\frac{1}{8}$

Sembreif   Minum   Crotchet   Quaver   Semquaver   Semdemquaver

Note.
A point before any note
means half as much more
as ⌂· = ⌂ ♩

to shew the names and values of all the notes, of which the crotchet
stands for the unite whereby the rest are

to

/ are to be measured, as in the diagram;[95] and the comon action of
the arme at length giveing the crotchet, all the rest will follow.[96]

45. The practise of multiplying and deviding times

For altho a beginner cannot imagin the length of a ⌂ at once, yet
if he strikes it at four pulses, he obtaines it, and these pulses may be
done so faintly, as not to be perceived, an[d] in a litle time it will be
done as well mentally, without any action at all; and that is the usage

---

[94] See ff.30–31.
[95] See f.32, Example 1.
[96] According to North, 'the reason why I pitch upon the crotchet to be the comon practick
measure, tho another might serve, is becaus according to the measure comonly used, a
crotchet movement is most easily kept steddy; for onely the strokes or swings of an arm,
will make the account, and that will be almost volens nolens by equalls' (*MG c. 1726*:
f.57v).

of t[he] best timists, who cannot undertake for a length without this artifice. And in the way of deminution the operation of the mind is no less needfull; for the hand or voice may fall into halving easily but not so easily into quartering and half quartering. To pass from ♩ to ♪ is no hard task, but from ♩ to ♪ scarce to be done without an act of the min[d], as for instance, these times: ♩ ♫♫. The expedient is this: ♫♫ ♫♫ [,] that is by breaking the crotchet mentally into semquavers, and then they goe on in series[;] so these notes[,] ♩ ♩ ♫♫♩ ♩ ♫♫ and the like of most ordinary occur- rence, [are][97] apt to puzle beginners. The practis may be thus: ♫♫♫ ♫♫ ♫♫♫ ♫♫. Numero[us]

examples

f.33   / examples of this kind might be brought to shew how difficult passages of time may become easy; but still the case is hard upon a sollitary practiser, who will certeinly loos his standard. Therefore as to time, no practise is usefull, or will ever make a consortier, but in consort it self. I need not stay to shew how the pauses are observed to a touch,[98] the whole being but a tacite accounting of the barrs, and lesser notes as they pass in the consort, wherein the same imployment of the mind gives the minutes.

46. Of varying the comon measure

It is not pretended here that the barrs which I have esteemed as totums,[99] should have a constant measure, for the unite or crotchet may be taken swifter or slower according to humour, and to say truth nothing is amiss when equallitys are fitly preserved. Masters may use their prærogative, and (as in some gavotts,) allow but two crotchets to a barr, and those very swift; so in doubling the o [they] make the o take the place of the unite, or crotchet[,] and measure the barr. These variations are misterys, for the use of them doth not appear, but masters having authenticated them, all is well.

I

f.33v   / 47. The use of signalls in time keeping

I mentioned the use of signalls, by which the performers regulate their totums and so keep together,[100] which in a consort of many, unless (as comon fidlers) they play by rote, and sometimes half

---

[97] MS has 'and'.
[98] I.e., by a touch of the finger.
[99] See f.32.
[100] See ff.26, 30, 32, 33.

asleep, cannot otherwise be done. But it is allwais fairer presented to the eye then to the ear, which (signall) els is not to be acted without some pulsation, and disorder. It is a wonder how the musick of our forefathers[101] was conducted, that had no barrs at all, and yet their consorts were solemne, of many parts, and full of restings but not given to catching* devisions. I guess that their movements were crotchety, which served to measure the longer notes; but now without barrs nothing is to be done. Those have occasioned the laying aside of the long marks of time, which are now exprest by numbers of ○ ○ ○, etc. the tale* of which answereth the barrs as they pass, but the pauses are still contracted, as ⟨figure⟩ . The old marks of comon time quickening, were C ₵ 𝄴 𝄵 . Now it is done by description, as adagio, grave, allegro, presto, prestissimo and for humour andante, ricercata,* affectuoso, manire-onico,* cantabile, and others dayly new, which need not be named nor interpreted, and this is all I shall say of comon time at present.

It

f.34 / 48. Comon time and tripla distinguisht by emphasis

It may be doubted whither in truth the tripla measures of time in reallity differ at all from dupla, or whither the seeming difference be not the result of emphasis, more then of proportion. For all the pulses are supposed to be equall, as a series of these sounds ♩♩♩♩♩♩♩♩ may be comon time, or tripla according to emphasis. For if with the duos,[102] the stroke falls a litle fiercer upon the first, and lighter upon the 2d, as they say of a foreward, and backward bow,[103] it is comon time, but if it falls hard upon the first, and slighter upon the second, and third, it is tripla. And as for the three against one, the same is found in comon time, as ♫♫ : ♫♫ which differs but litle from ♩ ♫ , or rather ♩. ♪♩ : ♩. ♪♩. Whereby the seeming want of tripla in the antique musick, which had no distinction of time but longum and breve, which was duple[,] is reconciled[,] for with a due

---

[101] '. . . musick of our forefathers': 'collections of musick no elder than Queen Elizabeth and since to the Resta[u]ration' (*MG c.1726*: f 63v).

[102] I.e., duplas.

[103] In instruments of the violin family, the down-bow is used for an accented beat (or part of beat) and the up-bow for unaccented ones. In instruments of the viol family, the strokes of the bow are in and out or, as Simpson expressed it, 'forward' and 'backward' (1665/ 1965: 2, 6, 7–9). These strokes are nearly equalized with respect to gravity and pressure, although the in-bow stroke is considered more naturally weighted than the out-bow stroke.

emphasis the ♫ made a dactyle as true as the tripla
♩. ♪♩ and may be so proved upon the first vers of Virgill.[104]
This hath made me suspect that if the cheif pulses of the sound, as
those they call barrs, (or when shorter are used

as

f.34v   / as such) it is not of great import how the breaking is managed,
provided the generall equallitys are maintained; on which account it
is that the capitall ma[s]ters in their performing, capreole* it in such
a manner as any one would think they kept no time at all, and yet
they never fail their gross measures.

49. The effect of emphasis

This that I call emphasis[105] prolongs and shortens notes, and
sometimes gives some paus which makes great distinction in time,
as of these   ♩ ♩ ♪ᵧ ♩ ♩ ♪ᵧ   that after the third note manifestly
casts the series into a tripla, which otherwise would run duple and
so when the tones vary as   ♩♩♩♩♩♩   they make a triple
account, for there is an emphasis at the beginning of every three, as
there is duple upon the first of every two, which is enough without
more to create the distinction, but when in tripla there is an
emphasis upon the first of two, it can scarce be knowne from
comon time as thus: ♩ ♩ ♩ ♩ ♩ ♩   etc. which in comon time is
♫ ♫ ♫ , and other like instances might be given. And in tripla
the subdevisions are duple, as also the ground on the oth[er]
sid[e][106] and when an emfasis, by a pulsation is forced

upon

f.35   / upon the ground notes so as to shew a tripla upon a tripla, it is a
constrained movement, and hath no vertue in the effect. And in a
word a tripla is an emphatick breaking the ground tones into 3 as the
comon time is into two, and wherein there are great libertys taken,
whilst the ground base moves equali passu,* and there is no rupture
or dislocation of the musicall current to check the attention and
satisfaction of the audience.

---

[104] Virgil (Vergil; Publius Vergilius Maro) (b. 70, d. 19 B.C.), Latin poet, wrote in
hexameters. In *MG c. 1726* (ff.61–61v). North refers specifically to the first 'vers' of the
Aeneid, as well as to the 'heroic tune' of the first *Eclogue,* for the latter of which he gives the
accents.
[105] See f.34.
[106] '. . . ground on the oth[er] sid[e]': 'the counter notes or base' (*MG c.1726*: f.62).

50. Tripla is but a manner of deviding upon equall times

Now laying aside all these speculations, wee condiscend to the plaine and comon notion, of 3 of one part against one of another, and the latter is comonly the lowest or base but it works all manner of ways, for there is no note in any part, but for humour it may be broken in 3 and it is a comon practise in compositions of late, to devide upon the base by duples and triples alternately without impeaching the steddy cours of the consort time, and it is marked onely by wrighting the figure 3 over the notes; but I medle no more with these capriccios. ⋆ The buisness here lyes chiefly among those triplas that are consigned to rule the whole peice and are indicated by a

proper

35v / proper mark at the entrance. The triplas now (whatever formerly was done) use the same caracters as the duple, onely for the most part a point is set afore sembreifs and cro[t]chets which turnes 2 into 3. But very often the base discovers no relation to tripla, but joggs on by even pulses, leaving partitions to the upper parts, which may act ad libitum by 2s or 3s so long as the equall steps of the gross tone are conserved.

51. The various triplas marked

It is impossible to make a diagram to express the various sorts of triplas that are used. They are all discovered to the performer by the entrance mark, which is very artificiall, and not by euery one understood. If the ○ or barr time is tripled by 3 minums there needs no more[;] but to write 3 for 3s, as many write is in that case improper, as will appear. [107] The manner and measures of triplas are so various, that without some direction it is hard to signallize them, for some times, a ○ or crotchet makes a barr, and sometimes the 3s are ♩s, ♩s, ♪s, or ♪s, and of them 3, 6, 9, or 12 to a barr, all which tending to confusion might breed much puzzle, if they had not this device to clear all

at

36 / at first. It's considered that the ○ contains 2 ♩s, 4 ♩s, 8 ♪[s], 16 ♪ [s], and then they take the number of the note, as 2 which signifyes [a] ♩, and 4 a ♩, and 8 a ♪, and 16 a ♪. Here is one figure to signifye the sort of note which is to make the barr; and this stands underneath; then the number of those that are to fill the time, that is

107 See f.36.

to be the barre, is wrote above with or without a litle line between as thus: 3/2 ♩ , 3/4 ♩ , 6/4 ♪ , 6/8 ♪ , 12/8 ♪ , 9/8 ♪ , and 3/8 ♪ . And for clearer explanation, I will bestow a scale upon each, and then the mistery will need no further key.

I must presume the masters have reasons for using these varyetys as they doe, but I cannot penetrate them in all. And particularly the ⅜: I have known that one of the swiftest movements and in another place grave as an adagio, but for what reason the same caracters are used to such different porposes, let the more skillfull answer.

f. 36v   / 52. [Of time in consort]

I have hetherto considered time in a musicall sence, with the usuall mensurations of i[t] but referred to single undertakin[g]s onely.[108] It remaines to consider the same in the practice of many undertakers in consort together; and that will admitt some further reflections; as that the nice measures in each part is not more

---

[108] See ff. 30–36.

considered then the company keeping together[,] the compassing which will allow libertys to be often taken by the particulars who may advance or relent a litle for[109] falling in with the rest.[110] And for this end, a new consort at sight (for practice reconciles all) requires a signall, not in gross by turnes or barrs onely but with some short expression of the unites, which by an artist is done by a slight★ of hand in the view of all, without which it is scarce like to succeed well, and the leader of the consort with a sort of favour★ upon long notes will intimate the time designed to the rest, especially at the entrance. As for chronometers by pendulum clock work [of which] some are so fond, viz. they are so very whimmish[,]★ that the success will not answer, but put more out then in.[111] And how should occasional shifting of time be catched, when time will be required to adjust the instrument? If such a device be good for anything, it is to regulate a private pra[c]tiser, but for consort [there is] nothing like a roll of paper in the hand of an artist; without nois and above board.

It

f.37   / 53. The key defined

It hath bin insisted that the septenary tones according to the scale, are fixed by a consonantiall relation to the first or leader (whatever that tone is) and by like relation of one to another.[112] The primary tone being prefixt[,] laying aside vocall syllables, and using (as, from henceforward I shall) only the letters, wee call it, (as hath bin hinted[113]), the key. And whither it hath the name of A, B or C, it is all one, for the proper consonances, and no other are attendant upon it. Whereupon the key in musick may be thus defined: the lower or leading tone of that scale which is chosen to determine the accordant notes of the following harmony. The word is often used loosly

[109] I.e., instead of.

[110] I.e., an 'elegance' or intentional 'error', perhaps of North's invention and, so, idiosyncratic (see *Some Memorandums, concerning Musick*: f.4v; *Notes of Me* ed. Jessopp 1887: 87; and *Cursory Notes of Musicke* ed. Chan and Kassler 1986: 279–80 (190:1)). Elsewhere, he writes: 'to my very great hazzard of reputation I have affirmed, that 2 violinos set to play the same lesson, if perfectly in tune to each other, it is better musick when one goes a litle before or behind the other, then when they play (as they zealously affect) to a touch together. For in that nothing is gott by the doubling, but a little loudness, but in the other way by the frequent dissonances there is a pleasant seasoning obtained (*MG c. 1726*: f.112v).

[111] A number of writers advocated the use of a pendulum for keeping time. Among these were Robert Boyle, Robert Hooke and Thomas Mace (see Kassler 1979: i/111–4; Kassler and Oldroyd 1983: 576–7; and Mace 1676/1968: 80–2).

[112] See ff.15–17.

[113] See ff.19v–20.

sometimes for the claves★ of instruments, and often declaring the
note of the scale, which is predominant in any peice of musick,
which may often change, but wee confine it striktly to the leading
tone, and doe not allow it to make any escapes for other porposes,
of any kind, whatsoever.

After

f.37v   / 54. Of accords according to the scale

     After the sound of the key note is determined[,] all the notes of its
proper scale follow in their order, and may be sounded either
ascending, or descending, untill the septenary scale either way is
exhausted. And then proceeding, the like notes recurre, and all the
variety is at an end, for octavarum eadem est ratio,★ as hath bin
observed.[114] Therefore I shall include all octaves in the consideration of the simple septenary. Wee shall have much to doe with
accords,[115] which word ordinarily means cosounding notes,
according to their places in the scale, but more striktly referred to
the key note. And these are tituled by the number of removes in this
manner.

	F	7th	
	E	6th	
Ascending	D	5th	
	C	4th	
	B	3d	
	A	2d	
1 . . . G . . . or key			
	2d	F	
	3d	E	
	4th	D	*Descending*
	5th	C	
	6th	B	
	7th	A	

As the accord G–B is a third, G–C a 4th, G–D a 5th, etc. ascending,
and so G–E [is] a third, G–C a fifth, etc. descending; and the manner
of these accords sounding is the same altho taken in any other place
of the scale as well as from the key[,] as, A–D or B–E ascending, so
F–C or E–B descending are fourths. But generally in musicall
accounts accords are taken from the lower note ascending with

unless

---

[114] See *T S 1728* (ff.131–131v).
[115] See ff.37v–56 *et passim*.

f.38 / (vnless the contrary is declared) the lower note as the leader of the scale, and the accords taken as derived upon that. It falls out that the accords descending are named a degree short of those ascending; for the scale is a septenary which will not be equally devided and the key note is numbred with the ascendants. So G-D rising is a fifth and falling but a fourth, and both ways meet in the octave D-D, as in the former scheme.[116]

55. Double accords ascending and descending
These consequences will be clearer explained by this scale,

which unites the accords rising and falling. Let the key note G be (obscurely) marked and all the scale notes plainely, and from the left to the right the accords ascendant appear, and reversly the accords descendant, and all by one and the same note. These are comonly denominated from the ascendants as if those were all single accords as they are figured, but in truth every sound is a double accord, one with the key and the other with its octave in this manner:
1}$^{2\ 3\ 4\ 5\ 6\ 7}_{7\ 6\ 5\ 4\ 3\ 2}$}8

38v / and so from the right to the left descending by a reverst process thus: 8}$^{7\ 6\ 5\ 4\ 3\ 2}_{2\ 3\ 4\ 5\ 6\ 7}$}1. These double accords inrich the sound as will be alledged when wee come to have more of them.[117]

56. Of intermediates and values of each accord
These [accords] taken as usuall singly, although derived upon the key note, and also others in the scale, which I call intermediates, as in the margin

A	C	
B	D	
C	E	thirds
D	F	
A	D	
B	E	fourths
C	F	
A	E	fifth

[116] See f.37v, Example 1.
[117] See f.46v, Example 2.

all being of the same denomination, have the like values, as to concord better or wors; which if I may venture to caracterise,[118] may be thus expressed, viz.:

G-g the octave, is (quasi) unison, without any advantage by sounding together, but loudness.

G-A the ♯2d carrys no ill sound, but in composition hath excellent propertys.

G-B the ♯3d a prime concord especially joyned with the fifth, as afterwards.[119]

A-C[120] the ♭3d the like but somewhat inferior.

G-C the 4th without offence; and much used in composition.

G-♮E⎱ the sixts flat and sharp some what inferior to their
G-♭E⎰ correspondent thirds.

f.39 / G-D the 5th the best accord and incident to every key[,] a distinguishing note, of which more afterwards.[121]

B-F[122] the flat 5th harsh, but usefull, and often elegant.

G-F the flat 7th includes the ♭5th and fairely accords with the key, 3d, and 5th [and] is frequently thereupon applyed.

G-♯G the first semitone, too harsh, and seldome used but in mixture for graceing, and the like of all other semitones, especially that between the ♭3d and ♯3d which is allwais insupportable.

57. Of accords that joyne well, or not

The comon tones are often permitted to sound together, but cautiously, and in consort, for being independent they are harsh, but not so as the semitones of the accords above. Some are permitted to joyn and others not, without incurring what is called discord, as G-B-D, the ♯3d, and 5th upon the key. These together are a consummate harmony, to which nothing can be added or detracted

---

[118] In *Musicall Recollections III,* North argues that the 'virtue' or 'morall caracter' of sounds derives from their 'materiall and disposition': 'I doe not mean of voices (which are of pure nature's provision). If the sounding instrument be not hard and elastick, the sound is dull as coming from rottenness and humidity' (f.15v). In *TS 1728* North provides a 'character' or 'account of the relish of the consonant sounds allowable in musick' (ff.113v–114). On the basis of the sound quality (i.e., more or less beating), he indicates how some intervals might be used to represent passions and affections. For example, he states that the semitone, 'the best and most flattering [of] sounds', 'is usefull onely in querelous cases, and much represents a sigh, but ordinarily serves as a stepp in the gradation of the scale when the key changes' (*ibid.*: f.114).

[119] See f.39–39v, 50.

[120] North cannot use G–B♭ here (nor in his description of the value of a flat fifth, B–F, on f.39), because he holds (f.41v) that 'the flat key note is not properly a key, but an intermediate of a sharp key'.

[121] See ff.40v, 50–50v.

[122] See f.38v, n.120.

to advance [the harmony], or rather without making it wors; for which reason it is called the full accord, and belongs to every scale, and so closely, that some have (fondly★) affirmed it to be included in every key note.[123] It will bear the ♭7th but as transient, and not for improvement.

39v / A-C-E, the ♭3d, and 5th is a compleat accord also, but inferior to the former. The difference is that here the ♯3d is superior, and before it was inferior,[124] that is, next the key note; so the 2 thirds have counter-changed scituations. And the lower note A obteins also to be called a key note, but with the addition of flat, becaus the flat 3d is next above it[.] And in contra★ to this, the other is called a sharp key, with respect to the ♯3d next above that. But the flat key is never termed the full accord nor is it properly a key, becaus the accord is among the intermediates, of which afterwards.[125]

$$\left.\begin{array}{c} \text{G-C-E} \\ \text{A-D-F} \end{array}\right\}$$ the 4th and ♯6th agree well,

but are not a compleat accord, becaus the fifth underneath brings it to the perfection of a full accord, as D-G-B by adding G underneath, and with the ♭6th [i.e. by adding g above] it is not much unlike.

$$\left.\begin{array}{c} \text{B-D-g} \\ \text{G-B-E} \end{array}\right\}$$ the ♭3d and the ♯3d[,] the sixt flat and sharp[,]

respectively are allwais, as thirds and sixes, well together, but not perfect accords, becaus the 3d underneath (added) gives them a perfection.

40 / G-D-F the fifth and the 7th is part of the full accord, topt with the 7th and cannot but sound well. But a transit is supposed.

G-C-D the fourth, and fifth, are not ill, but suppose also a change for the better, which comonly follows.

♯G-D-E the ♭5th and sixt, not ill but tending to change, for all harsh mixtures excite an expectation of some change for the better.

It is to be remembred that the values of these mixtures are shortly★ represented in abstracto★ and universally, but in formed

---

[123] Simpson (1667/1727: 34–6) was one of those who affirmed that every keynote comprehends the whole accord.
[124] I.e., on top . . . below.
[125] See ff.41–44v *et passim*.

musick will be as the cook's provisions for a choice dish of meat, or
the ingredients of a medicin, which put orderly together in composition, with salvo★ to the proper effect of each, shall acquire transcendencys not found in the simples;★ for so harsh sounds become
soft and mild, and those of most sweetness may be tempered, or set
off by contrarys[,] the contrivances of which will in some manner
be explicated, in what follows. [126] It must be again remembred that
all these notes simple and compound are derived upon the semitonian scale, [127] and that no sounds of any other scale or derivation will
by any means or in any degree joyne with them.

I

f.40v / 58. All concords extracted from the full accord
    I have already bestowed a short elogium of the full accord, [128] but
not as it deserves which I intend to supply here. And that will be
done by shewing that when the full accord sounds with its octave
every concord directly allowed in musick is heard and out of that
joynt sound of all the accords each may be extracted, as an automaton taken to peices and the parts exposed to examination. [129] As here

it is plain that in this sound all these accords are comprized, and
actually heard in the mixture; which is very wonderfull and rarely
observed. The next thing is to extract them, one or more, taking
and leaving as thought fitt.

    And first for the fifth, silence B and g and then the fifth G and D
sound pure.
    For the 3d sharp, silence D and g and it is hear[d] clear, viz. G
and B.
    For the ♭3d, silence G and g and that is heard B. [130]
    For the sixes[,] silence G, D[131] and you have 'em viz. B and g.

For

---

[126] See ff.40v–58v.
[127] See f.15, where North states that the derivation is from the septenary, not the semitonian,
    scale.
[128] See f.39.
[129] See I.2.1. The import is that complex ideas may be resolved into simple ideas, as North
    hints also at ff.46, 47 *et passim*.
[130] I.e., B and D.
[131] MS adds 'and g'.

f.41   / For the 4th[,] silence G, B[132] and then it remaines sounding with the octave as D-g.

I have not here medled with the ♭7th whose excellence lys in topping a combination of three 3ds tho it often in that manner attends the full accord, becaus it is not a regular but a contingent concord, nor [have I medled] with its inmate, the ♭5th called the tritone; but to discover where it (the tritone) lyes I may hint, that if the ♭7th be obscurely marked in the full accord as at F then silence all but B and F and then the tritone is heard.[133]

59. Of proper base notes and consort base notes

It is found that in consort, all accords whatsoever (in truth) have for base the key of the scale, but when intermediates happen, the lower note of the accord usurps the place of the key; and is termed the base of that accord. But the true base, that is the key note may resume its place, and whither so, or not, the musick is nearly the same. As if to the 4th D-g the key G is added, it onely joynes its complement the 5th underneath it. So if to the 6th B g the key G is added, it doth but joyne the 3d which is the complement; but the station* of the sound is either way the same. For this reason I am forced upon making a distinction between proper, and consort base notes; the former are key notes and the other intermediates.

41v   /Now wee must regard the place or station which these intermediate notes have in the full accord, and no concords can be put upon them but what the place allows; as if that proves to be a sixth and then if a 5th be imposed instead of a 6th the consort [bass note] turnes to a proper base [note], and the key is changed; as upon D; the scale allows a 4th and sixt, and upon B a 3d and 6th for so the order of the full accord hath predetermined. But a fifth upon either makes a change of the key. And whenever the proper base [note] is silenc't it may be rejoyned and both proper and consort [bass notes] without offence sound in consort together. And upon this scheme depends the knowledge when 6ths or 5ths are to be used, that is fifths when the base note is a key, or sixts when it is onely a member in its accords.

60. The nature of flat keys, and dependance on the sharp

It may seem an omission that the nature of flat keys hath not bin more considered, but the discours hath fallen altogether upon the

---

[132] MS adds 'and D'.
[133] See *TS 1728* (ff. 110–110v, 112–112v, 114).

full accord,[134] which in the scale is allwais a sharp key. As to that I may say once for all that thro out these papers, where flat keys have not bin (or shall) not be distinguished, the same method and rule will indifferently serve for both; but as to the state of the difference, which consists in the 3d next the note styled the key being sharp or flatt, I must observe that the flat key note is not properly a key, but an intermediate of a sharp key; and hath its place in the scale, which is the tone next above the leader. As in G key A and in C key D are the flatt key note. And becaus it falls

out

f.42   / out that the order of the scale allows a fifth, and then the ♭ 3d falls in of cours,★ this second tone (A) as also (D) hath the priveledg of being listed as a proper key [note] with the addition of flatt. And it appears to be a rule universall that whatever the order of the notes is, the fifth rising from any note of the base requires a ♯ 3d as from G the 5th is D to which the scale gives a ♭ 3d but the air makes for the ♯ 3d. The reason is that D there, and in all like cases is a key note and not a[n] [inter]mediate [note] and then the full accord that allwais attends a key gives the ♯ 3d. Therefore it is not strang[e] that the 5th of a flat key should have a ♯ 3d as well as from a ♯ key, to make for which latter the ♭ 7th from flatt turnes ♯ as F in G key. It is also to be observed that in the use of this flatt key, the scale in which it is seated, that is (for instance) of G is not disturbed by the dislocating any one note. But if you take C for the sharp key, and consequently D (the next note rising) for the flat key, the note B must be made ♭ which breaks the order of the scale of G. By this it appears that the scale of every proper [sharp] key includes one flatt key, which is the rising note and no more. But seeing every note may be flatted or sharped a semitone; it is ad libitum to make any key sharp or flat. As if B be reduced a semitone, and wrote ♭ then G becomes a flat key, but the comon scale is altered, and F the note next under G becomes the leader of the scale to both in regular order. And as the order of the scale C requires B to be ♭ so that of F requires E to be ♭ as appears in this

f.42v   / collation of the several keys

G 3d sharp   A 3d flat

---

[134] See ff. 37v–41v.

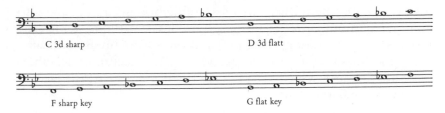

before mentioned,[135] and the proper scales that governe the stepps of them. And the like will fall out in every key, viz. that the next superior note maintaines the same gradation, and that every other note, taken as a key, breaks it; and it is remarkable that, lifting the key a 4th continually, at every remove one note further is altered, and no other, as from G to C flatts B and from C to F flatts also E, and from F to ♭B flats A et sic de ceteris;* as I think was noted before.[136] And this is the state of flatt keys, with respect to the various scales to which they belong; what the musicall influences may be, will be found elswhere.[137] But I may here advertise, that in the common language of the professors, no notice is taken of the relation of flatt keys, to the scale of the notes underneath, but they are joyned in the notes that bear the denomination, as being one and the same onely subject to the arbitrary power of making the 3d ♭ or ♯. As none says A in the scale of G but A with a ♭ 3d becaus it is in option to make the 3d ♯.

In

f.43

/ 61. A rule universall for change of keys

In musicall composition nothing imports more then a discretion in translating the ayre from one key note, to another; for the charming varietys which musick affords are cheifly derived there-upon. For a continuall sounding in the air of any one key is tiresome, and yet the shifting the key, if it be done improperly, is litle better then discord, till the remembrance of the former is worne out; for in musick antecedents and imediate consequents doe as it were coalesce. Now for the law of these changes, I must resort to our grand treasury of harmony[,] the full accord of the key of which the air is to be transferred to another. And from thence I extract this generall and infallible rule: the air of any key may pass immediately into that of any other key which is a prime accord,

[135] See f.25v and f.25, Example 1.
[136] See f.42.
[137] See ff.61v–62.

(that is a 3d or 5th) of the former ascending or descending; and into no other without large circuitions,* and interpositions, which the masters call preparation. Such preparation is sometimes necessary, and sometimes used for elegance, and often not needfull at all, altho there are formes* which usually take them[138] in. First, the change cannot immediately pass

into

f. 43v   / into any note which is not in the scale of the key you come from, as from G to ♯C. But wee reserve here, the consequences of many changes successive, which may carry the aire thro all keys, as elswhere [to be] shewed.[139] The air cannot pass from any note imediately into the 2d or 7th but by a circuition preparatory it may be done. So no cases are left to pass directly, but into some accord according to the rule, and of these matters I shall interpose a few observations.

62. Some reflections upon changing keys
    The reason of the rule is the concordance between the two notes a quo and ad quem,* supposing them sounding together; and alike successively. But there is a difference, for the change descending is much more naturall then ascending, for in the former, the key note stands a prime accord in the key into which the change is made; as from G to E is a ♭ 3d or a ♯ 3d is no solescism, being so well with E[,] so from G to C which is a fifth. Here preparation is perfectly useless; but sometimes by way of warning, or symptome of the change, some circuitions, or signalls will be made which may accordingly shew it is either at hand, or already done, and other varietys occur in changin[g] keys as

f. 44   / in the passing from C to A descending, which may be plain as in the (2d) instance,

or with a warning as by the 6th in the (3d) instance or implyed as if done, by the full 6th in the (4th) instance, or with some interposition, as in the first [instance], where B falls between. If that were a

[138] I.e., the circuitions and interpositions.
[139] See f.45 and Example 3.

short passing note, it takes no place in the harmony, but if it be, as here, held long, it must be considered it is a consort base, and the proper base [note], that is, E is shaddowed against it. And then the change is double, as here (5).

And by such interpositions when protracted, and diversifyed, as very often in composition ayerily contrived, a change of the key is perceived some time before it arrives. Here

by the fall of G a 5th to come to a cadence, there is a double change. For the note C by the rule may not turne into the next key note D and for that reason C is not a proper but a consort base note and mixt of C and A. And this is verifyed by the consort part, which is the accord both of C and of A in one sound which is hard to reconcile any other way[,] but more of this afterwards.[140] And the like methods

are

44v / are used to prepare, induce, protract, and adorne, the changes of keys ascending, but with a litle more circumspection becaus the note a quo doth not stand regularly in the accord of the note ad quem as it allwais doth descending. As the full accord ascending of E doth not take in C[,] so the full accord of G doth not take in C. But there are divers notes which are comon both ways, as will appear by the comparison of the full accords of C and E. But those of C and G are very divers, but from the affinity of those two key notes, each will nearly bear the accords of the other, of which complex cases further notice will be taken among the figurate passages.[141] But however the rule makes good the changes as well rising as falling, a temper may be added, (as) here.

140 See ff.51v–53v.
141 See ff.48v–58v.

(1) is plain, (2) with an interposing note D, which may be broke as at (3) and all (as many more instances might be given) for a more ayery change of a key ascending, which consortiers are well acquainted with, and may be called preparations. And the like is observable upon rising a fifth, as here,

which after the former needs no explanation. And then the whole scheme

f.45   / scheme of plain changes of keys in consort, according to the rule will stand thus;

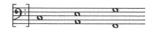

and the ayery dressing of them is left to the skillfull who will turne and disguise them many ways, but thro all the misty variations the rule will be discerned to take place, and if any scituation of notes seem to inferr otherwise, they will be readily resolved into it. As here;

the change may seem, from C to B, but in truth C is not the key becaus it is covered with a 6th, but A is it. And the change is legitimate from A to E and from E to B, and these relations to proper bases are allwais to be had in mind, tho not expressed. And the notes of the base that make the change must allwais be proper, and not consort notes, as the thing it self speaks. It will be remembred that changes into sixes are regular, becaus they are alternative of 3ds, as fourths are of fifths.[142] And it will readily appear that this rule of change will warrant a walk of the aire by note after note all over the scale of tones and semitones;

for if each note sounding is taken for the key [note] in its turne, and the removes not transgressing the rule, there

[142] See ff. 38–38v.

.45v   / will be no fault in the variety, provided a discretion is used in giving time for each key to hold the aire compleat, that another may not succeed before the former is well worne out; and also avoiding affectation and extreams, and remembring that no change of a key in possession is more gratefull, then that which returnes back into the same, which is allmost essentiall in cadences, as here.

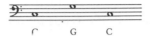

It is observable, that these removes of the key skipp over all intermediate notes, as must happen passing from concord to concord, which makes some authors say that the base parts affect to move in that manner, and the superior parts gradatim, but no reasons are given for it.[143] It is obvious therefore and I need not open the large prospect [t]here is of variety in musicall composition. For when the comon dispositions of the accords used in these transits of the air from note to note (of which more afterwards[144]) are knowne and familliar, as also the comon flourishing upon a key,[145] there is a fund provided for a continuation of ayre without limitation; and that is a subject most to be recomended to the speculation and practise of every one that courts composition.

f.46   / There are some passages that seem to impeach the rule of keys changing, as here

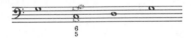

from C to D but I have further to answer that altho C may be (as a full close) a key note, it is not so here becaus it requires (not a fifth but) a 6th, viz. A, to cover it, and so is a consort note, as if A underneath had bin put in its place as is here shaddowed in the lines; and then the change is regular. But say that G should continue; that would not excuse A, which will continue also, and be mixt with it, as the comon practise in that case is. The like will fall out descending, from C to B 3[d]♯, but I answer the same that C is not a key but a consort note and carrys a 6th. And if the complement is added as at

[143] E.g., Simpson (1665/1965: 17, 1667/1727: 38–40, 127–8).
[144] See ff.46–48v, 50.
[145] See ff.47, 80–81v.

A below, even that is no key but a consort note and requires a ♉[,]
that is ♯ F as all composers know and is here shaddowed.

* MS has 7/8

These are mixt cases and being resolved into their elements will be
plainely understood, so the rule holds inviolably.

63. Of maintaining the key
   Now to finish this doctrine of accords wee must take in view
againe the key and its whole scale, and say it consists of that note
and its full accord, as G–B–D–g and the rest intermediate or consort
notes, as A, C, E, F. The

accord

f.46v   / accord notes (as I touched before[146]) are to be covered just as they
stand in the scale, as here

sound C in full accord and silence the key note, C; then E stands
with its proper harmony[,] the 3d G and sixth C, so when E is
silenced G stands with its proper accord the fourth c. Therefore
when the air of the key is to be preserved, it moves by or thro these
accords, els where a 5th is placed the key is changed; as at G. As for
the intermediates,

they are all in accord with the key or its accords, but those descending, as A is a 5th to D the fourth below; B [is a] ♯ 3d above the key
note; C is a key it self (having a 3d and 5th above it); E is a ♯ 3d above
C. F begins a different scale having B and E flatt. Now take the 8
notes as a lesson, to have the proper accords put upon it. And they
will be the same, as if composed upon the proper base note shadowed below, whereby it appears that all consort bases, have the
proper bases imaginarily underneath them; which may be produced
in sound or not without changing the air or rule of concords. And

146 See ff.40v–41v.

presupposing a due intelligence of these methods, no one can be at a loss in placing proper accords to any base lesson that can be (skillfully) proposed.

But

f.47 / But if these long notes were broke, diversifyed and adorned as consorts comonly are[,] it would appear to what plaine principles flourishing musick may be reduced, but of those matters afterwards.[147] But one thing will be seasonably advertised here, that there is a very great difference in the composition upon quick notes, and slow; which gives occasion to distinguish passing, from holding, notes. The latter, as in the foregoing instances,[148] dwelling long on the same tones, require accords to every note, but if they move swift, as in passing, many will fall under one accord, without altering, which is the case of most devisions, and what Mr. Sympson calls breaking of notes on a ground; of which no example is needed here.[149]

64. Observations of consecutions

I proceed next to consider the consecution of accords. Authors have distinguisht between the perfect and imperfect accords,[150] and consecution is denyed to the former, viz. unisons, 8ths and fifths becaus they are too luscious,[151] but it is free to the imperfect, as the two thirds and [two] sixes. In this scheme there is litle truth or reason, for 3ds are as perfect in their kind as any and the rule of perfection ought to be when they

are[152]

47v / admitt of no complement to mend them, so that if any are imperfect[,] it is the 2 sixes and the fourth, the former[153] admitt

---

[147] See ff.80–81v.

[148] See f.46v, Examples 1 and 2.

[149] Christopher Simpson (b. *c.* 1605, d. 1669), composer, viol player and writer on music, published two treatises, both of which North owned and studied (see *Notes of Me* ed. Jessopp 1887: 82–3). In his treatise on extemporized 'division' above a ground bass on a bass viol, Simpson defined division as 'the Breaking, either of the *Bass,* or of any higher Part that is applyable thereto' (1665/1965: 27). For North's examples of division, see *M G c. 1726* (ff.98v–99v).

[150] E.g., Butler (1636: 48–9) and Simpson (1667/1727: 32), who classed major thirds as imperfect or secondary consonances. North discards the traditional division of consonances into perfect and imperfect or primary and secondary, preferring a classification of them by degrees 'more or less' perfect (see above I.2.2.).

[151] E.g., Descartes (tr. Brouncker 1650/1653: 48–9); for a similar argument, see Simpson (1667/1727: 95).

[152] MS does not pick up the catchword at the beginning of f.47v.

[153] I.e., sixths.

lower thirds to be added, and the other[154] a fifth. Now unisons and octaves may follow, for what cls is doubling of parts? But so long as a better account is to be made by dispersing them, that is to be done, becaus an artist ought to make the best of his accords. But the consecution of fifths carrys great inconvenience, for every graduall succession changeth the key and most improperly, which dislocates and confounds the harmony[,] as hath bin already explained.[155] It is certainly best to intermix accords better and wors successively as after sweet to have sour, and è contra,* whereby the harshest sounds in the scale are allowed if better may follow. But as to the prohibited consecution of fifths, it must be understood between single parts and when the key is not to change. But as the key with its full accord, may change at every stroke, there must be a consecution of fifths accordingly, but then a discretion is to be used, and not to place the full accord notes in the same order, but if in one the 5th is above the 3d[,] in the next the 3d ought to be above the fifth. The 3ds and sixts have a variety of larger and lesser which much recommends them to a continued succession.

f.48   / There is a contrivance for consecution of 5th[s], and so as shall not be faulty as here ascending; the like may be done descending but nothing near so well.

I shall conclude this head with an example of key notes, all carrying 5ths marshalled with advantage, both upon the scale all together and also seperated, after the way of a score.[156]

---

[154] I.e., the fourth.

[155] See f.43.

[156] That North wrestled with the problem of how best to present practical demonstrations is clear in the penultimate draft of *MG 1728*, where he writes: 'It seems an incumbrance to load pages with diagrams of examples, but since it is found in most arts the hopefullest way of comunicating notions of things out of comon observation here[,] wee recurre to them and it is in truth an artificall language wherein musick may claime the same priveledg as other arts. And whoever is minded to study what he is about, will be thankfull for such a dialect. . . . And finding the need of such schemes as these to grow upon me, I have sometimes deliberated in what manner to dispence them; whither by expressing all the accords upon one set of 5 lines, which may be done very intelligibly, and so it is most prompt for perusal and examination, but then to the eye it seemed cluttered and confused; or whither by way of comon score, distributing the full accords

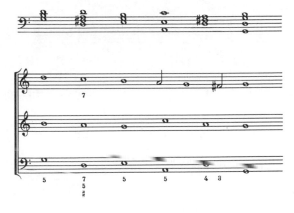

This latter is necessary when the decorum of the parts is to be shewed, as here in the first treble, the 2d note is a ♭7th to the base, which is better then any other accord that could be taken in that place, for it falls moving in thirds with the other treble, and that is allwais gracefull, besides[157] the proper elegance of that discord (as it is called) in that place. It is as I sayd[158] onely the accords and not the decorum of the parts that can be shewed fairely crowding the scale.

‾.48v   / 65. An example of a counterpoint[159] consort
    I have hitherto dealt altogether in plain notes of equall time, and [in] counterpoint,[160] in which a beginner better apprehends what is to be done, then by subdevided, and broken parts, the former understood soon draws the rest. And 2 up[p]er parts is more instructive then one, for it furnisheth a copia,★ and affords a choice, and helps to improve a single part of which I shall discours in particular afterwards;[161] in the mean time I have subjoyned [see p. 152] another counterpoint of 3 [parts]; with a litle more ayre, and change of key.

f.49   / 66. The method of instructions here conteined
    I have observed of authors designing to instruct the art of musick, that they affect★ to prescribe rules, by which a learner is to

    into severall parts set one over another as the usuall way is; this is more difficult to examine, but it is mighty advantageous, in shewing how single parts higher and lower are to be contrived; and being unwilling to part with any of these conveniences, I have thought fitt sometimes to use both ways' (*MG c. 1726*: ff.89–89v).

[157] I.e., in addition to.
[158] See above.
[159] I.e., note against note.
[160] See ff.12–36v ('equal time') and 37–48 ('counterpoint').
[161] See ff.60–66v.

G key   E key   C key

5   6   7   5   6   7   5   6   7

*

C   G   D   G

4   3

* MS has D♯

square all his proffers at composition; as the caracters of his concords, and which may goe before, after, or together; what passages
are legitimate, and what not; how to prepare, bind,* and let goe
discords with many other incidentall directions, all which are as it
were ex lata sententia,* how to act, but not why, nor imparting any
knowledg of the vertues of the musicall scale, or the nature, and
importance of keys, with their changes and comixtures, all which is
very proper in a view of teaching onely; and is the peculiar method
of grammer, and leaves intelligences to more philosoficall undertakers. And among those I am content to be listed, having no aim
but admitting what I find practised according to rules, or otherwise
with authority, to discover the common principles upon which all
depend, and from thence to resolve all that seems misterious in
musick, to the end that learners, and other persons that are curious
may understand the art

                                                    intus

.49v / intus et in cute;★ so that none of our saltinbanco★ pretenders may set up for conjurers, and value themselves upon more profound science then belongs to their profession. And accordingly I have endeavored to establish the authority of the single gamutt,[162] and the leading notes wee call keys,[163] and must further recommend the speculation of them, which are the helme of composition, for otherwise the vertues of musicall sounds cannot be knowne or found out. There are and ever were imitators, servile persons, who after patternes cutt out some work; but what is that to the undertakings of such as know all their patternes and skillfully advance upon them? The authority of these is the assurance of a beginner, but such must know that there is not any musicall sound that hath not relation to some key [note]; and whoever attempts musick must have actually or habitually a regard to that which is proper to every touch, els his success will be a sort of nonsense, as all contingent musick is. And in this, none are more concerned then the thro-base practisers, for their work is expresly referred to keys, and is but an exercitation★ of the variety of them. And now I shall advance in futher inquest of the same subject.

Hetherto

f.50 / 67. Of intermixtures of keys

Hitherto of single keys, with their full accords;[164] wee have next to consider what will be the effect of divers keys with their accords all or some of them sounding together.[165] It will be expected that generally such will prove no better then harsh confusion, and discord. But since there is a difference of keys, some being neerer related in harmony then others, it is reasonable to expect, that in mixtures the neerest should have the best effect; and those are the accord notes of any key [note] used as keys with certein of their accords, and joyned with the principall[,] and, of them, the best and neerest in accord is the fifth superior or inferior. As for instance G and D or G and C are neerer, and sounded full together are less resented then any other notes whatever[,] so sounding with G. For G changeth into C, or into D, and returnes, (which are the cadences or closes afterwards explained[166]) more harmoniously then into and from any other key notes, and these accords bear comixture the best of any. Now se[e]ing there will be disorder in these mixt

[162] See ff. 16–22, 25v.
[163] See ff. 37–48v.
[164] See ff. 37–49v.
[165] See ff. 50–56v.
[166] See ff. 51v–53v.

sounds more or less I will consider and extract that which I think hath least or which least needs to be retrenched.

68. The key with its fifth

And that for the reason given[167] will fall upon the fifth, and its accords for if there be any asperitys of sound upon the intermixture, the great harmony of the

two

f. 50v   / two prime keys will quallifye it, or rather make the clashings turne to ornament. And as they are ordinarily managed, exalt the harmony to a pitch [that] may be called sublime and so be a means, in a fair understanding to resolve the misterious use of discords as they are called in musick. In such cases the time or continuance of these sounds is considerable, for none but the legitimate concords will hold well sounding continually. And that priveledg is denyed to mixtures, which must cease in a reasonable time, or become offensive; and somewhat more orderly must succeed in their room. And since disorders are usually found more with the many, than the few, I will begin to instance in the most single case. And first of the ♯7th which with the key makes a very harsh sound, but by way of lift into the octave, is an elegance scarce ever omitted, as here.

Not   But

This is the foundation of the grace they call the beat up and is so qualifyed★ becaus it is a ♯3d to the fifth above the key, that is a member in the accord of D when G is the supposed key, as here for better demonstration is shaddowed underneath. And there is a

won-

f. 51   / wonderfull effect when this mixture is made with the accords full, as organists frequently shew at the entrance of a voluntary, for the fi[e]rceness of the 2 accords of G and D in conjunction creates an amazement, which excites an attention, in order to be aware of what is coming, and then the notes of the accord key being dropt one after another leavs the accords of the proper key in full and clear sound more pleasing then if it had never bin so embarassed. This grace may be thus expressed;

[167] See above.

nay more then this, the affinity of these 2 accords G and D is so great, that they may alternately change bases without offence; as here is noted;

for at a litle distance, these sounds mix, and yet [there is] no confusion.

69. The composition of the ninth
   And in like manner wee derive the vertue of the noble second or rather ninth[;] that is, of the note A upon G when that [G] is the key;

and it is a fifth upon the 5th. Or G–D is a fifth and D–A is also a fifth, that is the best accord of the best accord of the key both

soun-

51v   / sounding together. And in comon allegro musick, it is very often made to strike point blank upon the key, or any other note that hath place as such, which is frequently met with in Corelli.[168] But it is a perpetuall attendant upon cadences, for none come foreward without a clash of the key note and 2d or some octave of it. And the full composition of a cadence is a mixture of the key note and its fifth, and the capitall accords of them, as here,

with some notes in obscuro, ★ but plainer in the next,

---

[168] From their first appearance in England, the sonatas of Arcangelo Corelli (b. 1653, d. 1713) became the model for teaching composition until well after North's death (see Hawkins 1776 rev. 1853/1963 and Kassler 1979: ii/826 *et passim*).

where upon the cadence note D there sounds G, which is the key, and ♯F which is an accord of D, which kind of passages are termed binding, or sincopation, and are all no other but mixing of notes or accords so as to make a distinction of better and wors sounds to succeed each other.

70. Mixtures about cadences

There are other manner[s] of coming to cadences thro intermixtures which (as I hinted[169]) the masters call preparation and are an addition to the harmony, but not incident to all cadences of which the cheif may be as well plaine as prepared. The other instance I [shall] give[170] will be when the base falls a fifth

and

f.52   / and so comes up to the cadence note. This will bear as violent mixtures as any case whatever. The comon accords usually applyed are these,

but the next passage is more elegant,

and more apparently demonstrates the reconciling vertue of harmonious mixtures then any other, for here is 5th, ♯7th, and 9th all sounding and in a holding manner together, that is the full accord of the key upon the fifth below. There is another mixture of accords which may be either single or double. The upper is marked 9 8, and hath a great esteem in consort, thus (1)

<hr />

[169] See ff.43–44.
[170] MS has '⟨shall⟩ gave'.

and the lower as at (2) and both together in consort as at (3). And this may be carryed on to introduce a cadence as at (4), when notes as at (5) move in the proper air of the key, and of the accords, tho thro the harshest sounds, arising by comixtures of them, but continually comuting★ with better, will prove

an

f.52v / an exaltation of the harmony, as will be found by these notes,[171] and others of like importance which I shall exhibite,[172] and if protracted and broken with art, will make curious passages not seldome met with in consorts. I cannot pass by this schematisme, or (if you pleas) preparation for a cadence [note], which is pure Itallian, and not many years since unthought of in England (thus)

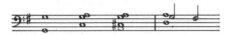

wherein it is to be observed that A (commixt with G) is a sixt upon C and the G also a ♭5th upon ♯C which supposeth a proper base wanted, and that is the lower A as here is shaddowed, and reconciles the mixture; making what seemed crabbed more harmonious. And this passage which was touched before[173] hath a futher complement; as when the parts fall so that a ♭5th is to meet a ♯3d, the former shall hang back half the time, and have a further mixture as is marked here.

No musicall scheme occurrs more frequently nor carrys a better air then this, and the holding the fourth, is so engaging and constant, that a skillfull player without any hint will use it. But it is expected the wrighting should express it least the master intend somewhat els.

Hereby

f.53 / Hereby it appears that the sincopations which authors propose about the cadence [note], is nothing else but a jangling of the accords of the fifths on each side of the key with the accords of that

---

[171] See f.52, Example 3(5).
[172] See below.
[173] See f.52, Example 1.

and of one with another comonly concluding with the flat 7th. And those notes single make a ground upon which most legitimate variety might be shewed.

And it is obvious how much melody of single parts, as well as consort, is drawne from these passages; wittness the arpeggio, which is the imperfect ape of consort.

71. Of the semicadences

There is another sort of close, which is usually called the half cadence. One manner is very solemne and often concludes grave musick; and it is onely by returning from a close [note] to the cadence note back again, and ending with a short flourish thus.

But the ordinary half cadences are when the base falls downe slowly from the key to the cadence note, and the 5th held on breaking onely a 7th upon the last note thus.

The midle part attends in plain counterpoint 3ds. This example is in a sharp key, and the 7th is sharp; it will be found that the notes are
resolvable

f. 53v   / resolvable into an whole cadence, by supplying the proper base in the room of the consort base as is there obs[c]urely hinted[174] but here

---

[174] See f. 53, Example 3.

more distinct. But the half cadence is of great use in musick, where the bases are more consort then proper. In a flat key the semicadence is wonderfull solemne, and is perpetually used in adagios, and moves thus,

with the 3ds attendant. I doe not find that these notes will admitt of any resolution, for they lye in order of the key descendant, unless D were, as a proper base[,] put in the place of F, but that would make Bb and so tend to a change of the key, to prevent which F the 3d upon D is made sharp, as (concerning flatt keys) was hinted.[175] But this semicadence hath found another come off, much in fashion among the Itallians, and was found out by accident, no ordinary cours of musick leading to it.

It succeeds well, but best with voices, becaus it carrys somewhat passionate, or sigh* with it. After all the semicadence hath so much authority that being absolutely harmonious, it comands the time[,] and performers are (as it were) agreed to hold longer upon it then the stated time requires.

Having

f.54   / 72. The manners of working upon the scale

Having undertaken to exemplifye divers schematismes or passages in musicall composition, which occur frequently and bear a good share in many consorts,[176] I shall proceed and display some more of them, and first of a kind I reserved to say a litle more of, which is the tormenting* the scale notes. There is a principall use of harsh notes in the discent of them, which I shall express plain, altho the masters disguise the matter with affected breakings and devisions. The nature of this passage

* MS gives a barline after the second crotchet
† MS has a semibreve

175 See ff.41v–42v.
176 See ff.51v–53v.

is pure mixture of better and wors alternately in consort, but tends
to no elegance or rapture, and the next

[tends] less, and [is] much rarer used. The next example

is of the same notes rising, which hath bin touched upon already, [177]
but is here more full and compleat. I know not whither
all these notes will be allowed of by crittiques but I am sure out of
them might be rambled★ a lively consort. But to shew how the scale
may be wrought to the

porposes

f. 54v   / porposes of musicall air, I subjoyne a set of descending notes
broken into fourths and fifths. And to avoid clutter I have put 3
consort parts upon them.

This may be called a consort of cadencys, which used to be regarded
for the wonderfull contrivance, when nothing is so trite as a ♭7th
upon the base rising a fourth and sinking a fifth, for which reasons
have bin given, [178] but this scheme hath spa[w]ned another, much
in use among composers and is a good help at need when better

---

[177] See f. 52, bass line of Example 3(5).
[178] See f. 48.

invention failes. The comon direction is in these cases to use 3ds and
sixts alternately, but se[e]ing it is not shewed how the notes and the
accords grow out of the notes of the plain scale; I have shaddowed
he[re]

the former base notes for a clearer illustration.

Out

f. 55   / Out of the same fountaine the great Corelli hath drawne a sublime
passage which he not seldome makes use of, and it is this, in 3 parts.

I have put them also distinct, and in the base cliff, for ready
comparison, but the 2 upper parts in consort should stand an octave
higher. And if any learner would well observe Corelli's opera
consorts,[179] no instruction for figurate musick would be wanted.
In the meantime let it be observed that halving notes one upon
another, avoids counterpoint and is perpetually usefull or rather
gracefull, in consort.

73. The like upon the semitones
    There is another scematisme much in use, which I may call the
semitonian rather then, as most of the masters improperly style it,

[179] *Sonata a tre*, Op. 1, Rome 1681; *Sonata da camera a tre*, Op. 2, Rome 1685; *Sonata a tre*, Op.
3, Rome 1689; *Sonata a tre*, Op. 4, Rome 1694; *Sonate*, Op. 5, Rome 1700. In Henry
Playford's 1697 *Catalogue of the last thirty years' Musick Books* (BL Harleian MS 5936: no.
145b), Corelli's Op. I–IV were offered 'printed or prick'd fair'. And in the spring of 1700
John Banister, the younger, then living at Brownlow Street, Drury Lane, issued to
subscribers Op. I–V.

the cromatique,[180] and it is at the base rising and falling by
semitones. And in the fabrick of these the onely care and circumspection is to discerne the proper keys to which the notes belong. For
it proceeds in continuall change; and then the composition is as
familiar as upon any other

notes

f.55v   / notes. I have added onely a single superior part, to avoid confusion, but that demonstrates the proceding as well as more. And
underneath I have marked the proper base notes as they fall sharp or
flat.

The next is the like descending.

* MS has D♭

These are difficult* notes but such as in these gradations must be
made use of for the extracting harmony out of such disorder;
seldome or never to be used but in representation of some passions,
and in such extraordinary cases allmost any thing suitable will pass
muster.

[180] I.e., North's instrumental scale which he distinguishes from the ancient chromatic genus.

74. Divers passages

I shall take notice of a few more singular passages,[181] before I come to composition.[182] As here

the first hard note is resolved into the lower D (obscure) with a 7th and is a charming accord. The other falling on a fifth was not allowed by our former English masters; they called

it

f. 56   / it dashing a 5th in the face.[183] But the fullness of harmony which it brings justifies it, but more the authority of Corelli who perpetually in his full consorts makes use of it. There is another accord properly en passant, but will not bear holding a long space, expecting to conclude in a 3d and fift[h]. The mistery of this accord is resolved by the G (faintly) added below, for that speaks it a plain 3d, 5th and ♭ 7th cadencing in C.

The Itallians use very much a querelous sort of cadence working with a semitone on each side of the key. This hath place onely in a flat key.

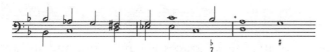

* MS has barline before the final G

The first barr is a mixture of consort upon 3 notes[,] ♭ B, C♭, D♯ and all in order thro ♭ E and C♭ to a cadence in G. There are not many such passages as these nor are they so useful in consort upon any account as to adorne cadences, which seem allwais to be persued and at last acquired thro difficultys. Therefore they should be used sparingly and upon occasion and not as some doe for ostentation of skill, like those, who in speaking affect hard words.

It

---

[181] See below and f. 56.
[182] See ff. 59–81v.
[183] E.g., Morley (1597: 75), who wrote about *'hitting the eight on the face'*.

/ 75. Of graces, and 1. tremolous

It is not amiss to say something of the graces added to musicall tones, by the dexterity of the performer either with voice, or instrument, becaus it is a sort of application of what hath bin held forth relating to accords and the mixtures of them.[184] And I must say that the practice of gracing, is the practise of composition, and without skill in the latter, the other will never succeed. Graces are comonly distinguisht into smooth and tremolous.[185] I shall have litle to doe with the latter becaus it is as I say'd[186] wholly a dexterity which words will not express, and onely imitation can acquire. But thus much may be alledged, that every tremolo★ is a mixing (in sound) of 2 notes, which will be well quietly together. Therefore it must be considered whither the commixt notes are in good accord or not; if so[187] they sound hard. The shake a litle softens them on this account. The joyning the key with the half note underneath is good, and called a beat up, becaus that (as I sayd before[188]) is a ♯3d to the fourth below. And if the accord of a cadence is mixt with a sixt it is good[,] for the cadence bears either a 5th or 6th and not unhappyly both. Therefore it is of universall regard in tremolous gracing to observe the

accords

/ accords, and touching onely what are legitimate. It is very dark work to describe these matters without some reall expression, therefore I have bestowed a scale upon them.

The comon fault of these graces is confusion, and so loosing the tone. Organs, harps and harpsicords succeed best becaus the sounds are stablisht, els the failing to touch them strong, and true hath that inconvenience; and at best the decor★ of them at a moderate distance is lost, therefore they are like lute lessons[,] a chamber elegance onely, otherwise the mixt sounds almost plain are more

---

[184] See ff. 37v–56.
[185] For a more detailed 'anatomy' of graces of the voice and hand, see *MG c. 1726* (see also *MS Frag*: ff. 62–65v). North seems to have had considerable difficulty in finding names that corresponded to particular graces, as a comparison of the *Grammarian* texts indicates. In some cases he tries various different names; in other cases he relies on a description.
[186] Missing from this text.
[187] I.e., not.
[188] See f. 50v.

effectuall. Perhaps it may be asked why shaking a 3[d] or any other accord is not good. The answer is easy, viz., becaus the consonance is lost, the sounds not having time to joyne. One great infirmity of the comon trill is, that according to the talent of the performer it is in time swift or slow allwais alike. Old Nicola Matteis was reputed to have no trill, and the reason was that in the grace of his play, he conformed to, and subdevided his time according as it was in the measure of the notes.[189] But of all these tremolous graces none succeeds

so well

57v / well as the wrist shake upon a violin, and the close shake upon the violl[,] for that doth not disturb the tone, of which the ultimate perfection is, to begin slow, and with a waver swell to the height, and then in like manner decay, and ceas.[190]

76. Smooth graces

Smooth graces are nothing but an extemporary acting [of] the artificiall improvements of harmony, such as I have before represented,[191] and are the elements of the sublime in composition. Scollars are taught them, but the adept, whose ears instruct them what accords reigne at present, and what are like to follow, ought to conforme their manner of handling accordingly. As in a flat key to slurr up to the 3[d] which done by the degrees of the scale, connect[s] the notes almost in consonance [as in] Example 1;

[189] Nicola Matteis (fl. *c.* 1670–*c.* 1702), Italian composer and violinist, was resident in England before 1671 (see f.140 and n.485). North is one of the principal sources of information about this musician, from whom he appears to have learned about bowstrokes on the violin. A detailed comparison of Matteis's printed works with North's comments about performance practice on the violin could be revealing. For example, Matteis used 'pointed notes', that is, notes in dotted outline, 'for Masters that can touch two strings for want of a second Trible' (see Tilmouth 1960). The same orthography was used for different purposes by the amateur violinist and composer, Francis Roberts (1692) and by North himself.

[190] The 'wrist shake' and 'close shake' refer to the left-hand vibrato, whereas the 'ultimate perfection' seems to be what North elsewhere calls the 'swelling wavee' or 'waived' grace (*MG Frag*: f.64 and *MG c. 1726*: f.111v): 'as when a long note is to be sounded, beginning as from nothing, and gradually swelling till it comes towards the loudest, and then waived (not as the beats of a drum, but as a bow of a tree waiving in the air, to and fro, and then failling by degrees like dying, into nothing which resembles distance, approach and departure[)]. This is the supra-philomelian sound which instruments of the bow and inflation may present, but the clavicalls cannot come up to, and how much is a trill inferior to this grace I need not expose' (*MG Frag*: ff.63v–64). North does not distinguish adequately between ornaments and bowstrokes, because he treats both as elegances or graces of the hand; moreover, in this text he uses the term 'tremolo' to refer to a class of ornaments ('tremolous' or 'curling' graces) as well as to a bowstroke (see f.72v, n.240; f.73, n.244).

[191] See ff.37–56.

* MS may have ♪.

and so from a sharp key, slurring up to the 3d and so to the fifth in such a manner as the notes shall seem to joyne in the full accord

for the reall sound as well as the memory continue one into another, and make a full accord, as in the 3[d] example.[192] And it is next to a rule

not

f. 58   / not to rise a 3d without a faint touch of the intermediate [note], and so descending[,] allwais emphasing the accords for that distinguisheth the nature of the notes, and [the] air of the key, which ought allwais to be observed, as in Example 1.[193]

But a competent skill will authorise such a passage as in Example 2.[194] And numberless instances might be given of their libertys, which belong to every performer of cours. For that reason masters are infinitely to blame that print these graces with their musick, which is an afront to an ordinary player, who may justly say, did not I know that? And by this means they make puzle and confusion in the notation. The elder Itallians in their finest cantatas have expres't no graces, as much as to say[,] whoever is fitt to sing this, knows the comon decorums. And in generall it is enough to say that it is the habit of a good performer, to express the harmony of the key and proper gradations of the scale, and he doth it without thinking which is enough to say of smooth gracing. It would be endless to call in all those elegant

turnes

[192] See f. 58, Example 1.
[193] MS has 'Example 3'.
[194] See f. 57v, Example 2.

f.58v / turnes* of voices and instruments[,] which are taught by the Itallian masters (and perhaps outdone by the English Banister[195]) [and] accounted glorious ornaments, and to subject them to a resolution. They are such as I may terme curling graces,* and are applyed often at cadences, and other principall passages, resembling a neat lesson contracted with a soft slurre more or less as there is occasion or time to lett it in. These are shewed as fine things neer [at] hand [in] solo[s], but have no use or effect at [a] distance or in consort, and for that reason the best masters in such cases decline them, and sound plain. Some presumer hath published a continuall cours of this sort of stuff in score with Corelli's solos, and is thereby intituled onely to a tolle for his reward;[196] vpon the bare view of the print any one would wonder how so much vermin could creep into the works of such a master. And nothing can resolve it but the ignorant ambition of learners, and the knavish invention of the musick sellers to profit thereby. Judicious architects abominate any thing of imbroidery upon a structure that is to appear great,[197] and trifling about an harmonious composition is no less absurd.

It

f.59 / 77. Entrance upon composition

It is time now to look for the fruit of what is gone before, which is to be found in the practise of musicall composition such as the masters of the art value themselves upon, in giving a pleasing enterteinement to the skillfull and unskillfull, and not without some inward joy, at the doing what many would, but few can.[198] It may

---

[195] I.e., John Banister, the elder (b. *c.* 1625, d. 1679) or the younger Banister (d. ?1725).

[196] On 19 September 1717 an advertisement appeared for Corelli's '12 Solos for a Violin and a Bass' newly reprinted and sold by D. Wright, 'which Solos have all their graces added to them by Corelli' (Tilmouth 1961: 99).

[197] I.e., Christopher Wren (b. 1632, d. 1723), who held that: 'Beauty, Firmness, and Convenience, are the Principles; the two first depend upon geometrical Reasons of Opticks, and Staticks; the third only makes the Variety] . . Views contrary to Beauty are Deformity, or a Defect of Uniformity, and Plainness, which is the Excess of Uniformity; Variety makes the Mean. Variety of Uniformities makes compleat Beauty . . . [but] much Variety makes Confusion [in things seen at once]. In things that are not seen at once, and have no Respect one to another, great Variety is commendable, provided this Variety transgress not the Rules of Opticks and Geometry' (Wren ed. Enthoven 1750/ 1903: 236–7). For some of North's responses to Wren's ideas, see *Cursory Notes of Building* (ed. Colvin and Newman 1981: 53–9 *et passim*).

[198] At f.56 North hints but explicitly draws here (also at ff.75, 76, 78v, 83 and n.272, 83v) on a notion of Hobbes, who, in enumerating the pleasures of hearing, identified one which 'happeneth only to men of skill in music, which is of another nature [than those enumerated], and not, as these, conception of the present, but rejoicing of their own skill; of which nature are the passions' (ed. Molesworth 1650/1962: 37). North reiterates this notion in a number of texts written before *c.* 1703 (see, for example, *Some Memorandums, concerning Musick*: f.1 and *Notes of Me* ed. Jessopp 1887: 73).

seem strange, that here hath bin so much stirre about tones, keys, accords, and ornaments, and all before any peice of work hath bin proposed, or begun. A magazine⋆ of hands, feet, heads, and members of litle use, untill there is occasion to joyne some in a decent⋆ figure, and then every litle peice in fitt place becomes significant. And for like end and porpose, all this provision of ingredients hath bin prepared, and are as wee suppose ready to be applyed in any attempt of musicall composition.

78. An artificiall base to be proposed

I doe presuppose that a raw composer may have learnt certein rules of accords, discords, consecutions, etc. such as are of cours taught; but yet that he may be at a loss, how to make an

appli-

f. 59v / application, by entring actually upon a peïce of work; in order to which, I think it necessary that he choos, or have prepared for him, some single base, upon which he may practise by putting thereto one or more parts. And it is not well for himself to be his own carver, but to have his base artificially made, for in that, (but more in the upper parts,) there must be what is called ayre; and by that wee understand a timely movement in the gradations of some key, and that not changing, but according to the rules already given.[199] But if the notes are set downe at a venture, or so unskillfully, that no regard is had to keys, and their changes, the whole is absurd, and will corrupt the endeavours of any one that shall offer to build upon it; for if ayre is not found in the base part, the superior, in which it should shine most, will be as a sort of nonsence, insignificant. I grant that of ayre there are of all degrees, better and wors, (of which in another place,[200]) but for an initiall lesson, if it be not absurd it may pass, and so lead a composer towards the framing his owne bases.

f. 60 / 79. Of accords

Thus furnished the composer hath 2 cares upon his spirits: 1st of the accords, 2d of the melody or tune. The first consists in finding out or at least choosing the proper accords; and in order to this he is to survey the lesson, and find what key is predominant, that is what note leads the scale that generally governes the move-

[199] See ff. 43–47.
[200] See ff. 83v–98v.

ment; for altho other keys, by changing, may have a share, yet they will (regularly) have relation to that. By this means divers places in the lines may be noted for being accords determined. As the key hath allwais a fifth, the 3d upon the key, a 6th, as also the semitone next under it. And the fifth upon it will have a fourth; and if not a fourth[,] a ♯3d; els thirds attend every note, according to the cours of the scale. I sayd[201] the fifth would have a ♯3d for [a] ♭3d upon that (the scale being from G) makes ♭B which alters the key, as was noted[,][202] and doth not agree with ♮B. Now since the base notes have each 2 accord notes to which wee may add octaves and unisons, (which to reconcile apt movements, may be used) there is a great latitude of forming an upper part smooth and aggreable; for if one of the accords fall not aptly the other may.

It is

60v / 80. Of counterpoint

It is usuall to direct the first essays to be by way of counterpoint, or note against note precisely. This is not amiss, but to be tyed to that soon grows fastidious; it is the genius of an upper part to be ayery, and that is acquired by vsing variety of movements, provided they swerve not from the degrees which the key regnant prescribes. A thro pac't counterpoint cannot be dull, and yet a mixture of it with other measures, especially by graduall sixts, and thirds, hath a lovely effect. Els★ the upper part may break upon a base note, or hold longer while divers [notes] pass according as fancy, or fluency of air may invite. Much of this doctrine depends upon precautions, as virtus est vitium fugere,★ and least dum vitant [stulti] vitia[,] in contraria currunt.★ Musick and oratory aggree strangely in principles. I have already obviated the errors of consecutions, with the reasons,[203] therefore wee proceed to the concerne about variety of keys.

81. Of keys and their changes

Strickt notice is to be taken, whither in the base the key changes, and into what notes, for saving the difference between flat and sharp (of

which

f.61 / [(]of which afterwards expresly[204]) the same rule of accords

[201] See above.
[202] See f.42.
[203] See ff.47–48.
[204] See f.61v.

returnes. Now to know these changes there are certein helps. As when the base riseth a fourth, or falls a fifth, and that not hastily but with deliberation, there is reason to expect a change of the key, by way of cadence by that fourth or fifth. So if the base moves to a note, and there stopps, or dwells long upon any note of the scale that will naturally bear a fifth, it is probable that note takes the place of the key; whereby a fifth will belong to it, and so they often become cadence notes. And the manner of the base moving, will distinguish which are passing notes, and are not intended to be key notes. As moving swift from G to D all the [inter]mediates are passing; but A may be made a cadence note to D and ♮B to E and E to F which the manner of the movement will indicate. And gener-ally those notes that lye between concord and concord, as A and C are[,] as I sayd[,]²⁰⁵ passing and not (without some signall) taken or used as key notes; but by express designe any of them will become emfatick and, prove²⁰⁶ a key of which there will be some antecedent discovery.

f.61v   / 82. [Theory of flat and sharp keys]

Nothing is more materiall to be well understood by a learner then the difference in the air of notes which as keys carry a sharp or a flatt third; for the carracter of the musick depends on that distinction. The sharp belongs to triumph, mirth and felicity, and the flat to querelousness, sorrow and dejection; and it is a wonder that so small a change in the cours of the scale should have such glaring consequences. As to the harmony it is to be observed, that the fifth note above a flat key, which in the order of the scale takes a ♭3d will require a ♯3d with the full accord. As in G♭ key F is a ♭3d to D the fifth but there F must be made sharp that D may sound with its full accord as hath bin touched before.²⁰⁷ And this is required upon several accounts. 1. respecting the cadence, for without such ♯3d the returning to, or falling upon a flatt key will want all the ornaments of a cadence, and sound dull and insipid; not to be endured in a plain cours, or without some humour or fancy designed by changing the key to be persued. But the sharp

there

f.62   / there maintaines the key, by making the going off and returning ayery and harmonious as here,

²⁰⁵ See f.47.
²⁰⁶ MS has 'to prove'.
²⁰⁷ See ff.41v–42v.

which compared with the same having ♭F would sufficiently
demonstrate the difference. And 2. the semicadence otherwise
would be utterly lost, which with the sharp is a glorious conclusion.
It is remarkable that this sharp in such company, surrounded with
flatts, as in G♭ key, there is F, E, and B flatt, should yeild such
harmony as is not onely pleasing but, circumstances considered,
unexpected, and yet necessary. But all this supposeth a designe to
maintaine the air of G♭ key. For if the intent is to goe further, as
from D to A, then the ♯3d is not required but the ♭3d as here.

Some think it odd if not a fault in the scale, that the 7th is allwais ♭ as
[to be] not so harmonious, as if it were ♯, but there is a difference
between the order of the scale, which respects one key note, and
harmony which respects divers; as the tune of 8 bells will not goe
well with ♭F descending, but requires it sharp, becaus that (as a ♯3d)
respects D and not G♭, which by the knowne tuning of 8 bells is
manifested thus.

And hereby wee see the importance of the science of keys, that is of
base notes such as wee have styled proper.[208]

The

62v / 83. Elegances of an upper part

The next care of a composer, fully possest of the genius and scope
of his base, to be used as a foundation, is to order his superstructure,
and his consentient notes with as much elegance as his fancy and
invention will prompt, using the precautions before given.[209] I
have shewed that he hath latitude enough for variety, and choice,[210]
therefore if the base be fitting, it is not without blame, if
the upper part is not melodious. One thing contributes to the

[208] See f.41.
[209] See f.60v.
[210] See f.60.

fullness and harmony of a treble and is much exercised in solos, and
that is to use the severall accords that belong to one note, as in the
example here;

* MS has 6 7 instead of 7 6

the sound thereby being as of a consort. And this gives me occasion
to hint how needfull it is to reflect back upon the many schematismes I have given of accords, commixtures of keys, and other
modes, and ornaments that continually occurr in consort
musick.[211] For out of them may be gathered most of the beautyfull
turnes that musick is capable of; which may be managed by a single
instrument, as most of the prime masters demonstrate in their
illustrious handling [of] a grave strain called an adagio.

It is

f.63   / 84. Examples rather then invention

It is hard to expect a beginner should invent those consort
passages, which are usually drawne over an harmonious base;
therefore (as other sciences) musick must have her learned authoritys, and there will be allwais opportunitys for observing the
manner of parts breaking, and holding against each other; which
taken notice of, may serve for patternes to use, or imitate upon
occasion. Nothing in musick, no more then in discours, ought to be
accidentall, as they say, quicquid in bucceam venerit,★ but either
skill, or example must warrant whatever is done. And there are not
a few conceipts, which some are fond of, with which beginners
ought not to medle, as swift devisions, and capricious movements,
which are rather dexteritys, then musick. There are indeed some
diversifications upon grounds, especially of Mr. Purcell[,] which
shew the many ways a base may be handled or rather tormented and
which as artfull example[s] may be usefull.[212] But there is one
excess seldome wanted in them, which is a wiredrawing★ of various keys and cadences out of the ground which the air of it doth not
in any manner lead

to

[211] See ff. 37–49v, 50–56, 56v–58v.
[212] Henry Purcell (b. 1659, d. 1695) used grounds in both vocal and instrumental music.

63v / to; certeinly the best musick is that which follows the plain tendency of the base. An upper part hath power, by applying 5th or 6ths, to vary the air of a base, but it is seldome to good porpose, and the masters, either to informe, or coerce those that play from thro bases, usually mark the accords, as 4th, 3d, 6th, 7th, 2d, etc. els the musick could scarce not be confounded.

85. Setting a base to a treble
     I should not turne the tables, and see what is to be done, when an upper part is proposed to have a base set to it. After so much discours of a treble to a base[213] there cannot be much left to say of a base to a treble, tho it seems harder to accomplish the latter, then the former; becaus that hath a more incertein tendency, and it is hard to guess at the designe. It is certein that divers bases may be applyed, and none jump with* the intended air. And if the notes were set downe at a venture it is still wors, and a base may be opus operatum* but of no value; therefore, as I think, in this work the aim should be, whatever the intent was, to joyne the notes so as shall make the

                                                                    best

f.64 / best consort that can be contrived and that either by holding, breaking,[214] cadencing, or otherwise, as ways may proffer, to improve, or perhaps to create, an harmony, neither of which often is practicable; as when dancing masters, comon fidlers, or other ignoramuses, make tunes, and then goe to their betters to put bases to them. And this makes so many unaiery lessons called dances, for the porpose whereof the touch of a tambour, as the French paisans* use, would serve as well; becaus nothing but the measure in those cases is essentiall to be regarded. To conclude therefore this exercise of basing under a formed treble, I cannot say but there may be advantage by it, especially when the part is skillfully set, and with designe to instruct; but not so much as in the other way; becaus the true guide of the ayre is wanted, and the work may be done fluctuating so many ways, as rather distracts, then informes a learner. For which reason I should prescribe very plain notes and such as should be determined in point of ayre, so as to admitt but one plaine base part and no other or more.

---

[213] See ff. 59–63v.
[214] I.e., syncopation (cf. broke f.44v).

f.64v / 86. Of imitation in composing

Hitherto wee have but crept along in the way to musicall composition;[215] and now it is reasonable to rise a litle higher, and enter upon matter of invention, for which there is scope enough in the work of composing a solo, or the small consort of 2 parts onely, for as that may be very plaine and low, so also it may rise to the culmen of musicall skill. I think it will be best now to lay aside the pedanterie of working upon any lesson after one part is prepared but to undertake the conducting [of] both parts together, and to advance one or other as the worm works, having allwais some [end in] view, as at the fruit upon a tree, which one would gladly reach. The matter or, (if I may so call it,) ayre must come cheifly out of pure invention, tho I know an imitation if not a direct filching out of other musick of it self will obtrude. And I cannot say it ought altogether to be chequed, for the best masters use the same figurate ornaments, and often the same passages, when they fall aptly in their designe; for consort is strait, altho the modes of it are

spacious

f.65 / spacious. Therefore I must insinuate these 2 tempers. One is to avoid direct imitation, and then [the other is] not to affect to be out of the way, as to deal alltogether in noveltys, which two are hard to reconcile, but have the like secret as language, wherein that style is best, which is plainest, and many by affecting somewhat superlative, have lost all. Now language hath a sence and signi[fi]cation at the bottom, which may be admired if some vanity of expression doe not spoyle it, so I affirme musick hath or ought to have a signification, about which the best inventions may be imployed, and to glorious effects, if some trifling in the expression doe not corrupt it.

87. Invention how regulated

Now that wee may not delude a begginner by exacting a vast excise of invention, without holding forth a fund of provision to answer it, I shall take the freedome to discours the matter at large. A composer of musick ought to look upon himself to be in a paralell state with painters or poets. And as they [do,] frame in his mind[216] some reall designe, to which as to

a

---

[215] See ff. 59–64.
[216] MS has 'their minds'.

:65v / a generall scope, he[217] is to direct his aimes. A poet puts his words together, not for the sake of meer sound, but to the intent that proper ideas may be excited in the peruser, whither lofty, serious, or jocular, as the subject proposed demands. So painters at first imploy their imaginative powers about forming the exact idea, and scheme of their intended peice, and having by divers essays satisfyed their minds, they fall to, and execute it. And whatever the designe is, the constituent parts must fall into due connexion, and unity, and not consist of incoherent scrapps, as if horses, bears, wolves, etc. were put in one peice, as having no concerne with each other. Besides if the subject be historicall, it ought to excite (quasi) the same passion, a[s] if the same were seen in the life. Whoever saw the famous pesthous of Rafael,[218] and felt not sorrow? Imagin that a skillfull master of musick were required to compose a symphony[219] proper for the spectators at that time[,] would not he strive[,]

by

f.66 / by some dolorous ayre, consentient with their minds at that time[,] to excite paralell ideas? Sure it would not be a jigg, no more then a painter would shew a saltinbanco in a cathedrall church. These instances are to shew that a musitian as well as painter or poet ought to forme in his mind the nature of his subject, and to temper his ayres accordingly. And so all kinds of actions, passions, buisnesses, and affections may come in their turne, [such] as variety, with due propriety of sound, and measures which the occasion may call for.

88. In the compass of 2 parts all musick [is] comprised

Having engaged our composer in forming a consort of 2 [parts] wholly of his owne invention, he is to esteem himself concerned to know all that belongs to composition in generall, not onely in 2 but in any number of parts, as the musick may be disposed. For there is no mode of consort that may not be expressed, if not in joynt yet in

---

[217] I.e., the composer.
[218] The art of Raphael (b. 1483, d. 1520) is thought to have embodied the highest aspirations and finest culture of the Renaissance. Seven of his 'cartoons' had been purchased by Charles I; and when the royal collections were dispersed, they were brought in for £300 by the express orders of Oliver Cromwell (Clinch 1890: 121–2). According to North, a 'good share' of the royal collections came into the hands of Peter Lely (see f.131, n.444), whose own collection included drawings by old masters. After Lely's death North, one of the executors, catalogued the collection for auction (see Notes of Me ed. Jessopp 1887: 202).
[219] I.e., a work for voices and instruments (see f.85v).

devided and (which memory will joyne) successive sounds, and the
comon practise declares the same; therefore I shall touch upon what
occurrs to me pro-

mis-

f.66v   / miscuously touching consort of all kinds, and first that, (as was
hinted[220]) the caracter of the subject be prefixed, and then that
nothing be advanced by accident, but with designe, respecting the
occasion, and never inconsistent with active nature or humanity.
And as to the latter [humanity], which is ever most to be regarded,
wee are to consider that it consists in thinking, and acting; and so
musick consists of harmony, and measure, which is called time.
And in effect harmony works upon the thoughts, and the time upon
the actions of humane kind. And consequently, from the thoughts
it passeth to affections, and passions and so to actions in conformity
with the time, of which when the musick is just and strong, few
persons that hear it will forbear conforming by some action or
other, as in dancing more egregiously. And it may be a rule, that no
musick can be well timed that may not be danced, or with which
men's actions may not conforme; and if there be any thing in those
old (suspected) storys of harping men out of one humour into
another, and so into fighting and madness, it is from hence.[221]

As

f.67   / 89. Of the passion of greif
    As for the passion of greif, it must be considered, that every man
living hath bin sensible of it in himself, or in others, and acquainted
with, or felt [it on] the funest★ occasions, and heard or made those
dolorous crys that proceed from it. And how aptly is this passion
(quasi) pictured in the ayre of a musicall flat key? as thus,

Ô   Je - su!   e che fa - ro,   sem - pre co - si

and the next example

Ahi   che   sem - pr'in - fe - li - ce

---

[220] See ff.65–66.
[221] North regards such stories as hyperbolical, although he accepts as miraculous the biblical
story about David's cure of Saul (see below f.108v).

is more passionate becaus it is put in F key,[222] with more flatts.[223] This should be sung in an upper octave but the accords are here which is enough for the porpose. It is wonderfull that sounds so pleasing as these should represent those made by persons in sorrow, but it is purely by vertue of the flatts; and it is so compleatly expressed in this latter canzona, that I have thought fitt to annex it in full harmony of 3 parts con basso continuo at the end of these papers where it will be found in score.[224] And the air is so interwoven thro all the parts that of 3 voices there is as it were but one single song.

These

/ 90. Divers musicall caracters

f.67v

These [examples][225] are sedate greifs, but the utterances of extream pain, torture, or fright in any creature can never be represented in musick, for they are allwais the worst of discord. But the extreams of joy and happyness are comonly exprest in the sharp keys, imitating trumpetts and merry songs usuall on such occasions, and all the dancing, theatricall, and festivous musick is cheifly of that kind. But the hardest task is to square with a state either of buissness or of comon conversation or traffick unless the allemand and fuge doth it. The adagios, are designed for pure and pute★ harmony, for which reason measure of time is so litle regarded in them. The grave comes neerer a sober conversation and the allegro light and chirping. The tremolo[226] is fear and suspicion; the andante is a walking about full of concerne; the ricercata is a searching about for somewhat out of the way; the affectuoso is expostulating, or amour; and so every other manner, as masters are pleased to titule them, are but so many states of humane life, as they have a fancy to represent, or imitate.

Is

/ 91. No musick accidentall, but from imitation or designe

f.68

Is it not therefore expected, that a composer should reflect which of these, or other humours he is to represent, and then to forme the style of his ayre accordingly? And is it not a low province, to make instruments speak in any contingent manner, and to have no designe, but (fidle fidle) sometimes quick, and sometimes slow,

---

[222] I.e., C key.
[223] (Exs. 1 and 2). Example 1 has not been identified; Example 2 is from the closing trio of *I Naviganti*, a cantata for two sopranos and bass by Carissimi (see below f.72, n.236 and ff.144v–147v).
[224] See ff.145–147v.
[225] See f.67, Examples 1 and 2, and ff.145–147v.
[226] I.e., not a grace (cf. f.56v) but a movement ('manner').

and often swift beyond all sence and reason, in all which sort of consorts the rationale is that it is so, becaus it is so, and no more? And if there happen a litle capriccio, then it is called very pretty, perhaps an arriette to a petit song, or a tune for a dance, or a levye in the morning; all which may be very well in their designe, but their vertue (if any they have) depends on the sparks of legitimate★ melody, which are owing to art, and may easily be perceived, by a skillfull ear. And in this respect it is not amiss that an early composer should try his skill in some short and plaine aires, without breaking his head with morallitys,[227] till he hath acquired a ready musicall style, and hath his memory filled with the comon places as I may

call

f.68v   / call them, or formes continually found in the works of the best masters; for those passages are matured by experience, and are to be gathered and not invented.

92. The invitatory kind tending to fuge

It is remarkable that melody is never so good the first, as at the 2d time of hearing, and few will hold much longer. For this reason the elder masters composed their musick after the manner of the lute, in straines, which were to be played twice over, and wee find the like in our sonnatas when it is fancyed they deserve it; and this is the warrant for repeats, and retornellos, and I may say even of fuges, whose cheif vertue lys in the same; and the reason is, the sence is allwais better satisfyed in a foreknowledg (tho faintly) of what is to come, then to be surprised with any thing intirely new, which comes, and is gone before it is enough reflected upon. For which reason also the masters affect an invitatory manner, which is not a fuge formed but tending to it as when one part begins and another follows in the same track and if the like be done in another key it beginns

to

f.69   / to take the shape of a fuge. But as to the invitatory manner, since it is hard to be well understood without examples, take this (1) plaine one.

---

[227] I.e., imitations of human characters (thoughts and actions).

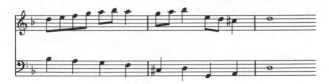

But that which follows (2)

is of the good Mr. Jenkins,[228] then which it is not easy to find a
better. But the most transcendent of the kind is that (3)

of Corelli's[229] which doth just not express, as it were, by words, a
calling, and then going away together; and according to these
examples, it will be allwais recomendable that divers parts should
be made to carry the same ayre, the base it self not excepted; for all

[228] (and Ex. 2). John Jenkins (b. 1592, d. 1678), noted for his consort music for viols, was one
   of North's teachers. He was a visitor, and from about December 1660 a resident, at
   Kirtling, the home of North's grandfather, Dudley (b. 1581, d. 1666), third baron North
   (1600), whose unpublished account book lists payments to Jenkins to 1669. Example 2 is
   an extract from one of Jenkins' two-part airs for treble and bass (see Dodd 1978–79: 84–5
   (Ashbee No. 161d)). The entire piece was printed as No. 21 in *New Ayres and Dialogues
   composed for Voices and Viols ... Together with lessons for viols or violins ...*, London 1678,
   collected by Banister, the elder and Thomas Low. No manuscript is extant.
[229] (Ex. 3). Example 3 is a sketch only of the opening of the 'Allemanda' from Corelli's
   Sonate a tre, Op. 4, No. 2.

notes have their proper accords, and the most precise treble may be brought downe to serve as base.

It

f.69v / 93. Of fuges and an example

It seems proper in this place to produce all I have to say concerning fuges; and first that they mean no other then a short parcell of notes distinguishable by their melody, and native of the key in which they are profered and variously repeated. And these the masters have called points, and the elder musitians professed wonderfull art in the management of them, which so far as was reasonable, consisted in pure repetition. But the point being once entered in the consort the parts took it one after another and in different keys, which they called reporting. But they went farther, for subtilety knows no bounds, and the point must be also reverted[,] that is, like a witch's prayer, to begin at the last notes, and so one way or other pass to and fro among the keys till it was worne thredbare. This latter art of reverting was nothing but taking a new point, for no sort of similitude of melody remained. But their fondness of this ornament of fuge was so great that, bating* meer harmony, they sought for no other, as I shall shew,[230] coming to those turnes. At present fuges are found copious in our

best

f.70 / best authors, and fail most in overdoing, for altho repetition is good, too much is fastidious, as may be observed in good Mr. Sherrard's sonnatas[231] which have no other fault. He wanted the philosopher's rule, ne quid nimis;* but the touchstone of fuge is Corelli. The great danger in conducting of fuges is the going too farr for variety, and so by tossing the point from key to key the ayre of the genuine key is lost, which is unwholsome for the musick; and in that respect Corelli's fuges are admirable, for tho driven thro variety enough, yet the air of the key is preserved.

Having sayd much of fuges,[232] I thought it reasonable to give a specimen which is here of 4 parts hunted from Corelli,

[230] See f.70.
[231] James Sherard (b. 1666, d. 1738), apothecary and fellow of the Royal Society, composed two sets of trio sonatas of the *da chiesa* type, Op. I of which, published by 16 September 1701, included a full-page dedication to Wriothesley Russell, second duke of Bedford (Tilmouth 1966). Katharine, the relict of North's eldest brother, Charles (b. 1635, d. 1691), married Russell's uncle. It is through this connection that North may have met the 'good' Mr. Sherard.
[232] See ff.68v–70.

* MS has G♯

but a very different peice of work.

I

.70v / 94. Of the grave or pavan

I cannot say that either the melody or harmony of this passage,[233] is exalted by the fuge, but both might be as well, or rather better, in plain consort notes, such as Corelli's graves are, which in my opinion excell his fuges. The old masters seldome affected fuges but in those peices, which are not unlike our sonnatas, and by them were called fancys. But for solemne musick they had a grave air which they called padoano or pavan, wherein they made the most they could of pure harmony without much of melody becaus, the parts were equally concerned to make good the consort and this .may be a short specimen in 4,

[233] See f.70, Example 1.

in which it is designed that no one part shall have advantage of air
above another, which such as it is seems to agree with the old pavan
and moderne grave; wholly void of fuge.

95. For parity of air
    Harmony is never so compleat as in full 4 parts; all inter-

                                                                woven

f.71 / woven and alike aiery, which is never so well when a part is thrust
in for repien as they terme it, against which I shall have more to say
elsewhere.[234] And now to conclude this matter of fuges, I am
perswaded the artists court them so much as they doe for want of a
lively invention. The fuge is a sort of scheme or model to work
upon, and the contrivances are to protract that, more then to persue
a vein of good air, and the work is easily done, for it is but
wrighting the fuge here and there foreward upon the score, and the
rest is but filling up. No wonder then that the practise is apt to run
out too much, and so to corrupt the ayre; especially when the point
(as sometimes) is but a break of a plaine note, over and over againe,

[234] See f.76.

which I need not animadvert in any of our moderne sonnatas. But the greatest vertue it hath is, letting all the parts into a parity of ayre, by persuing the point, one after another, in which cours a repien part is but a kind of drum, that accompanys the whistling of the rest. Therefore I cannot but wish that substantiall ayre were more in request then artificiall devises, which have more of ostentation, then harmony.

I

f.71v   / 96. Of the adagio and example

I have not yet done full right to the adagio musick, (usually intercaled for variety in our sonnatas) by any exemplar given of it; therefore, and becaus the designe of those verses (the adagios) is to preferre the riches of harmony, I subjoyne one here;

which perhaps may be faulty in affecting too much the hard accords but it is the

mode

f.72   / mode, errare cum patribus[,]* allwais excusable. But I have observed of the best Itallian canzoni, that thc straines were exquisitcly smooth and aiery, but the cadences as crabbed as might be, of which that before mentioned is an example.[235] It is a mistake therefore to think that good musick is purchased by hard accords, more then oratory by hard words. The magnificence of the sublime is found in the plainest dresses, and the practice of Signor Charissime,[236] and Signor Bassano,[237] with many others of the best note have bin accordingly, who allwais kept near to their key, as preists to their altar, and after a litle swerving, but never farr, made hast[e] to returne againe.

97. Of the grave by start or stopp
     There are two modes of the grave, which I shall just take notice of, the one may be called the start and the other the stopp. The first is striking upon a semiquaver rest thus.

* MS may have ♮

The manner was introduced by Mr. Babtist an Italianized Frenchman,[238] and all the

entrys

f.72v   / entrys of his branles,[239] as they were called, were of this action, but withall unexceptionable musick; and the hand nicely agrees with the foot, especially in the most stately step they call an entry. I fancy it is originally owing to the genius of the violin, of which one of the beautys is the stabb, or stoccata,* and the other is the arcata,* which latter hath given way and the other cheifly prevailes.[240] I

---

[235] See f.71v, Example 1.
[236] Giacomo Carissimi (b. 1605, d. 1674), Italian composer, was noted for his oratorios and cantatas. In England his reputation stood particularly high during the last thirty years of the seventeenth century.
[237] Probably Giovanni Bassano [Bassani] (b. *c.* 1588, d. 1617), Italian composer and cornet player, some of whose canzonettas were included in Morley's *Canzonets or Little Short Songs to Foure Voyces . . .*, London 1597.
[238] Jean-Baptiste [Giovanni Battista] Lully (b. 1632, d. 1687), Italian composer, dancer and violinist, resided most of his life in France. Foreigners considered him as the most representative of French composers, and at the time of his death he had already been enshrined in the French Parnassus.
[239] I.e., 'setts of lessons' (cf. f.135); suites.
[240] North first wrote about the arcata or 'long bow' before *c.* 1703, when he pointed out that performers 'will begin a long note, clear, without rubbs, and draw it forth swelling lowder and lowder, and at the ackme take a slow waiver, not trill to break the sound, or

have subjoyned a basso andante to shew how well that sober style joyns with the desultry action of the upper part,[241] as of one pacifying the rage of an angry person. The other mode is the stop, striking after a quaver rest altogether in this manner.

* MS has $\frac{b}{5}$ $\frac{5}{8}$

Harmony cannot be had with more advantage then by these stopps being of the whole consort at once, and (as ought to be) of the richest notes; for at every stopp there will be a kind of rattle,[242] which aided by the memory is softened, and so made purer, then taken from the gross strokes, as the eccho is allwais sweeter then the voice.

There is

f 73 / 98. Abuses of the tremolo

There is another mode of the grave that frequently occurrs in our Itallianczed sonnatas, which I have knowne intituled, tremolo,[243] and is now comonly performed with a tempered stoccata. And that I take to be an abuse, and contrary to the genius of that mode, which is to hold out long notes inriched with the flowers of harmony and with a trembling hand, which of all parts together resembles the shaking stop of an organ;[244] whereas the breaking the notes with

mix 2 notes, but as if the bird sat at the end of a spring, as she sang the spring waived her up and downe, or as if the wind that brought the sound shaked, or a small bell wer[e] struck, and the sound continuing waived to and again' (*Some Memorandums, concerning Musick*: f.8). In *Cursory Notes of Musicke* he refined this description, writing that 'the great arcatas, long strokes of the bow . . . shall begin from the least sound, and swell by degrees till you know it is at the top and there tremolo, and so wast[e] again till it is lost in nothing' (ed. Chan and Kassler 1986: 224). According to these descriptions, we may infer that the arcata is a species of that grace which North calls the 'swelling wavee' or 'waived' grace (see f.57v, n.190). There is no mention of stoccata in North's texts on music written before *c*. 1703.

[241] See f.72, Example 1.
[242] I.e., reverberation.
[243] I.e., not a grace (cf. f.56v) nor a movement (cf. f.67v) but a bowstroke.
[244] Modern sources describe this bowstroke as repeated notes, slurred or unslurred, but by 'tremolo' North denotes pulsations in the volume of a note (see *Cursory Notes of Musicke* ed. Chan and Kassler 1986: 223–4, where he first defines tremolo). His comparison to the shaking-stop of an organ indicates that his source is Simpson (1665/1965: 10).

repeated strokes, doth not well consist with the best of harmony, and of it self (out of consort) hath not so much as melody in it, but rather a fastidium, like the ticks of a spring pendulum,[245] nor is there any humane action to which it may be referred, unless it be stabbing often in the same place, or the andante or walking and not moving one stepp forewards, which is absurd; and not the less so, becaus it is a comon practise, as I have knowne plain tripla notes broken into snatches, which whole, if the performers could have afforded a full drawne sound, had bin more musicall; but the short windedness, or want of bow in those that performe often stabbs the musick.

There

f.73v   / 99. Of the aria and almanda

There are some other modes, which have pl[ace] between the grave and the allegro.[246] One is tituled, aria, but tho cheerfull enough, d[oes] not come up to the fury of an allegro, and hath this property, that it bears well the attendance of a plain consort base, and of that k[ind] this may be an example;

[245] Between 1670 and 1680 two important horological mechanisms were put into working practice: the anchor escapement and the spiral balance-spring. By 'spring pendulum' North probably refers to the latter, the invention of which has been attributed to the two most prominent figures in horology, Robert Hooke and Christiaan Huygens. In 1658 Hooke proposed the construction of a chronometer by attaching a spring to the arbor of the balance wheel, thereby replacing the pendulum with a vibrating wheel that could be moved because it oscillated around its own centre of gravity. In 1674 Huygens actually constructed a watch controlled by a spiral spring. For North's indebtedness to the work of these two men, see the 'Introduction' to *Cursory Notes of Musicke* (ed. Chan and Kassler 1986).

[246] Elsewhere, North argues that the andante is the most approved movement, because 'it expresseth steaddyness of mind' (*MG c. 1726*: f.147v).

and arias of duple time may [be] admi[t]ted into th[e] service of theaters, and fr[om] being for ch[eer]fullness a ma[tch] for the triplas. Another sort is the almanda[,] from a more heavy style, [which] is supposed to be [de]rived of the Germans, whose musick is good but very articulate★ and plaine as here.

★ The right-hand margin of the page has been lost in the binding

f.74 / 100. [Of the sarabanda]

The sarabanda deserves to be mentioned. It is an air purely spagnuola,★ and corresponds [to] the rodomontade humour of that nation. It is an ayre that bears a basso andante exceeding well; of which there are so many examples in our printed sonnatas, that no specimen is needed here. I have observed in other sorts of musick of the Spanish cutt, that fullness of harmony was very much affected by that nation; and there was a time when the English masters imitated them, as in those peices they called galliardos. It may be described by a small 3 part song printed in old Playford's catch book viz. Dellos ochos di me morena, etc.[247] then which the musicall scalle cannot launch a further consort, and, (as that is) freer from trespass upon melody and ayre. I had not sayd so much on the subject of Spanish musick but to second an observation viz. that nations are distinguisht in their musick, as apparently as in dress or any other humour; wittness the French and Spanish collated; and

[247] Both Francis and Roger North were personally acquainted with John Playford (b. 1623, d, 1686), whose 'catch book' went through many editions and, so, exemplifies Playford's method of book-making (see Krummel 1975: 115–23). The first edition of 1652 was compiled by John Hilton; but subsequent editions were collected and published by Playford himself. For one of the versions containing 'Del los ochos di me morena', see *Catch that Catch can, or The Musical Companion . . .*, London 1667, pp. 190–1.

tho the musick seems confined to the lines of the scale, it expresseth infinite variety.

f.74v   / 101. Of the allegro, and its sorts

It is time now to examine the state of the allegros about which I find so much variety, that I must owne my self in a willderness, and scarc[e] know which way to move. I think they will be partable into these two sorts: 1. such as run upon fuges, and 2. [such] that are quasi devisions upon a ground. As for the former, it seems that fuges and swift movements doe not agree well together, becaus being in many parts they will intermix and in the confusion loos the advantage of gracefull repeats; and unless it be at the entrance after a resting, the audience will have no knowledg of any point. Perhaps an ear placed in the midst of the performers may distinguish somewhat, but at a decent position, the sume is a musical dinn, and no better. And musick like picture, ought to have a just distance, els the parts whereof it consists, which in all enterteinements ought to be perceptible, will blend as in a mist. I guess it is for this reason that some masters write poco allegro, or assai to temper the impertinent hast[e] that some self conceipted performers are apt to make

more

f.75   / more for ostentation of hand then justice to the musick. When the master is for that sport, he writes presto, or prestissimo, but never when any fuge is thought of. But if in allegro-musick, the base part (without a thro-base attending) is made to spurr on with the rest as sometimes hath bin done, the whole consort turnes to a ratle indistinguishable. All objects of sence require time to impress, as red hot iron may be safely handled [if] swiftly changed, altho the iron flames. So sounds swiftly touched fail to affect our sence of their[248] quality.

102. In allegro of responses

In the allegros where is no express fuge, there is often used a sort of responce of one part to another, which I termed an invitatory⸱ manner.[249] But very often it is done by distribution of an ayre between 2 or more parts; as here,

---

248 ms has 'its'.
249 See ff.68v–69.

the ayre of one part is made to serve more elegantly in two, and I have shaddowed the proper base underneath,[250] with, (for fullness) a repien. It would take up a great deal of room to express how this comon base is diversifyed in the consort but having touched this case of an allegro before[251] I insist no further upon it.

It is

75v   / 103. 2 up[p]er parts moving swift and the changes

It is not easy to imploy 2 upper parts in a quick consort neatly; it is done oftenest in the manner touched before,[252] by making one part take an ayre (as it were) out of the mouth of another, with holding notes alternatim;* and sometimes by counterpoint accords as in triumph musick, which makes a continuall battery; but generally, and with most elegancy by consecution [in] thirds or sixts, and it is allwais a discovery when the ayre will allow that advantage, which the best masters catch at. And to shew how cleverly this will happen in some cases, observe this example

and remember how often it is met with in consort, either exactly or in paralell wise; as also when the moving part is given to the base, and the superiors hold, or els they take it alternatim and with various and desultory movements[,] an account of which with divers other capriccios, that allegros are stuff't with, must be referred to the consorts themselves.

Now

---

250 North has not 'shaddowed' the 'proper base'.
251 See f.74v.
252 See ff.74v–75.

f.76   / 104. Musick suffers by too much action

Now wee come to the other branch of the allegro musick, which is pure devision, with a ground attending, and often a midle part by way of repien, and that is called a second treble, which distinction ariseth from an abuse in composition, that now a days is most flagrant. I mean, when the whole air of a sonnata is designed to ramp in one part, for the sake of which, the rest are allowed to attend on foot. And this proceeds from a very usuall vanity of the masters, who by the work of their whole lives, having acquired uncommon dexteritys in performing, compose, not for musick, but for play, in that which shall best sett off their owne perfections, and if possible, that none els, at least, not out of their owne fraternity, or combination, shall doe the like. Hence, follows court-ship to them, as essentiall to all that's relevant in musick; whilst their desciples, who might make good consortiers, are worne out with practising their whimms, and musick it self imprisoned, as it were between 4 walls, and multitudes of lovers cast off. For now what are the celebrated consorts worth without a topper★ for the prime part

and

f.76v   / and whence should country familys, where in former times musick flourished in its best effects, be supplied with such, in case they had a mind to be troubled with them? In short the affectation of difficultys, and magnificence, hath gone a great way towards a suppression of good musick, and will soon bring it to perfection, unless a redicule or two more, such as the Beggar's Opera,[253] takes downe the rampant impertinence.

104. Musick seems but is not really advanced

I shall be told here that musick was never more in esteem, nor had more exquisite performers even of the best fortunes, and quallity in England then now. I grant the matter of fact, except in extent and number. As for the esteem, it is seen enough in the

[253] *The Beggar's Opera* is reputed to be the first ballad opera. The text by the poet and dramatist, John Gay, is a comedy of London low life in which the author satirises both the government and the Italian opera. North's neighbour in Norfolk, Robert Walpole, was ridiculed as Bluff Bob; and Walpole's mistress is said to have been identified with Polly, the heroine of the opera. The music interspersed in the dialogue consists of traditional English, Scottish, Irish and French melodies. An overture and basses for the melodies were provided by John Christopher Pepusch, music teacher to North's second son, Montagu (b. 1712, d. 1779).

scandalous, and insane subscriptions to forreiners. And for the quallity-performers, it had bin well if some of them had imployed a litle of their time about somewhat els. But for one of them gained, there are multitudes throwne off, and of those most of all such to whome musick would be most usefull, that is persons, studious, of imployments or in retiredment, who have not time or appetite to be devoted to the hunting of ayery perfections; and

if

f.77 / if they cannot content themselves with a moderate order of consort, they must not injoy the exercise of any. I shall conclude this reflection with an admiration of Corelli, who out of his immens abillitys in musick, hath condiscended to compose consorts fitted to the capacitys of the minor performers, but for musicall excellence transcending all others, and these are, and ever will be valued against gold, when the prestissimi and prestitissimi will have but little esteem.

106. In a quick motion the use of emphases

But to returne to the allegro devisions, they are either correnti, or arpeggianti; the former is when a part takes a carriere thro a whole strain without ceasing, and the other parts favour the action, by short touches in the accords. It must be observed, that whoever hath this part, never thinks he runs fast enough, and comonly being warm in his practise, he mends his pace. How wide this is from an harmonious consort, or any thing els but wonder, must appear to a judicious auditor, or rather spectator, who hath the greatest share. But if one

may

77v / may profer a temper to this extravagance, it should consist in two means. The one is some abatement of the hurry, so as to take along a midle part by way of andante, or some other melody by the attendants, which would have a reasonable agreement, and effect, by being reduced to a state of being understood. The other means is a powerfull application of emphases which[,] falling upon the accord places, would produce a shape of a consort; and the gross measures of the proper times would be seen (as it were) thro the tinsell devision; as if there were a kind of paus upon the first of every 4, 6, or 3, whereof the notion is obvious, and the effect manifest. However take this example upon a tripla ground;

which hath the emphases expres't and the touches of a midle part. It must be observed that all reference is here to the violin, but the like devision is performed upon violls, and particularly upon the base as Corelli and some others have advanced,

but

f.78   / but yet under the protection of a full thro base without which, as to the consort, it is a meer nothing, and at best an ostentation, or rather a complyance with some that have hands fitt for it, and for that reason expect to be gratifyed; with opportunitys of exercising their talents, without which the best musick will stand indicted of dullness.

107. Of the arpeggio
     The other sort of devision, which I termed the arpeggio,[254] tho exceeding the comon acceptation of that word, hath much more to be sayd for it becaus it carrys a perfect skill in the ornamentall or figurate composition of harmony. The movement is desultory or by way of breaking, and not onely of the notes of any single part but of the fullest consort that can be composed, and thro the devision may be heard all the concords, commixtures, and passing notes, as if they were all in full action, softness and deminution onely excepted. Examples, and florid ones, of this kind are frequently mett with, but I choos to add a note or two which shew the manner.

In

f.78v   / 108. Arpeggio an improper imitation
     In the performance of this arpeggio the usuall manner is, not to distinguish every stroke but to pass the notes with a slurr bow and

---

[254] See f.77.

rolling hand, which may be knowne but not described, and therein is the pride of the masters, whose skill and dexterity is shewed in nothing more then in this (proper) arpeggio.[255] For they will continue it wonderfully upon a single note, and changing, (as I sayd[256]) you heer a full consort. And that is the designe; and it is remarkable that musicall instruments should be made to imitate each other's defects; harpsicords, lutes, harps, etc. are imperfect, becaus they cannot continue a tone, and seek to make it good arpegiando. The violin holds out the tones in perfection; and is debased in straining to ape the defects of the others and that by tricks needless, or rather absurd. If an organist should imitate the manner, and touch of an harpsicord, he would be laught at. And when the violin is capable, by the finest tones, to move a passion in the hearers, why that should be waived to let in a faint resemblance of somewhat that in due order might be good, but as it is used, no better then a sort of a hum-drum devise that stirrs up onely an admiration, I know not.

Some

f.79   / 109. Why so litle sayd of the tripla

Some may think much that in all these discourses, and examples, there is very litle sayd, or shewn of the tripla movement; as if that had no great share in the variety of musick. I must answer that its portion in that province is very great; but I have thought that the difference between the duple, and tripla is not so much as many think it is, and that it consists cheifly in emphasis; otherwise the duple prevailes even thro that; and for this caus it hath seemed that reasons and examples apt for the one sort, are no less applicable to the other; and it had bin actum agere* to repeat them on every occasion. Take all the different styles, and both the times may be adapted; as in the ecclesiastick, can any thing be more august and solemne, then musick is in the grand tripla measure? And it is also introduced in the utmost levity and celerity; for the triple emphasis runns into the most minute touches, as ♫♫ ♫♫ and if cappacity of hand would allow, it might goe on tripla, but subdevisions fall more aptly into duple, which underneath also by equall pulses governes the measure, as in full latitude hath bin already observed.[257]

I would

[255] See f.78, Example 1.
[256] See f.78.
[257] See ff.30–36v.

f.79v   / 110. Of voluntarys and ayre

I would now expatiate a litle with some reflections upon musicall ayre and voluntary which are so connected in point of skill, that the knowledg of the one and practise of the other, and the like in revers are quater cosins[258] for any one that hath a ready and free hand upon any consort instrument, which is allwais to be presupposed, and a just notion of ayre, cannot but be a voluntarian. And the best hand upon earth, without it, cann never attain to be one and herein I must venture to reiterate some matters already set forth. The secret of ayre hath bin allready opened, but may bear a further explication. It consists in two or three points: 1st that the parts shall move in the scale of the key, allways emphasing upon the prime accords;[259] 2[d] that in all changes of the key, (which introduce a new scale), it shall be into some one of the prime accords of the former, and by those I mean the third or fifth, ascending, or descending;[260] and 3[d] that returnes back to the proper key be frequently made, which after a change will be better accepted; unless the spirit moves to ramble, and then allowing time enough, for the memory of the former to wear out, the musick in like order may pass into any key.[261]

The air

f.80   / 111. Air of a key exercised in flourishing

The air of a key is so well knowne or knowable that I am avers to the giving any examples of it. What is more comon then the flourish at the entry of a consort, which is onely a successive striking the key and its prime accords one after another, either distinct, or gradient according to the scale, or intermixt, and (in time) ad libitum, but ever observing to give the advantage, or emphasis upon the prime accords? What is easyer to doe then this? And what els is, or can be the ayre of the key note but this? As to the change and returne, into and from the fifth on either side, it is by way of cadence. And upon the fifth taken above, (G, D, G) the change is into (D) the cadence note, and returnes to the key or close note (G) againe; if to the fifth below, (G, C, G) there the key note G is the cadence note, and C the close, returning to the key (G) againe. But the passing into and from the upper, and lower thirds of the key and returning, requires some circumstance as first, into the lower, as from G to E may be plain or

---

[258] I.e., near relations.
[259] See ff.43–48v.
[260] See ff.50–58v.
[261] See ff.43, 45v. 50v, 56, 57.

notice given of it, which notice when it is given they call preparation, as in the following example,[262] which with what follows I
venture here to repeat.[263]

And the

8ov   / And the next

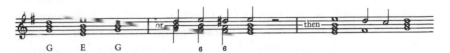

G   E   G   6   6

is with preparation or notice of the change, which in truth is
effected by the 6 which is as true a change altho the consonance is
not filled with the E below. The like will fall out, upon change into
the superior third, of which this is the example.

G   B   G   6   43

* MS may have a minim rest here

5   5   43

I must note that it is indifferent whither the 3d that takes the change
be flatt, or sharp, but fancy may determine it. Onely observe again
that the 6 that notifyes the change is really it self a chang[e] as the
obscure notes express. The following notes are proposed onely for
practise, which may be done by way of flourish; and if any habit is
acquired of flourishing properly, and freely upon such notes as
these, it will goe a great way in the art of voluntary, for great part of
composition lyes in the breaking of notes one upon another, all
which will bear this second, but more concise declaration.[264]

112. How musicall skill acquirable
    Now as for ayre, further than wee are ledd by the nature of keys,
and their accords, I must suppose, the inquiry is after good musick

and

81   / [(]and I must confess it would be rare if wee could prescribe to

---

[262] See f.8ov, Example 1.
[263] See f.8ov and n.264.
[264] See ff.43–58v for the more full declaration.

that,[)] and just as if one were to be shewed how to make a good speech or a good play, for ayre in musick is like witt in language, which supposing a genius must come by application, and industry, passing into an habit, and not by immediate instruction. There are authors of gramer, shewing how to put words together, and of rhetorick, how to enforce and adorne them; and all very well in ordinè ad,★ but there is more required to make an orator. So all our gamutts, times, keys, mixtures, fuges, and what els is couched under the musicall termes, are necessary in order to make a good musitian, but the good musick must come from one by nature as well as art compleatly made, who is arrived at a pitch to throw away the lumber of his rules and examples, and act upon the strength of his judgment, and knowledge of the subject matter it self, as if it had bin bred and born in him ab origine.★

113. Of artificiall[265] helps

But as in oratory there are certein formes and modes of speech so in musick there are certein passages, which are promiscuously assumed by the masters, and that I have termed comon places of ayre;[266] these will be very observable in consorts, and out

of

f.81v   / of them a beginner must make his collections, for he cannot invent, but must gather them. Of this sort are the cadences, both [the] whole, and the half; the commixtures of keys, which are called discords; transitions, and certein facetious★ turnes of ayre and the like which magazined in memory, and joyned with the exercise of the keys before hinted;[267] not declining an interposition of some- what of proper conceipt and fancy, (which amidst such furniture may make bold – audendum tamen★). And with these aids great things will come forth, and so great, that the whole art of compo- sition is by the same means acquired; and a voluntarian is no other then a composer, and composing it self is but following a fancy, as a voluntarian doth, onely the latter hath more of designe, contriv- ance, and exactness then the other, tho he (the voluntarian) in his flights shall often stumble upon passages, which he cannot recover however usefull he thinks they might be in a formed designe. And now in full contemplation of composition, I cannot but over look

[265] I.e., already existing (cf. f.8) or mechanical, used figuratively in opposition to natural, that which is invented by the aspiring composer.
[266] See ff.68–68v.
[267] See f.80.

the smaller performances, and fix an eye upon a full enterteinement
of musick as I fancy it should be, if not (readily) to be found in
perfection.

Musick

f.82   / 114. Distribution of musick and 1. solitary

Musick may be to various intents and those distributable into 1.
solitary, 2. sociall, 3. ecclesiasticall, and 4. theatricall. The solitary
hath 2 intents, 1. practise, in order to acquire a dexterity, or [2.]
perfection in the use of certein favorite instruments and nothing
more conducing[;] but on the other side, respecting time, and
application to consort, as much disabling; for the most exquisite
solitary practiser coming into consort is enervous, and at a loss how
to goe on; for he is not used to comand his pace,[268] and to act with
complyance. And besides his time is corrupted, for no one in the
exercise of difficultys, or when his private satisfaction in what he
doth is unequall can keep an equall measure of time long together;
but at hard places he will retard, and getting the better, goe too fast,
so also when he is better pleased; and when he comes to consort,
these failings, unthought of alone, will shew themselves grosly,
and spoyle all. Therefore solitary practise is good to make a hand,
but it corrupts consort; and in generall no practise is profitable to all
purposes, but onely in consort, yet with respect to amusement

and

82v   / and releif of an active mind distressed either with too much, or too
litle imployment, nothing under the sun hath that vertue, as a
sollitary application to musick.

115. The good and bad of solitary musick

It is a medecine without any nausea or bitter and is taken both for
pleasure and cure. It is most conducing to use such instruments as
touch the accords, for the harmony yeilds more pleasure then any
single toned instrument can doe, and the ear being once accustomed
to tast[e] that, can never have enough; and however the pleasure of
it cannot be described, it is sensibly knowne to those that have
found the way to be refreshed by it.[269] And the morall consequence is enough to recommend it, as a means of diverting other

---

[268] MS has 'pase'.
[269] That North himself was refreshed by music is clear from numerous passages in his
    writings on music and particularly, his encomium to the organ (see *Cursory Notes of
    Musicke* ed. Chan and Kassler 1986: 126).

ways of consuming spare time more pernicious, then this is pleasing. I knew one who was the greatest justician, and one of the best
men of his time,[270] who in his youth became a very good musitian,
and in his chamber used in a voluntary way to divert himself with
touching his lyra viol, lute fashion upon his knee and essaying his
voice thereupon. And I have heard him say that if he had not had
that refreshment, he had never bin a lawyer, that is he could not
have kept his chamber.[271]

The next

f.83   / 116. Of sociall musick in consort

The next partition of musicall enterteinement is the sociall or
what is called musica di camera; this hath 2 respects, 1. to the
performers, and 2. the auditors, for there is a vast difference both in
designe and event between these 2 nations. The former I presume to
consist of scollars advanced, or as it may be, adept in practise,
commixt with some of the musicall profession; but all cheifly
delighted in the exercise of difficultys; and in shewing their skill,
conceiting themselves envyed for the fine things they are able to
performe; tho there may be also a pleasure denuded of that vanity,
which lyes in the meer playing of tricks, as children love snappers.[272] And if any one seems to slight the enterteinement, he is
told that if he could attain to doe the same, he would be no less
pleased with it. But the fault is of the masters who to maintain their

[270] I.e., North's brother, Francis (b. 1637, d. 1685), first baron Guilford (1683) and lord
keeper of the great seal (1682), who has been treated callously by historians and still
awaits a more balanced interpretation. Roger North remains the main source for details
of the life of his brother, although the published version of his biography, 'censored and
mangled' by the first editor, Montagu North, cannot be said to represent the author's
intentions (see Clifford 1963: 277).

[271] Elsewhere North writes about Francis: 'I have heard him say, that if he had not enabled
himself by these studies ["ingenious arts, history, humanities, and languages"], and
particularly his practice of music upon his base, or lyra viol (which he used to touch lute
fashion upon his knees) to divert himself alone, he had never been a lawyer. His mind was
so airy and volatile, he could not have kept his chamber, if he must needs be there, staked
down purely to the drudgery of the law, whether in study or practice: and yet upon such a
leaden proposition, so painful to brisk spirits, all the success of the profession, regularly
pursued, depends. And without acquiring a capacity of making a solitary life agreeable,
let no man pretend to success in the law' (*Life of Francis North* ed. M. North 1819: i/15).
When Francis became lord keeper, he retired from social assemblies before midnight, and
'after a touch of his music, went to bed; his musician [Roger North] not leaving him till
he was composed. So that never any person had more assured witnesses of his
conversation than he had; and if ever music was a relief to a mind overwhelmed with
troubles, so it was with him' (*ibid.* ii/320).

[272] '... snappers': 'I grant that humane nature will ever have so much of the boy, to delight in
exercise of activity, and is loath to be outdone, as when one boy hath got snappers,
another waits with a longing appetite for his turne at snapping also, and all have inward
pride in so doing' (*MG c. 1726*: f.138v).

soveraignety, drive on the humour, to the prejudice of the auditory, who would be more affected with the full sound, well drawne
from the body of the instrument, then with an arpeggio upon a
violin tho never so admirably ratled with the 2d or 3d hand at the
sumit of the finger board.[273]

It

83 v   / It would be hard to deprive the masters from injoying the pride of
their skill, in the exercise of a swift hand, without a proffer of some
compensation; and that I think is to be had in managing the sound of
their instruments, with fullness, dulcor,* and grace, as divers have
done and continually doe, and which tho every one doth not
discerne it, hath more of difficulty, and also of the admirable, then
the swiftest measures they can pretend to. And so presuming on
this sort of performance, essentiall to all good musick, I proceed to
the auditory.

117. Sonnatas allwais to begin gravely and harmoniously
    The instrumentall musick of late hath bin listed mostly under the
title of sonnatas which being consorts of 3 and rarely of 4 parts, and
more hands requiring to be imployed, some parts have bin doubled;
but that not succeeding well (plainely) the very doubling hath bin
improved by art as in the conciertos, which have assigned the
separations and conjunctions with better effect; wittness those
nonpareil conciertos of Corelli.[274] But as to the disposition of the
consort varieties I take it to be most reasonable to

begin

84   / begin in a majestic style full of solemne and pompous harmony;
this will engage the hearers and make them attentive to what is to
follow. I have observed a method like this in most publick shows,
as fireworks for instance which enter with (as it were) thunder and
lightning and then fall into a cours of fire and nois, allwais increasing, and so without any relenting, (of which the least would be a
fault) to the end which is to be in a moment when all (with fire and
nois in extremity) are to ceas together. And I have observed the like
in musick, of which trumpetts and kettle drums have closed the

---

[273] I.e., in the higher positions.
[274] I.e., *Concerti grossi*, Op. 6, published posthumously, Amsterdam 1714. About December
    of that year they were played in England at the rooms of Jean Baptiste Loeillet, a Belgian
    composer, who settled in London *c.*1705 and held weekly concerts from *c.*1710 at his
    house in Hart Street, Covent Garden, and later at East Street, near Red Lion Square,
    where he died.

scene, for people are apt to censure the whole according to the first, and last relish. Nothing can begin more majestically then the Itallian canzoni of the last age, of which I have seen many and admired them. And what is more relevant then a solemne dancer's entry, with his lofty cutts,★ and no trifling stepps, which soon after follow fast enough? This consideration hath made me wonder at a certein sett of sonnatas I have seen[,] every one of which began with an allegro, and those

of

f. 84v   / of a buisy and nimble action, which is just as if a balle at court began with a morris-dance; or running barley-break[275] about the room. Any regular movement swift or slow will doe well in proper place, as after a grave, an allegro, etc. but even there a temper is to be used, and extreams avoided, that is out of very slow, to extream swift, without any interposition, which may not doe so well tho even Corelli hath once done it especially with fuges, which essentially require moderation. But not to dwell in these criticismes it is enough to say that, what with slow and quick, soft and loud, duple and tripla, there is unlimited scope for variety, which artificially disposed, as contraria juxta se, etc. will set each other off; but, with these cautions, that the same carracter be not spun out too long, for then without an extraordinary genious, it will grow dull, which is the worst effect musick can have. And next that there be a contin-uall regard to humanity; for if there be in nature any means to move the passions, and affections, which were never denyed to musick, those ought to be persued, as the best, or rather the onely means

to

f. 85   / to pleas. And lastly, as was prescribed,[276] after having made the consort to advance to a non plus ultra★ of action, and chorus, then to close all at once.

118. The basso continuo not ordinarily to ceas
      And during the whole sonnata, the basso continuo should not ceas one moment, altho divers of the parts may rest and perhaps all

---

[275] The barley-break was an old country game originally played by six people in couples. One couple, being left in a middle den termed 'hell', had to catch the others, who were allowed to separate or 'break' when hard pressed and thus to change partners, but when caught had to take their turn as catchers.
[276] See f. 84.

for a time, for any fissure in measures which thro swift and slow should be uniforme hurts the enterteinement, becaus they will run on in the auditors' minds, and ought to be attended by the basso continuo so long as that enterteinment lasts. But yet, to shew how for representation or humour, every thing, even (seeming) absurditys may be made use of, there is a passage in the Prince[277] Arthur where in the midst of a full chorus, a rurall deity enters, and with a loud base voice, sings, Peace. And then all the musique stopt all at once, and after a time the musick being resumed he sang, Silence, and was obeyed, a majesty in musick I have not observed in any I ever met with and even that silence kept the time.[278] I shall conclude this partition with one observation which is that the graver straines labour after harmony, and the lighter after melody, or tune.

The

85v / The former allows the inner parts a parity, but the other (except in fuges) as also all festivous musick, sets them on work to fill, as if the whole composition were designed onely for the sake of one part.

119. Of vocall musick

I may seem forgetfull, after having extolled vocall musick, as I have done, above all others,[279] and now in all this cours of varietys, to have mentioned litle or nothing of it. The reason hath bin that it seemed most proper to intercale it between the sociall, and ecclesiasticall, having a great interest in either, especially the latter, which allmost wholly consists of it. The musica di camera is allwais sublimed by the cooperation of good voices especially in the way of symphony, and the ecclesiasticks have used instruments to give a perfection to their voices; nay a single voice to an instrument is a consort of it self. Such are the prærogatives of voices. But since all pre-eminent vertues, and good quallitys are obnoxious to corruption or abuse, it is not to be wondered at, if the superior order of harmony by voices should not altogether escape; therefore I shall

be

f.86 / be so free to observe what I think amiss or amenable in the use of them.

[277] I.e., King.
[278] The passage is not from *King Arthur* but from *The Fairy Queen,* a semi-opera composed by Purcell and first performed in May 1692.
[279] See ff.9–10v.

120. Corrupted by imitation of instruments

The sounding part and how to make the most of it, hath bin at large held forth,[280] as also the errors that learners are lyable to, in the conduct of their voices;[281] that which remaines is to be answered for by the masters that compose for them rather then by the singers, unless they are of a forme pretending to be masters themselves. The cheif failings that I have to complain of proceed from the one mistake which is that they for the most part use or imitate the manner of ayre which is proper for instruments. The voice is of another genius, and capacity, and utterly unfitt for the movements practiced ordinarily upon instruments, whence many inconveniences; one is that it is apt to strain the compass too wide. Voices may reach great lengths one way and other, and thereby seem to have a large compass, but then it is done with loss of the good tone, (in that voice) peculiarly elegant[,] for the compass of a good tone, and [the] extent in the scale are very different. And it is not without just observation and skill, that this fault is obviated.

f.86v   / 121. The cackling manner, introduced

A greater inconvenience is that it introduceth the cackling manner of singing, that is a continued devision upon certein syllables, which may be A, I, E, O, or U, tho A hath the greatest share and may claime it, becaus it is most like children's crying. In the mean time the words are lost, nor is there much regard to them in the moderate way, for so many slurrs of divers notes to one syllable are used, that it is hard to pick out what the poem is that is sung. And this inconvenience is so gross, that the theaters are not ashamed, to allow weomen to sell the printed songs, that the audience (capable to read) may know what poetry is forthcoming. And yet this single point of being understood, is more materiall then all other graces; and that also demands another method then belongs to instruments which is in holding syllables to their time, and not to hobble over short and long in any manner, so the tune be made out. And in this the poets have their share who should versifye, (blank perhaps better then rhithme★) sonorously. Upon this measure the Italian language it self is reformed, for no word ends without a vowell, and all the hard syllables of the Latine are softened, as for objecta,[282]

---

[280] See ff. 12–14v.
[281] See ff. 10v–11v.
[282] MS has 'objectam'.

(which cannot be sung) ogetto, and for ex, ess, and the like. And if

if I

.87 / I had power to order, there should be no more sounds then syllables, and those to come as neer the manner of speech as might consist with song; and this is no novelty, since in our cathedrall churches some shaddow of it may be observed every day, enough to shew what is practicable, and may be improved to serve in all kinds of musick.

122. Voices not to ape the manner of instruments

It may not be pretended that such a manner would be any impediment to the full sound of a voice, for it gives all advantage to make the most of it. Nothing is so pernicious and destructive of sound, as devisions and curling graces, against which I have given some caution before.[283] Nor will it rescind all manner of graceing, so as to reduce a voice to a Dunstable plain[n]ess;* for there are elegances in passing from one note or syllable to another, which are derived upon the skill of harmonious composition, well knowne to all good singers, which by imitation may be communicated to beginners, but otherwise scarce expressible. The most skillfull of the elder Itallians leav all those matters to the performers, and

write

7v / write their musick plain; and all that I can ac[c]use them of is too much of the chachinnatory* manner, which sure they had from the Goths and Vandales since nothing in the nature or true use of things can be more barbarous.[284] But (with all that) they had the soul of musick in their compositions, which the Modernes, with their many motive and slurring ornaments, have corrupted; those affectations at best are but a cortex, and have not the nervous substance[285] of harmony. It had bin better if instruments of the hand, had affected to imitate the tones of the voice, and not the voice, them; for if there must be apeing in the case, that had succeeded better then to have the more perfect truckle to the manner of the less. But to add to this the authority of an example

---

[283] See ff. 54, 63, 76–78v; and f. 58v.

[284] The Goths, one of a Teutonic people, invaded the Roman empire; the Vandals, a Germanic people, ravaged Gaul and Spain in the fifth century, settled in Africa and in 455 sacked Rome. Afterwards, the names, Goth and Vandal, became synonymous with rude or barbaric persons.

[285] I.e., spirit.

* rauvivar: ?ravvivar
† di suspetto: ?di sul petto

I will take one of an elder style, of which the entrance is most sonorous and magnifique, and the tripla following falls into more air; and the whole if I could here shew it, would demonstrate what a recitative should be.

These

f.88   / 123. Of the rec[i]tativo manner

These frusta* of a celebrated canzon, shew the difference between the elder and moderne Itallian style, and give me a fair handle of discoursing more largely of the recitativo manner as now it is used in the operas. I have not found much, if any thing at all of it. In the canzoni of the elder masters, that flourished about the reigne of King James 1 and [King] Charles 1[,] and upon hearing that litle of it opportunity hath afforded me, I cannot say in generall that I like it. But I am sure that of those I have conversed with, who heard much more of them, very few had other sentiments, and many declared, that had it not bin for the cantati that were to follow they had not sate them out. Somewhat therefore must be amiss in them; for a musicall enterteinement ought to pleas every one, and (save faulty sence of hearing) either the composition, performance, or instruments, are not as they should be, and where are all these found so well as at the operas? No body ever was weary of an old Italian song by a celebrious* voice. Now a due observance of that manner, of which I have chose an example of the plainest,[286] compared with the moderne style of the recitativos, may strike a light for discovery of this great mistery.

The elder

/ 124. Difference between recitativo and speaking

The elder recitativos departed neither from the purest harmony (as may be seen in these few notes[287]) nor (by labouring after a style of comon speaking) from the elegance of melody or good ayre. Now the Modernes pass thro much variety of accords, but want the great ornament of harmony, melody or tune[,] and pass from note to note in such an exotick way that one cannot say, whither it is singing, or speaking. I know they intend both, which will not be; for so much as is musick must have melody, and so much as is speech, must not have any, but continue the same tone, and in that lyes the true difference between singing, and speaking. If it be sayd that the sonorous voices of them that read or speak to great auditorys are both speaking and singing; I answer[,] it's true that such deliberate and loud pronounciation falls into a tone, and measure, and is aptly termed by the ecclesia[s]ticks a singing, but it is not musicall, for it is perpetuall in the same tone, which would be a strange mess in an opera. And nothing that shifts the tone, as the recitativos, for the sake of accords doe, can be like speaking, so between one and the other, the consequence is a fastidium. I grant that speaking, as all humane actions[,] may in some sort be in music imitated, but then it

must

/ must not withdraw from the flowing aire of the keys that belong to the melody, but be perfect musick, as well as imitation, and not suffer the imitation to corrupt the musick, but afford the audience an uniforme satisfaction, which cannot be when pleasure and offence alternately affect them.

125. Example in Laneare's Hero and Leander[288]

I shall have occasion to touch these matters over againe in what is

---

[286] See f.87v, Example 1.

[287] See f.87v, Example 1.

[288] (and Ex. 1). Nicholas Lanier (b. 1588, d. 1666), composer, singer, lutenist and artist, travelled to Italy between 1625–28. After his return to England he composed his long recitative, *Hero and Leander*. This was first printed in the fourth book of John Playford's *Choice Ayres . . .*, London 1683 and reprinted in Henry Playford's *The New Treasury of Musick . . .*, London 1695. North refers to one, or perhaps both, of these as 'scurvily' printed (*Musicall Recollections III*: f.63).

to follow,[289] but in the mean time in favour of a melodious recitative, I cannot but reiterate a recomendation of Mr. Laneare's Hero and Leander,[290] as a compleat patterne of an Italian style, in an English recitative. I wish, for making good what I say, I might have given it all, but for a tast[e] here is a few words at the beginning,

the least remarkable. The basso continuo is underwrote, which I presume may not disturbe what belongs to the song; the rest expresseth

passion

f.89v / passion, hope, fear, and despair, as strong as words and sounds can bear, and saving some peices of Mr. H. Purcell, wee have nothing of this kind in English at all recommendable.

126. No imitation of inanimate things without action

It is an erroneous practise, but very comon, to strain hard in imitation of inanimate things, as place, or position. It would be rare if the musick should advance also in the quallity of picture, as when the subject mounts either really or metaphorically then the notes are upon wing and soon get above E la or discending, then they tumble downe grumbling to double D and so you have a description of

---

[289] See f.97v.
[290] North has not previously recommended *Hero and Leander* in this text.

heaven, and hell, all which as to touching the affections have no vertue or efficacy at all. If one looks upon the notation, there is a ladder indeed which shews the degrees of rising and falling, but sharp and flatt in tone, gives no idea of altitude or depression, unless somewhat like it may proceed (not from the thing but) from a prejudice, and having no relation to any state of humanity; such sounds lay hold of no passion and draw no locall resentment. ★

All actions

f.90 / 127. Any thing motive imitable

All actions being motive[,] and sounds of things animate or inanimate, admitt of a musicall immitation in some degree; as in a state of running a slow measure is improper, and a paralell quick-ness makes a sort of resemblance; and the alternate,[291] quick measures for slow proceedings, is equally absurd. And musick being all sound, may personate any sounds whither of things animate or inanimate; as the sea may roar, either in comon notes, or with iterations prolonging the ro[oooar][292] and as in the redicule[,] thunder may be plain, or with a thuuuunder.[293] But considering how these points are abused by a hurry hurry of insignificant devision, the plain way is best, at least when a laugh or the like is sung. If masters could have so much moderation, a short touch of 3 or 4 notes might serve the turne; for in truth the words, run, sit, roar, thunder and the like, if understood, touch the spirits without such imitations. As to other resemblances by sounds of joy, sorrow, and the like; enough hath bin sayd,[294] to which I add onely, that these attempts serve to help the fancy, and supply invention, which in composing very often wants such lifts.

f.90v The eccl-[295]

f.91 / 128. Ecclesiasticall musick, preferable

The ecclesiasticall style, as all agree, makes the best musick. It is

[291] I.e., alternative.
[292] MS has 'ro. . . .'.
[293] Wilson (1959: 266) suggested that the allusion is to *The Rehearsal,* a play written in 1663 by George Villiers, second duke of Buckingham, in which an actor, representing Thunder, is told by the producer to repeat the word 'in a voice that thunders it out indeed'. Wilson's suggestion is highly probable, since North's writings contain a number of references to 'Mr. Bayes', one of the characters in the play (see, for example, *Some Memorandums, concerning Musick*: f.24; *General Preface* ed. Millard 1984: 71; and *Cursory Notes of Musicke* ed. Chan and Kassler 1986: 225). *The Rehearsal* was produced in 1671 and printed in 1672; a fifth edition with amendments appeared in 1687, and a 'key' was published in 1705.
[294] See ff.64v–66v, 67–67v.
[295] The page is blank except for the catchwords at the bottom.

therefore fitt to inquire what reasons there are for it. One seems to be, that it is confined to a solemnity of ayre, and all levitys are excluded. Therefore the harmony is incomparably set off, which in light ayres is in great measure lost; and the melody hath no less advantage, becaus the movements are distinct as well as ayery. And within this compass there is scope enough for variety, for there will be a power of swifter and slower both in dupla and tripla measures, without running wild as the usages of other kinds of musick are apt to doe. And wherein those are most wanton, that is in the tripla measure[,] the church ayres surpass all[,] for no sort of musick expresseth the majesty of a grand pas★ like the slow tripla, which to diversifie upon fitt occasion, may inliven, but yet all are to keep within the bounds of decency, suiting the place, and intention. This is the standard of our church musick, and if, as they say, consorts and operas are introduced in some forrein churches, it is in the place of anthems, and belong to the theatricall kind (of which after-wards[296]) being intended for publik entertainement

and

f.91v   / and are no part of the service, as the hymnes, and psallmodys are which must retein their solemnity; and if the anthemes were as ours are, they might retein their appellation, ecclesi[a]sticall, which would not suffer by the greatest apparatus of voices and instruments that can be had, the style onely altered, and that, as many will judg, for the better.

129. The use of many voices in chorus

Another reason why church musick is preferred is becaus it is comonly heard in full chorus, or els in consort harmony, as in the dayly hymnes[297] according to the best services. When the chorus som[e]times pauseth, and then a consort of 3 or 4 voices continues the musick, till the chorus joynes again, here is a body of melody, and harmony to fullfill the sharpest appetite to musick. Some may choos a superlative voice, to an exquisite basso continuo, and think that best; I grant it is wonderfully delightfull, but then 2 such voices are better, and 3 then those. I have not knowne any musick so exquisite, as 2 prime voices in consort and from thence I had an idea of more added, the bright clangor★ of which must needs kill any single voice, but being disposed consort wise, as in the

canzona

---

[296] See ff.95–98v.
[297] I.e., canticle settings.

f.92   / canzona at the end of these papers,[298] mixt with some pauses, and so junto,* and solo alternatively is a consort in perfection, unless a chorus of many such, if it were to be heard, should claim that caracter.

130. The advantage of an arched church

Another advantage which church musick hath is the place, that is a spacious church, repleat with eccho[,] the very extent of which gives liberty to the sounds, as well to soften,[299] as to intermix. And I cannot allow that the musick proper for a great church would be so good in a chamber, for there the harmony would appear more broken, and all the roughnesses, and defects of the voices be more perceivable then in the church; and for the softening and polishing the composition of the musicall sounds that arrive at the sence all together there is a very apposite experiment which may be made at any time in King's College Chappell. Between the shell of the main arches and the timber covering, lay an ear to one of the holes thro which cords pass for carrying chaires when the inside of the roof is cleaned, and the organ with the quire sounding, such a delicious musick shall be heard, as I may call the quintessence of harmony, not otherwise to be described.[300]

There

92v   / 131. Magnificence in view exalts the musick

There is another means that advanceth the effect of church musick, and that is the magnificence of the structure in which it is heard.[301] I challenge any one to say that he enters into a stately cathedral and a barn, be it never so bigg, with the same temper of mind; for the former will strike a reverence, and raise the mind with a pleasure unknowne elswhere. And if the walls have such effect upon the spiritts, the sounds within them, whither reading or singing, will partake in the same influence. The very organ is not the same thing as in a chamber, and the voices also excell for where every thing resents grandure, it would be strange if musick should not have its share. Besides all this much is ascribed to the loudness of quire musick, for it is seldome that so many voices are heard together, even theaters, and operas doe not afford it, of which

---

[298] See ff.145–147v.
[299] I.e., make less harsh.
[300] The experiment was repeated by Wilson (1959: 268, n.28).
[301] North sampled the music in various cathedrals and churches whilst riding with his brother, Francis, on the western and northern circuit (see, for example, *Life of Francis North* ed. M. North 1819: i/230 on Exeter Cathedral, 263 on Durham Cathedral, 279–80 on the church at Litchfield).

afterwards.[302] And not setting aside all these advantages, I must place the very manner, and style of church musick, tho confined to an ordinary chamber, in the front of all that's excellent in the whole survey of harmony.

But

f.93   / 132. Means wanting and comon chanting an abuse

But I shall be asked what is the reason that these excellences are not found in many (if in any) of our cathedrall churches, so that except in [Saint] Paul's and the Royall Chappell, there are few that care much to hear it. I wish there were not reasons plenty to be given for it. I shall touch but a few particulars. And first as to the chanting the psalmes, when performed decently, the organ presiding, the musick, tho it chant most upon the key note, yet in vertue of the cadences which are artificiall, the harmony is exceeding good; but one may conceive how it might be much better, if the English language would allow it. And that is if the whole quire should pronounce the vers as well as the close in distinct counterpoint time with respect to long and short syllables, and then come off in the cadences all exactly together. But where the most deliberate chanting is, the pronounciation is at best a huddle unintelligible, as if all strove to have done first. And for this reason, where the organ is not used which keeps the quire upright, the chanting is scandalous, such a confused din as no one living not preinstructed could guess what they were doing. And I

suppose

f.93v   / suppose the monks where Erasmus came, chanted in that manner, which provoked him to say, their sound was more like the gaggling of gees, then the voices of men.[303] And with us, considering how litle, (or rather no) care is taken of this noble part of the service, but all run on, non passibus [a]equis,* it is a wonder that where the organ is used, it is so well performed as it is, and where it is not used, who expects better then the musick of Babell?[304]

---

[302] See ff.96v–98.

[303] Desiderius Erasmus (b. 1469, d. 1536), Netherlands humanist, whose attempts to regulate and reform music derived from his understanding of antiquity, his belief in biblical doctrine and his reaction to contemporary church music. The main focus of his attention was Gregorian chant, concerning which he criticised the accentuation of the texts and long melismata, the two features which undermined intelligibility of the words of the chant. In *Musicall Recollections III* (f.36v), North indicates that his source is 'lib. de pronun.' (see Erasmus 1528/1971), a work that gave direction to contemporary ideas concerning pronunciation of classical languages and at the same time provided the stimulus, particularly in England and France, for a closer examination of vernacular pronunciation and, hence, to the development of the study of phonetics.

[304] The confusion of tongues, which is recounted in Genesis xi: 1–9, became a major theme in writings of the sixteenth and seventeenth centuries.

133. Singing with melody or without, but never like comon speaking

The liturgie allows some passages to be sayd or sung; one would consider the difference. It seems not to be so much as is comonly understood, for in that sence singing is not according to melody and harmony, but in a distinct and sonorous voice without any modulation[305] at all, as the use is in our great churches in rehearsing the Pater noster, and Credo; and in that respect onely singing differs from common speech. For in speech the syllables are pronounced close, and in a customable disorder, but in singing, every syllable is pronounced at length, and in the same musicall tone; and doth not necessarily implye an harmonious composition. And if one may be so bold to guess, the singing [of] the Niceen

creed

f.94 / creed as if it were an hymne, proceeds from hence[,] for the requiring it to be sung, doth not implye melodiously, but distinctly, and with a sonorous voice all on the same tone. But our usage in the 2d service[306] is otherwise, and the true reason of vocall pronounciation in great churches, is that such vast congregations as were, or should be there, might hear and be edifyed, which would not be by comon speaking, and one may defie a good reader there to make himself well heard, unless he useth that manner which is called singing, and he shall fall into it incogitanter.* Hence wee have also a rationale of changing the tone, for by that the remoter people might know what the prayers are and also by the cadence tone at the end when the prayer is done, so also for the suffrages. The churches (generally) performe these parts well and in good order, and I have sayd thus much concerning them, purely in opposition to the stupid sectarys, who suppose singing to be a light exercise, and unfitt for churches.[307]

134. Why church musick failes

But it is very much to be lamented, that musicall skill, and

---

[305] I.e., inflexion.
[306] I.e., Communion service.
[307] I.e., the nonconformists of North's day (that is, after the Restoration) who, for a variety of reasons, opposed the inclusion of music in the church. Some, for example, objected to any singing; others, specially to the psalms as being unsuited to Christian worship. Some countenanced the psalms but scrupled about metre; others objected to anyone being heard but the minister. Some doubted that women should break their silence in the church (see f.94v, n.311); others condemned promiscuous singing in which good and bad alike took part. Besides these objections, all of which pertain to singing, others were made to the use of musical instruments.

abillity is so low, that it is very hard to get voices to make a quire. If most children were taught early, the best might be chosen, but

if any

f.94v / if any grown up and untaught, shew a good voice then such are taken in, and with what difficulty taught? And how monstrous is the comon way of teaching comonly found to be, as hath bin already complained of?[308] Wee will not complain of the great master, the organist, who must needs be [of a] Doctor's standing, nor of the failings of the men quiristers, among whom is rarely found a tollerable voice. Nor mention the taking from the cathedralls the most hopefull of their boys, to serve in the Royall chappells;[309] but it is certein the quires are poorly furnished, and one way or other the vocall performances are very mean; and I think an observation of good King Charles 2 at Canterbury may conclude this topick. He was asked how he liked Dr. Gosling's voice,[310] and he answered that all the rest sang like gees to him. One might without a desperate solescism maintain that if female quiristers were taken into quires instead of boys, it would be a vast improvement of chorall musick becaus they come to a judgment as well as voice, which the boys doe not arrive at before their voices perish, and small improvement of skill grows up in the room, till they come to man's estate. But both text and morallity are against it;[311] and the Romish[312] usage of castration is utterly unlawful, and is scandallous practice wherever it is used.

I come

f.95 / 135. Theatricall musick, comick and opera [and] 1. the comick

I come now to a sort of musick I ventured to terme theatricall,[313] which may be parted in two, [the] first comick, and the other,

[308] See ff.21–21v *et passim*.

[309] The master of the children had the power to impress promising choristers for service in the Chapel Royal. Visitations were made for this purpose at least until 1684, but when the practice actually ceased is not known.

[310] John Gostling (b. *c.* 1650, d. 1733), cathedral singer and music copyist, was educated at St. John's College, Cambridge; B.A. (1673). Subsequently, he was a minor canon at Canterbury Cathedral (1674–1733) and at St. Paul's Cathedral (1679–1733).

[311] The text is 1 Corinthians xiv: 34–5, where St. Paul admonishes: 'Let your women keep silence in the churches: for it is not permitted unto them to speak, but they are commanded to be under obedience, as also saith the law. And if they will learn any thing, let them ask their husbands at home: for it is a shame for women to speak in the church'. North's statement about women echoes that of Hobbes, who wrote: 'Prophecy in that place [1 Corinthians ii: 4,5], signifieth no more, but praising God in Psalmes, and Holy Songs; which women might doe in the Church, though it were not lawfull for them to speak to the Congregation' (ed. Macpherson 1651/1986: 457).

[312] I.e., Roman Catholic.

[313] See f.82.

opera. By the former I mean the comon entertainement and interludes of plays, which in former times were dispersed abroad by the
name of playhous tunes; and of this sort is all our comon musick at
feasts, and celebrated rejoycings. There is not much to be observed
of these, but onely that they are cheifly compounded of melody,
and pulsation or time. The consort is not much heeded, and if the
melody is ayery, or what they call pretty, the ground may be of a
comon style, and the more vulgar, the better. And all the force of
these consorts lyes in the upper part to which all the rest and even
the base sometimes is subservient. Therefore it is to litle porpose to
crowd in accords by inner parts, for if they could have any melody
care is taken, by doubling the superior to drowne them. And the
best accomplishment is by number and nois. But I must allow that
the attendance of instruments of the arpeggio kind, which rattle
plentyfully, as harpsicords, archlutes, and above all the pandora,
give a fullness as well as elegance to the sound, and

there-

.95v / thereby attracts attention. It is to my knowledg within the
memory of man, that in the (then) celebrated consorts divers of the
pandoras were used, which being a sort of double guitarres strung
with wires, and of those the bases double, and twisted, and struck
with a quill, strangely inriched those vulgar consorts which now
for want of a mixture of the arpeggio appear beggarly. And if
memory failes not very much, those pandoras, by way of thro base
had a better and more sonorous effect in the mixture, then now may
be ascribed to harpsicords. For the full sound of many instruments,
kills the best of them, and turnes the pulses to a timekeeping
service, more then any addition to the consort.

136. Vnfit for private uses, save dancing

As to the private enterteinement of such as call themselves lovers
of musick, this manner is very imperfect, if not useless; becaus all
runns into the melody of a single part, and the other parts, if any,
are no better then hum–drum drudges; and scarce any but hirelings
will be concerned with them; for which reason they are used mostly
in the theaters, where such allwais attend. And for this caus I think
that the musick of this class should be left to the proper owners, the
ordinary musitians. I have

observed

f.96 / observed some persons, lovers, and no mean performers, very
sollicitous to encourage the comon fidlers, that enterteined them at

mealls, to practise the celebrated sonnatas with which they were
used in private to divert themselves. But it seemed very unfitt, for
they must sitt and hear themselves out done, becaus those who play
all their live's long, will touch with more vigor[,] distinction and
swiftness, then persons of quality, that exercise onely for their
divertion, can doe. And they debase also the subject matter of a
considerable pleasure, by turning it up to be the joy of sotts in
alehouses, fair-booths, and tavernes. In a word this sort of popular
musick is most apt for driving away thinking and letting in dancing, and the former of these dispatched, all people's members are
apt to assume the other, and almost sencelessly to move one way or
other keeping the time as the pulses of the musick, wherein consists
the cheif efficacy, incites.

f.96v   / 137. Operas want no perfection

Now concerning the late operas, after so much discours as hath
bin had of most branches of musicall enterteinements[314] it cannot
be expected that I should have much of anything materiall to alledg
concerning them[,] the rather becaus I am not in the way to observe
them much.[315] But yet according to that litle I have personally
noted and had by prints and information of others, I shall be no
niggard in giving my thoughts of them. And first that they are an
assemblage of every kind that is good in musick, voices, action,
instruments of all kinds, performers, compositions, and what not
in perfection. If solemn musick is desired, nothing [is] more compleat then divers of the overtures, and so for other theatricall
consorts, which are intersperst in the enterteinement, and nothing
can be procured more efficacious for setting off the best voices then
is found there. The orchestre, as it is (improperly) called,[316] full-
filled with the best masters performing upon most usefull instruments, with such a clangor as sublimes the most vulgar ayre into
transcendent harmony: what in a chamber would be dull is there all
spirit; such is the vertue of magnificence even of sounds, to which
must be added

that

---

[314] See ff. 82–96.
[315] On 26 December 1690 North bought an estate at Rougham, Norfolk, and commenced
    rebuilding in 1692; he settled there permanently in 1701, when he rented out his rooms at
    the Middle Temple, London.
[316] In ancient theatres the orchestra was the place where the chorus danced and sang (see
    Vitruvius tr. Gwilt 1826: Chapter 8).

f.97   / that of the apparatus, decoration and illumination of a spacious theater, which with the splendor of the company, must needs affect the spirits of the auditory with a soveraigne pleasure. And with all this, it were to be wished that such perfections had never come amongst us, for they have allmost suppressed the ordinary copia of usefull musick, which comes not up to such heights, as I have particularly intimated before.[317] And it is notorious that in our comon theaters, as musick and decorations have advanced, good sence, witt, and action have declined.

138. Faction about voices

But to returne to our operas, setting aside the generall caracter here given and condiscending to particulars, there are some failings that might be amended. I know not whither the want of voices in parity, or neerer to it then they have, may be accounted one; and instead of one or two capitalls, a fuller chorus of such, would add to enterteinement. But as it is, the vocall composition is adapted to them and turnes to single ayres, and the censure passeth from the musick, to the dexterity of one or two singers;[318] and many that say nothing of the former shall

strive

97v   / strive mordicitus★ in favour of one singer against another and so transitur in partes.★ And the best voices care not to joyne in consort one with another which manner in a theatre[,] I mean consort[,] is doubdtless the best of the musick.

139. Recitative carrys neither air nor speech

But then respecting the forme of this musick it consists of 2 sorts: 1. ayery, and 2. recitative. I have observed that the recitative goes off from the ayre, and yet reacheth not a speaking tone. But certeinly it makes a different species, so that some who are fond of the aire will not bear the recitativo, and others may be as much delighted with that, which hath the same inconvenience, as when (in Mr. Betterton's semi operas) the drama was devided from the musick, and all the auditors were sure to be offended as well as

[317] See ff.76–76v.
[318] I.e., the Italians, Faustina Bordoni (b. 1700, d. 1781) and Francesca Cuzzoni (b. c.1698, d. 1770). Their rivalry became notorious during the 1726–27 opera season in London. On 6 June 1727, ovations, whistles, catcalls and hisses provoked a scuffle on stage between the two singers who supposedly were satirised as Polly and Lucy in *The Beggar's Opera* (but see f.76v, n.253).

pleased.[319] Therefore I should choos to quit the recitativo, or at least the manner of it, and conduct the whole opera thro a continued current of ayre, as in the elder Itallian operas (of which I have one by me) and recitativos (of which I have given peice of an example[320]) were used. But yet ayre is not to be so much courted as to loos the sence of the words in it, and of this error I can scarce excuse the best voices, who often loos the words in some fine turnes of ayre.

As to

f.98   / 140. Manner of the musick fiery, and litle or none of the mild sort

As to the instrumentall part it seemed to me that the orchestre was under based; of that part, the cheif were bassoons, which have more of the sound then effect of a base; for being sounded onely by a small reed the force is weak, and doth not urge the other instrument[s], as the double violls, doe. It is found that no pipes will make a sufficient base to an organ, but a double violl conjoyned supplyes what the faint blast wants, force; which beats all the rest of the sounds into order, and tune. The hautbois in the superior have a transcendent effect, and it is pitty they should not be sustained by the stoutest of bases. It may seem also an excess in the style of the opera musick, for (not medling with devisions and high flights upon the instruments, which have bin allready censured[321]) the whole manner is starting, * which doubdtless is very well, when the occasion requires, as to dancing or other like action, but when there is not that call for it, a softer, and more sedate manner intermixt, would not be amiss[,] for a true lucid harmony is never well in a passion, whither of joy or fright, or as if a man swore an oath at every word. For then

action

---

[319] Thomas Betterton (b. 1653, d. 1710), actor, theatre manager and author, was involved in different capacities in semi-operas, operas and plays with incidental music. In an early text North writes that both music and drama 'are principalls. And wee know not which to apply our attention to most. In such case, nothing is so sure, as that every one will be better pleased with one then the other, the consequence is this, that the delight of one, ills the other and makes it hatefull. And that must be a fault. I observed, this to Mr Betterton. He answered I was for dining on one dish rather then two, and so answered me with a simile. His better reason had bin, the true one, that the towne had not will or pallat enough, to know and relish what's good' (*Some Memorandums, concerning Musick*: f.26v; see also *Cursory Notes of Musicke* ed. Chan and Kassler 1986: 231). Hence, under the guise of 'auditors', North records his own reactions.
[320] See f.87v, Example 1.
[321] See ff.54, 63, 76–78v ('devisions') and ff.73, 78v, 83 ('high flights').

f.98v   / action becomes the principall; and harmony, or at least the flower of it, which consists in the interweaving of the parts is dropt, and onely a puls of an accord used in the room. The continuance of tones is richer then the memory of a stroke; as the sound of an organ, exceeds the touch of an harpsicord.

f. 102

/ Memoires of Musick
being
some historico-critticall collections
of that subject
1728

/Advertisement

Having dispatcht the Theory of Sounds [and the] grammaticall speculations of musick,[322] I doe not yet find in my self a full discharge of what I owe to that transcendent subject; but as a lover is not satisfyed in his rhapsodys to comend the beauty of his mistress, but he must needs search into her genealogie, cujus caput inter nubila★ – so am I in mind urged to look as farr back into the family of our dear art, as my faint opticks will permitt. And the result here I have intituled Memoires, as not pretending to a full history, a work for Herculean shoulders, but onely to collect and modifye some historico-criticall scrapps[323], hoping to be thereby eased of an incumbrance that as a dett lyes heavy upon my conscience.

[322] See *T S 1728* and ff. 1–101v above.
[323] MS has 'scarapps'.

/ 1. Antiquitys subject to extreams

In matters of Antiquity there are two extreams: 1. a totall neglect, and 2. perpetuall guessing; between which proper evidences
are the temper[,] that is if there be any, to make the best of them, if
none[,] to desist. So hounds in a cold s[c]ent are dilligent, and all
scent failing desist, and hopelessly trot away. This thought came
into my mind when I had a fancy to hunt after the antiquitys of
musick, and I had certeinly acted the despairing hound, if some
personall memory, and experience had not deteined me; for it hath
fallen in my way to observe, not to say practise, some species of
musick, long since antiquated, and in that respect may justly be
taken into the account of antiquitys; and now being engaged in the
recollection of those, the inquisitive spirit draws me back into the
dark speculation of what musick was in former ages and if the result
in what follows shall appear fond, erroneous or frivolous, in a pure
essay, it may be excused, the rather becaus neither religion, the state
or good manners are like to be hurt by it.

/ 2. Ancient modes of musick not intelligible

Wee have large and subtile accounts of the musick of the ancient
Greeks and after them the Latins with the addition of no less
copious, and subtile commentations* of moderne wrighters, and
notwithstanding all those, wee are yet ignorant how (so much as in
possibillity) to reconcile the misterious modes, and effects reported
of them; and many learned men have bin pleased to extoll the
antique musick, as farr excelling the moderne, and the Modernes no
less learned, but as I take it more skillfull, have pronounced the
other to be barbarous and unnaturall. This difference can never be
reconciled, first becaus in matters of tast[e], there is no criterium of
better and wors, and men determine upon fancy and prejudice, and
not upon intrinsick worth; and next becaus wee have no specimens
of antique musick left for us whereby (as it were) to tast[e] the
difference; and as for the skill, and manner of performance, lan-

guage is not sufficient to excite a just idea of it. Therefore, caracters apart, all wee have to doe is to inquire by what means the

Ancients

f.104   / Ancients found out and modeled the use of certein sounds to gratifie the sence of hearing and thereupon instituted the art called musique; and then to observe as well as wee may the changes that art hath undergone downe to our time. And that I may not appear to faile overmuch in so great an undertaking, I must aforehand declare that I pretend not to see further into the millstone then others have done, or may doe, but propose onely by conjecture to enlighten some obscuritys, whereof the reasons shall be shewed and submitted.

3. Ancient arts knowne by specimens and not by words

It is the misfortune of all arts of which the use happens to be discontinued, (leaving no reall specimens, which onely can demonstrate what the practise of any such art was, except some dark verball descriptions), and so to fall into the catalogue of the artes deperditæ,★ and be hardly, if ever recoverable, but yet by some cloudy expression found remaining to make work for crittiques, and the world litle the wiser; for arts have peculiar terms, that is a language understood by the professors, and some few els in the time; but in after times when such arts are attempted to be

revived

f.104v   / revived, who should make the dictionary, or adapt things to the words used by obsolete authors? It is certein that nothing, but the very things appearing by specimens (if any are left) can doe it; and without such authoritys, become enigmatick. The mathematical arts have come downe to us intire, becaus the subject (quantum) is knowne to every body. Rhetorick and poetry bring their proper specimens with them, the old speeches and poems; architecture but imperfectly, of which the antique is knowne almost intirely by the vestigia[324] yet actually, or in picture, remaining; and without the help of such formes of the ancient fabricks, had never bin gathered out of Vitruvius,[325] who wrote on porpose to instruct them;[326] and is not yet effectually understood.

[324] MS has 'vestigii'.
[325] Vitruvius (Vitruvius Pollio; Lucius Vitruvius Mamurra) (b. *c.* 84, d. 14 B.C.), Roman technical writer and architect, is known chiefly from his ten books on architecture (tr. Gwilt 1826).
[326] I.e., architects.

4. Old musick destitute of practique examples

And this inconvenience hath happened to the science and practise of musick in the highest degree, for among the Greek republiks, that art was had in veneration, as if law, liberty, justice, and all morallity depended upon it. And the modes and effects of it were the admiration, as well as delight of all men, both wise and unwise; and according to the disposition of the philosophers of

those

105 / those times, every naturall energye, was moulded into a formall science. So musick had its fate; and from following nature, and imitation, was made an art with laws and rules not to be temerated;* as they say, the adding a string to an instrument, was made almost high treason.[327] And of this subject wee have authors upon authors and comentators upon them. But for want of reall or practicable specimens it is not understood what their musick was, nor yet by means of all the pretended discoverys, can any peice be accordingly framed, that mankind will endure to hear. Altho Kercher hath vainely attempted it.[328]

5. Musick began with vocall pronunciation

I must observe that these assuming Greeks would needs have the orginall,* and invention of musick to have arisen amongst them. And for that end wee have poetick relations of dryed nerves* in tortois shells, smiths' hammers, and practi[ti]oners, as Apollo, Orfeus etc.[329] who might perhaps (as Homer,) sing well to a petite instrument at feasts.[330] But I am persuaded that, notwithstanding all these pretensions, musick had an higher originall and that is the use of voices, and language among men.

05v / And that having such facultys they must necessarily stumble upon the exercise of what wee call singing, that is pronouncing with an open and extended voice; and however the flexures might be rude at

[327] Strings were added by Timotheus (b. *c.* 450, d. *c.* 360 B.C.), whose 'new music' dominated the final decades of the 5th century B.C. and the succeeding period in Greece (see Plutarch tr. Einarson and De Lacy 1967: 421–3; see also Anderson 1966: 50 *et passim.*).

[328] In his *Musurgia* (1650) the German polymath, Athanasius Kircher (b. 1602, d. 1680), gave what purported to be the melody for the opening of Pindar's first Pythian ode. North is correct to be sceptical, since the melody is now regarded as spurious.

[329] North provides a naturalistic, not a supernaturalistic account of the origin of music; hence, the irony here.

[330] Homer (fl. 810–730 B.C.) may be the name of two authors, one who composed the *Iliad* and the other, the *Odyssey*. In 1673 Hobbes's translation of both works was published with his important critical introduction; a second edition appeared in 1677 (see Hobbes ed. Molesworth 1677/1962).

first, in process of time they would improve; especially considering
how usefull singing was in the pastoritiall★ life, the primitive race of
men ledd; among whom any one having a clear, and good voice,
tho purely naturall, must be a prime musitian; and per[ha]ps Tuball
Cain (or Vulcane) might be such a one, and merit the fame they
have had for it.[331]

6. Nothing express before King David[332]

But to drop all these reflections, and come to the time of King
David, for before him all the notice of musick wee have, is of some
songs in the Bible, of which nothing more is knowne, but that they
were songs; and that shews that in the highest Antiquity there was
vocall musick. But when King David for favour invited good old
Barzillai to his court, he[333] excused himself (partly) by his being
unable to hear the voices of singing men and singing weomen;[334]
which is a demonstration that then there was an establisht musick,
and not

onely

f. 106   / onely vocall, as is there expressed, but instrumentall also to attend
them, as appears in the account of David's harping before Saul,
with his hand and fingers[335] and by the epigraffs to divers of the
psalmes, directed to the cheif musitian,[336] and multitude of references to instruments and some particularly with ten strings (which
was not permitted to the Argives).[337] And these musitians were
not of a precarious quallity, as Homer etc.[,] to sing to the kill-
cows★ at feasts, but a royall consort, and the King himself who is
styled cytharædus★ and (probably) the cheif musitian, precenter

---

[331] According to the account in Genesis iv: 21–2, Tubal-Cain was the first metal-worker,
        and his half-brother, Jubal, the first musician. Scholars have supposed that the similarity
        of their names led various authors to speak of Jubal as Tubal; but context is important,
        since Tubal was sometimes linked with Vulcan, the first Roman metal-worker, and both
        were sometimes associated with the myth of Pythagoras' discovery of consonances by
        weights of hammers striking upon an anvil (see f.112, n.362). For examples of this
        linkage, see Hawkins (1776 rev. 1853/1963: i/245, 247; ii/617–8) and Münxelhaus (1976).
        In addition to their associations with metal-work and music, Tubal-Cain and Vulcan
        were important figures in the symbolism of alchemy.
[332] David (fl. 1000–975 B.C.) was founder, king and charismatic ruler of the united
        kingdom of Israel.
[333] I.e., Barzillai.
[334] See 2 Samuel xix: 32–7.
[335] See 1 Samuel xvi: 14–23. Saul was first king of Israel (c. 1050 B.C.).
[336] Of the 150 psalms in the book of Psalms, tradition assigns to David at least seventy-three.
        The 'cheif musitian' was his teacher, Asaph (see 1 Chronicles xvi: 7, xxv: 6).
[337] For the Argives, people of Argos, see Plutarch (tr. Einarson and De Lacy 1967: 441). For
        the 'multitude of references' to ancient Middle Eastern musical instruments, see the Old
        Testament.

amongst them. And if wee may suppose the great men of those times to have bin such scrib[b]lers as the Greeks were, and had works come downe to us, as theirs have done[,] what stately accounts had wee had of the musick of those times.

7. Greek musick cheifly song

But now to trace a little the history of musick, wee must come again among the Greeks, who have left us books enough to shew they had an art so called, upon which their restless witts, and philosofers had refined infinite ways; but their accounts to us are tantum non* hieroglifick; however according to what I have observed and may guess[,][338] their ancient musick (as that word implyes) lay cheifly

in

06v / in a concinnity of verses, which were sung to measures, or some long and short syllables combined, which the poets call feet, without much variation or flexure, and that onely as the accents require. So that a poem accented was without more adoe a song; and that pronoun[ced] in manner as singers use, might be aggreable musick even to us, especially if kept steddy as their use was, by an instrument attendant. Much here might be transcribed out of Plutarch, whose discours of musick is both critticall, and historicall but I can gather very little of distinct notion out of it.[339] It is sayd there, that three things are necessary to concurr in good musick, the sound, the time, and the syllable all together at once which is remarkable.[340] And instruments are scarce ever mentioned, but with respect to poeme. So that so farr as I can see, a poet and a fidler were termes

---

[338] MS has 'guess that'.

[339] Plutarch (b. before A.D. 50, d. after 120), Greek philosopher and biographer, whose treatise on music, *Peri mousikes,* is of doubtful authenticity. In the opening section the interlocutors make clear that music will be considered as a vocal art that comes after grammar (tr. Einarson and De Lacy 1967: 355).

[340] According to Plutarch, 'three smallest components must always simultaneously strike the ear: the note, the time [that is, the rhythmical unit], and the syllable or sound. From the course of the notes we recognize the structure of the scale; from that of the times, the rhythm; and from that of the sounds or syllables, the words of the song. As the three proceed in concert we must follow all with the ear simultaneously. Yet it is also evident that unless the ear can isolate [the note, unit and syllable from] each of the three, it is impossible to follow the details of the three movements and observe the beauties and faults in each. Before we can do this we must know about continuity. Indeed, continuity is required for the exercise of critical judgement, since beauty and the opposite do not arise in this or that isolated note or time or speech-sound, but in the series, as they are a blend of the smallest elements in an actual composition' (tr. Einarson and De Lacy 1967: 437).

convertible, and meant almost the same thing. But the changes afterwards happened to devide them, as will appear.[341]

8. Voices the originall of all musick

   During these elder times, which I may style, of the poets, and so downe to those of the philosofers, in musick the poem was

the

f. 107   / the principall, and instruments but accessionall,* and for melioration, which regulated the tones of the fraile voice, for those of cours would fall into accord with the instrument[.] Therefore the art of musick was originated in the vocall exercise.

9. Scales contrived from the manners of singing

   And the ordinary flexures of the voice in singing, however irregular, and perhaps contingent at first, gave occasion for the forming the severall musicall scales used by the Ancients; for nothing els could administer to the fancy such bizzarre gradations of sounds as some of them carryed; and that is a proof of what was sayd,[342] that singing was the first musick-master, and that nevertheless so becaus some notes in the scales are found just; for voices will naturally fall into a sort of tuneableness, which instruments might assist, and make steddy so as the voices might not swerve as they are apt to doe; but that the just tune of musicall notes in some sort or other is naturall, may be observed by the singing of some birds and the comon crys of the vulgar about the streets, but more especially when the songs were restricted by numbers poetically for the returnes fell into the same tones over and over againe. And it was

obvious

f. 107v   / obvious for the more curious, to observe the various tonations,* and reduce them to a certein order or scales, which I shall exhibite.[343] And then it was practicable to adjust instruments so as to humour, and attend the voice in unisons; it is as I sayd[344] rare to find any mention of musicall instruments, without regard to voices, as if in practise they were for the most part inseparable, and the poem equally allyed in both.

---

[341] See f. 113.
[342] See ff. 105, 105v, 106v.
[343] See f. 110.
[344] See f. 106v.

10. Originall of the scales or tetrachords

To make this genesis of the musicall art more familiar I shall use this image. Wee all know in what manner our stage players rehears their heroick verses, with many too-high-too-lows in a pedantick manner, as scoolmasters use to whine out verses of Virgill to their scollars; which is neither singing, nor speaking, but yet certein tones may be perceived in it. Now let an artist, or philosofer, come and observe those tones, and he·shall discerne the intervalls, and call them dieses,* semitones, tones, or fourths and accordingly forme scales of notes, whereby instruments may be contrived to accompany, in unisons, and choruses, and together make a pleasing sound

108 / and by usage, grow formall in the manner, and in the tones correct. One may guess that in these inceptives of musick, there was not any variations observed exceeding a fourth, but within that space divers orders of change. And a 4th is a consonance a voice is apt to fall into, and there stopp, therefore in early times the cycle of all the alterations was confined to that intervall and then all to returne by like stepps over again and this was the tetrachord, which regulated the tonations of the voice, and instruments from the beginning of the musicall art among the Greeks and continued (but with more latitude) for many ages, even, as I take it, to the time of Constantine, or lower, downe to the possession of the Goths in Itally.[345]

11. Musick various, and idolized

Of these tetrachords there was 3 of different orders establisht, as I shall shew,[346] and these were as laws among the Greeks, no other, or different order of notes being ever set up or pretended to in any of the cittys, or republicks, but in all other respects they had peculiaritys of manner or time, which were nominally distinguisht by countrys, as the Dorick[,] Phrigian[,] Lydian etc. And these manners were enterteined and used in

the

08v / the severall republiks, as happened or the governors thought most proper to incline the people to vertue and good order of living, and the philosofers recommended the same accordingly. I waive the

---

[345] Constantine, known in history as 'the Great' (Flavius Valerius Constantinus) (b. c. 285, d. 337), brought Christianity from the status of a powerful, though persecuted, minority to effective supremacy in the religious life of the Roman Empire. For the Goths and Vandals, see f. 87v, n. 284.
[346] See ff. 110–111v.

cure of Saul's frenzy by musick, as miracular, otherwise by what
charme it was, wee cannot demonstrate, but it is certein that
amongst the Grecian republicks musick was idolized (as I sayd[347])
as if all religion, governement, and good manners depended upon
it; and the states interested themselves to susteine and incourage it,
and to keep out innovations, so that to add to, or alter the instruments, or modes was almost piacular.[348]

12. Passions excited by musick, ascribed to the poem

After all my wonder at these representations I can fix upon no
resolution but this, which is that the d[a]emon lay more in the
poems, then in the musick;[349] for it is plain how those might
operate upon men's moralls but how meer modes of sound should
doe more then make men merry or sad is past all under[stan]ding;
and there is scarce any account of musick or of very litle which was
had without poetry, and it is likely that the severall modes, so much
spoke of for good or bad morall effects, referred to the subjects of
the poems sung with them, more then to the melody of the tunes.
For if some modes were apt for idleness and levity, and others for
                                                           solemnity

f. 109 / solemnity and good living, the words were allwais conformable,
and being as their manner was distinctly and intelligibly pronounced, no wonder that the publik authoritys in some places took
notice of them. But besides using one or other of the tetrachords, I
presume the cheif differences of these modes consisted in the manner of the puls or time. As if instead of German, Itallian, or French
modes, wee should say andante, allegro or currente and the like.
Wee use all modes promiscuously, but the Greeks affected the
modes of their peculiar country, and seldome any other. It is not
strange that neighbouring people, should have different usages
especially in their musick, which was their wonder, care, and
delight, and a subject of their philosofers' subtilety. But wherein
consisted the manner of their practice, so intirely in use and with

[347] See ff. 104v–105.
[348] MS has 'piacular, and'.
[349] The word dæmon (*daimon*), which in the works of Homer meant 'allotter' (of fate),
corresponds to the supernatural power not as a general conception but in its specific
manifestations and always with overtones of a personal agent. There is a good and an evil
dæmon in human individuals which follow them all their lives. Christianity, which made
the pagan gods evil, impressed upon the word the signification which 'demon' now has.
The ancient belief in dæmons as restless spirits continued on in alchemy and contributed
to the formation, in the seventeenth century, of the chemical concept 'gas' (see Kassler
1987).

effects discrepant from ours; I think cannot be made appear, tho many of our witts, and crittiques have sweat about it.

13. Musick subject to continuall change

But wee must also consider, that the people varyed their modes more or less in the consequence of time; for notions as well as practises are alwais in a way of alteration, especially among the Greeks, that swarmed with witts and

philosofers

109v / philosofers, who were allwais at work inventing some new thing. Their ordinary poetry and liricks diversifyed, as the singers contrived clusters of longum and breve syllables, called feet. In the first volume of St. Austen's works, there is an operose tract of musick, but more properly of poetry, for it is almost wholly upon feet, of which there is a catalogue enough to fright a minor poet; a meer prosodia, or any thing rather then musick, of which there is not the least discovery.[350] But admitting that changes, or as they accounted them, improvements (and those mostly of instruments)[,] advanced; yet the principles of their musick, by which the poetry and voices were regulated, that is the severall scales of tones, or tetrachords continued the same downe thro the empires even to the Gothick times. And however the instruments varyed in compass, yet they conformed to the modes of the voices, and were for the most part attendant upon them, seldome acting apart; but after tetrachords and diapasons were heaped one upon another, beyond the compass of song[,] instruments broke loos and often acted severally, as in the story of Themistocles[351] and other passages in Antiquity [although] it is not certein but song went along with the instrument even in that instance[.] But as to the grand revolution[s] of musicall affaires, I shall have them in consideration[352] when I have done with the tetrachords.[353]

The

---

[350] Aurelius Augustinus (b. 354, d. 430), bishop of Hippo and saint, was author of *De Musica Libri Sex*. The first five books are an account of the nature and properties of rhythm, as well as of the effects rhythms have on people. The sixth book, which may have been composed later than the first five, is a general discussion of the psychology of hearing.

[351] The 'story' of Themistocles (b. *c.* 528, d. 462 B.C.), an Athenian democratic statesman, is related by Cicero (tr. King 1960: 7) and by Plutarch (tr. Perrin 1959–62: xi/5–7). Although each author has a slightly different version and emphasis, they both hold that Themistocles showed a lack of culture in refusing to play the lyre at banquets.

[352] See ff. 117v, 118v, 122v, 125, 134v.

[353] See ff. 110–111v.

f.110   / 14. The 3 scales[:] 1. diatonick, 2. chromatique, 3. enharmonique

The tetrachords, or scales of musicall tones were three, which eo nomine* declares a fundamentall error, for in the truth of things, which wee call nature, there can be but one,[354] as later experiments have demonstrated, of which in proper time.[355] One of these scales was called the diatonick, and for degrees [upward] hath a semitone, and two tones to come at the fourth. This agrees well with the Orfean harp, and finally hath got the better of all the rest, and (with some improvement, as being most aggreable to nature) reignes in the moderne musick at this day. The next is the chromatick, which stepps by 2 semitones, and a trihemitone, or ♭3d into the fourth. And from hence our masters call all movement by semitones, chromatick. The other scale is called enharmonick; which by its name one would expect had most of harmony, but in truth there is litle or none belongs to it. For the steps are by 2 dieses or (as wee terme them) quarter notes, and then into the fourth by a ditone, or 3d sharp. And these 2 last seem to differ cheifly as a ♭3d and a ♯3d and that the comings to them, were but as graces, and the emfasis resting upon the fourth; for to begin with a semitone or less, when musick

requires

f.110v   / requires a tone to be the second sound, must be discordant upon any other account. And the ditonean scale as they used it is not without this fault, unless it is used as the comon beat up or rising into a sound from the semitone below as the [modern] musitians use at the entrance of their play.

15. Enharmonicks impracticable

It is difficult to tune these scales, and the enharmonick seems out of the power of ears to adjust; for who can hear when the dieses are right? And supposing them just, they can have no consonance with any other, for take any intervall that is musicall, and add, or detract a diesis, and it becomes damnable discord. It is sayd of Pythagoras,[356] (Plutarchus Zelandro interprete*), that he dissallowed the making a judgment of musick by the senses, but he would have it approved by the subtilety of the mind, and harmonicall proportion,

---

[354] I.e., the diatonic (cf. f.117v).

[355] See below and ff.110v, 111, 117v–118.

[356] Pythagoras (fl. 6th century B.C.), Greek philosopher and religious teacher, emigrated c. 531 B.C. from Samos to Croton (now Crotone) in southern Italy, where he founded a religious, philosophic and political society. His name became legendary, and from the 5th century onwards his followers constituted one of the principal scientific schools.

and not by the faculty of hearing.[357] Ô mirum!★ And there it is
complained, that of late the majesty of the ancient diatonicks are
slighted and many grow to[o] dull, to account the enharmonick
dieses insensible, and out of an hebetude of mind account what they
doe not perceiv as next to nothing, and unprofitable, with more of
such unintelligible geare, as would sooner burst, then edifye a
man's understanding, that should goe about to unriddle it. But as I
have pickt out a litle here, so another may squees out some further
misty conjectures and so with labour in vain, tire upon the subject
'till doomsday.

The

111   / 16. Chromatique litle better
       The chromatick hath not much advantage in practis, for it steps
by 2 semitones, and then leaps over a ♭ 3d into the fourth, which is
an inscrutable mistery, and inconsistent with melody; and, (as the
other) not to be reconciled, but by following an humour in singing
verses, which one may imagin to play to and fro, falling or rising
with the voice by small intervalls, and sometimes letting it vary a 3d
or a 4th[,] that is bringing irregular usages as the variegated sounds
of singing birds into an artfull discipline; and as for the diatonick I
shall say no more here,[358] but that it referrs also to singing, and by
help of instruments growing upon it, it became at length
Guidonian.[359]

17. Greek [music] continually disposed to change
       These scales were extended by setting one over another, and the
2d tetrachord came up within a tone of the diapason, but another
like tetrachord following did not answer by diapasons to the first,
therefore a stop was made there, and to fullfill the diapason, a note
was added below, out of all tetrachord[s]; which was called proslamb[an]omenas,★ as if 2 tetrachords reached from G to F[,] then ff
was the gained note, and thus the compass of a full diapason was
gained, which Pythagoras sayd was enough for the porpose of

---

[357] According to Plutarch, the 'grave Pythagoras rejected the judging of music by the sense
of hearing, asserting that its excellence must be apprehended by the mind. This is why he
did not judge it by the ear, but by the scale based on the proportions, and considered it
sufficient to pursue the study no further than the octave' (tr. Einarson and De Lacy 1967:
441). From North's parenthetical remark, it is evident that he has used an edition by
Guillaume Holtzmann (b. 1532, d. 1576), alias Xylander.

[358] See ff. 117v–118.

[359] I.e., the diatonic became the single scale with thirds and sixths (cf. f. 122v).

musick.[360] Wee must needs suppose that a buisy subtile people given to arts and sciences

and

f.111v / and all emolous of one and other, as the Greek republiks were, would never let their favourite arts of poetry, and musick be stagnant in any manner, without perpetuall profers of alteration, and some succeeding, by many thought for the wors, (as from the majesty of the Ancients or from the ditones to the chromes, and harmonicks, and with some noveltys of modes and versifying) but continually to vary, and that mostly by inlarging its territorys. And accordingly tetrachords were pyled up, and the notes honoured with distinct appellations, with marks to each which[,] set over the syllables of verses[,] instructed the musick, and the rations* of the intervalls subtilised, and the rationale of harmony drawn out of numbers, deferring litle to the sence of hearing, which it seems without mathematicks could not distinguish between right and wrong; and all with infinite refining, which is a demonstration that they were upon a wrong bottom, and worked upon fals principles; for as well in matters of arts and action, as in discours; trifling, verbosity, and cobling, are never so copious, and redundant, as when principles are fals, whence proceeds all manner of obscurity, and confusion both in notion and expression.

f.112 / 18. Of the tibia and fistula

It is a large branch of this subject, to gaine some cognizance of instruments. These were either flatile,* or nervous; the former were either trumpets (tubæ), tibiæ or fistulæ, and the other divers sorts of harps. The trumpets were used in warr, as the Roman litui, but were not drawne into any tetrachord, nor joyned with voices. The tibiæ, or fistulæ were allwais musicall. It is sayd the tibia had 4 foramina,* which I supposed answered some tetrachord; and in sonorousness imitated the trumpet; by which I guess it was voiced either by the lipps, as a cornett, or els by some reedall.* How the fistula was voiced I can scarce guess; if it had bin after the flute-manner, like our comon organ pipes, some discription would have shewed it,[361] but the unhappyness is such, that out of all the philo[so]phicks, and sculptures of Antiquity, there is no glimps of any device whereby these pipes were made to sound, tho it had bin a

---

[360] Pythagoras left no writings; but a fragment, supposed to be by Pythagoras, was translated into Latin by North's brother, John (b. 1645, d. 1683), and was included in Thomas Gale's *Opuscula Mythologica Ethica et Physica . . .* , Cambridge 1671 (see *Life of John North* ed. Millard 1984: 128, 132, 185n.).

[361] North treats the voicing of flue pipes in *TS 1728* (ff. 103–146v).

subject for Pythagoras to have observed as worthy as to note the
tones of a smith's anvill.[362] But it is certein they had no great
compass, and that not very just, it not being easy to

give

112v / give pipes and the foramina just accord on unison tones, and there
is reason to think the double mouthed or spread tibiæ used at
sacrifices were unisons and had no foramina; for in the [sculptured]
columnes the piping boy, is made to hold his hands upon the 2
tibiæ, full gripe, without any signe of foramina or fingering, which
one would think should, as well as greater nicetys[,] have bin
expressed if any such had bin in use. But at Baccanalls,[363] feasts and
weddings the antique bassreleivs shew double pipes, and (by the
posture of the fingers) foramina; but which were tibiæ, and which
fistulæ, for the formes are various, is hard to say. But it seems very
certein, that in the theaters onely the tibiæ were used, and not harps.

19. The tibiæ for loud musick

The mention of theaters puts me in mind to observe divers things
to confirme what hath bin sayd concerning musick following the
manners of the voice.[364] It is sayd that Gracchus, an impetuous
orator, had a piper stood behind him, to quallifie the tones of his
speeches to the people, which the straining to be loud had turned to
a right downe singing, with acutes and graves, so as a pipe might
conforme, which cannot be done to our

ordinary

113 / ordinary speaking or preaching.[365] And this was (nearly) the
same as tibiis canere,* and seems to unridle the wonderfull use of
the tibiæ in theaters of which I shall take notice afterwards.[366] A
man might be cytharædus and sing to his owne harp; and whilest
that instrument was used, the poet, and the musitian might be and
for the most part was the same. But when the song was to be
attended by wind instruments, the poet and the musitian or singer
devided; for one could not performe both. It is sayd by Plutarch,

---

[362] According to legend, Pythagoras discovered the ratios of perfect consonances by
listening to hammers in a blacksmith's shop. The fallacy was exposed by Galileo Galilei
in 1638 (see Hawkins 1776 rev. 1853/1963: i/xx; Kassler 1979: i/367–9; and McKinnon
1978: 22).

[363] Bacchanalia, the Dionysiac *orgia* or revels, included tumultuous processions in which the
spirits of earth and of fecundity appeared, their likenesses evoked by masks.

[364] See ff. 105, 105v, 106v, 107.

[365] The use of the pitchpipe or 'tonarian' by Caius Gracchus, Tribune in 123 B.C., was
recorded by Cicero (tr. Watson 1896: 400) and Quintilian (tr. Butler 1963: 173).

[366] See f. 114v.

that the poets were fain to hire the wind musick and pay 'em;[367] which was an excise upon witt, unless it were in order to some publik celebration, as in the theaters. For songs to the harp and to the fistula as I guess were proper for chamber musick, that required a tranquillity to be familiarly heard.

20. The Ancients had not our consort musick

It is probable that, after the harps were devided from the simplicity of a few strings, and new formes were devised, and many strings added, the handling became a peculiar art, and the performers, were, (as in latter times) proud of their play, and using their instruments perhaps singly and without voices, they shewed divers harmonious tricks upon them as wee doe now adays upon ours. But as for that

which

f. 113v   / which wee call consort musick, otherwise then by unisons, octaves, and diapentes, or[368] fourths clamming together in exact feet, I have not mett with any symptome of it, before the invention and use of organs. And it was not possible there could be any such, for the Ancients did not allow 3ds and sixths to be concords, and without them, their scales had no notes to sound together, but unisons[,] 4ths, 5ths, and 8ths. And the degrees were so desultory, that it was not possible to bring melody and consort to joyne. They affected onely the dulcor of sound, as the descriptions in authors shew, who have used for a simile, that persons of divers tempers should in actions aggree like divers musicall notes which sounding together are pleasing to the sence.[369] They had no imagination of counterchanging harsh, and mild consonances, or sour and sweet setting one and other off. Nor had they any knowledge of the monarchy of a key, with its full accord, nor of the least scruple in the way of our art of composition. It is therefore very hard to make a comparison of such meer disparata★ as the musicall harmony of the Ancients and Modernes are.

---

[367] Plutarch described a 'mercenary' manner derived from the so-called 'deposit' (*thematikoi*) contests which were for money (see Plutarch tr. Einarson and De Lacy 1967: 381 and note a). But the text says nothing about poets being 'fain to hire the wind musick and pay 'em'.

[368] I.e., and.

[369] Just as moral character is produced by music, by 'some manner of combining elements or of blending them or of both', so too moral character is produced in people (Plutarch tr. Einarson and De Lacy 1967: 427, 431 *et passim*). North's own equilibrium theory carries this implication for natural body (humans) as well as for body politic (society).

114 / It may be allowed that the former might be good, but in suo genere* not as consort, but somewhat els which for want of practick examples, wee cannot judg of.

21. Of the theater musick

But now to come downe to the theaters, where musick was in its altitude. It seems the enterteinement was made up of action, and singing like our operas about which many questions may be moved. As for the action it was visible upon the stage, but the voices were onely heard, and how could that be in an open theater, sub die,[370] with thousands of auditors in them? And knowing the disturbances incident to crowds how can wee imagin the actors could make themselves understood? As to that I consider first that they did not speak, as ours doe, but sung with all the utterance of sound they could make, and wee can conceiv that to double the strength of the voice. And next that they did not mumble, like our comon speaking but pronounced every individuall syllable according to its quantity, so that no confusion took place but all the language was distinct and clear. And then, as Vitruvious describes, a circle of brass vessels were planted, round the compass of

the

14v / the theatre.[371] Tho I cannot think that Pereault hath nicked the contrivance, by shutting them up in cavitys, which for the porpose should stand open.[372] That these might augment the voice is certein but then they must be tuned to the quadrichord,[373] or the generall tone in which they sung. Els they would not augment at all, nor answer to any syllable, that did not strike the true tone of the vessells.

22. Of choruses and pantomimes

But as great an assistance as all this, was the chorus of tibiæ, that sounded unison to all that was sung. This favoured the voices so much, that any one might performe his part with half the breath; as every one used to sing in our way, with or without a full thro base

---

[370] MS has 'sub dio'.

[371] Vitruvius is thought to provide the first reference to acoustic vases, along with an elucidation of how such a system of vases might be extended in a large theatre (tr. Gwilt 1826: Bk. V, Ch. 5).

[372] The edition of the French virtuoso, Charles Perrault (b. 1613, d. 1688), included an engraving of a Roman theatre, in which the vases were shown tucked away in 'petites chambres' under the tiers of seats. In *Notes of Me* North indicates that he favoured this edition 'because of the curiosity of the cuts, as the explanations and discourses annexed to the text' (ed. Jessopp 1887: 63).

[373] I.e., tetrachord.

can tell. But I have a farther prospect of advantage, which is that the actors did not sing at all, or but as single persons, and the matter of the drama was made out by choruses of many voices, and with so much vociferation as was easily heard, especially [with] the musick attending. And this manner with them did not run into gabble like our speaking or singing together, for nothing was more sacredly required then distinction of feet and syllables, in which the least disorder

made

f.115   / made a mutiny in the theater. And during all this the actors might be but pantomimes, and used the grimace and gesture as if they spoke, as well as acted. If this was not so, I desire to know to what end pantomimikery was so much used, and applauded? To see men act, saying nothing must be the dullest sight in the world; complements, and the like may be understood by drye action, but not in eisdem verbis,★ nor anything of science or reasoning. It's true one may act and another speak, and it shall be hard to say which is which. As Tully reports of Roscius, that he[374] was challenged to speak, and Roscius undertook to act what he sayd, as fast as he spoke it.[375] Therefore our paltry imitators are mistaken when they attempt to mime it upon a silent stage; but if the parts were rehearsed (near) and they acted, or (perhaps) as the Ancients to a chorus, they might be accepted as the ancient mimes were.

23. Of the tibiæ pares★ and impares,★ etc.

   I cannot drop this subject, before I have directed another bolt at the theatricall musick of the Ancients, aiming cheifly at the Terentian comedys which carry some mark of discovery in the short inscriptions.[376] It is certein they were sung or rather toned to musick, which were the tibiæ

pares

f.115v   / pares and impares, as it is there exprest, and also that the modes were made by a famed musitian.[377] There is nothing in the land of

---

[374] I.e., Tully.

[375] Marcus Tullius Cicero (b. 106, d. 43 B.C.), Roman orator and writer, was a friend of the actor, Gallus Quintus Roscius (d. *c.* 62 B.C.), whose name became typical for the consummate artist.

[376] The Roman playwright, Terence (Publius Terentius Afer) (b. *c.* 190, d. ?159 B.C.), provided prefatory information (*didascalia*) to each of his works, where he mentioned the kinds of double reed pipe used. These are 'equal' or 'unequal' in length, 'right' or 'left' and, for one play, 'Sarranian'. The edition used by North is hinted at f.116 below.

[377] According to Terence, Flaccus, a slave or freeman, was composer of the music (*modi*).

critiscisme more dark then the sence of those words, pares and impares. The tibiæ,* were pipes that sounded by a reedall device like those affixed to bag-pipes, and foraminated for changing the tone when there was occasion. They were also termed dexteræ* and sinistræ,* becaus two pipes met in an angle at the mouth, so that to manage them, there was work for right hand and left; but that position making no difference the crittiques allow not the distinction to be from there but from the scene; that is the right, and left of the stage. And as for the pares, and impares some will have it referre to magnitude, but there is no symptome of inequallity of the tibiæ in any peice of Antiquity. Others will have it to the foramina, in one odd, and the other even, by which the tones are unequall. But par and impar belongs neither to magnitude nor sounds but to numbers onely. My thought is, that after Aristotle[,] other philosophers had began[378] to esteem harmony by numbers mathematically, then all consonances must need be resolved thereby, and thence all the clutter about rations, bipartientes, superbipartientes, sesqui[-]

alteras

116 / alteras, sesquitertias, etc.[379] And so according to [the] 9th [of Euclid's] Elements which treats of parrs and impars etc. by like analogy, some consonances were styled pares, and others impares.[380] I should not have ventured upon a guess so wide from the ordinary, if I had not found enough in Plutarch (eodem interprete*) to lead me into it. The words are these – "His ergo partibus atque numeris harmonia, de Aristotelis sententia componitur. Idem aptissime ex finiti et infiniti, paris et imparis atque pariter imparis. Natura eandem constituit. Ejusque partes. Tota enim par est, cum constet quatuor terminis partes ipsius, proportionibus continentur, quorum termini sunt pares, impares, pariter impares;" – and exam-

---

[378] M S has 'after Aristotle and other philosophers had began'.

[379] Aristotle (b. 384, d. 322 B.C.), a pupil of Plato, founded the Peripatetic school in the Lyceum at Athens. The Academy he joined in 367 was distinguished from other Athenian schools by two interests: mathematics (including astronomy and harmonic theory) and dialectic. Plato regarded the first as preparatory and ancillary to the second, but Aristotle reversed these priorities. He held that mathematics was itself a science (or family of sciences) about the physical world, not about a Platonic world of transcendent objects. According to Aristotle, mathematics abstracts from those characteristics of the world that are the special concern of physics – movement and change and, hence, time and location. The Stoics were indebted to Aristotle, whose philosophy they modified and extended.

[380] Euclid (fl. *c.* 300 B.C.), Greek teacher of mathematics, was author of the *Elements of Geometry* in 13 books. Book IX is part of the arithmetical books (VII–IX), which deal with the theory of rational numbers and the elements of mathematics in general, containing propositions on the proportion of commensurable magnitudes (which are Pythagorean in origin) and on the theory of numbers (series, progressions and means).

ples follow.[381] If I am asked if I understand this, I must answer No, no more then the rest of the tract, but I can tell, that the tibiæ pares, and impares being so styled in Terence cannot be resolved according to any of the crittiques, but must be understood according to this mathematicall prescription (such as it is) or not att all. If any one would see a collection of these crittiscismes, they may be had in Rosinus' Antiquitatum[382] and in the variorum Terence[383] at the beginning there is a note of this subject ex professo.*

f.116v   / 24. The generall disposition of theater musick

It is impossible to state the mythologia of these descriptions, without repairing to the nature of the subject, which onely can discover what may or may not be intended by them. The the[a]ters being open to the skyes, and immensly filled, must require magnitude of sound to make an intelligible enterteinement which was to be the comedy sung to the sound of wind musick, called tibiæ, of which there were divers sorts, knowne by certein names, as pares, impares, dextræ, sinistræ, and sarannæ* mentioned in Terence and which soever were used, must sound concordant, and that could not be but as I sayd,[384] in unisons, octaves, (higher or lower) fourths or fifths. And this could not be otherwise then in counterpoint with the voice, which was governed by the accents (ab accinendo,*) that is recitative, with deflections as was prescribed, and the ever necessary rule cited out of Plutark, of the strikt coincidence of sound[,] time and syllable, observed.[385] And so the clangor of the musick could not drowne the voices, but augmented them, which was the effect of such nice coincidences. And of the pipes, the unisons and octaves to the tone

of the

---

[381]   The following is a paraphrase of the Latin quotation: 'Harmony, therefore (to follow the opinion of Aristotle) is composed of these parts and measures. These same most fitly from the finite and the non-finite, the equal and the unequal and the equally unequal. Nature established it [i.e., harmony]. The parts thereof. For as a whole it is evenly proportioned, although it is evident that the four parts of it are comprehended by terms [and] proportions, the terms of which are equal, unequal or equally unequal'. The passage does not appear in Plutarch's text and may have been an interpolation or comment by the editor, Holtzmann.

[382]   Joannes Rosinus (b. *c.* 1550, d. 1626) was the author of *Romanorum Antiquitatum Libri Decem . . .*, Basle 1585. Of the numerous editions, some reversed the two first words in the title.

[383]   Unfortunately, North's hint about 'the variorum Terence' does not enable us to make a positive identification, since there were numerous editions in Latin. The plays were published in an English translation in 1694; a second edition, published in 1698, included revisions by Roger L'Estrange (see f.140, n.487).

[384]   See f.113v.

[385]   For Plutarch's rule, see f.106v, n.340.

117 / of the theater or the vase mentioned by Vitruvius,[386] of which the numbers, being as 2, 4, 8, 16 might make them be styled pares, and the fourth as 3 to 4 or 5th as 3 to 2 might be the impares, and the dexter and sinister referre to shapes or modes of handling them or, as was sayd,[387] to the sides of the stage. And the modes (said allwais to have bin made,) might be, as I guessed, altering the time as sceenes changed and suited the subject and persons, and perhaps setling the accents, or tunes, of which with other circumstances, the nicety of those times, and the witts that courted them, from the examples of various nations and republiks, gave occas[i]on for endless variety, and might well render the performances no less admirable in their way, then the operas of our days are in our manner, and I might say more worthily, and give good reasons for it; but comparisons are odious. I must take one thing for granted which is that whatever the pipes were, the sounding part must be not like our bag pipes without stop, but so contrived that the tongue might comand the sound with distinction of touch precisely like our hautboys.[388] Els the feet and syllables could not be exprest, then which in the greatest nicety of time nothing was more essentiall; but neither in the lettered or carved descriptions, is there any symptome of such or of any manner of voicing whatever.

17v / 25. The diatonian the ancienter and juster scale

I have sayd litle of the diatonian tetrachord having considerations concerning that which are not proper to the others;[389] for in the first place the degrees are marked out by true harmony, as nature it self affords it; and when one [tetrachord] is set above another, it fullfills the septenary, which is the treasury of concord, and the whole becomes one scale, of which the tones are allyed to each other, as all are to the first [or keynote] saving that to accomodate some humour in singing the semitone hath bin put first, which in naturall order follows the 2 tones. It appears that the ancienter musitians affected this scale, as most magnifick, and proper for heroicks, or [for] the tragicall songs in prais of Baccus. But when the versifying vein turned fantasticall, and affected variety, and [when] lyricks in comon musick, and comicks in the theaters came in use, the other scales followed, and perhaps were at first invented for such melodys as had less of harmony, and more of passionate

[386] See ff. 114–114v and 114v, n.371.
[387] See f. 115v.
[388] *TS 1728* (ff. 139–139v 'Of pipes that are sounded by a reed').
[389] See ff. 110–111.

whining then suited with the diatonick intervalls, which difference will be manifest to those who

will

f.118 / will pleas to make a comparison of them. The antiquity of the diatonian among the Greeks, being probably the musick of Homer, inclines me to think it was also the scale of the Hebrean[390] [music], and that their polychord instruments were tuned accordingly, the other scales being the invention of the latter Greeks.[391]

26. Instruments establisht true harmony

And that which tended most to revive the diatonick musick among the Greeks, was the increas of compass in their stringed instruments; for so they rose to a disdiapason or higher, which with the proslamb[an]omenos, made a large catalogue of notes with names, and signatures, which are set forth particularly in most authors.[392] These must of necessity lead to the knowledg and practise of accords, however their dutyfull ears did not allow of 3ds and 6ths. And to lessen the wonder that must attend such mistakes of artificiall men I have to alledg that the numbers [which] the mathematick philosophers were pleas[ed] to annex to those accords[,] fell not into such cleaver[393] proportions, as they thought belonged to concords, and so the numerall estimates (annuente Pythagora★) and not the sence of hearing must governe in those cases. But it is usuall for arts to grow

by

f.118v / by degrees, and often very slowly, as men happen to be tenacious of old usages; so harmony, altho it was plainely revealed by the polychori[c] instruments, and probably divers of them might be used together in some sort of consort, yet the power of the vocall manner was so great, that it held musick to the tetrachords for divers ages, as wee find in the time of Augustus,[394] when Vitruvius wrote, who describes musick accordingly and is as hard to be

---

[390] I.e., Hebraic.

[391] The music of Homer was to become an important focus of the eighteenth-century debate about the origin of language. See, for example, Thomas Blackwell, *An Enquiry into the Life and Writings of Homer,* 2d edn., London 1736.

[392] Plutarch is critical of such authors, for he argues that they 'think the strongest demonstration of the truth of their view is in the first place their own dullness of ear … and next the fact that the interval [of a quarter tone] cannot be obtained by means of concords' (tr. Einarson and De Lacy 1967: 443).

[393] I.e., clever.

[394] Augustus (Caesar Octavius) (b. 63 B.C., d. A.D. 14) became the first Roman emperor in 27 B.C.

understood as any of the other authors of the Greek musick.[395] And in that manner, that is by tetrachords, the diatonian scale was used in theaters, and [in] ordinary singing till the use of organs, and other incidents, made a totall revolution of musicall discipline, as I shall shew.[396] But in the mean time I must observe, that after the grandees had a tast[e] of instruments in consort, voices became more slighted or els conformed, and the chromes and harmonicks (for the difficulty, as authors alledg) layd aside[,] instrumentall musick, post varios[397] casus,* hath got ground, and downe even to our days prevailes and voices have had much adoe to maintain their post in musicall enterteinements.

Being

119 / 27. Corrup[t]ion and decay of musick

Being come so foreward as the establishment of the Roman monarchy, there is to be observed a vast alteration of the methods of knowledge in the world. The philosofy of the Greeks especially the phisicall, slighted, the arts mathematicall under gross misconstruction; and the witts refined upon the arts of governement and warr; but most especially upon the nicetys of oratory, and its fellow, poetry. Most other pretensions to knowledg ceased, and matters went foreward more majorum,* onely the sluice gates of luxury were set open, and as an ingredient in that mixture, wee have reason to suppose musick to have bin enterteined or rather courted. Although verses were much in fashion, and lyricks plenty, which wee may suppose were intended to be sung ad lyram,* yet ordinarily, as I guess verses were repeated also plain; for whoever heard that among the Romans, either old Ennius, Lucilius, Horace's Sermones,[398] Virgill or any poems (out of theaters,) were sung? and in

the

19v / the theaters, not for the sake of poetry, but for augmentation of voice. The witts used to rehears their poems in assemblys, as wee

---

[395] Vitruvius devoted one of his ten books on architecture to harmonics (tr. Gwilt 1826: Bk. V, Ch. 4).

[396] See ff. 121–126v.

[397] M s has 'various'.

[398] Quintus Ennius (b. 239, d. 169 B.C.), Latin poet, was author of at least four books of satires, only fragments of which remain. His work is regarded as a model for subsequent Latin satirists, including the poets, Caius Lucilius (b. c. 180, d. c. 101 B.C.) and Horace (Quintus Horatius Flaccus) (b. 65, d. 8 B.C.). The *Satirae* (medleys) of the latter were treated as moral writings by Christian humanists, who frequently edited them under the title *Sermones* (talks), although Horace himself also called them by that name.

find in Pliny,[399] but no hint of any manner, musicall or otherwise. So that poetry and musick from being twinns, were scarce sisters. There is in Quintillian an exquisite encomium of musick where the originall laudable use, and the (then) moderne corruption of it, is set forth, as being mired in the theaters, and prostituted by light weomen (spadicæ★) with psalters,[400] and in short from a sober enterteinement of the wise and vertuous, was become a property of vice and intemperance. And so wee must conceive it proceeded, from bad to wors, till it sunk in the Gothick warrs, and by means of the Christian churches was happyly revived or rather preserved and thereby derived to us.

28. Musick in the East confounded by the Turks

This matter I shall resume afterwards,[401] but in the mean time have some regard to the devision of the Empire. This fell out after Constantine, and it was not long before instead of one, there was 2 Romes. The easterne had a succession of monarchs till in

the

f. 120 / year [1453] the Turks conquered Constantinople. There are historians that write of the eastterne governements, as Nicetas[402] etc. who have described the portentous luxury, with the abominable wickednesses of those courts, but no syllable of the musick used amongst them, either in the pallaces, or churches. Whence I may remarque that in times when men lived free and at eas, and which were deservedly accounted good, musick was a freind, and celebrated to posterity as such; but in factious, seditious, gluttonous, and debauched times, when men did tantum non eat one another; musick was made a slave, and tho perpetually held in exercise; yet so slighted, that no remembrance of it is left to posterity. But it is presumed the Greek patriark and bishops had solemne singing in

---

[399] Pliny (Gaius Plinius Secundus) (b. 23, d. 79), Roman writer on many subjects, was noted especially for his encyclopedia, *Historia Naturalis,* compiled from different authorities and arranged systematically as an account of all material objects that are *not* the product of man's manufacture. Nevertheless, the work contains a number of digressions (especially in Book VII) on human artifice, artifacts and institutions.

[400] Quintilian (Marcus Fabius Quintilianus) (fl. 1st century A.D.), Roman orator and writer on rhetoric, was author of *Institutio Oratoria*, a treatise in twelve books on the training of the ideal orator from childhood to maturity. Quintilian treats music chiefly as a propaideutic and as a handmaid of rhetoric. His 'encomium' on music seeks to demonstrate the antiquity, importance and power of music (see Quintilian tr. Butler 1963: 171–7).

[401] See f. 121v.

[402] Niceta Choniates (b. 1140, d. 1213), Byzantine historian, was author of a chronicle in twenty-one books covering the period 1118–1206.

their churches, of which together with that of the other Rome, I shall speak of afterwards,[403] but whither with or without instruments, is no where, that I know, declared but it's judged they used none. But that musick at large received a great improvement in that Empire I make no doubdt becaus it is very plaine that the invention

of

.120v / of organs with wind, (instead of working by the force of water) was first introduced there For it is reported that one of the Greek emperors sent to his brother at Rome one of them as bigg as a chariot for a present.[404] And the consequence of that most excellent invention must needs be a perfection of the diatonick scale, even as wee have it now, and that the harmony of musick must (as in time it did) setle thereupon; but yet it seems the use of tetrachords was not quite worne out there, for I have heard some merchants say,[405] that the Turks in their vulgar singing, have so much of the fourths in their emphasing, as smells strong of the tetrachords; as victors are often observed to lick up many usages from among those they have conquered.

29. Organs compleated

Now turning westward, as to the use of musick the scene is litle less deplorable. Wee allow it to have flourished in the courts of the latter emperors, for in one of the august historians it is complained that the emperor spent his time in his pallaces with hearing

of

.121 / of organs. This is the first notice taken of organs in history.[406] The word organon* is to be mett with in authors sooner, but crittiques say that organon was a word comonly applyed to most

---

[403] See ff. 120v–121.

[404] In 757 Emperor Constantine Copronymus sent an organ to Pepin, King of the Franks at Compiègne. According to Williams (1980: 30), this gesture was much commented on by scribes of the period.

[405] Two of North's brothers were Turkey merchants: Dudley (b. 1641, d. 1691), who resided in Constantinople between 1662 and 1680, where he was the leading merchant in the Turkey Company; and Montagu (d. 1710), who was taken prisoner by the French at Toulon and in 1693 returned to England a broken man.

[406] The emperor was Nero (b. 37, d. 69), who 'neglected to address either the Senate or the people; instead, he summoned the leading citizens to his Palace where, after a brief discussion of the Gallic situation, he devoted the remainder of the session to demonstrating a completely new type of water-organ, and explaining the mechanical complexities of several different models. He even remarked that he would have them installed in the Theatre' (Suetonius tr. Graves 1957: 234). North's statement notwithstanding, this is not the first mention of the organ in history.

musicall instruments, and the organon hydraulicon★ distinguish't the multifistular engin; and it may be depended on that this was the mother of our musicall scale, and of all consort harmony. And after the fabrick came once to be compleated, it was never in any times good or badd layd aside, but numerous artists, that call themselves organ builders, have ever bin, are, and probably will be imployed in the erection and voicing of them, and all along, and yet improving, and like to be so to the world's end. But as to the Greek musick planted in the Latine Empire[,] it is no wonder it fell, when the Empire it self could not stand, but was overwhelmed by deluges of bar[bar]ous nations who became possessors of Itally and the neighbouring territorys and even of Rome it self.

f.121v / 30. Poetry and singing turned Gothick

And in this disorder and commixture of nations, the Latine language lost its idiom, and from a vernacular speech became antiquarian or classick and the Gothick dialects prevailed, and then what must become of all the prosodies and poetrys, on which the musick of former times had depended? Whenever peace returns arts will revive, as poetry, for instance, but in a new forme, and dress. For in Province, as Bembo thinks a new sort of versifying was invented; and from thence brought into Italy, and the manner, that is rimes and stanzas, not onely setled there, but spread all over Europe.[407] This of cours introduced a new manner of singing and that could take into no channell but that of imitating the instrumentall musick of those ages, and what that was I may reflect afterwards.[408]

31. Ecclesiasticall musick unaltered

In the mean time wee must consider what became of musick among the ecclesiasticks. That there was a frequent usage of singing psalmes and hymnes from the beginning of Christianity, wherein consisted a great measure of their devotion is without all doubdt,

but

f.122 / but what that manner of singing was is hard to determine. And to referr to the Jewish psalmody, from whence it is supposed to have bin derived, is ignotum per ignotius.★ It is probable that having

---

[407] Pietro Bembo (b. 1470, d. 1547), Italian poet, literary theorist and cardinal, was author of *Prose della volgar lingua . . . ,* Venice 1525. This work is thought to have determined the aesthetic of the early madrigal by its stress on the sound of words and on the importance of rhyme and varied schemes for verse lengths (see Mace 1969).
[408] See ff. 124v, 126v.

been begun[409] by plain men as the Apostles were, the singing must be as plaine, and that is a sonorous pronunciation syllabically with some turnes in the nature of accents, to which a voice, even in speaking, is propens. A difference might be made between the manner of singing hymns and prayers, the latter with more delibe-ration and devotion. And so it continued untill the establishment of Christian churches and bishopricks, when great multitudes used to meet, and then singing was not onely for devotion, but necessity, for without choruses the church service could not be heard. And in times of calamity the letanys were sung processionally about the streets of great cittys in divers choruses. Otherwise the singing in churches continued (nearly) in the same manner downe to about the time of Gregory, called the Great; and wee must

look

22v / look abroad for the great metamorphosis of musick that happened after the fall of the Empire.

32. All instruments conforme to the organ

Wee must needs imagine that after the organ had broke the ice, and shewed the nature and connexion of accords in musick, that other instruments were made to conforme in that manner, that is to a single scale without tetrachords, taking in the 3ds and sixes, without which consort musick did not subsist. By degrees all the old instruments conformed, or by alterations and improvement came on, and new ones invented, and brought into comon use, so that the harmony of instruments subsisted in perfection, without a dependence up[on] voices to recomend it. And a match was soon made between the old harp and the organ, which produced the spinette kind, for since the harp was to be touched by a plectrum, why might not the keys of an organ be made to work the quills? And the harp it self gained a body of sound, but as to that, and other instruments that sound by nerves, I shall consider afterwards;[410] but first of the violl kind, or chelys as it is called, but for what reason I am to seek.[411]

Nothing

---

[409] MS has 'being began'.
[410] See ff. 123–124v.
[411] The Greek poets frequently referred to the lyre as 'tortoise' (*chelys*), a subject examined by Molyneux (1702). In medieval and renaissance usage, the term 'chelys' was used for lute and, latterly, for any arched structure. Simpson, for example, employed the term as the Latin equivalent for viol (1665/1965).

f. 123 / 33. The invention of the viol Gothick

Nothing made so great a denouement in musick as the invention of hors hair with rozin and the gutts of animalls twisted and dryed. I scarce think that the strings of the old lyra used in either the Jewish or Greek times[,] which in Latine are termed nerves, were such, becaus it was more or less piacular, to deal in that manner with the exta* of dead animalls. Nor is it any where, as I know[,] intimated of what materiall these strings were made, but I guess they were mettalline, as most sonorous; or of twisted silk. Nor is there any hint when the violl kind came first in use; had the Greeks known it, some deity, for certein, had bin the inventor, and more worthily then Appollo of the harp; for it draws a continuing sound, exactly tuneable to all occasions and compass, with small labour and no expence of breath. But as to the invention, which is so perfectly novell as not to have bin ever heard of before Augustulus the last of the Roman emperors[,][412] I cannot but esteem it perfectly Gothick, and entred with those barbarous nations, setled in Itally and from thence spread

f. 123v / into all the neighbour nations round about and now is in possession, and like to hold it as a principall squadron, in the instrumentall navy.

34. The invention perfected

I doe suppose that at first it was, like its native country, rude and gross. And that at the early importation it was of the lesser kind, which they called viola da bracchio, and since the violin, and no better then as a rustique zampogna used to stirr up the vulgar to dancing, or perhaps to solemnize their idolotrous sacrifizes. Those people made no scruple of handling gutts, and garbages, and were so free with humane bodys, as to make drinking cupps of their sculls. And when the discovery of the vertue of the bow was made, and understood, the vertueosi went to work, and modeled the use of it and its subject the viol with great improvement, to all porposes of musick, and brought it to a parallell state with the organ it self; and by adapting sizes to the severall diapasons as well above E la, as the doubles[413] below, severall persons take their parts and consorts

[412] Romulus Augustulus, commonly known as the last Roman emperor of the West (A.D. 475–6), was in fact a usurper and was not recognised in the East. He owes his diminutive name to the fact that he was still a child when his father elevated him at Ravenna in 475. When his father was killed, Romulus was deposed but spared because of his youth and sent to live on a pension in Campania. His subsequent fate is unknown.
[413] I.e., the notes below G (gamma ut).

are performed with small trouble, and in all perfection. The invention needs no encomium to recomend it to posterity; for altho

f.124 / it hath bin in practise many hundred years, no considerable alterations of it in forme or application have bin made which any memorialls can account for. And now no improvement is thought of or desired, but in the choice of the materiall, and curiosity of the workmanship I shall take leav of the violl with a remembrance onely of a merry discovery of Kercher's in one of his windy volumes, which is a note added to the pictures of a lute and a guittarre, that the old Hebrews used to sound them with the scratch of an hors tail bow.[414]

35. Spinetts, lutes[,] stopps or fretts, harp and wind musick

As the harpsicord or spinett kind was a composition of the old harp and organ, so the lute kind is a composition between the spinett and the violl. They are made of a shape not unlike a tortois, which suits with some of the practises, (if they are not fables) of the Ancients, but so done now for convenience of handling. The stopps or fretts of all these instruments are a further improvement wholly unknown to the Ancients, and make a distinct instrument with (almost) sufficient compass of every string. But the

lute

124v / lute kind cannot spare the fretts, as the violl may, and in many shapes succeeds better by plain stopps without them. The comon harp, by the use of gutt strings, hath received incomparable improvement but cannot be a consort instrument becaus it cannot follow organs and violls in the frequent changes of keys; and the wind musick, which by all stress of invention hath bin brought into ordinary consort measures, yet more or less labours under the same infirmity, especially the cheif of them which is the trumpet.[415]

36. Musick taken a new forme

Here is the furniture of the musick scool, and from hence, that is from the Gothick institution, I fix the epocha of all our moderne harmony; all the antique as well vocall as instrumentall together with their poetry, as to these porposes, being sunk in the pitt of

---

[414] See Kircher (1650: i/48–9); the pictures were reproduced in Hawkins (1776 rev. 1853/ 1963: i/94, figures 34–5).
[415] See *TS 1728* (ff. 129–133v.)

Lethe.[416] It is no wonder that the vertuosi made the best use and improvement they could invent or contrive for rendring musick compleat; and without being tyed up to the rules of prosodia and counterpoint, they spread their movements so as the parts might break one upon the other

with

f.125 / with sufficient variety, and comixtures unknowne to Antiquity, and so farr from prejudice, that I may securely add, with wonderfull and (barring some evill customes crept in) perfection of harmony. And all flowing (as well vocal as instrumentall) uniformely in the same channell without other restraint then the nature of things, and the comon sence of humane kind requires. And thus thro divers modes of operation, according to the various fancys and fashions of different times and nations, (but all founded upon the same principles) it is come downe to us, who have our turnes in prescribing disciplinary formes as others have had. And as others before us, so wee claim our performances to be the best.

37. Plainsong and figurate musick introduced by the clergy

But now, to stepp back a litle, wee must consider, that this revolution did not come on all at once, but gradually, and the church men were the means that brought it about. For their manner of singing the church services and hymnes was never according to the Greek or Latine

modells

f.125v / modells, but rather after the Jewish forme,[417] and they did not alter much till the time of Saint Ambrose who introduced the antiphones.[418] In those days Christians were so numerous, and their episcopall churches so great and splendid, that the prelates

---

[416] The word 'lethe', in Greek, originally meant forgetting, but in later classical mythology it was applied as a proper name to a river in Hades whose water caused forgetfulness of the past to those who drank it.

[417] Both Jewish and Christian psalmody were comparatively late developments which took place without benefit of mutual influence; but they had a common source from scriptural cantilation (see McKinnon 1979–80). North makes this point above f.122, despite his statement here.

[418] Ambrose (b. *c.*340, d. 397), Roman saint, bishop and doctor of the Church, is acknowledged as one of the three great Latin church fathers of the fourth and fifth centuries. Tradition assigns to him special significance as important in the development of Ambrosian (i.e., Milanese) chant, the authorship of the *Te deum*, the introduction of hymns and of antiphonal singing into the Latin church and the composition of a number of hymns. All these traditional attributions are no longer widely accepted, although there is still some debate about the issue of Ambrose's supposed contributions.

exalted the vocall services as much as they could, and indeed it was but necessary, for reasons touched elswhere.[419] It appears in Kercher and others, that there was no steddy scale of musicall notes, till the time of Pope Gregory, who contrived the order of them by a septenary of letters, and Guido added the vocall syllables, and the notation by lines; which was clumsily expressed before. This was sufficient for the use of plain-song in the churches, and gave latitude enough to vary the modulations for the more splendor of their musick; but yet all was plain-song, that is counterpoint unisonall, and without inequallity of time, sounding all syllables of a length[420] according to the notes. And this I take to have bin the state of church musick for many years after organs and various instruments, according to a more florid manner of composition, by concords interwoven, called descant, were in use abroad.

126 / And the churchmen having the skill of musick primarily amongst them, were cheifly concerned in those improvements, and associated with the laity in carrying them on, by teaching, and performing with them, and probably in time learning from them, who might become more florid and ayery then themselves. These exercises, which at first were cheifly of voices, at length took in the organ, and other instruments, but (very improperly) confined their skill to the Guidonian scale, and made the church plainsong the ordinary subject. No wonder therefore that organs and other instruments, with the descant manner at last entered the churches.

38. [Of descanting and In Nomines]
    Nothing shewed the influence of the ecclesiasticks over the spirits of the laity in those times more then the imposition of the church plainsong in almost all their figurate musick, from whence it was at first derived, and continued downe beyond the Reformation, and so near to our times, which must be ascribed to custome rather then any authority. But it is sure enough that the early discipline of musick in England was with help of the gamut to sing plainsong at sight and moreover to descant, or sing a consort part at sight

also

26v / also, with such breakings, bindings and cadences as were harmonious and according to art; and this not of one part onely but the art

---

[419] See *T S 1728* (ff. 120–121v); see also above f.27v, n.81.
[420] I.e., of a similar length.

was so farr advanced that divers would descant upon plaine song extempore together, as Mr. Morley shews.[421] And this exercise was performed not onely by voices and extempore, but whole consorts for instruments of 4, 5, and six parts were solemnly composed, and with wonderfull art and invention, whilst one of the parts (comonly in the midle) bore onely the plainsong thro out. And I guess that in some times, litle of other consort musick was coveted or in use, but that which was styled In Nomine was yet more remarkable, for it was onely descanting upon the 8 notes with which the sillables (In Nomine Domini[422]) agreed. And of this kind I have seen whole volumes, of many parts, with the several authors' names (for honour)inscribed.[423] And if the study, contrivance, and ingenuity of these compositions, to fill the harmony, carry on fuges, and interspers discords, may pass in the account of skill, no other sort whatsoever may pretend to more, and it is some confirmation that in two or three ages last bygone the best private musick, as was esteemed consisted of these.

I

f.127   / 39. The defects of plain-song musick

I would not have it thought that, by what is here observed, I am recomending this kind of musick; for in one principall article, nothing can be more defective, and that is variety or what is called air; I might mention other imperfections but that is enough. It is a sort of harmonious murmur, rather then musick; and in a time, when people lived in tranquillity and at eas, the enterteinement of it was aggreable, not unlike a confused singing of birds in a grove. It was adapted to the use of private familys, and societys; and for that porpose chests of violls, consisting of 2 trebles, 2 means, and 2 bases were contrived to fullfill 6 parts, and no thro base (as it is called) was then thought of; that was reserved to other kinds of musick, I shall mention;[424] but this began before organs came into churches, and while the pure plain song prevailed in them. And then the most celebrated formes came into secular use, and so continued in credit,

---

[421] Thomas Morley (b. 1557 or 1558, d. 1602), English theorist, composer, editor and organist, was author of a treatise in dialogue (1597, various editions), the purpose of which was to instruct the literate, upper-class amateur in the rudiments of notation (as employed between 1450–1600) and the arts of counterpoint, canon and extemporisation.

[422] MS has 'In Nomine Domine'.

[423] Rimbault (1846: 69 note) stated that he owned a volume, 'formerly in the possession of the North and L'Estrange families', with the title 'In Nomines and other Solfaing Songes of 5, 6, 7, and 8 partes, for Voyces or Instruments'. No such title appears in the sale catalogue of Rimbault's library (but see lot 1337 in Rimbault 1877: 86).

[424] See f.136.

in England at least, downe so low as the reigne of King Charles 1 which I can judg by some plain song consorts I have seen of so late composure. But in our days nothing can be more monstrous and insupportable then such a consort would be, so mighty is the power of custome and fashion in musick.

27v / Nor doe I pretend that the whole musicall imployment was restrained to these formes, for at the same time even from the first la[u]nching of descant, peices of musick were composed in different styles, and for various porposes, as for merriment, and dancing etc. which need not much to be inquired after; but thus farr is materiall, that the earlyer consorts were composed for 3, 4, and more parts, for songs in Itallian or Latine out of the psalmes; of which I have seen divers and mostly in print, with the names of the patroni inscribed. And in England when composers were scarce, these songs were copyed off, without the words, and for variety used as instrumentall consorts, with the first words of the song for a title. And of this printed musick vocally performed, many will shine against the best moderne compositions, and I suppose instrumentally would not loos much of their excellence. And as alterations with endeavour to advance are continually profered, so the Itallian masters, who allwais did, or ought to lead the van in musick, printed peices they called fantazias wherein was air, and variety enough, and afterwards these were imitated by

the

128 / the English, who working more elabourately, improved upon their patterne, which gave occasion to an observation, that in vocall, the Itallians, and in the instrumentall musick, the English excelled.

40. About [the time of] Henry 8 musick began to flourish

For want of registers or memorialls of times wee can scarce assert any thing cronically of musick, which is wholly destitute of those advantages, which few other arts want. But if one may guess[,] church musick was at its perfection in the reigne of Henry 8. He was a lover, and they say composed anthems. In some times royall familys were all fighters, and in others all scollars; for as he was learned, so he bred all his children to learning, and also to musick, as some of the historys shew.[425] Queen Elizabeth, had a good touch

---

[425] The specific histories have not been identified, but a number of writers on the Reformation (for example, Gilbert Burnet and Erasmus) reported that Henry VIII composed offices for the church.

on the harpsicord, and organ and sub Deo★ confirmed the musick
in churches upon the Reformation,[426] which the brutallity of the
Puritans would have throwne out, as the more brutall rebbells, in
Charles 1's time actually did.[427] But now taking a stand [in the]
reign [of] Henry 8 and looking backwards for some time and then
forewards downe to [the] reign [of] James 1 there will be small
show of skill in musick in England except what belonged

to

f. 128v / to the cathedrall churches, and monasterys (when such were) and
for that reason the consortiers wherever they went, (from ministers, as the word was) were called minstrells, and then the whole
faculty of musick [was called] the minstrelsie. And the word is
(nearly) so interpreted by Howell in his etimologys,[428] and by
Minshew in his Spanish dictionary.[429] And as for corporation and
mercenary musick, it was cheifly flatile; and the professors, from
going about the streets in a morning, to wake folks, were, and are
yet, called waits, quasi wakes. And that kind of musick did not ill
suit the minstrells, becaus wind musick was frequently used in
churches, instead of voices, or els to enforce the chorus. But in the
reigne of King James 1 and the paradisicall part of the reigne of King
Charles 1 many musick masters rose up, and flourished.

[426] Elizabeth I played the virginals, as well as a lute-like instrument called the 'polyphant'
(Playford 1655, various editions). Early in her reign she issued a proclamation that there
should be: 'a modest distinct songue, so used in all partes of the common prayers in the
Church, that the same may be as playnely understanded, as yf it were read without
syngyng, and yet nevertheless, for the comfortyng of suche as delyght in musicke, it may
be permitted that in the begynning, or in the ende of common prayers, eyther at morning
or evenyng, that there may be song an Hymne, or such like songue, to the praise of
almightie god, in the best sort of melodie that may be conveniently devised, having
respect that the sentence of the Hymne may be understanded and perceyved' (1559,
Injunction 49, before 19 July, quoted by Hawkins 1776 rev. 1853/1963).

[427] North probably refers to the ordinance, passed 4 January 1644, repealing the statutes of
Edward VI and Elizabeth I for uniformity in the Common Prayer. Hawkins (1776 rev.
1853/1963: ii/576–7) summarised the effects of this repeal, particularly as it relates to
instrumental music in divine worship and the 'havoc and devastation' of churches and
libraries, whereas Scholes (1934/1962) cited documents to counter the notion that the
'puritans' were against music.

[428] James Howell (b. 1594?, d. 1666), Welsh writer and from 1661 historiographer royal of
England, was an advocate of spelling reform along phonetic lines. In addition to political
and historical works, dictionaries and grammars, he published translations of alchemical
and other works. North probably refers to Howell's *Lexicon tetraglotton, or an English–
French–Italian–Spanish dictionary . . .* , London 1659–60.

[429] John Minsheu (fl. 1599–1617), lexicographer and teacher of languages, issued three
different Spanish dictionaries between 1599 and c. 1617.

41. The lute enlivened musik, which improved to [the] reigne [of]
Charles 2

Their works lay most in compositions for violls; but at that time
the lute was a monopolist of the ayery kind; and the masters[,]
gentlemen and ladyes for the most part used it. And the lessons for
that instrument were usually broke into straines, two to a lesson,
were it ayre[,] courant etc. but for pavans or more serious lessons
three and then

the

f. 129 / the musick masters fell to imitation of these, for after the fancys, In
which they had some ayre, they added a suit[e] of lessons called
ayres, galliards or other conceipt. The violin was scarce knowne
tho now the principall verb,⁴³⁰ and if it was any where seen, it was
in the hands of a country croudero*, who for the portabillity served
himself of it. And [music was] in this state when the troubles came
foreward;⁴³¹ and the whole society of the masters in London were
turned adrift, some went into the armyes, others dispersed about in
the countrys and made musick for the consolation of the cavalier
gentlemen. And that gave occasion to divers familyes to entertein
the skill, and practise of musick, and to encourage the masters to the
great increas of compositions. And this good humour lasted some
time after the happy Restauration,⁴³² and then decayed, which with
the reasons may be discourst of afterwards.⁴³³

42. The court masques in [the time of] James [1] and Charles 1 as
operas

In the reigne of King James 1 musick had the greatest encouragement, for the masques at court which were a sort of balles, or
operas,⁴³⁴ found imployment for very many of them, and in the
theaters at courts they were adorned with liverys, that is divers
coloured silk

mantles

⁴³⁰ For another example of North's use of 'verb', see the Glossary: riccercata. As Arthur
Danto has pointed out, in the Port-Royal *Grammaire Générale et Raisonée*, the verb is
'dynamic and performative', its role in speech being 'curiously analogous to that of the
cogito in thought' (Arnauld and Lancelot 1676/1975: 15).

⁴³¹ The civil wars began in 1642. North's knowledge of the 'troubles' would have come
from his father, Dudley (b. 1602, d. 1677), fourth baron North (1666), whose activities
during this period have been detailed by Randall (1983: Ch. 5).

⁴³² I.e., from 1660.

⁴³³ See ff. 132v–133.

⁴³⁴ North's grandfather (see f.69, n.228) was one of the masquers in Thomas Campion's *The
Description of a Maske, presented before the kinges maiestie at White-Hall, on twelfth night last, in
honour of the Lord Hayes, and his bride . . .* , London 1607. For the other masquers, see
Hawkins (1776 rev., 1853/1963: ii/508).

f. 129v   / mantles and scarfs with rich capps and the master in the shape of an
Appollo, for decoration of the scene. And they had the favour to be
made a corporation, with a charter whereby they had divers prive-
ledges, and a jurisdiction over the faculty;[435] no less formall then
the Colledg of Phisitians;[436] and this charter is still in force but not,
as I know, made use of.[437] The musick at these masques, (as must
be supposed) was of the ayery kind, with as much variety and
novelty as could be contrived to pleas the court and among other
conceipts there was a consort of 12 lutes, which must needs be (in
our dialect) very fine and pretty.[438] The enterteinements consisted
of consorts, singing, machines, short dramas, familiar dialogues,
interludes and dancing wherein the younger quallity had no small
share. And taking the whole together, and excepting the advantage
of a single voice or two, these diversions were not inferior to our
operas. And considering that the most vulgar composition in a
stately theater, comes not short of that which is more artfull, for
magnitude

and

[435] The earliest extant royal charter by which musicians in England were incorporated into a
craft-guild was granted by Edward IV to his minstrels on 24 April 1469. North refers
here to the Charter of Incorporation granted by James I on 8 July 1604. The company thus
instituted was styled 'The Master, Wardens and Commonalty of the Art or Science of the
Musicians of London'. The arms and crest of the company were approved in 1634 (see
Anon 1905: 82) and were described by Butler as follows: *'for their Arms, they bare Azure, a
Swan Argent, within a Tressure Counterflour Or: and, in a Chief Gules, a Rose between two
Lyons Or. And, for their Crest, the Signe called by the Astronomers, the Orphean Lyre'* (1636:
'The Epistle Dedicatorie' n.p.).

[436] The Royal College of Physicians was established by royal charter in 1518 not as a craft-
guild but as a new type of association which was emerging as the professions separated
from the crafts. After 1518 new charters were granted by Charles II in 1663 and by James
II on 11 March 1686/87. The charter of James II, which was in English, was intended to
supersede the charter of Charles II. It included all the rights he granted with an additional
function, for the College was to be allowed to print and publish. According to Clark,
'After the expiration of the Act of 1662 (14 Car. II, cap. 33) for the licensing of the press,
no printing or publishing on physic or surgery or the practice thereof was to be permitted
without approval of the president and censors. The Act did not expire until 1693, having
been continued in this same year 1685, but the College was already exercising this power.
By a private and in the beginning secret arrangement Archbishop Sancroft had
transferred to it his authority for licensing such books, which it continued to do until the
Act ran out and with it the whole system of censorship' (1964: i/356). The transfer of
authority may have been effected by North, who was steward to the see of Canterbury
from February 1679 to April 1692.

[437] The power of the guild had waned by the eighteenth century (see Kassler 1979: i/xxix–
xxxi, xlii–xliv). Nevertheless, two actions of the Company were recorded in 1718 and
1724, and there were a further two after North's death (see Crewdson 1950: 43).

[438] In Ben Jonson's *Hymenaei: or The solemnities of masque, and barriers . . .*, London 1606, the
first main masque dance was performed 'to a rare and full musique of twelue Lutes'.
Although payments to lute players were made for other masques, *Hymenaei* is the only
masque whose published description mentions that twelve lutes played in consort.

.130   / and force of sound is among the cheif excellencys of musick,
provided there is in it no absurdity wee must not brave it as some
doe that there never was good musick in England but in our time.

43. Of divers masters, and an account of Jenkins

It imports not much to the state of the world, or the condition of
humane life, to know the names and styles of those authors of
musicall composition, whose performances gained to the nation the
credit of excelling the Itallians in all but the vocall; therefore the
oblivion that is come over all is no great loss. But for curiosity, as
other no less idle antiquitys are courted[,] any professor would be
contented to know their names, and the caracters and works; and
much might be done that way, if there were means to come at some
gentlemen's old collections not yet rotten where many of them are
still delitescent* and there one might find some of Alfonso Fera-
bosco, Coperario (anglicè* Cooper), Lupo, Mico, Est,[439] and
divers others, especially of one Mr. John Jenkins, whose musicall
works are more voluminous and in the time more esteemed then all
the rest, and now lye in utmost contempt. I shall adventure to give

a

130v   / a short account of this particular master, with whom it was my
good chance to have had an intimate acquaintance and freind-
ship.[440] He lived in King James [the First's] time, and flourished in
King Charles the First's. His talents lay in the use of the lute, and
base or rather lyra viol; he was one of the court musitians, and once
was brought to play upon the lyra viol afore King Charles 1 as one
that performed somewhat extraordinary; and after he had done the
King sayd he did wonders upon an inconsiderable instrument.
After the court was disbanded[441] he left the towne, and past his
time at gentlemen's houses in the country where musick was of the
family, and he was ever courted and never slighted, but at home
wherever he went and in most of his freinds' houses there was a
chamber called by his name, for besides his musicall excellences, he

[439] All these men were noted especially as composers of music for viols: Alfonso Ferrabosco,
the younger (b. before 1578, d. 1628); John Cooper (Cowper) (b. ?c. 1570 or 1580, d.
1626), better known as Giovanni Coprario (Coperario); Thomas Lupo (d. 1628); Richard
Mico (Micoe, Micho, Meco, Myco) (b. c. 1590, d. 1661); and Michael East (Easte, Est,
Este) (b. c. 1580, d. 1648). The last-named composer was a tutor in singing of the
antiquary and alchemist, Elias Ashmole, whom North seems to have known (see Notes of
Me ed. Jessopp 1887: 43).
[440] In Notes of Me (ed. Jessopp 1887: 79–83), North provides his first 'character' sketch of
Jenkins, portions of which he repeats or elaborates on in later writings.
[441] I.e., in 1642.

was an accomplisht, ingenious person, and so well behaved, as never to give offence, and wherever he went was allwais welcome and courted to stay. Even in his extream old age, when as to musick he was almost effete, and withall obnoxious to great infirmitys, he was taken care of as a freind, and after having spent some of the last years of his life with Sir P. Wodehous[442] he dyed at Kimberly in Norfolk, and not poor but capable to leav, as he did, hansome remembrances to some of his freinds.

f.131   / I never heard that he articled with any gentleman where he resided, but accepted what they gave him, and he kept his places at court, as I understood to the time of his death, and tho he for many years was uncapable to attend, the court musitians had so much value for him, that advantage was not taken, but he received his salary as they were payd.

44. Of his compositions, new[,] ayery, and easy

It is not possible to give an account of his compositions, they were so many that he himself outlived the knowledg of them. A Spanish Don[443] sent some papers to Sir P. Lely,[444] conteining one part of a consort of 4 of a sprightly moving kind, such as were called fancys, desiring that he would procure and send him the other parts costa che costa.★ Lely gave me those papers, as the likelyest person to get them supplyed. I shewed them to Jenkens, who sayd he knew the consort to be his, but when, or where made he knew not, and could not recollect any thing more concerning them. It is supposed that when he first begun to compose he followed in the track of the most celebrated masters, of whom I have named some[445]

and

f.131v   / and consequently his style was, as theirs solemne and grave. I have seen an In Nomine of his of six parts, most elabourate; but his lute and lyra violl wrought so much upon his fancy, that he diverted to a more lively ayre, and was not onely an innovator, but became a

---

[442] Phillip Wodehouse (Woodhouse, Woodehouse) (b. 1608, d. 1681), third baronet (1611), was M.P. for Norfolk (1655–56, 1656–58) and for Thetford (1660).

[443] Woodfield (1985: 40–1) found evidence that the Spanish don was Don Juan, son of Philip IV, and that the compositions were either the twenty-seven fantasias for treble, two bass viols and organ or the twenty-one fantasias for two trebles and bass (no organ part is extant).

[444] Peter Lely (b. 1618, d. 1680), Dutch portrait-painter, came to London in April 1641. He painted most of the notable people of his day, including some members of the North family.

[445] See f.130.

reformer of musick. His fancys were full of ayery points, graves, triplas, and other varietys and his lesser peices imitated the dulcor of lute lessons of which he composed multitudes. And all that he did untill his declin[in]g age, was lively, active, decided, and (if I may be credited), cappriccioso.* And of this kind there was horsloads of his works, which were dispersed about, and very few came together into the same hands, but the private musick in England was in great measure supplyed by him; and they were coveted becaus his style was new, and (for the time), difficult, for he could hardly forbear devisions, and some of his consorts was too full of them. And if that, as the moderne caprice will have it, be a recomendation, his compositions wanted it not, but this is further to be sayd of him, that being an accomplisht master of the viol, all his movements lay fair for the hand, and were not so hard as seemed.

132   / 45. Fell short in the vocall, some peices humoursome

His vein was less happy in the vocall part, for tho he took pleasure in putting musick to poems, he reteined his instrumentall style so much, that few of them were greatly approved[.] Nor was his teaching scollars to sing (as for want of professed masters he did sometimes succeed) better, for he had neither a voice, nor any manner fitt for it; but some anthems of his remain in the cathedralls, where they are in cours sung, and in that service are not amiss. He would be often in a merry humour; and make catches, and some strains he called rants, which were like our stoccatas.* He made a peice called the Cryes of Newgate, which was all humour, and very bizzarre; but of all his conceipts, none flew about with his name so universally as the small peice called his Bells.[446] In those days the country fidlers were not so well foddered from London, as since, and a master that made new tunes for them, was a benefactor; and these Bells was [in] such supply, as never failed to pass in all companys. It was a happy thought, and well executed and for the variety, might be stylled a sonnata; onely the sound of bells being among the vulgaritys, tho naturally elegant enough, like comon sweetmeats, grows fulsome, and will not be endured longer then the humour of affecting a novelty lasts.

[446] Jenkins' music for viols has been catalogued in The Viol da Gamba Society provisional index of viol music. The index includes, under two-part airs for treble and bass, several rants as well as 'The Bells', consisting of an 'Almaine', 'Corant' and 'Saraban' (Dodd 1978–79: 82, 84 and 80–1). Two other works also have 'bells' in the title: 'Mr. Jenkins Bells', which is listed under three-part airs for two trebles and a bass (ibid. 1977: 83), and 'The Bell Pavan', which is listed with the fancies (ibid. 1969: 51). The 'Cryes of Newgate' seems not to be extant, but its title is reminiscent of an In Nomine which Jenkins based on London street cries (ibid. 1971: 34).

f. 132v   / 46. Why now layd aside

It will be now asked how it can consist, that the musick of Mr. Jenkins, if it were such as here is pretended, should be now so much layd aside, or rather contemned as it is, when the art is thought to be arrived at a perfection? This would be harder to answer if it were not a great truth, and notorious, that every age since Appollo did not say the same thing of the musick of their owne time, for nothing is more a fashion then musick; no[,] not cloaths, [n]or language, either of which is made a derision to after times. And so it is of all things that belong to the pleasures of sence. For allowing that there is somewhat preferable in right reason, as some cloaths may be more convenient and language concise, and significant, yet there is a great deall indifferent, and so much, that the prejudice of custome will gett the better of it. And the grand custome of all is to affect novelty and to goe from one thing to another, and despise the former. And it is a poorness of spirit, and a low method of thinking that inclines men to pronounce for the present, and allow nothing to times past. Cannot wee put ourselves in loco★ of former states, and judg pro tunc?★ Therefore as to all bon gusto wee ought to yeild to

the

f. 133   / to the authority of the proper time and not determine comparatively where one side is all prejudice. It is a shallow monster that shall hold forth in favour of our fashions and relishes and maintaine that no age shall come wherein they will not be despised and derided. And if on the other side, I may take upon me to be a fidling★ profet, I may with as much reason declare, that the time may come when some of the present celebrated musick will be as much in contempt as John come kiss me now now now,[447] and perhaps with as much reason, as any is found for the contrary at present.

47. First compositions lost, and his caracter

But as to Mr. Jenkins in particular, there is somewhat more to be sayd. His style is thought to be slow, heavy[,] moving from concord to concord and consequently dull; and I grant that he was obnoxious to an excess the English were, and I beleev yet are, obnoxious to, and that is perpetually moving up and downe [the notes of the scale stepwise], without much saltation or battering as

---

[447] For details of seventeenth- and eighteenth-century settings of 'John, come kiss me now', see Simpson (1966: 396–8) and Ward (1967: 50–6).

the Italian's use. But els as to activity of movement, and true musicall ayre in his passages, none had more then Mr. Jenkins; but the unhappyness is, that all his earlyest and most lively compositions are sunk and lost, and none remaine but those of his latter time, when he lived

in

33v / in country familys, and could compose no otherwise then to the capacity of his performers, who could not deal with his high flying vein. It is no wonder that few or none but those of the latter sort are to be met with; and so the whole force of a man is measured according [to] a member that is lamed. But in his old age he made some essays of his art, which not being usefull where he resided I had the honour to carry as a present from him to good Mr. Stephkins, who was much esteemed by him;[448] whither they are extant or not I know not. He was certeinly a great master of devisions, and encouraged Sympson the devision violist by a copy of verses at the beginning, and some exemplars of devision at the latter end of his book.[449] But as plaine as his latter compositions are, if performed (not with dull but) [with] brisk hands, distinguishing the graves and allegros, I may challenge the most skillfull of the masters (fashion apart) to find fault with the musick; for his ayre is unexceptionable; and if he hath not so many hard notes, as are now used, (which by the way are not absolutely necessary, but onely as an ornament to harmony) a skillfull hand will supply enough of them, for there are very few, but what occurr in the comon gracing of musicall performances. And

now

.134 / now to conclude as to Mr. Jenkins, he was certeinly a very happy person, for he had an [un]interrupted health and was of an easy temper, superior in his profession, well accepted by all, knew no

[448] Theodore (Dietrich) Steffkin (Steofkin, Stefkin, Stephkin) (d. 1673), viol player, was one of the musicians of Charles II. In *MG* c. 1726 (f.171), North has the 'old gentleman Stephkins' esteeming the music of Jenkins (see also *Notes of Me* ed. Jessopp 1887: 81).

[449] The poem appeared in the first edition of Simpson's treatise on viol playing, which was published by Playford in 1659 as *The Division Violist*. It was not included in the second edition with the altered title, *The Division-Viol* (1665/1965). All the divisions at the end of the volume conclude with the initials 'C S', but in the text preceding the divisions Simpson observed: 'if you desire written Copies of that sort, (a thing most necessary for those who intend to Compose such like themselves) none has done so much in that kind, as the ever Famous and most Excellent Composer, in all sorts of Modern Musick, Mr. John Jenkins' (1665/1965:61).

want, saw himself outrunn by the world, and having lived a good
Christian, dyed in peace.

48. Mr. M. Lock a good composer, in the old and new way[450]

Mr. Mathew Lock was the most considerable master of musick
after Jenkins fell off. He was organist at Somerset Hous chappell as
long as he lived, but the Itallian masters, that served there, did not
approve of his manner of play, but must be attended by more polite
hands; and one while[451] one Sabinico,[452] and afterwards Signor
Babtista Draghi used the great organ,[453] and Lock (who must not
be turned out of his place, nor the execution) had a small chamber
organ by, on which he performed with them the same services. In
musick he had a robust vein and many of his compositions went
about. He set most of the psalmes to musick in parts, for the use of
some vertuoso ladys in the citty; and he composed a magnifick
consort of 4 parts after the old style which was the last of the kind
that hath bin made[,][454]

so

f.134v   / so wee may rank him with Cleomenes King of Sparta[455] who was
styled ultimus heroo[r]um. ★ He conformed at last to the modes of
his time, and fell into the theatricall way, and composed to the

---

[450] Matthew Locke (b. 1621 or 1622, d. 1677), composer, writer and controversialist, was
noted for his chamber and dramatic music. He was organist at the Catholic chapel at St.
James's Palace (1662–71) and at Somerset House (1671–77). In 1673 he was demoted at
the latter place when the position of first organist was given to Draghi (see f.134, n.453).

[451] I.e., at one time.

[452] Giovanni Sebenico (b. c. 1640, d. 1705), organist and tenor of Croatian origin, studied
and worked in Italy. He was at the court of Charles II between April 1666 and the summer
of 1673. He returned to Italy in 1683.

[453] Giovanni Batista Draghi (b. c. 1640, d. 1708), Italian composer, harpsichordist and
organist, was taken to England in connection with Charles II's abortive plans to establish
opera in London. He was appointed first organist at Somerset House (1673) and organist
of James II's private chapel (1687). For a time he was also music master to the king's
daughters. In the 1690s Draghi was active as an impresario for concerts in the York
Buildings (BL Sloane MS 1388), and in 1698 he was pensioned.

[454] Two holograph manuscripts survive of Locke's *Consort of fower Parts* (twenty-four pieces
in six suites). Rimbault claims to have owned the 'original MS of the Psalms' composed
by Locke for virtuoso ladies. According to his description, the manuscript 'is written in a
small neat hand on forty-nine folio pages, and contains the following anthems (the words
selected from the Psalms), for three and four voices: – Blessed is the man; O Lord, rebuke
me not; O Lord, how marvellous; Let God arise; Behold, how good and joyful; Praise the
Lord, all ye Gentiles; When I was in tribulation; Sing unto the Lord; From the depths; O
Lord, hear my prayer; In the beginning, O Lord; Arise O Lord; Lord, now lettest thou.
At the end are several latin hyms for voices and instruments, probably composed for the
Chapel of Queen Catherine' (1846: 96). Although Rimbault did own a copy of Locke's
Consort of fower Parts (see lot 1374 in Rimbault 1877: 90), the sale catalogue of his library
does not seem to contain a manuscript that corresponds to the above description.

[455] Cleomenes III (b. c. 260, d. 219 B.C.), son of Leonidas, was the last king of Sparta.

semioperas divers peices of vocall and instrumentall enterteinement, with very good success; and then gave way to the devine Purcell, and others, that were coming full saile into the superiority of the musicall faculty.

49. The band of violins[,] Mr. Baltesarr,[456] and the style of Babtist[457]

But now to observe the stepps of the grand metamorfosis of musick, whereby it hath mounted into those altitudes of esteem it now enjoys; I must remember that upon the Restauration of King Charles [2], the old way of consorts were layd aside at court, and the King made an establishment, after a French model of 24 violins, and the style of the musick was accordingly. So that became the ordinary musick of the court, theaters, and such as courted the violin. And that instrument had a lift into credit before, for one Baltazarre a Sweed came over, and did wonders upon it by swiftness, and doubling of notes, but his hand was accounted hard and rough, tho he made amends for that by using often a lyra-tuning, and conformable lessons which were very harmonious, as some

coppys

.135 / coppys now extant in divers hands may shew; but this manner, which was but a complement to the lute, and not fitt for consort, did not take at all. But during the first years of Charles 2d all musick affected by the beau-mond run into the French way, and the rather, becaus at that time the master of the court musick in France, whose name was Babtista (an Itallian Frenchifyed) had influenced the French style by infusing a great portion of the Italian harmony into it; whereby the ayre was exceedingly improved. The manner was theatricall, and the setts of lessons composed, called branles (as I take it) or braules, that is beginning with an entry, and then courants etc. And the entrys of Babtist ever were, and will be valued as most stately and compleat harmony, and all the compositions of the towne were strained to imitate Babtist's vein; and none came so neer it as the honourable and worthy vertuoso, Mr.

[456] Thomas Baltzar (b. ?1631, d. 1663), German violinist and composer, came from Sweden to England (by 4 March 1656). On 23 December 1661 he was appointed musician-in-ordinary for the violin in the king's private music. The copies of his works referred to below and on f. 134v are described by North in *MG c. 1726* (f. 173) as 'neat lute-fashioned lessons' and 'also some of his rough pieces'. Montagu North presented a manuscript collection of Baltzar's pieces to Charles Burney (1776–89: iii/428; see also Holman 1984).

[457] The style in question is that of Lully, whom North here refers to as 'Babtist' and on f. 135 as 'Babtista'.

Francis Roberts.[458] But the whole tendency of the ayre had more regard to the foot, then the ear. And no one could hear an entree with its starts, and saults but must expect a dance to follow, so lively may human actions be pictured by musick.

f.135v   / 50. King Charles 2d a novellist,* and a comparison of nations

King Charles 2 was a professed lover of musick, but of this [French] kind onely, and had an utter detestation of fancys, and the less for a successless enterteinement of that kind given him by Secretary Williamson,[459] after which the Secretary had no peace, for the King (as his way was) could not forbear whetting his witt upon the subject of the fancy-musick, and its patron the Secretary. And he would not allow the matter to be disputed upon the point of meliority, but run all downe by saying, have not I ears? He could not bear any musick to which he could not keep the time, and that he constantly did to all that was presented to him.[460] And for the most part [he] heard it standing and for songs he approved onely the soft vein, such as might be called a step tripla, and that made a fashion among the masters, and for the stage, as may be seen in the printed books of the songs of that time. Once the King had a fancy for a comparison to hear the singers of the severall nations, German, Spanish, Italian, French, and English performe upon the stage in Whitehall. The Itallians had that mentioned elswhere – [Amante] che dit[t]e che fatti, etc.[461] The English brought up the arrere under great disadvantage, with – I pass all my hours in a shady old grove, etc., for tho the King chose that song as the best, others were not of his opinion.[462]

[458] There is considerable circumstantial evidence that North was personally acquainted with Francis Roberts (Robartes) (b. 1650, d. 1718), politician, virtuoso and amateur musician. Contact with the North family may have come in the first instance through Roberts' father, John, viscount Bodmin and earl of Radnor, who was a member, with Francis North, of the reorganized privy council (1679).

[459] Joseph Williamson (b. 1633, d. 1701), knight (1672), was a man of affairs and amateur viol player, a biography of which would involve an almost exhaustive survey of political and social England from 1665–80. He was called to the bar from the Middle Temple (1664) and afterwards served as M.P. for Thetford (1669) and Secretary of State (June 1674, removed 1678). In all these capacities, he must have come into contact with the Norths. He was elected a fellow of the Royal Society (1663) and served as second president (1677–80). Evelyn was present at two 'consorts' of music at the home of Williamson, and in his brief sketch of the man states that 'Sir *Joseph* was a Musitian' (ed. de Beer 1955: iii/601, iv/39, 277).

[460] North's statement is corroborated by Pepys (22 November 1663): 'here [at chapel] I first perceived that the King is a little Musicall, and kept good time with his hand all along the Anthem' (ed. Latham and Matthews 1970–83: iv/394).

[461] See ff.144v–147v.

[462] The text was by the king himself, and the music was composed by Pelham Humfrey (b. 1647, d. 1674).

f.136 / 51. Old musick and forrein, reteined by some

This French manner of instrumentall musick did not gather so fast as to make a revolution all at once, but during the greatest part of that King's reigne the old musick was used in the country[463] and in many meetings and societys in London; but the treble violl was discarded, and the violin took its place. In some familyes organs were used to accompany consorts, but the old masters would not allow the liberty of playing from a thro base figured, as harpsicords of late have universally practised, but they formed the organ part express; becaus the holding out the sound required exact concord, els the consort would suffer; or perhaps the organists had not then the skill as since, for now they desire onely figures. There were also divers societys of a politer sort, who were inquisitive after forrein consorts, and procured divers, as from Itally Cazzati,[464] and Vitali;[465] and one from Sweeden by Becker composed for from 2 to 6 parts which was too good to be neglected and lost, as it is at present.[466] And however England came to have the credit of musicall lovers, I know not, but am sure that there was a great flocking hither of forrein

masters

f.36v / masters as from Germany[,] Sheiffar, Vvoglesank, and others, and from France, Porter[467] and Farinell;[468] these latter for the violin and they found here good encourag[e]ment, so that the nation, (as I may terme it) of musick was very well prepared for a revolution.

---

[463] MS has 'countrys'.
[464] Maurizio Cazzati (b. *c.* 1620, d. 1677), Italian composer and organist, was noted for his music for trumpet and strings.
[465] Giovanni Battista Vitali (b. 1632, d. 1692), an Italian composer, string player and singer, helped to establish the baroque and, especially, the trio sonata.
[466] Dietrich Becker (Bekker, Baekker) (b. 1623, d. 1679), a German (not a Swedish) composer and violinist, published *Musicalische Fruehlings-Fruechte*, Hamburg 1668 (2d edn. as *Musicalische Lendt-Vruchten*, 1673), a collection of chamber music for three to five instruments.
[467] Sheiffar (?Shaeffer, ?Sheffer), Vvoglesank (Vogelsang) and Porter (?Porte) have eluded positive identification by Rimbault (1846), Wilson (1959) and the present editors.
[468] Probably the composer and violinist, Michel Farinel (fl. 1675–89), member of a French family of musicians and pupil of Carissimi in Rome. He visited England between 1675–79 and returned to France in 1688. Among his compositions is a set of variations for violin and continuo on the folia which was known in England as 'Farinel's Ground'.

52. Publik meetings and 1. Ben Wallington[469]

A great means of bringing that foreward was the humour of following publick consorts, and it will not be out of the way to deduce them from the beginning. The first of those was in a lane behind [Saint] Paul's [Cathedral], where there was a chamber organ that one Phillips played upon, and some shopkeepers, and foremen came weekly to sing in consort, and to hear, and injoy ale and tobacco;[470] and after some time the audience grew strong, and one Ben Wallington got the reputation of [a] notable base voice, who also set up for a composer, and hath some songs in print, but of a very low sence;[471] and their musick was cheifly out of Playford's catch book. But this shewed an inclination of the citisens to follow musick. And the same was confirmed by many litle enterteinements, the masters voluntarily made for their scollars, for being knowne they were allwais crowded.

f.137   / 53. Banister's in White fryers[472]

The next essay was of the elder Banister, who had a good theatricall vein and in composition had a lively style peculiar to himself. He procured a large room in Whitefryars, neer the Temple back gate, and made a large raised box for musitians, whose modesty required curtaines. The room was rounded with seats and small tables alehous fashion; 1s. was the price and call for what you pleased. There was very good musick, for Banister found means to procure the best hands in towne, and some voices to come and

---

[469] Ben (Benjamin) Wallington (Walington) (fl. 1664–68) was by trade a goldsmith. According to Pepys (15 September 1667), Wallington and 'Piggott' came to his home, the former 'whereof, being a very little fellow, did sing a most excellent bass, and yet a poor fellow, a working goldsmith, that goes without gloves to his hands' (ed. Latham and Matthews 1970–83: viii/437; see also 557).

[470] North alludes here to the Musick Society, Old Jewry, which met first in the musick house at the Miter in Fleet Street, near the west end of St. Paul's Church, and then towards the end of 1664 moved to the Old Jewry. When the Society first began is not known for certain, although it is possible that the date of its inception was 1660. According to Pepys (21 January 1660), a music room at the Miter was 'being in fitting for Banister [the elder] to come thither'; the room was ready by 18 February 1660 (ed. Latham and Matthews 1970–83: i/25, 59). The Society's organist, Phillips, has eluded identification by Wilson (1959), Spink (1965–67) and the present authors (but see Rimbault 1846: 108). The Society was defunct by January 1665. It is probable that North's information about the Society came from his brother, Francis, who had contact with at least one member of the Society (George Piggot) but may have known the other members who went to the free school in Bury St. Edmunds, to which he was sent for 'finishing' before university.

[471] Only three of Wallington's compositions seem to have appeared in print: (1) a glee, (2) three duets and (3) a song for bass alone.

[472] Music meetings began on 30 December 1672 at Banister's house called 'The Musick School', over against the George Tavern in Whitefriars near the Temple back gate. They continued from 25 January 1675 at Chandos Street, Covent Garden; and from November 1678, at Essex Buildings over against St. Clement's Church, Strand (to 1679).

performe there, and there wanted no variety of humour, for Banister himself (inter alia) did wonders upon a flageolett to a thro base and the severall masters had their solos. This continued full one winter, and more I remember not.

54. The gentlemen's meeting[473]
There was a society of gentlemen of good esteem, whom I shall not name for some of them as I hear are still living, that used to meet often for consort after Babtist's manner, and falling into a weekly cours, and performing exceeding well, with bass violins (a cours instrument as it was then which they used to hire), their freinds and acquain-

tance

37v / tance, were admitted and by degrees as the fame of their meeting spread, so many auditors came that their room was crowded; and to prevent that inconvenience, they took a room in a taverne in Fleet Street,[474] and the taverner pretended to make formall seats, and to take mon[e]y; and then the society disbanded. But the taverner[,] finding the sweet of vending[475] wine and taking mon[e]y, hired masters to play, and made a pecuniary consort of it to which for the reputation of the musick, numbers of people of good fashion and quallity repaired.

55. The York musick hous, and how failed[476]
The masters of musick finding that mon[e]y was to be got this way, determined to take the buissness into their owne hands; and it proceeded so farr, that in York Buildings a fabrick was reared and furnished on porpose for publik musick. And there was nothing of musick valued in towne, but was to be heard there. It was called the

---

[473] North's membership in this meeting is hinted in *Notes of Me* (ed. Jessopp 1887: 84–5). It commenced *c.* 1677 and met weekly or oftener in private chambers or taverns. About 1689 North and other 'gentlemen' dropped out of the meetings, making it a solely professional society which was then renamed 'The Musick Meeting'. From circumstantial evidence, it seems that one of the professional members was the elder Matteis and one of the gentlemen, Francis Roberts.

[474] North indicates that most of the gentlemen were violinists and identifies one of the locations for their concerts as the Castle Tavern (*MG c. 1726*: ff. 174v–175). There was a tavern by this name in Paternoster Row which burned down in 1770 (see Deutsch 1955/1974).

[475] MS has 'venting'.

[476] The concert room in York Buildings, Villiers Street off the Strand, was built *c.* 1680 as the first room in London designed specifically for public concerts. North states: 'I observed well the musick here' (*MG c. 1726*: ff. 175–175v). Advertisements for concerts began on 23 November 1685 and continued more or less regularly to 5 December 1711; they reappeared on 13 June 1717 and then only sporadically to 1718 (Tilmouth 1961).

musick meeting; and all the quallity, and beau mond repaired to it but the plan of this project was not so well layd as ought to have bin, for the time of their beginning was inconsistent with the park[477] and the playhouses,[478] which had a stronger attraction. And

what

f.138   / what was wors the masters' undertakers were a rope of sand, not under the rule or order of any person, and every one foreward to advance his owne talents, and spightfull to each other, and out of emulation, substracting their skill in performing, all which together scandalized the company, and poysoned the entertainement. Besides[,] the whole was without designe or order; for one master brings a consort with fuges, another shews his guifts in a solo upon the violin, another sings, and then a famous lutinist comes foreward, and in this manner changes followed each other, with a full cessation of the musick between every one, and a ga[b]ble and bustle while they changed places, whereas all enterteinements of this kind ought to be projected as a drama, so as all the members shall uninterruptedly follow in order, and having a true connexion, set off each other. It is no wonder that the playhouses got ground, and as they ordered the matter, soon routed this musick meeting.

56. The semi-operas at the theaters

It had bin strange if the gentlemen of the theaters had sate still all this while, seeing as they say a pudding creep, that is a violent

inclination

f.138v   / inclination in the towne to follow musick, and they not serve themselves of it. Therefore Mr. Betterton who was the cheif inginerr of the stage, contrived a sort of plays, which were called operas but had bin more properly styled semioperas, for they consisted of half musick, and half drama; the cheif of these were Circe, The Fayery Queen, Dioclesian and King Arthur; which

---

477 By 'park' North denotes pleasure gardens which levied a small entrance fee and supplied refreshment and entertainment. In North's day the parks, and the date they were founded, were Marylebone Gardens (*c.* 1659), Vauxhall Gardens (1661), Belvidere Tea Gardens (*c.* 1664), Sadler's Wells (1684), London Spa (*c.* 1685), Cuper's Gardens (1691) and Lambeth Wells (*c.* 1697).

478 The playhouses or theatres existing in North's day, with date of opening, were Lincoln's Inn Fields (1661), Drury Lane Theatre (i.e., Theatre Royal 1663, reopened 1674), Dorset Garden Theatre (1671), New Theatre in Little Lincoln's Inn Fields (1695), King's Theatre (1705) and Little Theatre, Haymarket (1720).

latter was composed by Purcell and is unhappyly lost.[479] These were followed at first, but by an error of mixing 2 capitall enterteinement[s], could not stand long. For some that would come to the play, hated the musick, and others that were very desirous of the musick, would not bear the interruption, that so much rehearsall gave, so that it is best to have either by it self intire.[480]

57. Of the prize musick, and the ill effects, of competition

But nothing advanced musick more in this age then the patronage of the nobillity, and men of fortunes, for they became encouragers of it by great liberallitys, and countenance to the professors; and this was made very publik by a contribution amongst them, to be given as a premio* to him that should best entertein them in a solemne consort.[481] And divers of the masters entered the lists, and their performances were in the theaters successively

heard

39 / heard, and the victorys decided by the judgment of the subscribers; but this method gave no satisfaction, for the lords and the rest that subscribed, (as the good King Charles 2) had ears but not artificiall ones and those were necessary to warrant the authority of such a court of justice. I will not suppose, as some did, that making interest as for favour, and partiallity influenced these determinations; but it is certein, that the comunity of the masters were not of the same opinion with them. And so instead of incouraging the endeavours of all, the happy victor onely was pleased and all the rest were discontented and some who thought they deserved better, were almost ready to relinquish the faculty. And Mr. G. Finger a German and a good musitian[,] one of the competitors who had resided in England many years, went away upon it; declaring that he thought he was to compose musick for men, and not for boys.[482] So much a mistake it is to force artists upon a competition,

---

[479] The semi-operas were produced between *c.* 1683 and 1695. For *Circe; The Prophetress, or the History of Dioclesian; King Arthur;* and *The Fairy Queen,* see Price (1984), who classes the last three as semi-operas and the first as a 'tragic extravaganza'.

[480] See f.97v and n.319.

[481] The competition was announced 21 March 1699; the music of the contenders for the 'Musick-Prize' was played at Dorset Garden Theatre in 1701 (Tilmouth 1961: 27, 37, 38).

[482] Gottfried (Godfrey) Finger (b. *c.* 1660, d. 1730), Moravian composer and instrumentalist, came to England as one of the foreign musicians in the service of the Roman Catholic chapel of James II. The chapel opened 25 December 1686, and Finger's appointment is dated 5 July 1687. The chapel musicians were disbanded in 1688, when Finger pursued an independent career. Finger, who was placed fourth in the competition, left England sometime before 25 November 1704.

for all but one, are sure to be malecontents. And wors happened upon a competition for an organ at the Temple Church in which the 2 competitors[,] the bests artists in Europe, Smith and Harris, were but just not ruined.[483]

f. 139v   / 58. Italian musick, and the caracter of the elder N. Matteis

But as yet wee have given no account of the decadence of the French musick, and the Itallian coming in its room; this happened by degrees, and the overture was by accident, for the coming over of Signor Nicolai Matteis gave the first start.[484] He was an excellent musitian, and performed wonderfully upon the violin. His manner was singular, but in one respect excelled all that had bin knowne before in England, which was the arcata; his stoccatas, tremolos, devisions and indeed his whole manner was surprising and every stroke of his was a mouthfull. Besides all that he played was of his owne composition, which shewed him a very exquisite harmonist, and of a boundless fancy, and invention; and by all that I have knowne of him, and other musick of Itally, I cannot but judg him to have bin second to Corelli. When he came over first he was very poor, but not so poor as proud, which was the reason that kept him back, so that he had no acquaintance for a long time, but a merchant or two who patronized him. And he valuing himself at an excessive rate, sque[e]zed considerable sumes out of them. By degrees he became more taken notice of. He was heard play at court but his manner did

not

f. 140   / take, and he behaved himself fast[u]ously;* no person must whisper while he played, which sort of attention had not bin the fashion at court. It was sayd that a nobleman, the Duke of Richmond (I think it was)[485] would have given him a pension, but he did not like his way of playing, and would needs have a page of his

---

[483] North was directly involved in the competition between the organ builders, Bernard Smith (Bernard Schmidt, Baerent Smit) (b. *c.* 1630, d. 1708) and Renatus Harris (b. *c.* 1652, d. 1724). In February 1683 North and other benchers of the Inner and Middle Temple invited the two builders to design a new organ. The so-called 'battle' of the organs was waged until 21 June 1688, when North's name appears on official papers for the Temple Church organ purchased from Smith. Later, North hired Smith to build his own organ at Rougham (see *Cursory Notes of Musicke* ed. Chan and Kassler 1986).

[484] Standard biographical sources usually state that Matteis came to England in the 1670s, but see f. 140 and n. 485.

[485] Charles Stuart (b. 1639, d. 1672), sixth duke of Lennox, third duke of Richmond and tenth Seigneur d'Aubigny, went as ambassador to the Danish court in 1671, where he died. Since Williamson was Stuart's brother-in-law and one of Matteis's patrons, it is likely that North's identification here is correct. If so, Matteis would have been in England by 1670 and possibly earlier.

shew him the best manner, and he, for the jest sake, condiscended to learne of the page, but learn't so fast, that he soon out-run his master in his owne way. In short he was so outrageous in his demand especially for his high peices[,] solos, that very few would come up to him, and he continued low and obscure a long time.

59. Susteined and civilised by Dr. Walgrave;[486] printed, and not imitable.

And he had continued so but for 2 or 3 vertuosos, Dr. Walgrave a prodigy of an archlutinist, Sir R. L'estrange[487] an expert violist, and Mr. Bridgman the Undersecretary,[488] a thro base man upon the harpsichord. These got him into their acquaintance, and courting him in his owne way, by discours shewing him the temper of the English who if they were humoured would be liberall, but if not humored would doe nothing at all. And by putting on an air of complaisance, and doing as they desired, he would not want imployment or mon[e]y. They brought him by degrees into such good

temper

ᴸᴼⱽ / temper as made him esteemed, and sought after, and having got many scollars, tho at moderate rates his purs filled apace, which confirmed his conversion and he continued very mansuete* as long as he lived. And he found a way of getting mon[e]y which was perfectly new[,] for se[e]ing his lessons, (which were all duos), take with his scollars, and that most gentlemen desired them, he was at

---

[486] William Waldegrave (Walgrave, Wallgrave) (b. *c.* 1636, d. 1701), Roman Catholic, M.D. (Padua 1659) and knight (10 June 1688), was physician to the duke of York (*c.* 1684) and to the queen (*c.* 1687). He became an honorary member of the Royal College of Physicians (1664) and was elected fellow (1686). On 19 November 1674, Evelyn heard a number of 'rare Musitians', including the elder Matteis and 'that rare *Lutenist*' Waldegrave (ed. de Beer 1955: iv/48). Pepys wrote that Waldegrave, an 'Englishman bred at Rome, . . . plays the best upon the lute that I have ever heard' (ed. Latham and Matthews 1970–83: v/119–20).

[487] Roger L'Estrange (b. 1616, d. 1704), pamphleteer and Tory journalist, came from a musical family in which Jenkins and Thomas Brewer were resident musicians. L'Estrange was taught by Brewer and became noted for his skill as a bass viol player. In 1660 he was made a licenser of the press (to 1688). In this capacity he licensed the second edition of Simpson's *The Division-Viol* (1665/1965) and the first full edition of his *Compendium of Musick* (1667/1727). A number of musical works were dedicated to him, including Locke's *Melothesia* (1673). L'Estrange was also one of the performers at the Thursday music meetings held from 1678 to 1714 at the rooms of Thomas Britton, Aylesbury Street, Clerkenwell.

[488] William Bridgeman (b. *c.* 1646, d. 1699) was a clerk in the Secretary of State's office (from 1669); a clerk of the council (1685–88 and 1692–99); M.P., for Bramber (1685); in Secretary of State's office (1692–97); secretary of the Admiralty (1694–95); and joint secretary (1695–98). On 18 December 1680 he became a fellow of the Royal Society.

some charge to have them graven in copper, and printed in oblong octavos, and this was the beginning of ingraving musick in England.[489] And of these lessons he made books, and presented them, well bound to most of the lovers, which brought him the 3, 4, and 5 ginnys and the incouragement was so great, that he made 4 of them.[490] And a capriccio came in his crowne, to make the like for Paris, as he did, and went over to fiddle it off there,[491] but soon came back re infecta. ★ For tho he pretended to compose in the style of all nations, and of the French in particular[,] he soon found, that pistolls did not walk so fast as ginnys. But he vended his [French] copys (for they were not printed) in Ingland to very good porpose. He made another book, which was designed to teach composition, ayre, and to play from a thro base. And his exemplars were for the guittare, of which

instrument

f.141   / instrument he was a consumate master, and had the force upon it to stand in consort against an harpsicord. This book was printed, but few of the copys are to be found.[492] These books of his were of

[489] The first music in England to be printed from engraved plates was published in 1613. Nevertheless, North's statement is substantially correct, since Thomas Cross, the younger, had a monopoly of the music engraving trade at the end of the seventeenth century. Cross, who was also a music printer, publisher and seller, issued his first engraved work in 1683. This was Purcell's *Sonnata's of III Parts*, printed for the author and published by Playford and Carr. Both publishers had shops in the Temple. North himself attempted to improve the method of engraving, for he writes about one of his 'gimcracks': 'I attempted to shew them [the masters] that without the charge of a graver or composing characters they might print by buying copperplates grounded, and etching themselves their music upon them, and a little habit would perfect them in the reverse writing, which seemed the hardest part. The copper so prepared, that is polished and ground, might be bought for 1s. 6d. per lb. and sold again after it was done with for 1s. 2d., which was but a small charge. And to give a demonstration of this, I bought a plate, etched a sonata or two upon it in score, and entitled it "Tentamen calcographicum". This miscarried a little by the fury of the aquafortis, that made the character too coarse, but might have prevented by tempering it with water. But this I thought might shew how practicable the thing was, and I gave the plate to Carr, but found none to follow the industry of my example' (*Notes of Me* ed. Jessopp 1887: 88–9). The incident took place before 1684 (see Wilson 1959: 29, n.40), so that through Carr, North could have influenced Cross's decision to engrave on copperplates (he later changed to pewter which was cheaper). There also may be some lost works which followed North's plan, as Krummel has suggested (1975: 158, from evidence in Tilmouth 1961: 14, 15, 16, 18).

[490] Probably the *Ayres for the Violin* (i.e., preludes, fuges, allemandes, sarabands, courants, gigues, fancies, divisions), the fourth part of which seems to have been published in 1685.

[491] Matteis went to France at the end of 1678, the year of the Popish Plot (Mabbett 1986: 241).

[492] This was published by Carr as *The False Consonances of Musick or Instructions for Playing the True Base upon the Guitarre, with choice examples and cleare directions to enable any man in a short time to play all musicall ayres . . .* , London 1682. An earlier, Italian version was issued in London *c.* 1680.

grounds and short peices or lessons onely; his full consorts and solos were not printed, and I think are very scarce if at all to be mett with. But one thing to be observed was very extraordinary, which is that while folks were acquainted with his manner of playing[,] as he often did in full companys out of his books, no person pretended to doe the like, for none could comand that fullness, grace, and truth as he did, so that in his time his books suffered for the difficulty, and since as much becaus unknowne, and yet there is nothing in them puzling or seeming difficult for the hand, and now no person can have an idea of this that I have observed here, who was not a wittness of his playing in person. In short his books well observed, are a sufficient tutor of artfull composition.

60. Well attended to

Another observation of him was that when an assembly for musick was, as divers were, appointed, and he onely to entertein the company having his ministers Waldegrave, Lestrange and Bridgman[493] about him and flaming[,] as I have seen him, in a good humour he hath held the company by the ears with that force and

.141v / and variety for more then an hour together that there was scarce a whisper in the room, tho filled with company. In short, waiving the mention of other excellences in particular, he fell into such credit and imployment, that he took a great hous, and after the mode of his country, lived luxuriously, which brought diseases upon him, of which he dyed. He left a son Nicholai[494] whom he taught upon the violin from his cradle; and I have seen the boy in coats play to his father's guittarre. He grew up and was a celebrated master upon the violin in London for divers years; hee being invited went over into Germany and hath ever since bin there and now resides at Vienna, in full payment for all the masters wee have received out of those countrys.

61. Itallian musick, and Corelli

After this wee cannot wonder, that among the courters of musick an Itallian tast[e] should prevaile; but there were other incidents that contributed to establish it, one of the cheif was the

---

[493] MS has 'Bridgm^t'.
[494] According to standard biographical sources, including Burney (1776–89: iii/516), Nicola Matteis, the younger (fl. *c.* 1682–1700) studied under his father and left England before 1 July 1700 to enter the service of the Habsburg court. Presumably, then, he was not the same as John-Nicola, who was christened on 27 December 1694.

coming over of the works of the great Corelli.[495] Those became the onely musick relished for a long time. And there seemed to be no satiety of them, nor is the vertue of them

yet

f.142   / yet exhaled, and it is a question whither it will ever be spent, for if musick can be immortall, Corelli's consorts will be so. Add to this that most of the yong nobillity and gentry that have travelled into Itally affected to learne of Corelli,[496] and brought home with them such favour for the Itallian musick, as hath given it possession of our Pernassus; and the best utensill of Apollo, the violin, is so universally courted, and sought after to be had of the best sort, that some say England hath dispeopled Italy of viollins. And no wonder after the great master made that instrument speak as it were with humane voice saying to his scollars – Non udite lo parlare?* But not satisfyed with that, the gallants must have the voices themselves, set off in operas as amply as hath bin knowne in Ittally, but how long this humour will hold without backsliding into balladsinging I cannot foresee tho a fair proffer hath bin made of it in the celebrious and beloved enterteinement of the Beggar's Opera which made a nightly assembly of the beau mond at the theater for above a month uninterruptedly.[497]

f.142v   / 62. Conclusion

A large scene might be opened here, to present a view of the present state of musick in England but why all that which every body knows, and most hearers better then my self? And what a work would it be to enumerate the masters regnant, with their caracters, and the number of consorts, sonnatas and conciertos, besides solos innumerable bredd and born here or brought from abroad; the magnificences of the operas, the famous organs[,] organists, and builders; the various societys and assemblys for

[495] In *MG c. 1726* (f.179), North refers to 'Corelly's first consort that cleared the ground of all other sorts of musick whatsoever'. This could mean Corelli's Op. 1 (*Sonate a tre*, Rome 1681), or it could mean the first concerted work by Corelli to reach England.

[496] According to Hawkins (1776 rev. 1853/1963: ii/675), Richard Edgecumbe (b. 1680, d. 1758), first baron of Mount Edgecumbe (1742), was a pupil of Corelli, a point of some interest, since North states that Edgecumbe's mother, Matilda, daughter of Sir Henry Furnese, Bart., was a 'near relation' (*Life of Francis North* ed. M. North 1819: i/232).

[497] The Beggar's Opera opened on 29 January 1728 at Lincoln's Inn Theatre and was performed sixty-two times before the end of the season. William Hogarth depicted a performance of the opera in its first production, showing the more important London theatre-goers present.

musick; especially the new Royall Society,[498] (if it continues now as formerly,) with many other varietys which musicall gentlemen hereafter would be glad to know, if there were a genius apt and sufficient to transmitt it to them.[499] But I should be very presumptious to undertake it, being for many years an alien to the faculty, and at present in deprivado;★ and should rejoyce to receiv such information as I wish my self able to give, and pretending to that is beyond my lines for what hath history to doe with the present? And if any thing of that kind hath already escaped, it is ultra crepidam,★ and pardon desired.

[ff. 143, 143v, 144 are blank.]

f. 144v / Sung at a muster of voices in the theater in White hall reign [of] Charles 2[500]

> Amante che ditte che fatte
> lagrimate piangete,
> sospirate piangete,
> fatte quanto sapete.
> Non si cangia in amor
> fortuna o fato.
> Ahi che sempr' infelice
> un sventurato.

[498] The Royal Academy (not, as North has it, 'Society'), an association of noblemen supported by the king, was founded 1719 for the promotion of Italian opera. The Academy opened 2 April 1720 under the musical direction of George Frederick Handel. The 1727–28 season was the Academy's last, and the doors closed on 1 June 1728. A second Academy was then formed, the season opening on 2 December 1729. North's nephew, William (b. 1678, d. 1734), sixth baron North (1699), was one of the original subscibers (Milhous and Hume 1986).

[499] The task set out by North was fulfilled by Hawkins (1776 rev. 1853/1963).

[500] Giacomo Carissimi, *Sciolto havean dall' alte sponde (I naviganti)*, serenata composed before 1653; the last section, 'amante che dite', survives separately.

A 3 voci con basso continuo

* MS has a bar line in the upper voice part between the 3d and 4th notes.

[f. 146]*

tu - na o fa - to[.]   Non si cang - 'in a - mor for -

tu - na o fa - to[.] Non si cang - 'in a - mor for - tu - na for -

non si cang - 'in a - mor for - tu - na o 'fa - to[.]

[f. 145v]

tu - na o fa - to.

tu - na o fa - to[.]   Ahi che

Ahi †che sem - pr'in - fe - li - ce un sven - tu -

[f. 146]

Ahi   che sem - pr'in - fe - li - ce che sem - pr'in - fe - li - ce un

sem - pr'in - fe - li - ce che sem - pr'in - fe - li - ce che sem - pr'in - fe - li - ce un

ra - to   Ahi   che sem - pr'in - fe - li - ce un

* North transcribes across the opening, ff. 145v and 146.
† At f. 147v North indicates the text underlay like this: 'che sempr - 'in - fe - li - ce'

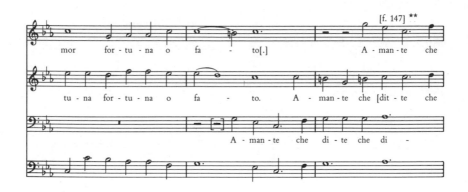

* MS has–'pe-te'. Cf. the first bar of this voice part on f. 145v.
† MS has a barline in the upper voice part between 2d and 3d notes.
** North transcribes across the opening, ff. 146v and 147.
†† MS has 'nangete'.

[f. 146v]

quan-to sa-pe - te non si cang-'in a-mor for-tu - na o

get - te non si cang-'in a-mor for - tu - na for-tu - na o

fat - te quan-to sa - pe - te non si

[f. 147]

fa - to[.] Non si cang-'in a-mor for - tu - na for-tu - na o

fa - to[.] Non si cang-'in a - mor for - tu - na o

cang-'in a - mor for - tu - na o fa - to for - tu - na o

[f. 147v]

fa - to[.] Ahi che sem-pr'in - fe - li - ce che

fa - to[.] Ahi che sem-pr'in - fe - li - ce che sem-pr'in - fe - li - ce che

fa - [to.] Ahi che

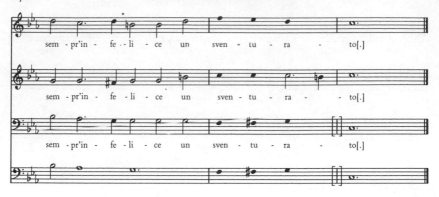

sem - pr'in - fe - li - ce un sven - tu - ra - to[.]

sem - pr'in - fe - li - ce un sven - tu - ra - to[.]

sem - pr'in - fe - li - ce un sven - tu - ra - to[.]

★ MS has a barline in the upper voice part between the 3d and 4th notes.

GLOSSARY

Words that have been glossed from the sources itemized in the Editorial guidelines (section 6) are given in the spelling and form in which North first uses them. The gloss is given next, followed by other spellings and forms in alphabetical order and the folios on which all these words appear.

ab accinendo: (*Lat.*) by singing f.116v
ab origine: (*Lat.*) from the beginning f.81
accessionall: accessional; additional, accessory f.107
actum agere: (*Lat.*) to act an act; superfluous f.79
ad lyram: (*Lat.*) to the lyre f.119
admonition: authoritative counsel (*OED, 1. but without the sense of implied reproof*) f.13v
ad quem: *see* a quo
affect: aim, aspire (*OED, 1.*) f.49
alternatim: (*Lat.*) alternately, by turns f.75v
anglicè: (*med. Lat.*) in English f.130
anima: *see* materia . . . anima
annuente Pythagora: (*Lat*) as Pythagoras would agree f.118
a quo . . . ad quem: (*Lat.*) from which . . . to which; i.e., the keynote from which one is changing and that into which one changes ff.43v, 44v.
arcata: (*It.*) arch; i.e., bowstroke ff.72v, 139v
artes deperditæ: (*Lat.*) lost arts f.104
artfully: skilfully (*OED, 1.*)
    artfull ff.9v, 30v, 63, 111, 129v, 141
articulate: (of sound) divided into distinct parts (*OED, 6.*) f.73v
artificially: in accordance with the rules of art, skilfully (*OED, 2.*)
    artificiall ff.8, 35v, 57v, 59, 59v, 71, 84v, 93, 118, 139
audendum tamen: (*Lat.*) notwithstanding boldness f.81v

barbare: barbar (*Fr.* barbare); barbarian f.16
bating: lowering in estimation (*OED, 4.*) f.69v
bind: syncopate
    binding, bindings ff.49, 51v, 126v

cantable: (*Northism*) singable ff.23ᵃv, 24v
capreole: capriole; (*Northism*) alter the time; from the intransitive verb to leap, skip, caper f.34v

capriccios: caprices; whims (*OED, 2., caprice 1.*)
    capriccio ff.35, 75v, 140v
cappriccioso: capriccioso (*It.*); in a free style f.131v
carriere: carrière (*Fr.*); career, swift course ff.23ᵃv, 77
catching: North could mean unexpected (*OED, II.9*), or he could mean canonic
    (*as adj., Northism*) f.33v
celebrious: famous, renowned (*OED, 2.*) ff.88, 142
chachinnatory: (*Northism*) cackling; from cachinno: (*It.*) a loud laugh or cackle
    f.87v
circuitions: goings round and about, encirclings
    circuition ff.43, 43v
clangor: (*Lat.*) the sound of a trumpet; any loud, resonant, ringing sound ff.91v,
    96v, 116v
claves: (*Lat.*) keys f.37
commentations: expository notes, comments or glosses (*OED, 1.a.*) f.103v
compos: (*Lat.*) having mastery or control ff.13v, 27v
comunis mensura: (*Lat.*) common measure f.31
comuting: commuting; exchanging (*OED, 1.*) f.52
contraria juxta se: *see* varia . . . contraria juxta se
copia: plentiful supply ff.48v, 97
costa che costa: (*Sp.*) at any cost f.131
croudero: crowder, one who plays a crowd (crwth); a fiddler f.129
cujus caput inter nubila: (*Lat.*) whose source is among the clouds f.102v
culmen: the top or summit; (*fig.*) the height, acme, culminating point (*OED, 1.*)
    ff.13v, 64v
curious: ingenious, skilful (*OED, I.4.*) ff.10v, 52v
curling graces: (*Northism*) 'tremolous', i.e., trilled or shaked graces ff.58v, 87
    see also tremolo
cutts: cuts; steps in dancing, consisting of springs from the ground and, while in
    the air, rapid movements of the feet one in front of the other alternately
    (*OED, 30.*); from the verb to cut f.84
cytharædus: (*Lat.*) singer to a cithara ff.106, 113

dans les formes: (*Fr.*) in proper form f.21
    see also formes
decent: suitable, appropriate or proper to the circumstances (*OED, 1.*)
    decently ff.59, 74v, 93
decor: beauty f.57
delitescent: lying hidden f.130
deteriority: poorer or lower quality f.9v
dexteræ: (*Lat.*) right-handed
    dextræ, dexter ff.115v, 116v, 117
dieses: (*in North's usage*) quarter tones ff.107v, 110, 110v
difficult: unaccommodating (*OED, 2.a.*); hard, harsh f.55v
disparata: (*Lat.*) different things f.113v
dulcor: sweetness, pleasantness ff.83v, 113v, 131v

Glossary 281

dum vitant [stulti] vitia[,] in contraria currunt: (*Lat.*) while they are avoiding one fault fools rush into others (*Horace, Satires, I.2.24.*) f.60v

Dunstable plain[n]ess: Dunstable, the name of a town in Bedfordshire, was linked to London by the Edgware Road, part of the ancient Roman road called Watling Street, notable for its long stretches in direct line; hence, directness, straightforwardness, plainness (*OED, 1.b.*) f.87

è contra: (*late Lat.*) the contrary f.47v

egregious: remarkably good or great (*OED, 2.b.*); remarkable, notable egregiously ff.7, 66v

els: in another case, under other circumstances (*OED, 4.*) f.60v

en passant: *see* passant

eodem interprete: (*Lat.*) in the same interpretation; i.e., of Zelandrus (*see* f.110v) f.116

eo nomine: (*Lat.*) in itself f.110

equali passu: (*Lat.*) by equal steps f.35

errare cum partribus: (*Lat.*) to stray with the elders; i.e., to make the mistakes the experts make f.72

et sic de ceteris: (*Lat.*) and so of the rest f.42v

exercitation: an exercise or display of skill, especially literary or oratorical f.49v

ex lata sententia: (*Lat.*) according to general opinion f.49

exotick: exotic; outlandish, barbarous, strange (*OED, 2.b.*) ff.19v, 88v

ex professo: (*Lat.*) openly f.116

exta: (*Lat.*) entrails f.123

facetious: polished, agreeable, urbane (*OED, 1.*) f.81v

fastidious: disagreeable, unpleasant (*OED, 1.*)
fastidium ff.8v, 14v, 60v, 70, 73, 88v

fast[u]ously: haughtily, with arrogance f.140

favour: 'inclination' (*MG c. 1726: f.19v*) f.13

favour: partiality towards (*OED, 4.*); emphasis f.36v

fidling: fiddling; busy about trifles (*OED, 2.a.*) f.133

flatile: wind (of musical instruments) ff.112, 128v

flexures: curvatures (*OED, 1.*); inflexions of the voice
flexure ff.12v, 105v, 106v, 107
see also warping

fondly: foolishly (*OED, A.4.*)
fond ff.39, 103

foramina: (*Lat.*) openings; finger holes
foraminated ff.112, 112v, 115v

formed: drawn up according to rule (*OED, 2.a.*) ff.9, 19, 40, 68v, 81v

formes: styles of expressing the thoughts and ideas in literary or musical composition, including the arrangement and order of different parts of the whole (*OED, 9.*)
forme, formall ff.43, 68v, 81, 105, 108, 121v, 125, 125v, 127v

frusta: (*Lat.*) fragments f.88

funest: fatal, disastrous f.67

gimcracks: mechanical contrivances (*OED, 2.b.*); e.g., monochords f.9v

gradatim: (*Lat.*) step by step; i.e., gradually ff.13v, 45v

gradatory: proceeding by steps
   gradation, gradations, gradient, graduall ff.12, 15v, 18, 26v, 42v, 47v, 55v, 58, 59v, 60v, 80, 107

grand pas: (*Fr.*) majestic pace f.91

harvest men's largess: *cf. the proverb* 'good harvests make men prodigal' f.16v

ignotum per ignotius: (*Lat.*) the unknown through the more unknown f.122

impares: (*Lat.*) unequal
   impar ff.115, 115v, 116, 116v, 117

in abstracto: (*Lat.*) abstractly f.40

incogitanter: (*Lat.*) without thought f.94

in contra: (*Northism*) by contrast f.39v

in cours: *see* of cours

in deprivado: (*Northism*) in a state of deprivation f.142v

indifferently: indiscriminately, without difference or distinction (*OED, 1.*) f.23ª

in eisdem verbis: (*Lat.*) in those very words f.115

inferior: *see* superior

in loco: (*Lat.*) in the place f.132v

in obscuro: (*Lat.*) in the dark, obscurely; referring to North's style of notation which in this text he describes as 'shadowed', i.e., in dotted outline f.51v

in ordinè ad: (*Lat.*) in turn towards; in its proper place f.81

in suo genere: (*Lat.*) in its own kind f.114

intercaled: intercalated; inserted or introduced between the members of an existing series
   intercale ff.19v, 23ªv, 28, 71v, 85v

intus et in cute: (*Lat.*) within and on the surface f.49v.

jump with: agree completely with (*OED, 5.*) f.63v

junto: a body of people joined or combined for a common purpose (*OED, 1.*); i.e., chorus f.92

kill-cows: swashbucklers, bullies (*OED, A.1.*) f.106

languefies: 'apt to fall off' (*MG c. 1726: f.20v*); becomes weak or languid (*OED, 2.*) f.14

legitimate: genuine, real as opposed to spurious (*OED, 1.b.*) f.68

magazine: a storehouse or repository for goods or merchandise (*OED, 1.*)
   magazined ff.59, 81v

manireonico: (*Northism*) possibly a conflation of manieroso (*It.*): affected, and malinconico (*It.*): melancholy f.33v

mansuete: mild, gentle f.140v

materia ... anima: (*Lat.*) matter ... spirit f.13

mediety: a middle or intermediate state (*OED, 2.*) f.18

meliority: the quality or condition of being better; superiority ff.17, 135v

memoriter: from memory f.21

modallity: modality; manner f.15v

monitor: one who gives advice (*OED, 1. but without the sense of warning*); instructor
monition ff.13v, 14

mordicitus: (*Lat.*) with the teeth, clamorously f.97v

more majorum: (*Lat.*) according to the usage of the majority f.119

ne quid nimis: (*Lat.*) nothing in excess (*Terence, Andria 1.1.*) f.70

nerves: strings of sinew (of musical instruments) (*OED, 4.c.*)
nervous, nerves ff.105, 112, 122v, 123

non passibus [a]equis: (*Lat.*) with unequal steps f.93v

non plus: nonplus; a state in which no more can be said or done (*OED, 1.*) ff.9v,
23v

non plus ultra: (*Lat.*) nothing more beyond f.85

non udite lo parlare?: (*It.*) do you not hear it speak? f.142

novellist: novelist; innovator f.135v

octavarum eadem est ratio: (*Lat.*) the proportion of the octaves is the same f.37v

of cours: in ordinary or due course, according to the customary order (*OED,
36.b.*)
in cours ff.42, 58, 59, 107, 121v, 132

Ö mirum!: (*Lat.*) O wonder! f.110v

opus operatum: (*Lat.*) a labour of labours f.63v

organon: (*Gr.*) instrument, implement, tool; method of science f.121

organon hydraulicon: (*Gr.*) hydraulic organ f.121

originall: original; beginning, origin f.105

paisans: paysans (*Fr.*) peasant f.64

pares: (*Lat.*) equal
par ff.115, 115v, 116, 116v, 117

passant: en passant (*Fr.*); in passing
en passant ff.26v, 56

pastoritiall: pastoral f.105v

per arsin et thesin: (*Lat.*) by raising and lowering the hand (to establish the beat)
f.30

per saltum: (*Lat.*) by leap f.17

plausible: praiseworthy (*OED, 1.*) f.28

Plutarchus Zelandro interprete (*Lat.*) Plutarch interpreted by Zelandrus f.110v

polite: (of persons) refined, civilised, cultivated (*OED, 2.b.*)
politer ff.11v, 134, 136

post varios casus: (*Lat.*) after many accidents or events f.118v

prattique: pratique (*Fr.*); practice f.22

premio: (*It.*) prize f.138v

pretended: put forward as a reason or excuse; used as a pretext (*OED, I.6.*) ff.9v,
87, 132v

pricked: (of music) written or set down (*OED, III.13.*) f.22v

professor: one who makes a profession of any art or science (*OED, II.5.*)
 professors ff. 1v, 30v, 42v, 104, 128v, 130, 138v

propens: propense; inclined (*OED, 1.*) f.28

proslamb[an]omenas: the name of the lowest note, added below the lowest
 tetrachord, in the later scales or systems of ancient Greek music ff. 111, 118

pro tunc: (*Lat.*) according to that time f.132v

pure and pute: pure, clean f.67v

qualifyed: qualified; described, designated (*OED, I.1.*) f.50v

quantum in nos: (*Lat.*) so far as concerns us f.1v

quicquid in buccam venerit: (*Lat., usually with dicere or scribere, to say or to write*)
 whatever comes uppermost f.63

radix: (*Lat.*) root f.14v

rambled: rumbled; furnished up (*OED, 5.c.*) f.54

rations: ratios (*OED, 2.*) ff. 111v, 115v

reedall: reedal; reed ff. 112, 115v

re infecta: (*Lat.*) with the thing not done f.140v

resentment: feeling, sensation (*OED, 5.*)
 resents ff. 89v, 92v

rhithme: rhythm: riming or rimed verse (*OED, I.1.*) f.86v

ricercata: (*as tempo mark, Northism*) 'And hence it is that straines are denominated
 according to men's acting. As andante, is the measures of the step in
 walking. And so currant, and jigg a species of running, and others relating to
 the art of dancing inumerable. Then the recercata, is a this-way-that-way
 manner, like searching; then, adagio, malencholico[,] affectuoso[,] allegro,
 grave, and some others all relating to the ordinary behaviour of men under
 such passions; therefore masters that have not nature, and truth to direct
 their measures, want the principall verb in their syntax' (*MG c. 1726: f.63*)
 f.33v, 67v

saltinbanco: saltimbanco; mountebank or quack ff. 49v, 66

saltuatim: (*Lat.*) by leap; i.e., suddenly f.31v

salvo: a reservation or saving clause (*OED, 1., citing legal expressions as 'salvo iure':
 without prejudice to the right of*); with salvo, having regard to f.40

sarannæ: sarranæ; (*Lat.*) belonging to Sara, the city of Tyre in Phoenicia f.116v

septenary: the seven notes of the diatonic scale (*OED, B.4.*); another term for
 gamut, i.e., North's 'vocall scale' ff. 15v, 16, 16v, 17, 18v, 19, 19v, 22v, 23ª,
 37, 37v, 38, 117v

shortly: concisely (*OED, 1.*) f.40

sigh: (*as adj., Northism*) expressing lament or longing f.53v

simples: single or uncompounded things, especially those serving as ingredients in
 a composition or mixture (*OED, B.7.*) f.40

sinistræ: (*Lat.*) left-handed
 sinister ff. 115v, 116v, 117

slight: sleight; artifice, ruse, stratagem (*OED, 6.*) f.36v

spadicæ: (*Lat.*) female players of the spadicum, a stringed instrument condemned
as effeminate f. 119v

spagnuola: Spagnuolo (*It.*) Spanish f.74

stage: position (*OED, I.2.*) f.26v

starting: causing one to undergo a sudden involuntary movement of the body
resulting from surprise (*OED, 5.*) f.98

station: position (*OED, II.*) f.41, 41v

stoccata: (*It.*) thrust, stab; i.e., bowstroke
stoccatas ff.72v, 73, 139v

stoccatas: (*by analogy to rant, Northism*) a short country dance of the jig variety in
binary form and either simple or compound duple rhythm f.13a

sub Deo: (*Lat.*) under God; i.e., as God's representative on earth f.128

sub die: (*Lat.*) under the sky f.114

tale: numerical statement or reckoning; enumeration (*OED, II.6.*) f.33v

tantum non: (*Lat.*) all but ff.106, 120

temerated: violated f.105

tibiis canere: (*Lat.*) to play on the pipes f.113

tonations: (*Northism*) the action of toning or producing musical tones ff.107v, 108

topper: something surpassingly or exceptionally good (*OED, sb² 1.*) f.76

tormenting: disturbing (*OED, 3., 3.b.*); i.e., by syncopation
tormented ff.54, 63

totum: whole (*OED, 1.*); unit
totums ff.32, 33, 33v

tout accomplié: tout accompli (*Fr.*); completely accomplished f.28

transitur in partes: (*Lat.*) they take sides f.97v

tremolo: (*It.*) trembling; i.e., a trill or shaked grace (cf. ff.67v and 73) f.56v
see also curling graces

turnes: modification for particular effect or as a grace or embellishment, especially
applied to language and literary style (*OED, 32.*) ff.58v, 62v, 69v, 81v, 97v,
122

tyrones: tiroes, tyroes; beginners or learners in anything; novices f.9

ultimus heroo[r]um: (*Lat.*) the last of the heroes f.134v

ultra crepidam: (*Lat.*) not sticking to my last f.142v

unum necessarium: (*Lat.*) single necessity f.12v

varia . . . contraria, juxta se: (*Lat.*) changes . . . contraries, next to one another; (*an
old rule of logic proverbial in England from the sixteenth century*) contraries appear
more evident when they are set off one against the other ff.8v, 84v

vestigii: vestigia (*Lat.*) ruins (of buildings) f.104v

virtus est vitium fuere: (*Lat.*) it is virtuous to flee from vice (*Horace, Epistles,
I.1.41.*) f.60v

vociferacious: (*Northism*) vociferous, loud, clamouring; from a combination of
two words: vociferation (an instance of loud speaking or shouting; *see* ff.12,
114v) and vociferate (to cry out loudly) f.29

warping: 'any flexure' (*MG c. 1726: f.19*) f.12v
   see also flexures
whimmish: (*Northism*) whimsical, capricious f.36v
wiredrawing: drawing or prolonging to an inordinate length, protracting exces-
   sively (*OED, 3. fig.*) f.63

REFERENCES AND BIBLIOGRAPHY

1. References to North's writings

In the references below North's writings have been listed under four periods: early (*c.* 1690–*c.* 1703), middle (*c.* 1704–*c.* 1720), late (*c.* 1720–1734) and posthumous (from 1735). Within each period writings are entered alphabetically, not chronologically. The assigning of manuscripts to the first three periods has been based on study of the paper. While this is reliable for most of the texts cited, two texts on early paper have been grouped according to references within the texts (*Of Humane Capacity, Some Essays*), and one on late paper almost certainly belongs to the early-middle period (*Of Etimology. Concerning Laws*). A short title or abbreviation has been assigned to each work for the purposes of citation; full bibliographic particulars then follow.

1.1. Early period

Cursory Notes of Building (ed. Colvin and Newman 1981) see Section 1.4 below
Cursory Notes of Musicke (ed. Chan and Kassler 1986) see Section 1.4 below
Notes of Me (ed. Jessopp 1887) see Section 1.4 below
Prejudices
   Prejudices, BL Add MS 32526: ff.2v–7v
Some Memorandums, concerning Musick
   Some Memorandums, concerning Musick, BL Add MS 32532: ff.1–26v (for details see Hine, Chan, Kassler 1987)
The World Part I
   A group of essays, each with short titles, BL Add MS 32546: ff.1–18v
Vossius de viribus Rithmi
   Vossius de viribus Rithmi, BL Add MS 32531: ff.53–58v (for details see Hine, Chan, Kassler 1987)

1.2. Middle period

An Essay of Musicall Ayre
   see *Musicall Recollections III*
Change of Philosoficall Methods
   Change of Philosoficall Methods BL Add MS 32549: ff.94–102v

Essay on the Reciprocall Forces of Body and Spirit
 Essay on the Reciprocall Forces of Body and Spirit influencing each other, BL Add MS
  32549: ff.77–81.
Of Humane Capacity
 Of Humane Capacity, BL Add MS 32526: ff.34v–47
Musicall Recollections I [Prencourt Tracts Annotated]
 *Short[,] easy, and plaine rules to learne in a few days the principles of musick, and
  cheifly what relates to the use of the espinette[,] harpsicord or organ*, BL Add MS
  32531: ff.8–23v
 The treatis of the continued or thro-base, BL Add MS 32531: ff.29–41v
Musicall Recollections II
 *The Theory of Sounds taking rise from the first principles of action that affect the sence of
  hearing, and giving phisicall solutions of tone, harmony and discord, shewing their
  anatomy, with the manner how most instruments of musick are made to yeild
  delicious, as well as triumphant sounds, with intent to leav no mistery in musick
  untoucht. Being the 2d part of the Musicall Recollections*, BL Add MS 32534:
  ff.1–82v
Musicall Recollections III
 *An Essay of Musicall Ayre. Tending cheifly to shew the foundations of melody joyned
  with harmony, whereby may be discovered the native genius of good musick, and
  concluding with some notes concerning the excellent art of voluntary. Being the 3d
  and last part of the Musicall Recollections*, BL Add MS 32536: ff.1–90
Of Etimology
 Of Etimology, BL Add MS 32430: ff.1–83
Power of Humane Understanding
 Power of Humane Understanding, BL Add MS 32526: ff.88–89v
Preface
 Pr[eface], BL Add MS 32545: ff.2–6
Prencourt Tracts
 *Short and easy plaine rules, to learne in a few days time, the true principles of musick and
  cheifly what relates to the use of the spinette[,] harpsicord or organ*, BL Add MS
  32549: ff.1–16v
 The treatis of the continued or through basse, BL Add MS 32549: ff.17–30v
Prencourt Tracts Annotated
 see *Musicall Recollections I*
Some Essays
 Some Essays, concerning the manner of our sence, or perception of things, BL Add MS
  32526: ff.8v–33v
The Theory of Sounds
 see *Musicall Recollections II*
Untitled Essay
 Untitled essay, BL Add MS 32546: ff.247–262v

1.3 Late period

A Discourse on the Study of the Laws ed. Anon 1824
 see Section 1.4 below. The paper of the original manuscript was not examined;

hence, its placement here in North's last period is based on a letter written to his second son, Montagu, and dated 17 April 1732: 'As to directions for the study of the law, which you desire, it is a copious subject, and I remember that formerly I have wrote somewhat about it, which, if I can find it, shall be committed to you . . .' (*Notes of Me* ed. Jessopp 1887: 273; see also 280)

General Preface (ed. Millard 1984)
   see Section 1.4 below

Life of Dudley North (ed. Jessopp 1890)
   see Section 1.4 below

Life of Francis North (ed. M. North 1819)
   see Section 1.4 below

Life of John North (ed. Millard 1984)
   see Section 1.4 below

Life of Lord Keeper North
   The Life of the Lord Keeper North, St. John's College, Cambridge, MS James 613, 10 vols.

The Musicall Grammarian Fragments (cited in notes as *MG Frag*)
   Fragments with the running head 'The Musicall Grammarian', BL Add MS 32537: ff. 1–65v (for details see Chan, Kassler, Hine 1988)

The Musicall Grammarian c. 1726 (cited in notes as *MG c. 1726*)
   The Musicall Gramarian or a practick essay upon harmony, plain, and artificiall with notes of comparison between the elder and later musick, and somewhat historicall of both, BL Add MS 32533: ff. 1–151v (for details see Chan, Kassler, Hine 1988)

The Musicall Grammarian 1728 (cited in notes as *MG 1728*)
   The text edited and presented in this volume (see also Chan, Kassler, Hine 1988)

Of Etimology. Concerning Laws
   Of Etimology. Concerning Laws, BL Add MS 32530: ff. 84–88v (in the hand of Montagu North on the late paper, although the text probably was written during the middle period)

Physica
   Physica[.] Being a congeries of discourses upon most subjects in natural philosofye, Rougham MS (in North's hand); BL Add MS 32544: ff. 1–274 (in the hand of Montagu North)

Theory of Sounds 1726 (cited in notes as *TS 1726*)
   Theory of Sounds shewing, the genesis, propagation, effects and augmentation of them reduced to a specifick inquiry into the cripticks of harmony and discord, with eikons annexed exposing them to occular inspection 1726, BL Add MS 32535: ff. 1–73v (for details see Chan, Kassler, Hine 1988)

Theory of Sounds (cited in notes as *TS 1728*)
   Theory of Sounds shewing, the genesis, propagation, augmentation and applications of them reduced to a specifick inquiry into the cripticks of harmony and discord, with eikons annexed exposing them to occular inspection 1728, BL Add MS 32535: ff. 74–149 (for details see Chan, Kassler, Hine 1988)

1.4 Works published posthumously

Cursory Notes of Building (ed. Colvin and Newman 1981)
 Roger North's writings on architecture edited by Howard Colvin and John New-
 man, Oxford 1981
Cursory Notes of Musicke (ed. Chan and Kassler 1986)
 *Roger North's Cursory Notes of Musicke (c. 1698–c. 1703): A physical, psychological
 and critical theory* edited with introduction, notes and appendices by Mary
 Chan and Jamie C. Kassler, Kensington, N.S.W. 1986
A Discourse on the Study of the Laws (ed. Anon 1824)
 A Discourse on the Study of the Laws now first printed from the original MS in the
 Hargrave collection with notes and illustrations by a member of the Inner
 Temple, London 1824
General Preface (ed. Millard 1984)
 Roger North: General Preface and *Life of Dr John North* edited by Peter Millard,
 Toronto, Buffalo, London 1984
Life of Dudley North (ed. Jessopp 1890)
 The Lives of the Norths edited by Augustus Jessopp, 3 vols., London 1890,
 ii/1–265
Life of Francis North (ed. M. North 1819)
 *The Life of the Right Honourable Francis North, baron of Guilford, lord keeper of the
 Great Seal, under King Charles II and James II, wherein are inserted, the characters
 of Sir Matthew Hale, Sir George Jeffries, Sir Leoline Jenkins, Sidney Godolphin,
 and others, the most eminent lawyers and statesmen of that time*, 3d edition, 2 vols.,
 London 1819 (1st edition 1742)
Life of John North (ed. Millard 1984)
 see *General Preface* (ed. Millard 1984)
Notes of Me (ed. Jessopp 1887)
 The Autobiography of the Hon. Roger North edited by Augustus Jessopp, London
 and Norwich 1887

2. References to other writings

In the list below the abbreviated manner of citation is given first with date of
publication. For reissues, translations or reprintings, the date of the original
(though not necessarily the first edition) is also given. Bibliographic particulars
then follow.

Alexander 1985   Peter Alexander, *Ideas, Qualities, and Corpuscles: Locke and Boyle
 on the external world*, Cambridge and New York.
Anderson 1966   Warren D. Anderson, *Ethos and Education in Greek Music*, Cam-
 bridge, Massachussetts.
Anon 1905   *The Worshipful Company of Musicians*, 2d edition. Issued by the Livery
 Club of the Company for Private Circulation (London).
Ariotti 1971–72   Pierro E. Ariotti, 'Aspects of the conception and development
 of the pendulum in the seventeenth century', *Archive for History of Exact
 Sciences*, 8: 329–410.
Arnauld and Lancelot tr. Rieux and Rollin 1676/1975   [Antoine Arnauld and

Claude Lancelot], *General and Rational Grammar: the Port Royal grammar* edited and translated with an introduction and notes by Jacques Rieux and Bernard E. Rollin with a preface by Arthur C. Danto and a critical essay by Norman Kretzmann, The Hague and Paris.

Arnauld and Nicole 1662/1970 [Antione Arnauld and Pierre Nicole], *La Logique ou l'art de penser contenant, outre les règles communes, plusieurs observations nouvelle propres à former le iugement*, Hildesheim and New York.

Arnauld and Nicole tr. Anon 1685 [Antoine Arnauld and Pierre Nicole], *Logic: or, the Art of Thinking . . . To which is added an index to the whole book*. For the excellency of the matter, printed many times in French and Latin, and now for public good translated into English by several hands, London.

Arnauld and Nicole tr. Dickoff and James 1685/1964 [Antoine Arnauld and Pierre Nicole], *The Art of Thinking: Port-Royal logic* translated by J. Dickoff and P. James with a foreword by C. W. Hendel, Indianapolis, New York, Kansas City.

Atcherson 1973 W. T. Atcherson, 'Key and mode in seventeenth-century music theory books', *Journal of Music Theory*, 17: 204–32.

Bacon 1626/1818 Francis Bacon, 'Sylva sylvarum', 2 vols., *The Works of Francis Bacon, Baron Verulam, Viscount St. Alban, and Lord High Chancellor of England*, a new edition, London.

Barker and Goldstein 1984 Peter Barker and Bernard R. Goldstein, 'Is 17th-century physics indebted to the Stoics?', *Centaurus*, 27: 148–64.

Borgerhoff 1950/1968 E. B. O. Borgerhoff, *The Freedom of French Classicism*, New York.

Burney 1776–89 Charles Burney, *A General History of Music*, 4 vols., London.

Butler 1636 Charles Butler, *The Principles of Musik, in Singing and Setting: with the two-fold use thereof, [ecclesiasticall and civil.]*, London.

    1636/1970 Charles Butler, *The Principles of Musik in Singing and Setting*, introduction by Gilbert Reaney, New York.

Cannon and Dostrovsky 1981 John T. Cannon and Sigalia Dostrovsky, *The Evolution of Dynamics: vibration theory from 1687 to 1742*, New York, Heidelberg, Berlin.

Carlin 1973 Betty Lee Carlin, *The Harmony of the Spheres in Seventeenth-century Thought*, Johns Hopkins University doctoral dissertation [UM No. 73 – 12,122].

Chan 1986 Mary Chan, 'On editing Roger North's writings on music', *Early Music New Zealand*, 2: 3–9.

Chan, Kassler, Hine 1988 Mary Chan, Jamie C. Kassler and Janet D. Hine, *Roger North's The Musicall Grammarian and Theory of Sounds: digests of the manuscripts with an analytical index of 1726 and 1728 Theory of Sounds*, Kensington, N.S.W.

Chenette 1967 Louis F. Chenette, *Music Theory in the British Isles during the Enlightenment*, Ohio State University doctoral dissertation [UM No. 68 – 2695]

Cicero tr. Watson 1986 Marcus Tullius Cicero, *Cicero on Oratory and Orators: with his letters to Quintus and Brutus*, translated and edited by J. S. Watson, London.

Cicero tr. King 1960   Marcus Tullius Cicero, *Tusculan Disputations* with an English translation by J. E. King, London and Cambridge, Mass.

Clark 1925/1965   A. F. B. Clark, *Boileau and the French Classical Critics in England (1660–1831)*, New York.

Clark 1964   George Clark, *A History of the Royal College of Physicians*, 3 vols., Oxford.

Clifford 1963   J. L. Clifford, 'Roger North and the art of biography', C. Camden (ed.), *Restoration and Eighteenth-century Literature: essays in honor of Alan Dugald McKillop*, Chicago, pp. 275–85.

Clinch 1890   George Clinch, *Bloomsbury and St. Giles's: past and present; with historical and antiquarian notices of the vicinity*, London.

Cohen 1981   Albert Cohen, *Music in the French Royal Academy of Sciences: a study in the evolution of musical thought*, Princeton.

Cohen 1984   H. Floris Cohen, *Quantifying Music: the science of music at the first stage of the scientific revolution, 1580–1650*, Dordrecht, Boston, Lancaster.

Cohen 1977   Murray Cohen, *Sensible Words: linguistic practice in England 1640–1785*, Baltimore and London.

Crewdson 1950   H. A. F. Crewdson, *A Short History of the Worshipful Company of Musicians*, London.

De la Fond *c.* 1724   [John Francis de la Fond], *The Truth of the 12 Notes; and one of their great uses, viz. facilitating transposition. Illustrated in 2 general preludes: together with the method of writing music without clefs: and 2 other most considerable advantages of the 12 notes, viz. figuring of compound bass truer, and rendering the playing of that noble branch of music vastly easier than it is now, and indeed as easy as it possibly can be, fully exemplify'd in Corelli's VI sonata, IV work, fitted for the purpose*, N.p., n.d.

   1725   John Francis de la Fond, *A New System of Music, both Theoretical and Practical, and yet not Mathematical: written in a manner entirely new; that's to say, in a style plane and intelligible; and calculated to render the art more charming, the teaching not only less tedious, but more profitable, and the learning easier by three quarters. All which is done by tearing off that veil that has for so many ages hung before that noble science*, London.

Descartes tr. Brouncker 1650/1653   René Descartes, *Renatus Des-Cartes Excellent Compendium of Musick: with necessary and judicious animadversions thereupon. By a person of honour* (William Brouncker, 2d Viscount), London.

Deutsch 1955/1974   Otto E. Deutsch, *Handel: a documentary biography*, New York.

Dodd 1969, 1971, 1973–74, 1977, 1978–79   Gordon Dodd (ed.), 'The Viol de Gamba Society provisional index of viol music [John Jenkins]', *Chelys* 1: 45–53, 3: 35–8, 5: 86–95, 7: 73–85, 8: 71–85.

Dostrovsky 1974–75   Sigalia Dostrovsky, 'Early vibration theory: physics and music in the seventeenth century', *Archive for History of Exact Sciences*, 14: 169–218.

Ehninger 1946   Douglas Ehninger, 'Bernard Lami's *L'art de parler*: a critical analysis', *The Quarterly Journal of Speech*, 32: 429–34.

Erasmus 1528/1971   Desiderius Erasmus, *De recta latini graecisqui sermonis pronuntiatione 1528*, Menston, Yorkshire.

Evelyn ed. de Beer 1955   John Evelyn, *The Diary*. Now first printed in full from the manuscripts belonging to Mr. John Evelyn and edited by E. S. de Beer, 6 vols., Oxford.

Fearing 1930/1964   Franklin Fearing, *Reflex Action: a study in the history of physiological psychology*, New York and London.

Gardiner, Metcalf and Beebe-Center 1937   H. M. Gardiner, R. C. Metcalf, and J. G. Beebe-Center, *Feeling and Emotion: a history of theories*, New York.

Gaukroger 1986   Stephen Gaukroger, 'Philosophical responses to the new science in Britain, 1644–1799: a survey of texts', *Metascience*, 4: 60–71.

Gouk 1980   Penelope Gouk, 'The role of acoustics and music theory in the scientific work of Robert Hooke', *Annals of Science*, 37: 573–605.

     1982   Penelope M. Gouk, 'Acoustics in the early Royal Society 1660–1680', *Notes and Records of the Royal Society of London*, 36: 155–7.

Gregory 1938   Joshua C. Gregory, 'Chemistry and alchemy in the natural philosophy of Sir Francis Bacon, 1561–1626', *Ambix*, 2: 93–111.

Harding 1938   Rosamond E. M. Harding, *Origins of Musical Time and Expression*, London, New York, Toronto.

Hawkins 1776 rev. 1853/1963   John Hawkins, *A General History of the Science and Practice of Music* with a new introduction by Charles Cudworth, 2 vols., New York.

Heawood 1950   Edward Heawood, *Watermarks Mainly of the Seventeenth and Eighteenth Centuries*, Hilversum.

Helmholtz tr. Ellis 1885/1954   Hermann von Helmholtz, *On the Sensations of Tone as a Physiological Basis for the Theory of Music*, 2d English edition, translated, thoroughly revised and corrected, rendered conformal to the 4th (and last) German edn. of 1877, with numerous additional notes and a new additional appendix bringing down information to 1885, and especially adapted to the use of music students by Alexander J. Ellis, with a new introduction (1954) by Henry Margenau, New York.

Hine, Chan, Kassler 1987   Janet D. Hine, Mary Chan and Jamie C. Kassler, *Roger North's Writings on Music to c. 1703: a set of analytical indexes with digests of the manuscripts*, Kensington, N.S.W.

Hobbes ed. Molesworth 1650/1962   Thomas Hobbes, 'Human nature, or the fundamental elements of policy. Being a discovery of the faculties, acts, and passions, of the soul of man, from their original causes: according to such philosophical principles, as are not commonly known or asserted', *The English Works*; now first collected and edited by Sir William Molesworth, Bart. (reprinted), Scientia Aalen, Vol. 4: 1–76.

     ed. Macpherson 1651/1986   Thomas Hobbes, *Leviathan*, edited with an introduction by C. B. Macpherson, Harmondsworth, Middlesex.

     ed. Molesworth 1656/1962   Thomas Hobbes, 'Elements of philosophy. The first section, concerning body, written in Latin ... and translated into English', *The English Works*; now first collected and edited by Sir William Molesworth, Bart. (reprinted) Scientia Aalen, Vol. 1.

     ed. Molesworth 1677/1962   Thomas Hobbes, 'The Iliads and Odysses of Homer translated out of the Greek into English, with a large preface concerning the virtues of an heroic poem; written by the translator', *The*

English Works; now first collected and edited by Sir William Molesworth, Bart. (reprinted) Scientia Aalen, Vol. 10 (1st edition 1673).

Hollander 1961/1970   John Hollander, *The Untuning of the Sky: ideas of music in English poetry 1500–1700*, New York.

Holman 1984   Peter Holman, 'Thomas Baltzar (?1631–63), the "incomperable *Lubicer* on the violin" ', *Chelys*, 13: 3–38.

Homer tr. Hobbes 1677/1962   see Hobbes ed. Molesworth.

Howell 1956   W. S. Howell, *Logic and Rhetoric in England, 1500–1700*. Princeton.

Hunt 1978   Frederick Vinton Hunt, *Origins in Acoustics: the science of sound from antiquity to the age of Newton*, New Haven and London.

Kassler 1972   Jamie C. Kassler, 'Burney's *Sketch of a Plan for a Public Music-School'*, *The Musical Quarterly*, 45: 210–34.

   1973   Jamie C. Kassler, 'The systematic writings on music of William Jones (1726–1800)', *Journal of the American Musicological Society*, 26: 92–107.

   1976   Jamie C. Kassler, 'Music made easy to infant capacity, 1714–1830: Some facets of British music education', *Studies in Music*, 10: 67–78.

   1979   Jamie C. Kassler, *The Science of Music in Britain, 1714–1830: a catalogue of writings, lectures and inventions*, 2 vols., New York and London.

Kassler and Oldroyd 1983   Jamie C. Kassler and David R. Oldroyd, 'Robert Hooke's Trinity College "Musick Scripts", his music theory and the role of music in his cosmology', *Annals of Science*, 40: 559–95.

Kassler 1984   Jamie C. Kassler, 'Man – a musical instrument: models of the brain and mental functioning before the computer', *History of Science*, 22: 59–92.

   1984a   Jamie C. Kassler, '*Organon:* musical and logical instrument', *Problems & Solutions: occasional essays in musicology presented to Alice M. Moyle* edited by Jamie C. Kassler and Jill Stubington, Sydney, pp. 122–48.

   1986   Jamie C. Kassler, 'The emergence of probability reconsidered', *Archives Internationales d'Histoire des Science*, 36: 17–44.

   1987   Jamie C. Kassler, 'Breaking wind', *New Journal of Chemistry*, 11: 451–3.

   Forthcoming   Jamie C. Kassler, 'The paradox of power: Hobbes and Stoic naturalism' Stephen Gaukroger (ed.), *The uses of antiquity: The scientific revolution and the classical tradition*, Dordrecht.

Kircher 1650   Athanasius Kircher, *Musurgia universalis sive ars magna cansoni et dissoni . . .*, 2 vols., Rome.

Korsten 1981   F. J. M. Korsten, *Roger North (1651–1734) Virtuoso and Essayist: a study of his life and ideas, followed by an annotated edition of a selection of his unpublished manuscripts*, Amsterdam.

   1981a   F. J. M. Korsten, 'Roger North (1651–1734), and his writings on science', *LIAS*, 8: 203–24.

Krummel 1975   D. W. Krummel, *English Music Printing 1553–1700*, London.

Lamy ed. Harwood 1676/1986   Bernard Lamy, *The Rhetorics of Thomas Hobbes and Bernard Lamy* edited with an introduction and critical apparatus by John T. Harwood, Carbondale and Edwardsville, Illinois.

Leeuwen 1963   H. G. van Leeuwen, *The Problem of Certainty in English Thought 1630–1690* with a preface by R. H. Popkin, The Hague.

Leyden 1968   Wolfgang von Leyden, *Seventeenth-century Metaphysics: an examin-ation of some main concepts and theories*, London.

Locke 1690/1985   John Locke, *An Essay concerning Human Understanding* edited with a foreword by Peter H. Nidditch, Oxford.

Locke 1673   Matthew Locke, *Melothesia: or, certain general rules for playing upon a continued-bass. With a choice collection of lessons for the harpsichord and organ of all sorts . . .*, London.

Longinus tr. Dorsch 1965   Longinus, *On the Sublime* translated with an introduction by T. S. Dorsch, Harmondsworth, Middlesex.

Mabbett 1986   Margaret Mabbett, 'Italian musicians in Restoration England (1660–90)', *Music and Letters*, 67: 237–47.

Mace 1964   Dean T. Mace, 'Musical humanism, the doctrine of rhythmus, and the Saint Cecilia odes of Dryden', *Journal of the Warburg and Courtauld Institutes*, 27: 271–92.

   1969   Dean T. Mace, 'Pietro Bembo and the literary origins of the Italian madrigal', *The Musical Quarterly*, 55: 65–86.

Mace 1676/1968   Thomas Mace, *Musick's Monument*, Vol. 1, reproduction en fac-similé, Paris.

Malcolm 1721   Alexander Malcolm, *A Treatise of Musick, Speculative, Practical, and Historical*, Edinburgh.

Markus 1957   R. A. Markus, 'St. Augustine on signs', *Phronesis*, 2: 60–83.

McKinnon 1978   James W. McKinnon, 'Jubal vel Pythagoras, quis sit inventor musicae?', *The Musical Quarterly*, 64: 1–28.

   1979–80   James W. McKinnon, 'The exclusion of musical instruments from the ancient synagogue', *Proceedings of the Royal Musical Association*, 106: 77–87.

Milhous and Hume 1986   Judith Milhous and Robert D. Hume, 'The charter for the Royal Academy of Music', *Music and Letters*, 67: 50–8.

Millard 1973   Peter Millard, 'The chronology of Roger North's main works', *Review of English Studies*, n.s. 24: 283–94.

   1984   Peter Millard (ed.), *Roger North: General Preface and Life of Dr John North*, Toronto, Buffalo, London.

Molyneux 1702   Thomas Molyneux, 'A letter . . . to the Right Reverend St George, Lord Bishop of Clogher in Ireland, containing some thoughts concerning the ancient Greek and Roman lyre, and an explanation of an obscure passage in one of Horace's odes', *Philosophical Transactions of the Royal Society*, 23: 1267–78.

Monk 1935/1960   Samuel H. Monk, *The Sublime: a study of critical theories in XVIII-century England . . .*, Ann Arbor, Michigan.

Morley 1597   Thomas Morley, *A Plaine and Easie Introduction to Practicall Musicke, set doune in forme of a Dialogue: deuided into three parts . . .*, London.

Morris 1932/1966   Charles W. Morris, *Six Theories of Mind*, Chicago and London.

Münxelhaus 1976   Barbara Münxelhaus, *Phythagoras musicus: Zur Rezeption der pythagoreischen Musiktheorie als quadrivialer Wissenschaft in lateinischen Mitte-lalter*, Bonn-Bad Godesberg.

Norris 1678/1710   John Norris, 'A letter concerning love and music', *A Collection* of *Miscellanies: Consisting of poems, essays, discourses and letters, occasionally written*, 5th edition, carefully revised, corrected, and improved by the author, London.

North 1677 [Francis North], *A Philosophical Essay of Musick directed to a Friend*, London.

Pepys ed. Latham and Matthews 1970–83 Samuel Pepys, *The Diary* . . . a new and complete transcription by Robert Latham and William Matthews, 11 vols., London.

Playford 1655, various editions John Playford, *An Introduction to the Skill of Musick. In two books* . . . , London.

Plutarch tr. Perrin 1959–62 Plutarch, 'Themistocles', *Plutarch's Lives* with an English translation by Bernadotte Perrin, 11 vols., London and Cambridge, Mass., vol. 2.

Plutarch tr. Einarson and De Lacy 1967 Plutarch, 'On music', *Plutarch's Moralia* with an English translation by Benedict Einarson and Phillip H. De Lacy, London and Cambridge, Mass., vol. 14: 344–455.

Pocock 1980 Gordon Pocock, *Boileau and the Nature of Neo-Classicism*, Cambridge.

Polybius tr. Paton 1960 Polybius, *The Histories* with an English translation by W. R. Paton, 6 vols., London and Cambridge, Mass.

Porter 1985 Roy Porter, 'Making faces: physiognomy and fashion in eighteenth-century England', *Études Anglaises*, 38: 385–96.

Price 1984 Curtis A. Price, *Henry Purcell and the London Stage*, Cambridge.

Quintilian tr. Butler 1963 Quintilian, *The Institutio Oratoria* . . . with an English translation by H. E. Butler, 4 vols., London and Cambridge, Mass.

Randall 1983 Dale B. J. Randall, *Gentle Flame: the life and verse of Dudley, fourth lord North (1602–1677)*, Durham, N.C.

Rees 1975 Graham Rees, 'Francis Bacon's semi-Paracelsian cosmology', *Ambix*, 22: 81–101.

  1980 Graham Rees, 'Atomism and "subtlety" in Francis Bacon's philosophy', *Ambix*, 37: 549–71.

Rees and Upton 1984 Graham Rees assisted by Christopher Upton, *Francis Bacon's Natural Philosophy: a new source*. A transcription of manuscript Hardwick 72A with translation and commentary, Chalfont St. Giles, Buckinghamshire.

Rimbault 1846 Edward F. Rimbault (ed.), *Memoirs of Musick by the Hon. Roger North, Attorney-General to James II*, now first printed from the original MS and edited, with copious notes, London.

  1877 *Catalogue of the Valuable Library of the Late Edward Francis Rimbault, LL.D. comprising an extensive and rare collection of ancient music, printed and in manuscript* . . . which will be sold by auction by Messrs. Sotheby, Wilkinson & Hodge . . . Tuesday, the 31st of July, 1877, and five following days . . . , London.

Roberts 1692 Francis Roberts, 'A discourse concerning the musical notes of the trumpet, and trumpet-marine, and of the defects of the same', *Philosophical Transactions of the Royal Society*, 17: 559–63.

Salmon 1672 Thomas Salmon, *An Essay to the Advancement of Musick by casting away the perplexity of the different cliffs, and uniting all sorts of musick, lute, viol, violins, organ, harpsichord, voice etc. in one universal character,* London.

Scholes 1934/1962   Percy A. Scholes, *The Puritans and Music in England and New England: a contribution to the cultural history of two nations,* London.

Shapiro 1983   B. J. Shapiro, *Probability and Certainty in Seventeenth-Century England: a study of the relationships between natural science, religion, history, law, and literature,* Princeton.

Simpson 1665/1965   Christopher Simpson, *The Division-Viol or the art of playing extempore upon a ground:* a lithograhic facsimile of the 2d edition, London and New York.

1667/1727   Christopher Simpson, *A Compendium: or, introduction to practical musick. In five parts. Teaching, by a new and easy method, I. The rudiments of song. II. The principles of composition. III. The use of discords. IV. The form of figurate descant. V. The contrivance of canon.* The 7th edition, with additions: much more correct than any former, the examples being put in the most useful cliffs, London.

Simpson 1966   C. M. Simpson, *The British Broadside Ballad and its Music,* New Brunswick, New Jersey.

Smith ed. Black and Hutton 1795   Adam Smith, *Essays on Philosophical Subjects* [ed. by Joseph Black and James Hutton]. To which is prefixed, an account of the life and writings of the author; by Dugald Stewart, Dublin.

Spink 1965–67   Ian Spink, 'The old Jewry "Musick-Society": a 17th-century catch club', *Musicology II* [Publication of the Musicological Society of Australia] 35–41.

Suetonius tr. Graves 1957   Gaius Suetonius Tranquillus, *The Twelve Caesars* translated by Robert Graves, Harmondsworth, Middlesex.

Tilmouth 1960   Michael Tilmouth, 'Nicola Matteis', *The Musical Quarterly,* 46: 22–40.

1961   Michael Tilmouth, 'A calendar of references to music in newspapers published in London and the provinces (1660–1719)', *R.M.A. Research Chronicle,* 1: vii, 1–107, 2: 1–15.

1966   Michael Tilmouth, 'Sherard', *Music and Letters,* 47: 313–22.

Vaucanson 1737/1979   Jacques de Vaucanson, *Le mechanisme du fluteur automate/ An account of the mechanism of an automaton or image playing on the German-flute . . . ,* Buren.

Vitruvius tr. Gwilt 1826   Vitruvius, *The Architecture . . . in ten books* translated from the Latin by Joseph Gwilt, London.

Vossius 1673   Isaac Vossius, *De Poematum Cantu et Viribus Rhythmi,* Oxford.

Waite 1970   William G. Waite, 'Bernard Lamy, rhetorician of the passions', *Studies in Eighteenth-Century Music: a tribute to Karl Geiringer on his seventieth birthday* edited by H. C. Robbins Landon in collaboration with R. E. Chapman, London, pp. 388–96.

Wallis 1682   John Wallis, 'De veterum harmonica ad hodiernam comparata', *Claudii Ptolemaei Harmonicorum Libri Tres . . . ,* Oxford, pp. 281–328.

1698   John Wallis, 'A letter of Dr. John Wallis, to Mr. Andrew Fletcher; concerning the strange effects reported of music in former times, beyond what is to be found in later ages', *Philosophical Transactions of the Royal Society*, 20: 297–303.

1693, 1695, 1699 John Wallis, *Opera Mathematica* . . . , 3 vols., Oxford.

Ward 1967 J. M. Ward, 'Apropos *The British Broadside Ballad and its Music*', *Journal of the American Musicological Society*, 20: 28–86.

Warren 1725 Ambrose Warren, *The Tonometer: explaining and demonstrating, by an easie method, in numbers and proportion, all the 32 distinct and different notes, adjuncts, or suppliments contained in each of 4 octaves inclusive, of the gamut, or common scale of musick* . . . , London.

Webster 1962–66 Charles Webster, 'The discovery of Boyle's law, and the concept of the elasticity of air in the seventeenth century', *Archive for History of Exact Sciences*, 2: 441–502.

Williams 1980 Peter Williams, *A New History of the Organ: from the Greeks to the present day*, London.

Williamson 1935 George Williamson, 'Milton and the mortalist heresy', *Studies in Philology*, 32: 553–79.

Wilson 1959 John Wilson (ed.), *Roger North on Music: being a selection from his essays written during the years c. 1695–1728*, London.

Wood 1972 Theodore E. B. Wood, *The Word 'Sublime' and its Context 1650–1760*, The Hague and Paris.

Wood 1983 Neal Wood. *The Politics of Locke's Philosophy: a social study of 'An Essay concerning Human Understanding'*, Berkeley, Los Angeles, London.

Woodfield 1985 Ian Woodfield, 'The first earl of Sandwich, a performance of William Lawes in Spain and the origins of the pardessus de viole', *Chelys*, 14: 40–42.

Wren ed. Enthoven 1750/1903 Christopher Wren, *Life and Works of Sir Christopher Wren. From the Parentalia or Memoirs by his son Christopher* edited by E. J. Enthoven . . . , London and New York.

Yolton 1983/1984 John W. Yolton, *Thinking Matter: materialism in eighteenth-century Britain*, Oxford.

3. Bibliography

Biographie universelle ancienne et moderne, ou histoire, par ordre alphabétique, de la vie publique et privée de tous les hommes qui se sont fait remarquer par leurs écrits, leurs actions, leurs talents, leurs vertus et leurs crimes. Ouvrage entièrement neuf, rédigé par une société de gens de lettres et de savants, 52 vols., à Paris 1828

The New Catholic Encyclopedia, 17 vols., New York 1967–79.

Anderson, W. D. 1979 'What song the sirens sang: problems and conjectures in ancient Greek music', *R.M.A. Research Chronicle*, 15: 1–16.

Ashbee, A. (ed.) 1981 *Lists of Payments to the King's Musick in the Reign of Charles II (1660–1685)*, Snodland, Kent.

(ed.) 1987 *Records of English Court Music*, Vol. 2 (1685–1714), Snodland, Kent.

Berry, W. Turner and Poole, H. Edmund 1966 *Annals of Printing: a chronological encyclopaedia from the earliest times to 1950*, London.

Bynum, W. F., Brown, E. J. and Porter, R. (eds.) 1983 *Dictionary of the History of Science*, London and Basingstoke.

Cross, F. L. (ed.), 1957 *The Oxford Dictionary of the Christian Church*, London.

Dijksterhuis, E. J., 1961 *The Mechanization of the World Picture* translated by C. Dikshoorn, Oxford.

Foster, J., 1887–92 *Alumni Oxonienses: the members of the university of Oxford. . . .*, 8 vols., Oxford and London.

Gillispie, C. C. (ed.), 1970–80 *Dictionary of Scientific Biography*, 16 vols., New York.

Hammond, N. G. L. and Scullard, H. H. (eds.), 1970 *The Oxford Classical Dictionary*, 2d edition, Oxford.

Herford, C. H. and Simpson, P. and E. (eds.), 1925–52 *Works of Ben Jonson*, 11 vols., Oxford.

Highfill, P, H., Jr, Kalman, A. D. and Langhans, E. A., 1973–(in progress) *Biographical Dictionary of Actors, Actresses, Musicians, Dancers, Managers, and other Stage Personnel in London 1660–1800*, vols. 1–, Carbondale and Edwardsville, Illinois.

Humphries, C. and Smith, W., 1970 *Music Publishing in the British Isles*, 2d edition, with supplement, Oxford.

Musgrave, W., 1899–1901 *Obituary prior to 1800 (as far as relates to England, Scotland, and Ireland)* edited by G. J. Armytage . . ., 6 vols., London.

Sadie, S. (ed.), 1980 *The New Grove Dictionary of Music and Musicians*, 20 vols., London, Washington, Hong Kong.

Schlager, K. *et al* (eds.), 1971–81 *Répertoire Internationale des Sources Musicales (Series A.I.1–9): Einzeldrucke vor 1800*, 9 vols., Kassel, Basel, Tours and London.

Schnapper, E. B., 1957 *The British Union-catalogue of Early Music printed before the year 1801. A record of the holdings of over 100 libraries throughout the British Isles*, 2 vols., London.

Schneider, B. R. (comp.), 1980 *Index to The London Stage 1660–1800* . . ., Carbondale and Edwardsville, London and Amsterdam.

Stephen, L. and Lee, S. (eds.), 1885–1901 *The Dictionary of National Biography* . . ., 66 vols., London.

Venn, J. and Venn, J. A., 1922–54 *Alumni Cantabrigienses. . . .*, 10 vols., Cambridge.

Warmington, E. H. (ed. and tr.), 1959–61 *Remains of Old Latin. . . .*, 4 vols., London and Cambridge, Mass.

INDEX OF NAMES

Note: names are listed under their modern spellings. The index includes groups of people meeting as professional societies (e.g. the Royal Society) and music societies.